COAL

RIVER

Fairb

TANANA   RIVER

S K A

OLD   RIVER

SUSITNA   RIVER

Anch

GOLD

Kenai

Seward

OAL

COAL

ROUTE

COAL

GOLD

COAL

Yakutat

COAL

GOLD

Chilkoot   Pass

Whit

OLD

GOLD

ay

GOLD

neau

GOLD

Wrangell

H OF 53°

Al   Yukon

ning

F   ntier

0-1914

NORTH OF 53°

NORTH OF 53°

The Wild Days of the Alaska-Yukon Mining Frontier

1870–1914

William R. Hunt

MACMILLAN PUBLISHING CO., INC.
NEW YORK

COLLIER MACMILLAN PUBLISHERS
LONDON

MAPS DRAWN BY ERIK VAN VEENEN

Macmillan Publishing Co., Inc.
866 Third Avenue, New York, N.Y. 10022
Collier-Macmillan Canada Ltd.

Library of Congress Cataloging in Publication Data

Hunt, William R
North of 53°.

Bibliography: p.
1. Klondike gold fields.   2. Alaska—History—1867–
1959.   3. Yukon Territory—History.   I. Title.
F931.H86   917.98'6'033   74-12404
ISBN 0-02-557510-4

FIRST PRINTING 1974

Printed in the United States of America

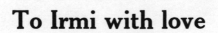
To Irmi with love

Acknowledgments

I OWE MUCH TO the University of Alaska's staff and faculty. The pace of my research and writing was accelerated by a sabbatical leave granted for 1972–73. Several University of Alaska scholars read this manuscript and made valuable contributions. My thanks to Dr. Earl Beistline, Dr. James Foster, Dr. Claus–M. Naske, Dr. Herman Slotnick, and Dr. Ernest Wolff. Dr. Naske read the entire manuscript twice with meticulous care. Students at the university have also contributed; particular mention should be made of Bill Evans, John Halterman, Donald Markham, Jeanne Ostnes, and Erik Van Veenen.

Dr. Richard Solie has been most helpful in providing secretarial assistance for the typing of the final draft. To all the typists who have labored over my wayward handwriting during the past four years, I express my deep gratitude. Doris Nichols presided over the final stages of preparation with concern and interest. Jeanne Rodey, a very talented young woman, typed much of the final draft, and timely assistance was given by Mary Hayes, Joanne Floretta, and the good people of the Institute of Marine Science. Pat Little, Linda Bailey, and Judy Brogan have also helped. Mrs. Brogan typed most of the first draft at great speed and still managed to find time to be an excellent student of history and a charming person. She understood the importance of getting a scribbled draft into a presentable form with dispatch and greatly facilitated the progress of my writing.

During my sabbatical leave I benefited from the kindness rendered by the staff of the Scott Polar Research Institute. Dr. Terence Armstrong, my ideal among scholars and gentlemen, was always encouraging. Dr. Alan Cooke edited the first section of this book and made many knowledgeable suggestions.

Ed Isenson and George Hohman made it possible for me to visit the ghost town of Iditarod.

Contents

Maps

Chronology of Northern Gold Rushes

1870	Gold found at Sumdum Bay, Southeastern Alaska.
1871	Discovery made in Cassiar district, British Columbia.
1872	Stewart mine opened near Sitka.
1873	Jack McQuesten and Arthur Harper begin prospecting along Yukon River.
1880	Gold discovered at Juneau.
1886	Forty Mile gold located.
1888	Gold discovered on Kenai Peninsula.
1893	Gold found near Circle and Rampart.
1896	Original discovery made on Klondike River.
1897–98	Klondike stampede.
1898	Gold discovered on Seward Peninsula.
1899	Mining begun on beaches of Nome.
1899–1900	Nome stampede.
1902	Felix Pedro finds gold in Tanana valley.
1906	Gold discovered in Chandalar district.
1909	Iditarod discovery made.
1910	Stampede to Ruby.
1911	Kennicott copper mines begin production.
1913	Gold found at Marshall.
1914	Livengood gold found.

NORTH OF 53°

Introduction

ALASKA'S EXCITEMENT TODAY is being generated by the development of its oil resources. Huge construction projects, most notably the North Slope–Valdez pipeline, are underway. While the drilling rigs on the Arctic coast are being readied, exploration parties are seeking still more petroleum in the Arctic and elsewhere.

For all its impact and importance, the great oil boom falls into a familiar pattern in Alaska's history. What is occurring has occurred before. Over the last 100 years other riches have attracted outsiders: first, the fine furs of the region's sea and land mammals; then its fabulous stores of precious gold; and, still later, its fisheries. Now it is oil.

This book is concerned with an earlier era of Alaskan excitement. It is the story of Alaska–Yukon gold seekers, the men and women whose intense, lusty efforts opened America's northern frontier. Their adventures span the years from the first, tentative quests of the pioneer prospectors in the 1870s, through the heightened frenzy of the Klondike and Nome stampedes in the lates 1890s, to the excitement sparked by later gold discoveries in Tanana valley, Ruby, Iditarod, and Livengood—altogether some 40 colorful years.

A chronicle of the mixed lot of characters who rushed North with such golden expectations does not gain from any exaggeration of their qualities or of their travails in the rigorous subarctic climate. Saints and sinners, whores and housewives, swindlers and laborers alike attempted a hasty adjustment to novel conditions in a land that seemed strange and forbidding. If they determined to be miners, they had to face up to the realities of the physical environment, their own capacities, and the probabilities of success. For many, a short trial against such odds was enough, and they were glad enough to abandon the effort. A few succeeded and became millionaires. Others were lucky just to make a living. Many died—victims of frostbite, exposure, scurvy, or misfortune along the trail. Those who kept to town life did not lead as perilous an existence, but they traveled no surer road to fortune. Pimps, gamblers, and sober businessmen were among those who experienced varying degrees of success. Entrepreneurs, like miners, were either victims or beneficiaries, according to their talents and luck.

The story of such a disparate group as the gold stampeders must focus on a comparatively small number of individuals, and they should be chosen with care. To avoid distortion, the flagrant careers of Soapy Smith, Judge Alfred Noyes, Swiftwater Bill Gates, Tex Rickard, and Wilson Mizner have to be balanced by a consideration of steadier characters such as George Pilcher, Carl Lomen, Judge James Wickersham, Will Ballou, Rex Beach, Captain Charles Farnsworth, and J. F. A. Strong. Professionally, these men represent miners, gamblers, newsmen, judges, soldiers, con men, and wood choppers. Some were wastrels, criminals, and parasites; others were significant achievers. By reviewing their deeds and misdeeds, one can obtain a comprehensive picture of the Alaskan gold era.

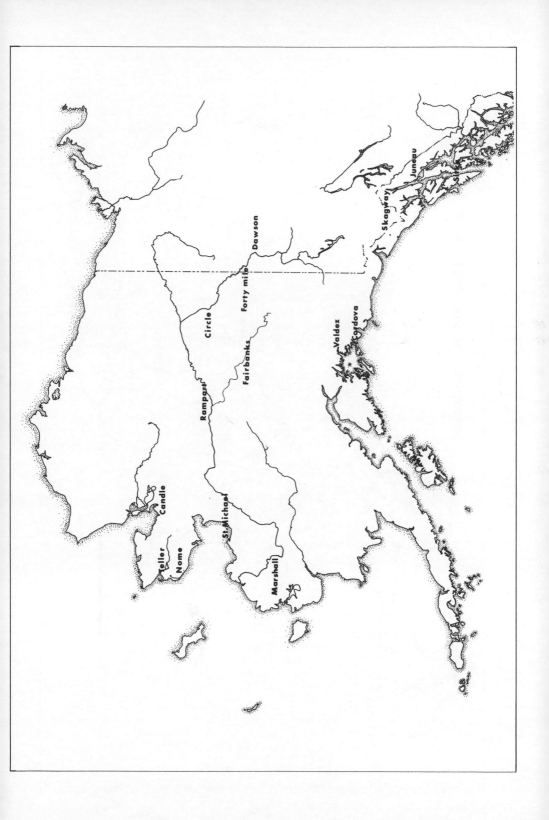

Juneau

Skagway

Dawson

Forty mile

Circle

Fairbanks

Valdez

Cordova

Rampart

St. Michael

Candle

Teller

Nome

Marshall

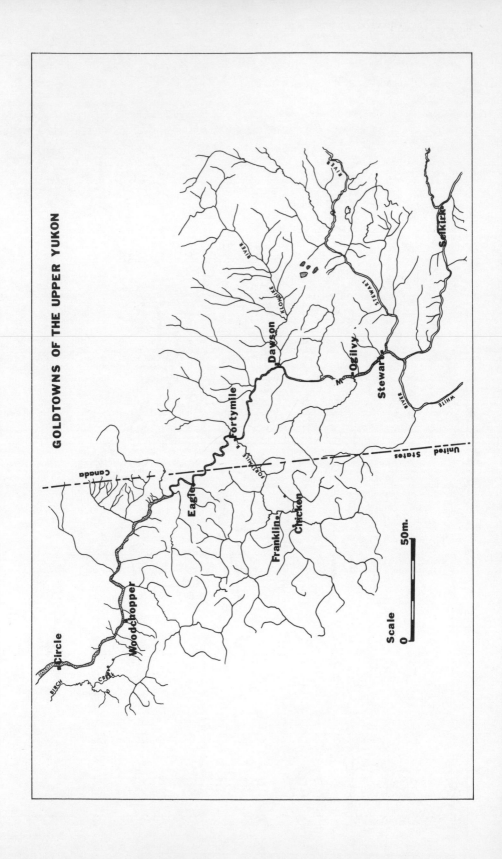

GOLDTOWNS OF THE UPPER YUKON

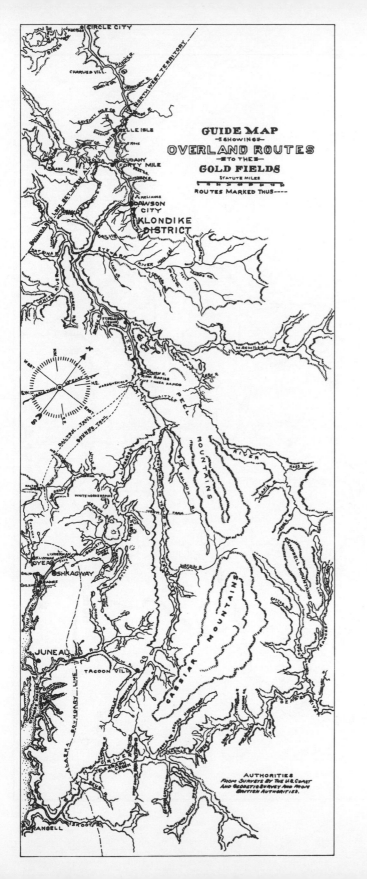

GUIDE MAP
—SHOWING—
OVERLAND ROUTES
—TO THE—
GOLD FIELDS

STATUTE MILES

ROUTES MARKED THUS----

AUTHORITIES
FROM SURVEYS BY THE U.S. COAST
AND GEODETIC SURVEY AND FROM
BRITISH AUTHORITIES.

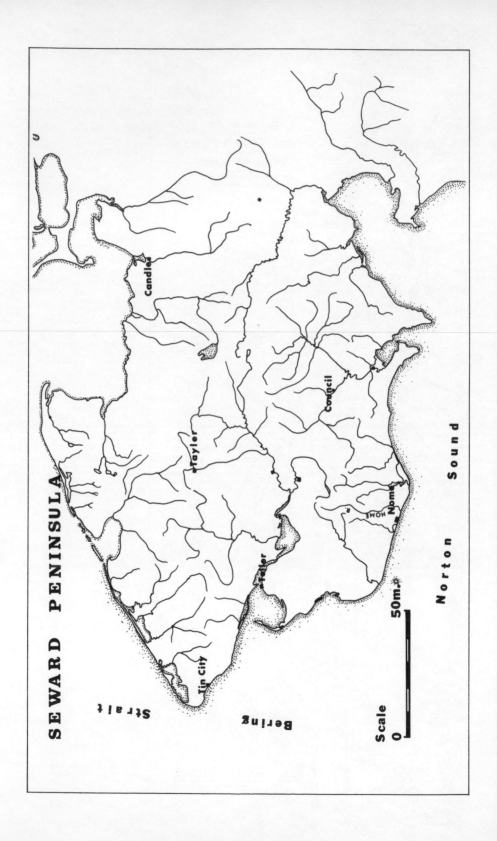

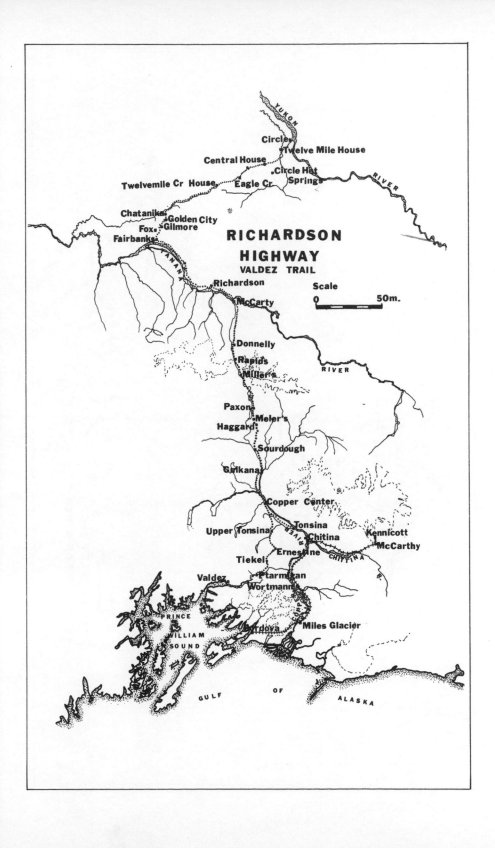

RICHARDSON HIGHWAY

VALDEZ TRAIL

Scale

0   50m.

Yukon

Circle

Twelve Mile House

Central House

Circle Hot Springs

Twelvemile Cr House

Eagle Cr

RIVER

Chatanika

Golden City

Gilmore

Fox

Fairbanks

TANANA

Richardson

McCarty

Donnelly

Rapids

Miller's

RIVER

Paxon

Meier's

Haggard

Sourdough

Gulkana

Copper Center

Tonsina

Upper Tonsina

Chitina

Kennicott

McCarthy

Ernestine

CHITINA

COPPER RIVER

Tiekel

Valdez

Ptarmigan

Wortmann

PRINCE WILLIAM SOUND

Cordova

Miles Glacier

GULF   OF   ALASKA

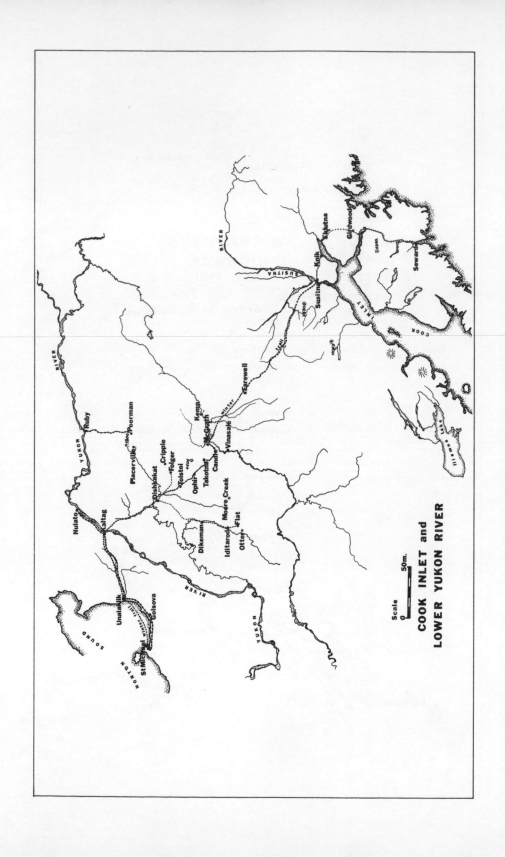

COOK INLET and
LOWER YUKON RIVER

Part I

EARLY DAYS ON THE YUKON

1

Opening the Land

In May 1883 a small exploration expedition steamed north from Vancouver, Washington, to the head of southeastern Alaska's Lynn Canal. The expedition was composed of seven U.S. Army soldiers, led by a 34-year-old officer, Lt. Frederick Schwatka; their purpose was to chart the Yukon River from its source to its mouth.

A glance at a map of Alaska and northernmost Canada reveals the significance of the great Yukon River. From its Canadian origins the river flows in a majestic arc for 2,300 miles before finding its way to the Pacific Ocean at Norton Sound. The Yukon is navigable during the summer for virtually its entire course; in the winter its frozen surface serves as a highway for sled trails.

Rivers were the transportation network of the frontier west. In 1792–93 Alexander Mackenzie followed rivers westward to the Pacific Ocean to make the first crossing of Canada; in 1805 Lewis and Clark reached the Pacific coast at the mouth of the Columbia River; later, trappers, gold stampeders, and settlers explored other river and overland routes westward.

In the North the Yukon River offered the best and most obvious route for the penetration of the interior. The Yukon River was known to Europeans very early. Before Alaska was purchased by the United States in 1867, the Russian–American Company had established trading posts along the river as far as Nulato, and Russians had ventured upriver for trading. A portion of the Yukon was well known to English traders also. In 1841 Alexander H. Murray of the Hudson's Bay Company built Fort Yukon within the Arctic Circle and in Russian territory; in 1848 another Hudson's Bay Company trader, Robert Campbell, built Fort Selkirk on the Pelly River. In 1869, following the Alaska Purchase in 1867, U.S. Army Capt. Charles W. Raymond steamed up to Fort Yukon and raised the American flag over the post, and the Hudson's Bay Company traders withdrew.

Campbell's Fort Selkirk did not last long. Indians in the region were glad to have a Hudson's Bay Company post because it ended their dependence upon the coastal Chilkats for the white men's trade items. Soon after Campbell had completed his post, a party of twenty Chilkats arrived from Lynn Canal. They were "a hard looking set" and, unlike the interior Indians, were given to thieving and bullying.[1] "Fair dealing was unknown among the Chilkats, whose motto was 'might is right,'" observed Campbell.[2] Four years later, in 1852, the Chilkats attacked the traders at Fort Selkirk, disarmed them, pillaged all the stores, and burned the post to the ground. The Chilkats would brook no rivals in their expansive territory and the Hudson's Bay Company made no attempt to reestablish the post.

Despite this activity, over many years parts of the Yukon River, particularly its upper course, were still not well charted. It was for this reason that the U.S. Army despatched Lt. Frederick Schwatka, commissioned at West Point 11 years earlier, to follow the entire length of the river in 1883. The Army's authority to conduct the survey was perhaps somewhat questionable, since it had been withdrawn from Alaska some years previously. (The Army, after supervising the Russian removal from Sitka, had maintained garrisons at Sitka and other coastal towns from 1867 to 1877. After this 10-year occupation, the U.S. Navy was assigned the Alaskan patrol for a short time; then the work was taken over by the U.S. Revenue Cutter Service.) Authority or not, Gen. Nelson A. Miles, Commander of the Military District of the Columbia, launched the Yukon expedition, ostensibly to investigate threats of Indian hostility; Schwatka, an experienced Arctic explorer, was put in charge of it. Schwatka's first exploring experience covered a two-year period from 1878, when he successfully searched the Arctic islands north of the Canadian mainland for relics of the lost party of the British explorer Sir John Franklin.

Schwatka's party landed near the mouth of the Chilkat River, where there was an Indian village and a salmon cannery operated by the North-West Trading Company. There he negotiated with the Chilkat Indians for packers to carry the expedition's supplies over the Chilkoot Pass. Indians and whites alike were amused by his plan to build a raft for transport once the soldiers reached the Yukon headwaters, but he was able to hire the needed sixty packers.

A few years earlier Schwatka probably would have had trouble securing Indian labor, for the Chilkats had maintained a monopoly of the route to the interior, jealously guarding it against the intrusions of interior tribes and profiting from an exchange of fish oil for furs. In 1879 they had denied a party of twenty American prospectors the use of the pass, and the prospectors had appealed for assistance to Capt. L. A. Beardslee.

Beardslee commanded a naval ship, the U.S.S. *Jamestown*, and his was the only American military force in that part of the world. According to one account, a naval officer exhibited the wonders of a Gatling gun to the Indians and they got the point, but more likely it was Captain Beardslee's tact and diplomacy in negotiating with the Indians that secured the passage. In 1880 and thereafter American prospectors crossed Chilkoot Pass without interference and in increasing numbers.

So, on June 6 Schwatka set out from the coast. Indian canoes carried all the army provisions to the head of Dyea River. From that point the Chilkat packers, carrying loads of 100 pounds and more, transported the expedition's provisions over the Chilkoot Pass to Lake Lindemann. At Lake Lindemann logs were gathered and the soldiers constructed a raft. Their first 500 miles of lake and river navigation was entirely in Canadian territory, although neither the Canadian nor the British governments had been consulted. This fact later caused some ire in Canada, and so did Schwatka's practice of renaming prominent geographical features for his friends.

On June 14 Schwatka inspected the raft his men had constructed and deemed it a fit vessel for the long voyage ahead. The soldiers started across the small lakes that are the mighty Yukon's source. The twin scourges of interior travel, mosquitoes and black flies, accompanied them in persistent clouds, but the beginning of the voyage was otherwise not especially arduous. However, the rivers connecting the lakes were more difficult, and soon the expedition encountered dangerous rapids. Where the rapids were especially swift, the raft's cargo was unloaded and carried around them, while the unburdened raft, which was too cumbersome to control, was allowed to shoot the rapids alone and then retrieved later. Treacherous "sweepers"—trees hanging into the river from undercut banks—had to be avoided. It was hot work, for even in these high latitudes the summer temperatures reach 100° F., which "made one feel as though he were floating on the Nile, Congo or Amazon."[3]

They rarely saw Indians on the lakes or the upper river, for the aboriginal population was small and scattered; the village sites they passed were more often than not deserted. Game was scarce, and to them the land seemed inhospitable and forbidding. Yet, even in their quick passage, they noted the presence of gold in the sands of the river bars, and they met two American prospectors, the "most woe-begone objects I ever saw," commented Schwatka.[4] An American prospecting party had left the coast shortly before Schwatka arrived there; the two prospectors were returning to Lynn Canal because the party's food supplies were dwindling. Schwatka later heard that the party had been saved from starvation by Indians in the Dyea valley near the coast.

These prospectors were precursors of the flood of men who would pour over the Chilkoot Pass in 1897–98. Most of the prospectors at this period were drifting away from Juneau, where Alaska's first substantial gold strike had been made in 1880–81. But even before the Juneau strike, gold had been mined in the 1870s near Sitka, the old Russian–American capital. These quartz mines of southeast Alaska and the placer discoveries of the 1870s in the Cassiar district of British Columbia encouraged prospecting in the interior of Alaska and northern Canada during the 1880s. But the miners from the southeast coast were preceded by a number of men, many of them American, who had prospected along the Mackenzie River and then had crossed over to Alaska in 1873, following the Porcupine River to the Yukon River. Among these pioneers were Arthur Harper, L. N. "Jack" McQuesten, and Alfred H. Mayo, all of whom doubled as traders and established posts for the Alaska Commercial Company within Canadian territory.

But in 1883 Schwatka and his party drifted through a region that had changed little over the centuries. The aboriginal pattern of life had of course been somewhat disrupted by the appearance of Russian traders and priests in the early years of the nineteenth century on the lower Yukon River and by their British counterparts from the Mackenzie River (the Reverend Robert McDonald had founded an Anglican mission at Fort Yukon in 1862), but life for the natives had not been altered essentially. The Indians greeted Schwatka's raft with salutes from firearms and asked for tobacco and tea but otherwise behaved in their traditional manner. Bows and arrows were more common than firearms; brush huts and skin tents were their habitations. Their livelihood depended in large part upon the summer run of Pacific salmon, the unfailing resource that dictated the natives' seasonal movements, and they dressed and sheltered themselves as their ancestors had done. Schwatka and his soldiers had encountered a region poised on the threshold of the momentous changes that had occurred everywhere else in North America where white traders or trappers had been joined by miners and settlers.

Schwatka swept into the middle Yukon, passing the ruins of Fort Selkirk (burned in 1852 by the Chilkats) and the mouth of the Stewart River (a spot where Jack London would later spend the winter of 1897–98). For some 400 miles beyond Fort Selkirk the river flows through mountainous country that Schwatka called the Upper Ramparts, likening its first 100 miles to the "stupendous grandeur" of the Yosemite or Yellowstone rivers.[5] No longer blue and clear but now muddied by its junction with the glacier-fed waters of the White River (which the expedition passed on July 17), the Yukon courses its way past Forty Mile River and across the international boundary into Alaska. Not far from the boundary, the expedition passed what would later be the site of Eagle, a well-wooded section bounded on one side by a steep bluff, and about 100 miles further on, the site of Circle, to be called 10 years later the largest long-house town in the world. Here the bluffs hemming in the Yukon River fall away; its waters spread out over a broad area of flat lands, and its many channels flow through innumerable islands and sand bars. Schwatka's expedition spent three weeks working their raft through the mazy network of these channels of shallow water. The tedium of this portion of their voyage was only slightly relieved by meeting another trader–prospector, Joe Ladue, whose sawmill would later furnish the building materials for Dawson City.

Below Fort Yukon the Yukon River narrows once more, enclosed by high bluffs on both sides. This 100-mile stretch of the river, called the Ramparts, was a welcome contrast to the dreary flats, and its rapids were no threat to the raft party. Ten years later, in 1893, a major gold strike in this region resulted in the founding of Rampart City, one of the most important towns along the Yukon River during the gold era. Below the Ramparts, the Yukon is joined by a major tributary, the Tanana River, from the south. The Tanana River, which at its mouth appears to be almost as large as the Yukon itself, drains an area that was then little known. The Tanana Indians discouraged white intrusions, but they turned up at Nuklukayet, a village near the confluence of the two rivers, to trade during the summer. At this point the expedition abandoned its raft, which had carried it 1,300 miles, in favor of a schooner lent by trader Arthur Harper. The soldiers encountered no surprises on the remaining portion of the river, which was well known. At St. Michael, just upcoast from the Yukon River delta, they took passage on August 30 back to Fort Vancouver.

Schwatka's published narrative, *Along Alaska's Great River* (1885), increased public interest in the area. Leading journals published articles on the expedition, and it is probable that his remarks on the presence of gold and on the few American prospectors searching for a big strike encouraged others to make the same effort. Certainly the U.S. Army expedition's survey of the upper 500 miles of the Yukon River, the first record of its course through Canada, proved to be of great practical value. It charted the principal route to the Klondike goldfields that were soon to be the goal of tens of thousands of prospectors.

2

Early Trading

THE ALASKA COMMERCIAL COMPANY (A.C.C.) fell heir to the commerce of the Russian–American Company after the United States purchased Russian America in 1867. Its major operation—an extremely lucrative one—was based on the Pribilof Islands in the Bering Sea where, in return for the maintenance of natives there and annual fees to the U.S. Treasury, the company held a monopoly over the teeming fur seal rookeries from 1870 to 1890. But the A.C.C. also took over the Russian company's fur-trading activities in the interior.

Although the A.C.C. was not given a monopoly over the Yukon River fur trade, freelance traders could not compete effectively against it. Transportation was the key factor in dominating the trade, and for some years the A.C.C., a firm based in San Francisco, maintained the only steamers on the Yukon River and the only regular ocean service between St. Michael and the Pacific coast ports. In 1868 the company sent George R. Adams to St. Michael, 70 miles upcoast from the Yukon's mouth on Norton Sound. There the United States' flag was raised over the fort that the Russians had built in 1831, and twenty-one Russian–Indian Creoles, who had been employed by the Russian–American Company, signed on, agreeing to hunt and trade exclusively for the American concern.

In 1869 the A.C.C.'s first river steamer, the *Yukon*, made its maiden voyage upriver to establish a trading station at Nulato, 600 miles upriver from St. Michael. One passenger on the *Yukon's* maiden voyage was Capt. Charles Raymond, U.S. Army Corps of Engineers, who made a reconnaissance survey of the Yukon River, in the course of which he ascertained that Fort Yukon, a Hudson's Bay Company post, was in American territory.

By employing prospecting partners Jack McQuesten, Arthur Harper, and Alfred Mayo, the A.C.C. directly subsidized prospecting. Later, when the three partners became independent traders, they relied on the A.C.C.

for their supplies. Until the early 1890s virtually all of the trade on the Yukon River above Nulato was in their hands, but they looked upon the fur trade primarily as a means of supporting their widespread prospecting activities. As might be expected, the partners, especially McQuesten, were sympathetic traders and extended liberal credit to other prospectors, and their letters to friends and others in the States describing the attractions of the country brought many other prospectors into the region. For all of their work and foresight, the partnership received small reward, for not one of them shared directly in any of the great bonanzas.

The life of a Yukon trader was hard, and once the river's brief navigation season had closed, there was no way of resupplying any of the posts. Jack McQuesten's post at Fort Reliance, 1,700 miles upriver from St. Michael, almost always ran short toward the end of winter. It was impossible to forecast accurately the quantities of beans, bacon, other foodstuffs, clothing, and tools that a constantly varying number of miners needed for their work. The natives wanted firearms, blankets, beads, black tea, brown sugar, and bolts of cotton print cloth in return for their beaver, lynx, bear, deer, and fox skins. The A.C.C. men did not hunt or trap themselves but depended upon the furs brought to them by natives.

Security of the post was another source of anxiety. Friendly relations with the Indians were essential to profits—and to survival. Breaches of peace occurred frequently enough to keep traders apprehensive. In 1878 James M. Bean and his wife set up a post at Harper's Bend on the Tanana River. Indians of the vicinity took exception to the prices Bean offered for furs and decided on his destruction. Two of them, armed with flint-lock muskets obtained earlier in trade with the Hudson's Bay Company, hid near the post and waited. Their chance came one night as the Beans sat before their fire, in full sight of their assassins. One of the Indians shot Mrs. Bean dead; the other's weapon misfired. James Bean escaped and made his way downriver to McQuesten and Mayo's post at Nuklukayet. Although the three traders returned to Bean's post to bring back Mrs. Bean's body and to remove the stores, they made no effort to punish the Indians. There was no military or police authority in the interior of Alaska, and the traders were not strong enough or numerous enough to impose law upon the natives by themselves; they could only turn the other cheek. In 1886, when the white population had greatly increased, a similar murder of prospector John Bremner on the Koyukuk River was met with swift retribution when a party of miners hanged the Indian involved, but in the 1870s and early 1880s nothing could be done.

Like the Tanana Indians, the Indians of the Copper River were also inclined to be hostile. A trader of the A.C.C., George Holt, was killed by one of them in 1884. Copper River Indians had traveled to Holt's post at

Knik on Cook Inlet and became resentful because of the low prices offered for their furs. Holt's questioning of the Indians concerning a rich
mountain of copper ore said to exist in their country was an additional
annoyance. In any event the other white men made no attempt to avenge
Holt's slaying, and in the following decade prospectors did not dare to
venture into the Copper River country, despite the rumors of rich ore.

McQuesten, Mayo, and Harper also had their troubles with Indians.
The Indians had offered no resistance when the three had established Fort
Reliance in the Canadian Yukon in 1874, but they were clearly not
pleased with the traders' presence. In 1875 the partners cached their
goods and temporarily left the area. McQuesten returned the next season
to see whether his absence had softened their mood. Apparently it had, for
the Indians were willing to trade, but they insisted on compensation first.
It was revealed that some of the Indians had broken into the traders'
cache to get flour but had taken rat poison instead. Two elderly women
and a young blind girl had eaten the poison and died. McQuesten must
pay for the girl, they argued, but he need not pay for the old women.
McQuesten accepted their reasoning and settled for a cash payment of six
dollars, which restored good feelings.[1]

The gold strikes at Forty Mile River and Stewart River in 1886, which
involved about 300 miners, increased the A.C.C.'s business. At this time
the A.C.C. had no competitors, but it did not abuse its monopolistic
position. Extra provisions were sent up to the new camps from St. Michael
with the company president's caution. Wrote Louis Gerstle, "It must not
be understood, however, that the shipment referred to is made for the
purpose of realizing profits beyond the regular schedule of prices hereto-
fore established." The company intended these additional provisions to be
a reserve against the possibility of an influx of miners with insufficient
provisions. "The Company cannot permit itself to be made an instrument
of oppression towards anyone that they may come into contact with."
Furthermore, the president ordered "that in case of absolute poverty or
want, the person or persons placed in that unfortunate position should be
promptly furnished with the means of subsistence without pay."[2]

In 1892 a formidable competitor to the A.C.C. appeared on the Yukon
River, the North American Transportation and Trading Company
(N.A.T. & T.), organized by John J. Healy with backers who included
such wealthy Chicago interests as the Cudahy family, Portus B. Weare,
and the Corn Exchange Bank. Healy had convinced them of the potential
profitability of trading in the interior of Alaska and had assured them that
the A.C.C. could be successfully challenged. A prospector himself, Healy
had hunted gold in Montana before coming to Juneau in 1885. For a time
he ran a trading post at Dyea, founded in 1886, and it was there he had
become convinced of the region's great commercial possibilities.

The N.A.T. & T. built a post at St. Michael and launched a steamer, the *P. B. Weare*, for trade upriver. After a slow start—the *Weare* was caught by the freeze-up at Nulato and was held there during the winter of 1892–93—the new traders opened their assault on their veteran rival. At every place on the river where the A.C.C. had a post, the N.A.T. & T. built a rival store. Advertisements in the *Yukon Press*, founded at Fort Adams in 1893, blazoned the N.A.T. & T.'s threat: "STAND FROM UNDER! GOODS ARE FALLING, WE HAVE COME TO STAY."[3] By 1895, when this particular advertisement appeared, the N.A.T. & T. had good reason for such confidence. By then there were approximately 1,000 miners along the upper Yukon and its tributaries, and there was trade enough for both companies. The senior firm held the edge, partly because of its experience and partly because of its credit policy. N.A.T. & T. advertised business "on a strictly cash basis," but its customers were assured of quality service: "Our stock of goods for the season of 1895 has been selected with great care by [our] manager, who has devoted many years studying the wants of miners and mountaineers."[4]

The competition between the A.C.C. and N.A.T. & T. was beneficial both to the miners already in the country and to those who were yet to come. Transport was improved, larger stores of provisions were available, and more stations were established. An increasing number of persons gained experience in trading and river transport that served them well when the great stampede of miners began.

3

Mining

JUNEAU IS LOCATED on Lynn Canal, some 100 miles south of its head, from which rise the steep trails that lead across passes to the headwaters of the Yukon River. A lovelier setting for a town can hardly be imagined—steep, heavily forested hills ascend from the water's edge to tower over the city that has grown up from the cluster of cabins and shacks built by the miners. The town of Juneau, originally known as Harrisburg, was established in 1881 after Richard T. Harris and Joseph Juneau had made placer and quartz discoveries in 1880.[1] Both men had worked in the Stewart mine near Sitka and were financed by George E. Pilz, a German assayer who had come to Sitka to erect a stamp mill for the Stewart mine and other Sitka men.

Harris and Juneau had staked their claims on placer deposits in Silver Bow basin in the hills that encircled the camp, but the richest claims in the area were developed by John Treadwell, a California contractor and mining engineer. Treadwell bought a quartz claim on Douglas Island, just opposite Juneau, and began digging the "Glory Hole," which eventually would cover over 13 acres and penetrate 2,000 feet into the earth. Quartz or hard-rock mining requires techniques different from those used to work the placer deposits that were found in stream beds (virtually all of the interior mining was of placer gold). The Douglas Island quartz ore was low grade, but Treadwell had foresight enough to realize its potential. Over the years 1882–1916 the four mines of the Treadwell group produced some $60 million in gold from ore processed by what became the largest stamp mill in the world before its flooding closed operations.[2]

Henry Davis, a typical prospector of the period, arrived in Juneau in May, 1884. He did some prospecting in the area and made a little money, but not much. Rumor had it that more favorable geological conditions could be found in the interior, and Davis worked at various odd jobs—storekeeping and logging—to earn enough to buy a Yukon outfit. Davis refused to work in the Treadwell mine in Juneau because he thought work there was too dangerous: "Men were getting hurt and killed there every day."[3] Prospectors like Henry Davis did not linger in Juneau any longer than necessary—laboring for wages did not interest them. Why work for someone else when they dreamed of the possibility of striking it rich in the interior? By May, 1886, Davis and his partners had their outfits and followed the now well-worn path of others over the Chilkoot Pass to the headwaters of the Yukon River.

The first Yukon prospectors followed stream after stream, panning the sand of their innumerable sandbars. If, after washing the sand away, enough glittering flakes of gold dust remained, that stretch of the river was worked more thoroughly. The prospectors shoveled the sand into a crude rocker, which caught the heavy gold as the sand passed through. With luck and hard work a man could pan enough gold by this method to keep himself in provisions. Once winter had set in and the ground was frozen and snow-covered, little work could be done. Some intrepid men continued to prospect, even after the freeze-up, until the snow grew too deep for travel, but most settled quickly into what comfort they could supply in their winter shelter, spending their time cutting wood for the stoves and hunting for game to supplement their food stores.

With adequate food on hand the Davis party built a log cabin 14 by 16 feet for the winter, laid in a good wood supply, and settled down on the Upper Yukon to a leisurely routine for the winter. Time passed slowly. They celebrated Christmas with a feast: moose meat, a big plum duff with bear fat, and an invigorating rum sauce. Diary entries made by Davis at intervals throughout the winter depict the life of the isolated men:

January:
   My, but it is cold today, makes you cough whenever you open the door . . . We just stay indoors and pile on wood.
   Chris is not feeling good and I guess he is homesick, as it is his first time away from home.
February:
   Buckskin came down today for some Epsom salts for Bob English and said he was sure it was scurvy. We gave him some meat and Lubeck [dried?] potatoes and onions. It is still very cold and Chris is making himself a fiddle. I am making fish nets and Nick and Charley are playing poker at one cent a chip.
   We made a spring camp, and Chris and I will live there as the cabin is very dusty and we are getting bored looking at each other.[4]

In January news of the strike at Forty Mile River reached them. By mid-March the days were long, the weather was growing warmer, and the men began rocking the bar sand once more, a welcome relief after the mo-

notony of winter. When the ice finally broke on the river in early May, the
party had plenty of excitement: They had to climb onto their cabin roof
because the Yukon overflowed its banks. For two days and a night they
perched there, eating dried raisins and peas, until the ice jams broke up
and the river flowed more freely.

With the breakup the months of monotony and isolation were ended.
Other prospectors came in from the coast with news of events in the
outside world that was most welcome, for now fresh ideas for conversation were available. Men traveling upriver, with reports of prospecting and
other activity on the lower Yukon, were just as eagerly received.

In retracing the steps of the prospectors of the 1870s and 1880s—
Arthur Harper, Alfred Mayo, Gordon Bettles, Henry Davis, Jim Bender,
Frank Buteau, and others too numerous to name—the legend that gold
was suddenly discovered in bonanza proportions is soon dispelled. Unlike
the military and other explorers who preceded and followed the prospectors into the Yukon basin to reconnoiter its principal geographic features,
these tireless pioneers investigated the region pace by pace, "necking it"
—hauling their own sleds—in the winter and backpacking their gear in
summer over unmapped hills and mountain ranges and along every creek
and river that drained into the great basin. The swift winter travel that was
common at the height of the stampede period, when heavy traffic kept the
trails open, was unknown. Dogs were scarce—neither Indians nor whites
yet owned large dog teams for sled transport, although it was common to
use one or two dogs as pack animals or to help pull a sled. A full decade
of such arduous foot-slogging and sandbar rocking preceded the first
major placer finds in 1886, and another decade of patient exploration and
incalculable man-hours of hard labor along the river sands and gravels
passed before the great Klondike strike was finally made.

The Yukon was no quicker to reveal its treasures to experienced mining
men with large resources than to individual prospectors with pick and
shovel. The only well-equipped and large-scale expedition to try its luck in
the interior during this period had no more success than other pioneers. In
1882 Ed Schiefflin, a professional prospector and the discoverer of the
gold fields at Tombstone, Arizona, took a party from San Francisco by
schooner to St. Michael, carrying with him a small river streamer, splen-
didly named the *New Racket*. Before this only traders had maintained
steam-powered vessels on the Yukon River, and the *New Racket* gave the
Schiefflin party mobility and independence. The expedition wintered near
the mouth of the Tanana River, and in spring 1883 they took the *New
Racket* about 20 miles up the Tanana and made extensive investigations
there. They discovered signs of gold but not enough to encourage another
season's work.

The first major break in the pattern of Yukon prospecting came in the fall of 1886, when Howard Franklin made his strike of a rich placer field on a tributary of the Forty Mile River. All the gold strikes before his had been found on sandbars along the Canadian stretch of the Yukon River. Just before Franklin's strike the mining picture had been brightened a bit by the relatively high yield of the Stewart River sandbars, where about seventy-five miners took some $75,000 in 1875–76. But the gold on Forty Mile River was not confined to sandbars—it was there all over the region in rich bedrock deposits that straddled the American–Canadian border. Paydirt was found on Chicken Creek, Miller Creek, Franklin Gulch, and other tributaries of Forty Mile River. A stampede, small by later standards, of the prospectors on the Stewart River and elsewhere— Henry Davis and his partners among them—led to the development of the first mining community on the Yukon River. The settlement sprang up on a site approximately 25 miles from the American border, 34 miles down-river from McQuesten, Mayo, and Harper's post at Fort Reliance, which had been the supply center of mining along the upper Yukon River since 1874. With the Forty Mile discovery the pace of events on the Yukon River was accelerated.

4

Forty Mile

THE HEADWATERS of the Forty Mile River are in Canadian territory, but the river follows a looping southerly course that crosses the United States boundary and forms a wide arc before flowing north to recross the border and join the Yukon River. The diggings at Bonanza Bar, Franklin, Chicken, Jack Wade, and Steel Creek were all on the American side of the boundary. In 1887 the gold taken from these diggings totaled $30,000; the amount increased each year until in 1896 it reached a high of $800,000.[1] During the same decade the summer mining population increased from about 200 to about 1,000, half of whom wintered in the region.[2]

Prospecting and mining were done simply, without machinery. Typically, a gold stream was small, perhaps only a few yards wide, although the flats over which it meandered might be a half mile or more in width. The tributaries might be in shallow valleys that wound between rounded hills where trees grew sparsely, or even extended above timberline.

In this wild, beautiful setting the prospector scooped sand or gravel from the stream banks or bottom into a pan like a pie plate. He would fill the pan with water and shake it vigorously. Gold, if present, would settle and the higher sands would be washed out. Careful washing often revealed a few golden specks. A bonanza? Perhaps, but more likely not. The answer to that question could be determined only after a shaft had been sunk to the bedrock of the valley, a distance of from 15 to over 100 feet. Sinking the shaft was no easy task. If the ground was unfrozen, as it might be near the stream, there was no way in which digging could be carried on below the water table, since the early prospectors did not have pumps. Frozen ground—permafrost—was also difficult to dig, but a shaft could be sunk with great effort. It was impossible to pick frozen gravel, so the practice was to build a wood fire at the site of the shaft some distance laterally from the stream bed and to excavate the ground thus thawed. Each day's fire permitted the excavation of about eight inches of gravel. The walls of the shaft remained frozen and as strong and safe as if they had been composed of hard bedrock. Shoring them with timber was unnecessary. Wood for the fires could usually be found close at hand but even so it had to be laboriously carried or sledded by the prospector. Above timberline, this became a formidable task. When the shaft finally reached through the frozen gravel to bedrock, the miner scanned the bottom for signs of gold. If the area was very rich, he could see the gold but usually he would take a sample out for panning. If the gravel was rich he would excavate the ancient stream bed by lateral digging or by sinking other shafts to aid in the work.

Through the winter miners working in a shaft hoisted the gravel thawed by the fires and heaped it in conical mounds beside their diggings to await the spring cleanup. These mounds, which grew to dwarf the miner's cabin, were called dumps, or winter dumps, and grew wherever underground or drift mining was practiced. When spring came and the dump began to thaw, the miner shoveled it into a sluice box through which water was flowing. The heavy gold would remain in the riffles of the box as the lighter materials were washed away. An adequate water supply for sluicing was essential, and the miners always tried to sluice the dumps during the spring thaw, for a particularly dry summer could stop this work.

Eventually, during the Klondike rush, steam points replaced wood fires for thawing and this greatly speeded the mining work. A steam point consists of a short length of iron pipe connected to a rubber hose that carries steam from a small nearby boiler. The point is driven into the frozen earth until the earth is thawed and can be removed; then the process is repeated.

Forty Mile did not resemble a cosmopolitan center, but it did reflect the steady increase in population that had been taking place in the region. The town consisted of about eighty log cabins, most of about 12 by 14 feet. A wood-fired "Yukon" stove, either square or round bottomed, and containing a small oven at the back end, provided cooking facilities and kept the cabin warm in the winter. Other buildings in town included stores, a barber shop, two bakeries, two restaurants, several saloons, a billiard parlor, and a theater. Gambling and drinking were the chief amusements, and an occasional dance, in which Indian women participated, rounded out the social calendar.

But there was far more work than play in a miner's life on the Yukon, as a brief consideration of the life of A. E. Ironmonger Sola, a typical miner, will show. Soon after his arrival in 1894 Sola bought a mining claim on Miller Creek near Forty Mile. He hauled his provisions and hardware from Forty Mile out to the diggings, built a cabin, and chopped and hauled in firewood from a nearby hillside. Thawing and digging several shafts kept him busy all winter. In the spring he hired several men at $10 a day to help him with digging and sluicing, but he did not clean up enough gold to pay their wages. To pay off his debts, Sola whipsawed lumber for other miners at 10 cents a foot, then sold his mine for $250. He had originally paid $500 for the claim and, after a year's work, had not even realized his investment. But Sola did not give up; instead of continuing to work for wages, he borrowed $700, bought a dog team, and freighted goods from Forty Mile to other men's mines during the winter. After eight months of working hard for 12 hours a day, he had paid back the $700 loan and earned enough to try another mining venture.

Most of the miners at Forty Mile were men who had already been working along the Yukon River when the strikes were first made there, but others came inland from Juneau, where they had been working at the Treadwell or other mines. A few arrivals had come to Forty Mile directly from the Outside. One of them, Madame Emilie Tremblay, who arrived with her husband in 1894, is believed to have been the first white woman to cross the Chilkoot Pass. The small, polite society of Forty Mile, which Madame Tremblay joined, included very few other white women. Trader John J. Healy's wife was one, and Charlotte Selina Bompas, the wife of Anglican Bishop William Bompas, was another. For relaxation Mrs. Bompas was fond of reading Dante in the original. Perhaps she found it agreeably warm work during the cold winter.

Healy and Bishop Bompas together brought about a momentous change in Forty Mile, one that was resented locally at the time but that accomplished much for the orderly development of the region. Bishop Bompas believed that Forty Mile was within Canadian territory, and as the town grew, he urged the Canadian government to establish a garrison of the North-West Mounted Police there. In 1893 Healy, angered by an edict issued by a Forty Mile miners' meeting—the only government in the town—also called for the Mounties. It happened that Healy's wife had a hired white girl who enjoyed the town's night life too much for the Healys' taste. One night, to punish her for keeping late hours, Healy locked the girl out, and she, or her boyfriend, appealed to the miners. Healy was not popular with the miners, perhaps because the N.A.T. & T. Company did not extend credit at its stores, and the Forty Mile men appear to have used the incident as an excuse to spite the trader, for they ordered him to pay the girl a year's wages and to pay her transportation to the Outside.

In response to Healy's and Bompas' petition, inspector Charles Constantine made an investigatory journey in 1894. In 1895 a detachment of twenty Mounties was dispatched to keep the peace at Forty Mile. Bishop

Bompas was not resented by the miners—he was, after all, a man of the cloth and English—but the men of Forty Mile did not soon forgive Healy for invoking the aid of the Canadian government.

By the time the Mounties arrived, Forty Mile was no longer the only town along the upper Yukon River. In 1893 gold discoveries on Birch Creek, 240 miles downriver from Forty Mile, had led to the founding of Circle. In 1894, when the gold discovery was confirmed by arrival of the A.C.C.'s *Arctic* on her first voyage, many residents of Forty Mile returned with her to the new strike. By 1895 this new town had far surpassed Forty Mile in population.

5

Circle, 1893-96

JACK MCQUESTEN'S STOREKEEPING did not allow him any time for prospecting, but it permitted him to grubstake others. In 1893 two Creoles, Pitka and Sorresco, whom he had outfitted, discovered gold in paying quantities on Birch Creek. Their find led to the founding of Circle—also known as Circle City—240 miles northwest of Forty Mile and well within American territory. Its founders thought the town site was within the Arctic Circle, hence its name. Circle boomed, to become the first mining settlement on the Yukon River that could be fairly dignified as a town.

To the north of Circle the Yukon River flows through open flats as it makes a great loop across the Arctic Circle at Fort Yukon before arching southward to find a more direct course to the Bering Sea. Miners built log cabins at Circle and used it as a supply base and winter residence. Soon after the first cabins went up, the A.C.C. built a store; saloons were erected, and, wonder of wonders, an opera house was opened.[1]

By 1895 Circle had a population of 500, including a few women. Until the Klondike stampede it was the largest community on the Yukon. For a few years Circle was the only American camp of any size, and its residents had to govern themselves without the benefit of constituted authority. Miners in Circle could depend upon the trading companies for food and equipment, but the solution of the problems of living as an orderly community was entirely in their own hands.

The Birch Creek mines were easily worked because they were shallow. The removal of a few feet of overlay revealed bedrock. The shallowness of the diggings spared the miners a good deal of work, although it meant the mines could be worked only during the summer. In other areas, where deep shafts had to be sunk to bedrock, miners could work underground in relative warmth and comfort throughout the winter.

Most Circle miners backpacked all their provisions and equipment the

65 to 80 miles from town to the scattered mines of Birch Creek. In summer the trail crossed a swampy plateau of muskeg and scattered ponds; clouds of mosquitoes and black flies made a living hell. Game avoided such country during the summer, and the few pack horses available had to be shielded in canvas against the insect plague. With the first autumn frosts the mosquitoes disappeared, and the first snowfall made the use of freight sleds possible.

Freighting was the first service industry that developed to meet the miners' needs in Circle. Men with strength and capital enough—sled dogs cost from $75 to $200 each—made good money hauling to the diggings. Arthur T. Walden, a husky 24-year-old who reached Circle in 1896 after a three-month, 1,000-mile journey from the coast via the Chilkoot Pass, was one of many who went into the freighting business. In the summer freight to Birch Creek cost 40 cents a pound, so miners got by with as little as possible and waited to hire Walden or the other freighters to haul necessary supplies at much cheaper rates during the winter.

Miners themselves did not usually own sled dogs, although their use was becoming more widespread and those who had dogs usually made them pay as mail carriers or as freight teams. A mail carrier could skim along at a quick pace with a light load, whereas a freighter was pleased to make three miles an hour. Walden's six-dog team, hitched in single file, pulled three sleds lashed together carrying loads of 600, 400, and 200 pounds, respectively, or 200 pounds for each dog. Walden reckoned that his team could pull loaded sleds 20 miles a day on a long trip. (Sixty miles a day would not be unusual for a team hauling an empty sled.) Of course, mileage varied with the terrain, the condition of the animals, and the availability of feed for them, which was usually dried or frozen salmon.

Residents of Circle were proud of the place, but visitors sometimes were slow to discover the charms of the town. Harry DeWindt, an Englishman who stopped there in the summer of 1896, was frankly critical. On the misty day he arrived, Circle presented "a truly dismal and depressing appearance."[2] Jack McQuesten's storehouse, a corrugated iron shed that was an unusual structure in the region, was noted but not appreciated by DeWindt. But as a visitor, he could not have been expected to understand what a comparatively fireproof building meant to an isolated trading center, nor what its presence suggested in a region that had developed so slowly and painfully. DeWindt was a supercilious outsider, yet his observations reveal more of Yukon life than he might have thought. What he found tawdry and mean, the pioneers—particularly in remembrance—found exciting and glamorous.

Thus DeWindt, wading through the sticky muck, viewed the "motley collection of sodden dwellings and dripping roofs," and reflected with some asperity on the enthusiasm of Yukoners who referred to Circle as the "Paris of Alaska." He "failed to trace the slightest resemblance to the beautiful French city," but he did find more "gaiety, or life, of a tawdry, disreputable description than at Forty Mile, for every tenth house was either a gambling or a drinking saloon, or a den of even worse description."[3]

Circle's entertainments did not appeal to the English visitor. He had heard that the previous year a theatrical company of six women and five men had struggled over the Chilkoot Pass to present a "drama of the blood-curdling type," but only the dance halls were operating at the time of his visit. "I attended one of these entertainments . . . The orchestra consisted of a violin and guitar—almost drowned by a noisy crowd at the bar, where a wrangle took place, on an average, every five minutes."[4] Mud-stained men paid a dollar a dance to a painted woman and thought it well worth the price, but DeWindt was shocked.

Residents such as Arthur Walden recorded a different picture of Circle. He dispelled the image of a "roaring mining camp" and described a "City of Silence," broken in the summer only by the plodding of pack trains through the mucky streets, the rare whistle of a steamboat, and the howling of dogs.[5] People were about at all hours, for little distinction was made between day and night through the summer season of almost constant light.

Winter was even more silent. The snow hushed the sound of what little movement there was, and outdoor activity diminished. Wind rarely disturbed the calm. No birds sang. "The brown, dirty river turned to a sheet of white. Frost and snow hung over everything, and the cold was intense."[6] On one moonlit night, as Walden approached the town from the mines, he saw that "every stovepipe in the city was belching forth a column of fast-rising smoke which, when it cooled at a certain height, formed a sort of canopy over the entire city, with the smoke columns as posts to hold it up. From under this canopy the lights shone through the uncurtained windows, promising warmth, food, and rest."[7] Men who looked to Circle for "warmth, food, and rest" knew a town that a casual passerby such as DeWindt could hardly appreciate.

Miners' Meeting
It was at Circle that the self-government of a community by common agreement reached a kind of apogee. Miners at Juneau, Forty Mile, and Circle all followed a precedent set in the early days of the California gold rush and established mining regulations. The rules had always been supported by the American courts. At the first meeting in a new camp the men agreed upon the boundaries of their district, the extent of individual claims, and the method of staking and of giving notice. Then they elected

a recorder to note all the locations that had been claimed by prospectors. The acceptance of this procedure by the miners and later by the courts prevented widespread chaos and disorder.

In Alaska, as elsewhere, the miners' meeting served another necessary function—that of keeping civil order. For lack of any other recognized authority, the miners' meeting acted as judge and jury to punish those accused of transgressions. Opinions varied on the effectiveness and integrity of the collective body in this role. Some considered the miners' meeting to be the purest form of democracy; others regarded it as akin to mob rule.

Arthur Walden's Circle "was a town of some three or four hundred inhabitants which had no taxes, courthouse, or jail; no post office, church, schools, hotels, or dog-pound; no rules, regulations, or written law; no sheriff, dentist, doctor, lawyer, or priest." Despite these deficiencies—or because of them—"there was no murder, stealing, or dishonesty, and right was right and wrong was wrong as each individual understood it. Here life, property, and honor were safe, justice was swift and sure, and punishments were made to fit the case."[8]

Most pioneers shared Walden's high opinion of the miners' meeting as conducted at Circle, and veterans of Forty Mile bitterly resented the intrusion of the North-West Mounted Police's authority there. Among the most heartfelt legends of the Yukon mining frontier, are those that extol the purity of the miners' meeting.

The meetings at Circle were generally conducted in a saloon because no other structure in the young town was large enough for the assembly. And the setting could certainly affect the course of justice. Once, in a bootlegging case brought before the meeting by the customs officer, the men wanted to make sure that the confiscated goods actually consisted of whiskey. Bottles continued to circulate until all the evidence had disappeared and "case dismissed" was proclaimed.

On another occasion a prominent prostitute called May brought her grievance to the miners and demanded a jury trial for her civil suit. The regular miners' meeting, she argued, was nothing but a "damned kangaroo court."[9] May sought $2,000 damages from an ex-lover for boarding his dog team and for bodily services. Meanwhile, she was holding the valuable dogs. Unfortunately for the course of justice, the jury considering May's case was locked for its deliberations in the storeroom of the Pioneer Saloon. There the "twelve men good and true" were overpowered by temptation. After sampling two gallons of the best whiskey, the jury staggered out to report: "We the jury find the amount sued for is excessive and fine the defendant and assess the costs of the case to the plaintiff."[10] The boozy inclarity of the verdict left some confusion.

However, in their deliberations the jury had decided to thwart May by taking certain measures. While she was still attending court, one of the miners was dispatched to steal the dogs and head upriver. When May refused to pay the costs, the miners prepared to sell her cabin. A few of the boys thought it would be a good idea to spend the cash from the sale with May, but wiser heads prevailed. At any rate May mushed out of Circle, never to return, raging at the travesty of justice meted out to her.

Keeping order by way of a miners' meeting could result in injustice. Yet in the absence of more effective means, something had to be done, and the miners themselves took the institution seriously enough. Josiah Spurr, a government geologist, visited Circle in 1896 and found warning signs posted on all the saloons in town and on roadhouses along the trail to the mines:

NOTICE

TO WHOM IT MAY CONCERN

At a general meeting of miners held at Circle City it was the unanimous Verdict that all thieving and stealing shall be punished by WHIPPING AT THE POST AND BANISHMENT FROM THE COUNTRY, the severity of the whipping and the guilt of the accused to be determined by the Jury.

SO ALL THIEVES BEWARE[11]

But miners did not depend upon posters for protection. Those coming in from the creeks with their gold packed revolvers and kept a wary eye. The fruits of a year's toil had to be protected.

Selling whiskey was illegal in Alaska, but it was regularly floated down the Yukon to Circle from Canada. Generally, the United States customs official posted at Circle overlooked this traffic, for it could be dangerous to interfere with thirsty miners. Spurr's arrival, however, coincided with a very tense situation. Customs officials had seized two barrels of whiskey from smugglers and had stored it in the customs house. Word reached them that the saloon keeper and others were planning to take the valuable spirits from them, by force if necessary. They recruited Spurr to aid them, and all three men, armed with rifles, watched nervously.

A group of miners approached the customs house and called for a parley. If the officials would be reasonable, argued the mob's spokesman, no one would get hurt, and they would be paid "a nice little sum as a plaster" for healing wounded dignities.[12] The officials refused to barter.

They barricaded themselves in the customs house, where they maintained a night-long vigil. The mob did not carry out its threat of an attack.

Spurr attended a miners' meeting while in Circle City, and its proceedings showed how swiftly public opinion could shift. The recorder had called for a meeting because his lot, which he had chosen for his office, had been jumped. Sandy Jim was named chairman, whereupon he mounted a box in the midst of the miners who were assembled at the river bank. The miners buzzed sympathetically on hearing the complainant explain that his town lot had been jumped. Another man climbed on the box to argue forcibly that the jumper "had acted in defiance of the miners' meeting, which was the only law they had." He proposed a fine. If the culprit resisted he should be "put in a boat and set floating down the Yukon."[13]

Before appointing a committee to execute the tribunal's judgment, the chairman asked that the jumper be identified. The miscreant turned out to be Black Kitty, one of Circle's soiled doves. After revealing this, the complainant himself pleaded for less severity. "I don't think we ought to be so hard in this case . . . She's a woman, even if she *is black* and a fighter, and she's alone and working for a living." The miners agreed. A speaker moved that Kitty be left alone. "I don't think anyone wanted to quarrel with a woman, and black one at that."[14] Anyway, he argued, there is plenty of land for public purposes out in the bush. A chorus of approval greeted this statement, and the crowd scattered even before the chairman had time to formalize the decision.

Sourdough C. S. Hamlin participated in several miners' meetings at Circle. Thievery was usually punished by banishment. If banishment was decreed, the convicted had 24 hours to clear the region. On one occasion a "blue ticket," an order to leave town at once, was issued to a businessman who had resorted to gun play in a dispute over a dog. The thermometer recorded 60 degrees below zero at the time, but no account was taken of it and the man was dismissed into deadly weather.

Even breach-of-promise suits came up on the "court" docket. It happened one year that after the ice breakup the steamer *Bella* docked with an expectant bride aboard, but the miner who had promised to marry her had changed his mind. She appealed to a miners' meeting. The reluctant miner rested his defense of two grounds: his poor health and that the plaintiff had once vamped a married man. Circle's only doctor, a veterinarian, testified that the defendant looked healthy enough to him. Several orators declaimed against an abandonment of the girl merely because of a slight tarnishing. A wedding was decreed.

In a similar case noted by James Wickersham, a young woman appealed to the miners because a dance hall fiddler had enjoyed her favors, had made her pregnant, and had then reneged on his promise to marry. A meeting was swiftly called and a judge and sheriff elected. Then a warrant was issued, and the fiddler appeared before the meeting. Evidence was taken and the miners unanimously resolved without debate:

> *"that the defendant pay the plaintiff's hospital bill of $500.00, and marry her as he promised to do, and that he have until 5 o'clock this afternoon to obey this order; and resolved, further, that this meeting do now adjourn till 5 o'clock."*[15]

The miners enjoyed a spell of leisure in the saloon until the afternoon session convened. Then, having received verification of the nuptials, the court, along with the bride and groom, adjourned to the saloon once more to toast the blushing couple.

Klondike Discovery

Miners at Circle and Forty Mile first heard about the Klondike discovery in the late fall of 1896. Robert Henderson had found good prospects there and had passed the word along to George Washington Carmack. Then Carmack and two Indians, Skookum Jim and Tagish Charley, found gold in quantities never before seen in the Yukon country. In one pan they scooped up $4 worth of the glistening metal and realized they had a bonanza. To prospectors who, having found as little as 5 or 10 cents' worth of gold in a pan, did not hesitate to sink a shaft to bedrock, $4 to a pan was unprecedented. It was August 17, 1896, when Carmack staked the first claim in the region that would soon become world-famous. By one of those quirks of fate, Henderson himself had not bothered to stake any claim and was thus denied any part of the fortune that his efforts had revealed.

Carmack did not keep his discoveries to himself, but still the stampede did not begin immediately. Miners at Forty Mile were skeptical of "lying George" at first. Carmack was married to an Indian and consequently did not enjoy a good reputation. Besides, he had never been a very zealous prospector; the Indian life—fishing and hunting—had always appealed to him more than the hard grind of gold hunting. Still, miners could not ignore such an electrifying report, especially after Carmack had shown them a shotgun shell filled with coarse gold. Soon men traveled upriver from Forty Mile to have a look, and by the time winter came on, the reports of other miners confirmed the strike. It became clear that this time the great strike was neither a hoax nor a delusion. By early winter most of the men of Forty Mile had rushed to the new ground and staked claims.

Circle was farther away, and the first rumors to reach that camp were not believed either, until in January, 1897, when Arthur Walden mushed in with letters for saloon keeper Harry Ash. Ash's partner had hit it big and was now summoning the saloon keeper. According to legend, Ash tore off his apron and invited the boys to drink up his stock. Within hours he was mushing for the new goldfields, while free booze detained some of the miners in the saloon. For riotous hours they swilled away, while cooler heads were trying to buy sled dogs. From the normal price of $25 to $50 for a single dog, the price soared to $1,500. Virtually everyone in Circle rushed to the Klondike. Some of them would make a fortune in Dawson. When the news did spread to the outside world, the whole of it was crazed by "Klondikitis." A new day had dawned for the Yukon and Alaska.

Part II

THE KLONDIKE ERA

6

Seattle Gets the News

AT FIRST it was just a rumor discussed in the saloons along First Avenue and in some business offices and homes during the 1896–97 winter. Seattleites who had relatives or friends in the North were getting word that great things were happening on the Yukon, that a huge goldfield of unparalleled wealth had drawn the men of Forty Mile and Circle upriver to the Klondike. True or not, it was stirring news for a city still in the throes of a depression. Work was scarce everywhere in the States, and unemployed men, then as now, were restless and volatile. Some Westerners were demanding that the government adopt a free silver standard that would free the national economy from the relentless grip of a specie shortage; others, like the young and footloose Jack London, joined the grim ranks of Coxey's Army on a long trek to Washington, D.C., to demand relief.

Few people in Seattle had any firsthand knowledge of Alaska or northern Canada. What was there to know? Fishermen from Ballard sometimes brought in catches from Bristol Bay and other Alaskan waters, and the cannery operators shipped in their seasonal salmon pack. But these activities did not contribute to any consciousness of the interior. Fur merchants in San Francisco followed developments in Alaska, but only a few persons were involved in this small industry. It took sensational events to change the prevailing dim awareness of Alaska among inhabitants of the Pacific coast into high interest.

The arrival of the *Portland* from St. Michael on July 17 ended speculation. Rumors were confirmed in flamboyant fashion by banner headlines in the *Seattle Post-Intelligencer:*

GOLD! GOLD! GOLD! GOLD!

Sixty-Eight Rich Men on the Steamer <u>Portland</u>

Stacks of Yellow Metal

Some Have $5,000, Many Have More, and A Few Bring Out $100,000 Each

The Steamer Carries $700,000

Special Tug Chartered by the <u>Post-Intelligencer</u> To Get the News[1]

The *Post-Intelligencer* made its scoop by dispatching newsmen to meet the *Portland* off Cape Flattery, and its extra was already on the streets as the Seattle crowds flocked to greet the *Portland* at the dock. Another ship, the *Excelsior*, had reached San Francisco two days before the *Portland* arrived in Seattle without attracting as much attention, although its twenty-five passengers carried $189,000 in gold. Another ship, the *Annie Maud* from Calcutta, commanded headlines in the Bay City because the bubonic plague had been reported aboard. Seattle thus stole a lead on its California shipping rival—a lead it never lost.

The news from Seattle swept across the nation—and the world:

A TON OF GOLD ON THE <u>PORTLAND</u>!

Eager Seattleites at the dock gaped as the *Portland* passengers disembarked. Wells Fargo Express Company guards were there in armed force to protect the precious cargo. Down the gangplank marched John Wilkerson with $50,000 in gold; Dick McNulty had $20,000; Frank Keller had $35,000; and Frank Phiscator landed with $96,000. Others had smaller sums; all had rousing stories to tell. In a moment these fortunate prospectors had created a legend. Fortunately for posterity, some of them had style and were more than willing to declaim on the wonders of the Klondike to newsmen and saloon crowds and to emphasize the extent of their gains by the reckless spending that the tradition has always demanded. They told of the fortunes still in the ground, described the methods of mining, identified the most bountiful creeks, and pointed out the most expeditious routes to the goldfields. Never was a city so far removed from the actual scene so instantaneously and thoroughly altered by a gold discovery. Seattle accepted the gold madness gleefully; the city fathers realized Seattle's advantageous position and determined to secure it. Now the

"Queen City of the Pacific Northwest" was also to be the "Gateway to the Goldfields."

Seattle got a huge jump on other west coast cities competing for the northern trade. The city was fortunate in having a chamber of commerce public relations man of striking energy and imagination.[2] Erastus Brainerd set out to let the world know that Seattle was the northernmost rail terminal and seaport and that it was the most experienced center of northern outfitting. Thousands of advertisements were placed in newspapers all over the Midwest. In Illinois alone, 488 weekly newspapers carried ads for Seattle. To find out anything about the Klondike and Alaska, Brainerd advised, just write to the Seattle Chamber of Commerce. National periodicals—*Mussey's, McClures, Harper's*, and others—also carried Seattle ads. When migrants reached Seattle they were encouraged to write to their local newspapers to describe their good reception in the Queen City. Brainerd provided stationery, postage, and even the message. A special Klondike edition of the *Seattle Post Intelligencer* of 212,000 copies was sent to newspapers all over the country. In addition, 70,000 copies went to postmasters all over the United States, 6,000 to the public libraries, 4,000 to city mayors, and 15,000 to the transcontinental railroads.

Brainerd established a special information office within the chamber of commerce to follow the Klondike news that appeared in the nation's newspapers, and he relentlessly corrected any erroneous reports on the North or on Seattle. He churned out information in an endless stream. Potential argonauts were warned against river rapids, were advised to take care in fording streams, and were assured that the Seattle Chamber of Commerce would provide all the travel particulars needed.

Foreign countries were not forgotten. Crowned heads received photographs of Alaska and the Klondike, and the foreign embassies were sent stacks of information brochures, including Brainerd's masterpiece, an official proclamation of the State of Washington, issued over the signature of the Secretary of State, which boosted the Seattle gateway.

With this kind of promotion, coupled with obvious geographic advantages, Seattle's rivals—Vancouver, Tacoma, Portland, and San Francisco—could not keep pace. In the late 1890s Seattle's population increased by 88 percent.[3] Shipbuilding and transportation companies zeroed in on the Alaska trade, and vendors of everything from lumber to machinery prospered with the mining boom. Seattle could boast of being "the only city in the world that owned a territory."[4]

Victims of Klondike fever numbered in the tens of thousands; casual laborers, farmers, students, cowboys, professional men, bakers, journalists, entertainers, saloon keepers, seamen, businessmen, and even miners were among those infected. Men such as George Pilcher, Wyatt Earp, Rex

Beach, and J. F. A. Strong preferred to go on their own; others such as Will Ballou and John Hewitt formed joint companies with like-minded neighbors who were willing to pool their resources and talents. Many individuals and companies were backed by investors who wanted a share of the northern enterprise but did not care to undertake the adventure in person.

Much discussion and planning went into the preparation of the northern ventures. Publications issued by the Seattle Chamber of Commerce represented only a small portion of the literature available for consultation. There were also guidebooks or handbooks purporting to give all the information required by an argonaut: how to get there, what to take, what to expect. Publishers did not waste any time getting these wares on the market. A 550-page volume, the *Chicago Record's Book for Gold Seekers*, was in the bookstores in the fall of 1897, just a couple of months after the bonanza news reached the Outside. Other similar works followed hard and fast.

The *Chicago Record's* book advised readers that transportation on the all-water route to the goldfields from the west coast would cost about $200 and would allow the voyager to take along 200 pounds of baggage. There were cheaper ways to get there: steerage passage from Seattle to Skagway could be had for $15, then one could hike into the interior over the Chilkoot Pass, packing his own provisions if he did not care to hire the Indian packers who specialized in the work.

Another guidebook published in 1897 which was "carefully prepared" by Ernest Ingersoll, was *Gold Fields of the Klondike and the Wonders of Alaska*. Ingersoll knew what qualifications were needed for a man to be a success as a northern miner, although he did not reveal how he garnered such wisdom. "To be well prepared is half the battle won." The conditions of the frontier were certain to make a man resourceful and self-reliant, "but these things being equal, it is the one who has just the right equipment who will have the advantages when the going is hard and to all appearances pretty even." Of course, Ingersoll noted, "to be sober, strong, and healthy is the first requisite for any one who wants to battle successfully for a year or two in the frozen lands of the far North." And it was not just the physical aspect that was important. "Temperament counts for a good deal in the miner's life. Men should be of cheerful, hopeful dispositions and willing workers. Those of sullen, morose natures, although they may be good workers, are very apt, as soon as the novelty of the country wears off, to become dissatisfied, pessimistic, and melancholy.[5]

Many thousands of men and women studied such guidebooks as a preparatory step for the great gold-seeking adventure. One may forget why they were so eager to gamble so much on unknown prospects until one reads the stipulations of such writers as Ingersoll: "If a man is able to meet these conditions he is almost sure of making a good living and takes chances with the rest in making a fortune."[6] That certainty of "making a good living" was quite a lure in a depression-ridden nation, although in fact no such certainty existed. Much of the lore of the North hinges on the "gold fever" of the argonauts, but perhaps a better understanding of the pioneers, particularly of those who remained in the North, comes through an appreciation of their desire for steady employment. What could be more attractive, despite the rigors of climate and remoteness, than a land where a man could find work, work that would provide him a decent income and, beyond that, the possibility of a fortune?

Most of the 1897–98 argonauts chose Seattle as their port of embarkation to the North. Opinions about Seattle and its role as northern outfitting and shipping center varied. Will Ballou and his Vermont party found the city fascinating and prices reasonable. One had a bed for 50 cents a night and good meals for 20 to 25 cents. All the hustle and bustle was stimulating, and Ballou was not put off by "fakiers trying to sell you a gold crusher, a Klondike stove or a dog team with one lame dog which would get well by tomorrow."[7]

Reputable brands of dried and canned foods, clothing, and tools vied in the marketplace with fanciful contrivances: a special "Klondike" bicycle and machines designed to scoop out paydirt effortlessly could be purchased. Clairvoyants were willing to tell where rich placers existed. Con men, often posing as returning prospectors, were on hand to separate the gullible from their money. One could buy a map to a glittering "lost mine," invest in sure-thing mining stock, or grubstake a miner who already owned valuable ground.

Special trains came into Seattle from the East loaded with stampeders. Spielers met them at the King Street station, crying their wares. Newspaper reporters interviewed arrivals of interest. Carl L. Lokke's Minneapolis group attracted attention because it included ten Norwegians, two Danes, two Swedes, and two Americans. The Scandinavian party had been warned that Seattle was a "dirty, dingy, hilly, nasty, foggy, ill-kept, God-forsaken little country town." Lokke found the city a "hot town . . . the liveliest city in America," where one could buy indispensable items like Klondike protection hats, Klondike frost extractors, or Klondike sectional boats; stay at the Klondike Bar Hotel; and get a haircut at the Klondike Barbershop.[8]

Arthur Arnold Dietz found Seattle unbearably crowded and full of cheats. "I thought that nothing could surprise a New Yorker. But I was sadly deluded and to my sorrow . . . we were relieved of hundreds of dollars through schemes that looked perfectly good until we got to Alaska and found that we had been defrauded in every way."[9]

Dietz's impressions of the city were recorded after his return from an

Alaskan experience marked by disaster. His bitterness can be understood and his outraged moral tone discounted: "That western city was more wicked than Sodom; the devil reigned supreme. It was a gigantic chaos of crime and the city government as an institution protected evil. Every kind of illicit business flourished."[10] Among the provisions laid in by the Dietz party were 100 pounds of evaporated eggs that turned out to be corn meal.

Dishonest dealers could be avoided by wary travelers who kept their wits about them, but they could still suffer at the hands of greedy shipping companies and their agents. Carl Lokke bought second-class tickets for the steamer *City of Seattle* in Minneapolis and boarded the vessel to find that only tourist accommodations were available. The passengers "were treated not like men but dogs."[11] Every hulk that could steam or sail north was loaded beyond its registered capacity; overcrowding, poor service, and indifferent food were the normal conditions, and nothing could be done about it. If one chose to join the exodus, the price was high in fare and in discomfort. Despite all, the compelling motive was to get out of Puget Sound and to the scene of action.

7

Skagway and Soapy Smith

WILLIAM MOORE was a man of vision. When the *Al-ki*, the *Portland*, and other ships landed stampeders from Seattle, Tacoma, Victoria, and San Francisco in late July, 1897, the 74-year-old man's foresight was rewarded. Moore, a seasoned veteran of 50 years' experience in Western gold camps, concluded in 1888 that in time there would be a major stampede to the Alaskan interior and that the route would be over the passes at the head of Lynn Canal. After examining the two passes, the White, which he named himself, and the Chilkoot, Moore built a cabin on Skagway Bay not far from the base of the White Pass. The White Pass was 45 miles long and not as precipitous as the Chilkoot, which was shorter by 10 miles. Three miles west of Moore's cabin was Dyea Inlet; just inland, the Chilkoot Pass, or Dyea Trail, commenced. John J. Healy, also a man of vision, built his trading post at Dyea in 1886.

Skagway is a beautiful place, well wooded, embraced by lofty mountains that stand back a few miles to allow breathing space, watered by the Skagway River, which dashes through the forest to join the clear, blue waters of Lynn Canal. Winter weather on the coast is never severe, although rain and snowfall are heavy; strong winds sometimes prevail, but the excruciating cold of the interior is unknown.

Into this enchanting setting swept a continuous wave of men and women in 1897 and 1898. They were in a hurry and did not concern themselves overmuch with the sylvan beauty of the region, nor with Moore's claim to legal title of the site. Frank Reid, a former Indian fighter and a surveyor, laid out Skagway's streets, and carpenters labored through the remaining weeks of summer and the fall to erect stores and dwellings. Moore was ordered to move and was forced to do so when he resisted. Orderly legal processes would have to wait; immediate urgencies demanded that saloons, stores, hotels, and houses be erected to serve the argonauts. Four years later a court would recognize Moore's claims, but in the first frenzied days of Skagway's existence there was little time for niceties.

Skagway's name derived from the Indian word "Skagus," meaning the home of the north wind, and the town arose as fast as if it had been swept in by a wind. At the same time neighboring Dyea grew into a town of a few buildings and many tents—not on Skagway's scale, however, because Skagway's anchorage was better.

The first issue of the *Skagway News* appeared on October 15, 1897. Skagway's newspaper was by no means the first in Alaska: Juneau and Sitka papers had been publishing for years, and even the interior had the *Yukon Press*, a semiannual issued from 1894 to 1899. But the *Skagway News* was the first Alaskan newspaper of the Klondike era. It soon had rivals, however, in the *Skagway Daily Alaskan* and the *Dyea Trail*. After the fashion of frontier newspapers, each boosted its community, holding its neighbor up to scorn.

The *Dyea Trail* was first published in January, 1898. Its editor, Charles D. Ulmer, lit into the Skagway press with fierceness. Naturally the two Skagway papers had been berating Dyea as a terminal for passage into the interior, while extolling the merits of Skagway. "As bad as we are here, and as contemptibly as both the alleged *News* and *Alaskan* have used us, we refrain from answering such drivelling rot." The *Alaskan*'s "putrid" article is "a stain on their city and a horrible botch upon its authors." Ulmer raged against his neighbor's "glowing headlines too foul to reproduce" and the "vile language" used. "Authorities should suppress papers for obscenity or indecent exposure."[1]

New Alaskan towns were sensitive to derogatory reports made by outsiders. Among the stories in the first edition of the *Skagway News* was one describing a public meeting that illustrates this sensitivity. Major J. F. A. Strong of the *Skagway News* read to the meeting from a copy of the *Seattle Times* in which Skagway was pictured in very black terms. According to the Seattle newspaper, Skagway teemed with "1,500 starving and desperate men" caught by the winter before they could cross the Chilkoot Pass into the Klondike. Skagway did not, of course, lack food, and the meeting hooted at the false report of the Seattle "prevaricators."[2] Such stories were annoying: argonauts feared that their relatives would become alarmed, and businessmen were concerned that such gloomy tidings would divert rushers to other places.

Alaska's first post-Klondike gold camp differed measurably from Circle, the earliest interior town. Circle had a certain stability that Skagway lacked; its population was much smaller and therefore more controllable; it had a clearer purpose and more civic pride. Unlike Circle, Skagway possessed some of the amenities of civilized centers from the outset—a newspaper and churches existed by the autumn of 1897. Yet these evidences of a gentler culture could not stem the lawlessness that gripped Skagway through the 1897–98 winter. Neither could the much-vaunted miners' meeting system of justice cope with the turbulent conditions of the coastal town. The effectiveness of the miners' meeting depended upon the existence of a manageable number of men with the common purpose of mining in the immediate region. Skagway was a place of passage for all but a handful of entrepreneurs and a class of hoodlums. New arrivals, intent upon crossing the mountains, were not community builders, nor were those returning from the interior, whose only concern was to book passage south.

Little wonder then that Skagway fell into the hands of an organized gang of criminals who imposed a reign of lawlessness over the town and its environs for a good six months. Much has been written about the "King of Skagway," Soapy Smith. Smith, a man of imposing appearance —tall, slim, handsome, black bearded—had worked at cardsharping and shell games for years in western mining camps. In 1892 he and his gang had manged to take complete control of Creede, Colorado, by rigging the election of cronies as officials. In occasional brushes with the law, Smith indicated some capacity for humor. Once, when a criminal court judge in Denver thought to sanction him for maintaining an illegal gambling house, the articulate con man explained that his institution existed for an educational purpose—to cure afflicted men of the gaming habit. As proof of this claim, he exhibited the Latin sign that stood over the entry to his place: *Caveat Emptor* (Let the buyer beware).

Alaska was made to order for Soapy Smith. After looking the situation over in the autumn of 1897, he rounded up a number of rogues and set up an organization. Smith planted his men on Seattle docks, on incoming ships, all around Skagway, and on the trails to guide newcomers to his various establishments, which included a saloon and gambling house, the telegraph office, merchant's exchange, cut rate ticket office, reliable packers, and information bureau. The moment the unfortunate victim showed a wallet of substantial proportions in any of these places, he was a marked man. If a bold thief did not grab it at once and take off, another waylaid the traveler later. Even the hue and cry that attended such open robberies was carefully staged. The robber was never caught, and the stolen goods remained lost, yet the frustrated stampeder could usually depend upon the benevolent Smith's loan of boat fare back to Seattle.

Among the 100 or more ruffians who leeched on the stampeders and on those returning to the Outside from the Klondike were a few whose talents compared with their leader's. "Reverend" Bowers looked and talked as if he were the refined preacher he pretended, and was always ready to give advice. "Slim Jim" Foster, youthful and good-looking, seemed eminently trustworthy and could easily steer gullible men to Smith's saloon and gambling emporium. "Old man Tripp" played the part of a Klondike veteran, dispensing information to new arrivals while he sized up their potential as victims.

Soapy's gambling ventures at his saloon, Jeff's Place, were all rigged in favor of the house, and there was no town official, policeman, or judge to whom a fleeced rusher could effectively complain. Some of the Smith enterprises bordered on the legitimate. Family men liked to leave a message at the telegraph office announcing to the folks at home their safe arrival. What lonesome traveler minded the expenditure of $5 for the telegram and another $5 for the collect reply that was sure to come within a few hours? Of course, in 1898 Skagway did not yet have a telegraph line.

Smith also exploited the opportunities presented by the outbreak of the Spanish–American War by setting up a recruiting station for "Klondike Volunteers." Broke and discouraged stampeders were lured to an enlistment tent, where a "doctor" conducted physical examinations. Applicants were probably not as interested in serving in the U.S. Army as they were in getting free transportation to Seattle or San Francisco. "No, sir! It won't cost you a cent," cried a pleasant-spoken member of Smith's gang. And there was absolutely no obligation to join the army, "but you must pass the doctor. The War Office made that imperative."[3]

Henry Toke Munn was an interested witness of this larcenous charade. Men responding to the recruitment fraud stripped down to their boots in the enlistment tent, then stood by helplessly as an armed thug emptied pockets, demanded money belts, and ordered the fleeced patriots out the back of the tent. New victims appeared with regularity and were robbed in the same manner. Robbery victims could not appeal for police protection but some helped themselves. Munn stayed six nights in Skagway and observed shoot-outs on the street each night. Colonel Sam Steele of the North-West Mounted Police was roused from his sleep one night by sounds of gunfire just outside his cabin. Curses and shouts mingled with the pistol shots as the battle raged. Steele and another Mountie officer, Maj. Zachary Taylor Wood, kept low and did not intervene; the Queen's rule did not extend to beleaguered Alaska. "Bullets came through the thin boards [of our cabin], but the circumstance was such a common event that we did not even rise from our beds."[4]

Steele considered Skagway "about the roughest place in the world." Robbery and murder were daily occurrences. Smith's gang, over 100 strong, "ran the town and did what they pleased; almost the only persons safe from them were the members of our force . . . Neither law nor order prevailed, honest persons had no protection from the gangs of rascals who plied their nefarious trade. Might was right."⁵

Foolish men who wandered into Skagway's variety theaters in search of entertainment were besieged by "actresses" who preyed on spectators during intervals, cadging drinks in return for their attentions. A soft young man engaged in hauling Steele's freight over the White Pass paid $750 for a box of cigars and $3,000 for drinks in one of the theaters. The clip joint proprietor had gall enough to complain to Steele because the young freighter still owed $1,000 for the night's fun. Steele refused to collect the money and warned the owner to stay on the American side of the summit.

The Mounties did have one direct encounter with the archrogue of Skagway. By the late spring of 1898 the Mounties had accumulated $150,000 in customs fees from the rushers and wanted to ship it out. Their precautions in doing so were testimony to a high respect for Soapy's operation. Major Zachary Taylor Wood, named for his grandfather, the former president of the United States, was given the job of transporting the money. Rather than ship the money to the coast under a conspicuous Mountie guard—and perhaps occasion an embarrassing shoot-out in American territory—Wood and his escort packed it in ordinary saddlebags. To explain the journey, Steele announced beforehand that Wood had been transferred to new duties. With these precautions Wood got over the trail safely, yet the gang dared an interception after the Mounties set out from Dyea to Skagway by boat to board a waiting steamer. Wood held off the boatload of thieves until he reached the Skagway wharf. There the Canadian Pacific Railway ship *Tartar* was docked, and other Smith men lined the dock. Because the *Tartar's* sailors were armed with rifles, the gang's attempted robbery got no further. Wood refused Soapy's gracious invitation to visit Skagway, and boarded the *Tartar* without interference.

Smith's enlistment endeavor was not his only stratagem to capitalize on the Spanish–American War. In keeping with his pose as a respectable leading citizen, he organized a civilian militia composed of his gang and notified the War Department that the group was available for foreign service. Washington responded with thanks, but declined the acceptance of the Skagway force. This rejection came as no shock to Soapy, and did not discourage his patriotic enthusiasm. Rather than disband the "militia," he paraded it in town as a visible sign of his power. On the Fourth of July, 1898, Soapy, mounted on a white stallion, proudly led his force down Skagway's main street. As the town's first citizen, he was called upon to give the leading address in the Independence Day celebrations. The occasion was quite a triumph for Smith, and his speech rang with patriotic spirit. American institutions and character merited eloquent praise, and stalwart frontiersmen were exalted; the absence of effective federal courts and marshals in Skagway went unmentioned.

In the summer of 1898 some of Skagway's citizens determined to restore order to the town. Frank Reid, a civil engineer, and J. F. A. Strong, a newsman, were among those forming the vigilante committee, the Committee of 101. A public notice was issued:

WARNING
A word to the wise should be sufficient. All confidence sharks, bunco men, sure-thing men, and all other objectional characters are notified to leave Skagway and the White Pass. Failure to comply with this warning will be followed by prompt action!

Signed — COMMITTEE OF ONE HUNDRED AND ONE.[6]

Not to be outdone, Smith returned the challenge with an announcement from the Committee of 303:

ANNOUNCEMENT
The business interests of Skagway propose to put a stop to the lawless acts of many newcomers. We hereby summon all good citizens to a meeting at which these matters will be discussed. COME ONE, COME ALL! Immediate action will be taken for relief. Let this be a warning to those cheechawcos who are disgracing our city! This meeting will be held at Sylvester Hall at 8:00 p.m. sharp.   (Signed) Jefferson R. Smith, Chairman[7]

At the public meeting Smith harangued a large audience. Outsiders, he cried, were trying to take over the town from the true pioneers. Riffraff from all over the world were attempting to disrupt order. The Bunco King was cheered noisily.

A good number of the people in town were bamboozled by Smith's pose as a keeper of order. Others knew better but, sensing that trouble loomed, hoped to stay out of the line of fire if the two mobs clashed.

Another notice was posted by Smith:

PUBLIC WARNING

The body of men calling themselves the Committee of One Hundred and One are hereby notified that any overt act committed by them will be met promptly by the law-abiding citizens of Skagway and each member and their property will be held responsible for any unlawful act on their part. The Law and Order Committee of Three Hundred and Three will see that justice is dealt out to its fullest extent and no Blackmailers or Vigilantes will be tolerated.

(Signed) LAW AND ORDER COMMITTEE OF THREE HUNDRED AND THREE[8]

For a while the vigilantes lay low. Most were prudent men. They appealed to the small U.S. Army garrison at nearby Dyea for help, but the military had no authority in such a matter. No officer in his right mind would dare to intervene unless ordered to do so.

In Dyea people were noting these doings in Skagway with fascination and disgust—and feeling quite self-righteous about their orderly community. In March the *Dyea Trail* quoted the bulletins issued by the two committees and commented: "And there you are!"[9]

In the end, it did not take representatives of law to overthrow the notorious con man. A few days after the glorious Fourth of July festivities, a vigilante meeting was called by the Committee of 101 to consider Smith's activities. Such daring defiance of the first citizen of the town could not go unchallenged. Smith, no respecter of conventional law and order agencies, could not tolerate a rival order.

The vigilantes concluded their meeting and sent a notice to Smith that he had 24 hours to return all the gold dust he had stolen from a recent victim. Knots of men stood about on the streets, watching and talking excitedly. Members of Smith's gang broke the groups up and forced their dispersal. The vigilante committee called for another meeting to be held at 11 P.M. that night.

Smith's critics assembled at the appointed hour but had not long to discuss the course of events before their adversary bore down on them. Boldly striding up to the assembly place, Smith, armed with two revolvers and cradling a double-barreled Winchester repeating rifle, shouted to the crowd, "Chase yourselves to bed."[10] A bodyguard of fourteen of Smith's men were backing up their leader; although they displayed no arms, they were known gunfighters.

At the door of the meeting place surveyor Frank Reid confronted Soapy. Smith leveled his Winchester at the poor man's breast. Both men fired at the same instant and fell together in a confused heap on the ground. Smith was dead; Reid did not live long. The bodyguards charged forward, then backed off as one of the vigilantes picked up Smith's Winchester. Just four days before, mounted on a white horse, Soapy had proudly led the Fourth of July parade. *Sic transit gloria mundi!* Soon the bodyguard and all the other men of the gang took to their heels. With the posting of guards at the passes into the interior and on the wharves, their hope of escape was thwarted, and most were rounded up. Those who were not prosecuted were banished from town.

Soapy's reign extended through the 1897–98 winter to July, 1898, a long period considering the audacity of his minions and the character of some of the stampeders. Stampeders were customarily armed and not all were gentle city folk: Many were veteran frontiersmen well accustomed to defending themselves. Descriptions of Skagway during this period give the impression that the tens of thousands of gold seekers quaked under the tyranny of the Smith mob. This is somewhat farfetched. Incontestably, the mob's predations were frequent and outrageous, yet they must have exercised a great deal of discretion. They, too, knew something of the frontier and had long since learned to avoid men of character and experience, the hard-eyed individuals who disdained shell games and fingered their weapons if anyone seemed too curious or pressing. Hoodlums preferred the gullible, the drunks, and the naive gamblers as victims. Men who looked to their own concerns in a purposeful way were rarely molested. Thieves and con men found prey enough among the weak and stupid; after all, hardened criminals have never been inclined to look for unnecessary trouble. One stampeder, Jim Geoghegan, recalled that he had passed through Skagway without seeing Smith or any of his men. "If you don't get drunk, you don't get rolled" was Geoghegan's assessment.[11]

What maintained Smith's position was his plausibility, the support he drew from other Skagway citizens, and the general indifference of the many who did not suffer at the hands of his mob. Smith knew the frontier and recognized the quality of its hardier men. Arthur Walden, the Forty Mile freighter, "knew Soapy personally and was proud of it." He was safe because he had no money "and knew enough to keep my mouth shut."[12] Mike Mahoney, another experienced dog musher, claimed that Smith offered him a job, which he refused. Mahoney, if his story can be believed, had attracted Smith's attention by warning miners about the card cheating in Jeff's Place, yet was unmolested. Both Walden and Mahoney were obviously impressed by Smith's personality.

But most of the stampeders were like Lynn Smith, an 1898 stampeder who watched the Smith gang openly rob a man in Wrangell. "About one hundred of us were watching—all afraid to make a move." When Lynn Smith got to Skagway he also witnessed a shooting, but he and other spectators did not get involved. They had learned "that no matter what kind of a crowd you may be in, if you keep your mouth shut and attend to your own business, you are never in danger of harm from outsiders . . . especially if you are broke and green."[13]

Soapy Smith's killer, Frank Reid, was honored by Skagway's citizens. His grave was marked with a marble slab inscribed: "He gave his life for the honor of Skagway." But as the gold seekers moved on it was Soapy they remembered better. Smith became firmly enshrined in the gold rush legend, and, for good or bad, is still one of the best known of Alaska's historic figures.

8

Chilkoot and White Passes

AMONG THE 60,000 STAMPEDERS of 1897–98 was a husky 21-year-old, Jack London of Oakland, California. London and his partners were among the 30,000 to 40,000 argonauts to choose one of the passes from the head of Lynn Canal as their route to the Klondike. Most, like London, favored the Chilkoot over the White Pass. Both passes reached the lakes that form the headwaters of the Yukon River some 30 to 40 miles inland from Skagway and Dyea. From the coast to Dawson City the distance was more than 600 miles, mostly a water route in summer. But it was the first 18 miles from Dyea to the summit that caused most anxiety to travelers. In all of the American frontier experience not another stretch of trail has been so widely and diversely reported on. Its rigors were described in the numerous personal narratives of participants, in guidebooks, brochures, and thousands of newspaper articles—and, of course, in the stories of Jack London.

By the summer of 1897, when London made his crossing, the Chilkoot had long been a well-established entry to the interior of the North. Its passage had always entailed a hard grind for travelers, but only with the major stampede did the trail come to be represented as something more than a steep, rugged stretch of terrain. Great movements of people always contribute to legends; the mundane and ordinary become spectacular, transformed by mass participation into something of heroic proportions. So it was with the Chilkoot and the rest of the Klondike trail, which became, in legend, an awesome obstacle, a towering challenge, the maker or breaker of character.

From Sheep Camp, at the base of the mountains eight miles from the coast, the slope ascended sharply for 10 miles to the summit, an elevation of 3,500 feet. Extra hard scrambling was required over the last 1,000 feet, as the grade by then is about 35 degrees. But such statistics do not define the reality of the Chilkoot, nor explain why it loomed so awesome in the imagination of tens of thousands of stampeders. What made the Chilkoot a terrifying barrier were the conditions of 1897–98. Crossing the pass under ideal weather conditions on the hard-packed snow of early spring was one thing; undertaking it during a winter blizzard through deep, soft snow quite another. When Lieutenant Schwatka, Henry Davis, Arthur Walden, and other early travelers had crossed the pass, they had not been crowded by thousands of anxious men and women, some of whose excitement bordered on hysteria. Nor had the early climbers been pressed by companions fresh from offices and shops, little inured to demanding physical feats, by travelers too old or too young for strenuous effort, and too careless and inexperienced to wait on the weather for advantageous traveling circumstances. Stampeders made the Chilkoot forbidding by the pressure of their own numbers and their highly charged mood. Its passage inspired fear because so many of those attempting it were ignorant or misinformed, inept, disorganized, and weak. And those who made it across had good reason to feel triumphant over those who arrived at Skagway—and there were many of them—who saw the challenge of the Chilkoot and decided forthwith to return to their homes without testing the trail.

Any proper assessment of the mental state of the stampeders as they approached the passes is impossible. How did they react to the turbulent crowd at the beachhead at Skagway and Dyea? Their view of the route depended upon reports read and heard; their ability to withstand the mob frenzy and to maintain good judgment depended upon individual stability. Misinformation created more apprehension than did existing physical hazards, and contributed to the tension of the experience. Little of the product of alarmed rumor can be traced to its source, yet its effect on the atmosphere on the trail and in the camps was felt throughout the whole gold rush era. Rumor fed on the dazzling expectations of gold seekers and on their morbid fears as well. Rumors stimulated and depressed the thousands of restless fortune hunters, sometimes sparking them to endure extreme hardship, other times inclining them to panic and quit.

What made the Chilkoot trail a cruel punishment for most stampeders of 1897–98 was the necessity of tackling it time after time, weighed down by unaccustomed backpacks. The average argonaut brought from 1,000 to 2,000 pounds of supplies into the country, and most lacked money enough to hire packers. This meant that up to twenty or more crossings had to be made after one's base depot was made at Sheep Camp.

Jack London and his companions expended two days of arduous labor in advancing only two miles on a hard piece of the trail, and they were lucky with the weather. London took a great deal of pride in the prowess he developed in the course of such relay packing. By the time his party reached the last stage of the pass, a three-mile descent to Lake Linde-mann, London's performance equaled that of a Chilkat: "I back-tripped it four times a day, and on each forward trip carried one hundred and fifty pounds. This means that over the worst trails I daily traveled twenty-four miles, twelve of which were under a burden of one hundred and fifty pounds."[1]

In a novel, *A Daughter of the Snows*, London depicted the long line of straining backpackers in more vivid terms:

Time had rolled back, and locomotion and transportation were once again in the most primitive stages. Men who had never carried more than pencils in all their lives had now become bearers of burdens. They no longer walked upright under the sun but stooped the body forward and bowed the head to the earth. Every back had become a pack-saddle, and the strap galls were beginning to form. They staggered beneath the un-wonted effort, and legs became drunken with weariness and titubated in diverse directions till the sunlight darkened and bearer and burden fell by the way.[2]

The White Pass was attempted by many in the autumn of 1897 who assumed that it afforded an easier passage to the interior. It was lower than the Chilkoot and much less precipitous, yet had its own peculiar hazards. Pack animals could not make it over the Chilkoot, and travelers so provided were attracted to the gentler ascent of the trail that began from Skagway. But the White Pass trail proved a death trap for horses and mules. Hundreds fell from the twisting, narrow trail into the valley below; others foundered in deep snow or mud, or broke their legs fording the rocky streams. All the animals were worn by the crushing weights they carried, particularly when the long line of progress was halted time after time due to obstructions on the trail. Bruised and torn by their loads and exertions, driven by men brutalized by their inexperience, the wretched animals fell along the way. The trail lined with their rotting carcasses became known as "Dead Horse Trail." Men who loved horses were ap-palled at the horror of it.

Snows closed the trail during the winter of 1897–98, covering the stinking carnage. In the spring thaw the uncouth procession started up again, but the mire cut movement to a snail's pace. Travelers were warned against using the trail because of the mud and stench. Angelo Heilprin counted nearly 1,000 festering remains, enough to average one carcass for each 60 feet of the trail. In 1898 railroad construction began on the White Pass, and by 1899 trains operated on the route that was remembered chiefly for the viciousness of its animal drivers.

All was not grimness and labor on the Klondike trail; there was recreation as well. At every stage where men halted to cache their supplies before going back for another load, a tent city arose. Tired men could call at saloons for liquid refreshments or to patronize the gamblers. Even hotels, of sorts, were on hand. Mrs. George Black paid $1 for a bunk at Sheep Camp's Grand Pacific Hotel. Although the hotel looked more like a woodshed to Mrs. Black, it offered the basic comforts, including meals at $1 each. Prices of food rose on the other side of the divide; meals generally went for $2.50 and coffee with donuts for four bits. Hard liquor and bunks kept to a standard price of $1 everywhere.[3]

Gamblers ran their games wherever a number of people gathered. Some of the operators belonged to Soapy Smith's Skagway gang and hoped to fleece the unwary who had managed to get through the tidewater town with money belt intact. Others were freelancers enroute to Dawson themselves, not unwilling to give the boys along the way a run for their money and to help them pass the time.

All the entrepreneurs along the trail contributed to the carnival mood. There was nothing gloomy about the "instant" towns at Sheep Camp and along the lakes and river. Some argonauts seemed more interested in fun than gold and did not mind spending their money for recreation. If they could hit it big in Dawson, they would soon recoup the money laid out for booze and their gambling losses. Men reasoned that they should occasionally have a chance to forget all the nonsense told of the dreaded trail and relax: hard work merits hard play. Others, more cautious types, were amazed to see money thrown away so recklessly on drink and gambling. Storytelling and interminable comparing of mining plans would do them for diversion.

On the American side of the border there was some disorder, and, for lack of any other authority, the stampeders punished malefactors in their own way. Three Californians had cached their provisions near Sheep Camp in the autumn of 1897 and returned to the Outside for the winter. When they came back, they found their cache had been plundered. Two men, Hansen and Wellington, were caught with some of the Californians' gear in their possession. A miners' meeting was quickly held in a saloon tent at Sheep Camp, and the two men were convicted of theft. Wellington broke away from his captors and took to his heels—but there was no way to escape pursuit. As the miners reached him, Wellington shot himself in the head fatally. Hansen was whipped with a knotted rope and, after receiving fifty strokes, was conducted to Dyea wearing a large sign inscribed with one word, "Thief." According to Carl L. Lokke, Governor Brady of Alaska, who made an inspection trip to the region just after the affair, issued his approval. "This may not be legal," the Governor declaimed, "but it will be salutary for thieves for some time upon the trail and will be better than a whole lot of moral suasion."[4] Brady had little option but to approve of such impromptu justice because the federal authorities had done nothing either in Skagway or on the trail to see that order was maintained.

Order did exist on the Canadian side of the divide—the Mounties saw to that. Early in the stampede the Mounties had established a customs station on Tagish Lake; then, to prevent ill-provisioned rushers from coming into the interior, a post was manned right at the Chilkoot summit. No one knew whether the summit was in Canada or in United States' territory, but, in the absence of any American effort to police the pass, the Mounties moved in. No one was allowed to get beyond the summit unless he had a year's provisions, about 1,000 pounds of food. Many tried to circumvent this elementary precaution only to be turned back by the armed police who were on watch day and night.

During the winter and early spring, traffic along the pass varied with the weather. Cold, clear weather aided travel, but snow storms were a menace. From March until the first of May storms swept the mountain almost incessantly. Travelers holed up wherever they found themselves, and waited for the weather to break. The Mounties established a post on the White Pass too, and officers at both stations collected customs on all goods that had not been purchased in Canada. The rushers grumbled as they paid, but there is no doubt that they benefited by the Mounties' presence. Officers treated the sick and put an end to the provocative gun-toting so dear to American frontiersmen. Guns had to be kept secured in one's baggage, a restriction that made conditions much more secure for everyone. Furthermore, the dregs of Skagway, Soapy Smith's hoodlums, dared not venture as far as the Mounties' posts. Their proper milieu was disorder, and the Canadians' efficient exertions in keeping the peace were not to their liking. "I noticed the difference in the demeanour of the people of all nationalities when they arrived under the protection of our force," wrote Colonel Sam Steele of the North-West Mounted Police, "everyone went about his business with as strong a sense of security as if he were in the most law-abiding part of the globe."[5]

On two occasions thundering avalanches of snow and ice hurtled down on hapless travelers. In September, 1897, fierce winds forced loose the glacier's edge, releasing a lake that heavy rains had built up on the glacier. Tents and gear were strewn for miles around as miners fled to high ground. Three lives were lost.

In April, 1898, after weeks of heavy snowfall, a second avalanche occurred. Men engaged on the most treacherous part of the trail, ascending "The Scales," the steps cut into the face of the mountain on the last stage to the Chilkoot summit, were swept off the cliff into oblivion as they raced back down the trail before a roaring, massive burden that buried an area of 10 acres under 30 feet of snow. Frantic rescuers pulled over 100 men to safety; between forty and sixty others died under the snow.

Typhoid fever was another killer. A score or more men were struck down in Dyea in the spring of 1898; and more than eighty succumbed in Dawson at the same time. Drownings on the upper Yukon accounted for many other deaths, although their numbers are uncertain. Government reports estimated that fewer than one percent of the tens of thousands of participants in the 1897–98 stampede met their end on the trail.[6]

Still another menace was spinal meningitis. Just after crossing the Chilkoot, Al McLeod fell victim to this disease. A doctor from Los Angeles tried to help him, but had no medicines. "Use whiskey," advised the doctor, "there is nothing better available." Left to himself, McLeod lay in his tent for five weeks, eating a mixture of whiskey and sugar. His big problem was keeping the camp stove going. When he was able to, he gathered wood. Most of the time he remained in his sleeping roll, feeding the fire when necessary without getting up.[7]

Once the Chilkoot was passed, the most dangerous portion of the trek was over, but the next stage of the journey called for a halt for boat-building. Lake Lindemann, or Lake Bennett for White Pass travelers, or another part of the headwaters of the Yukon River, were the sites of the necessary boat-building activity. Winter arrivals at these lakes had plenty of time, for there was no further travel until spring. Men sweated through the arduous work of building boats without the benefit of sawmill products. The logs to be sawed rested on a simple platform about seven feet above ground. Two men, one on the platform and one below, worked their way through the length of the logs on either end of the seven-foot whipsaw. This work, said to be the hardest known to man, strained men beyond endurance, ended partnerships long held, and dissolved families. Each sawer felt in his aching muscles that the other loafed while he strained. Addison Mizner and his brother, Wilson, never regained quite the same fraternal rapport they had once had after going through this experience:

The man on top has to be almost a tight rope walker with new back muscles to pull it through. The one below gets just as dizzy looking up and trying to follow the line, while he gets his eyes and mouth full of sawdust. There is little choice between the two, and I changed forty times with Wilson the first day. Each time he argued that I had all the best of it. In fact, we spent most of the time climbing up and scrambling down.

At the end of two hours we had half a board sawed, and he asked me

*if I was tired. Of course, I wouldn't acknowledge that I was nearly dead.
He called me a "big stupid dumb brute," which started a slight un-
pleasantness.*[8]

Mizner also related the story of the two partners who went to school
together, worked in the same bank, and married sisters, because they
could not bear to be separated. Whipsawing ended all that and drove them
to such bitterness that in dividing their property they insisted on a precise
halving of all—even of their twenty sacks of flour, which they severed in
half rather than divide whole.

Jack London and his party reached Lake Lindemann in September.
Once their craft was fashioned, it did not take them long to reach their
destination. After spending two weeks building their boat, it took them
only four days to cross Lakes Lindemann, Bennett, Tagish, and Marsh;
one day to get through Box Canyon and the dreaded White Horse Rapids;
a week to cover the next 30 miles of river and cross Lake Laberge—then
the going was pleasant for the 400 miles of river navigation to the goldfields.

Although London and his companions accomplished this stage of their
journey in a month's time and without suffering any notable mishaps,
other parties were less fortunate. Many of the stampeders dared the rapids
rather than portaging their property around them. The rapids claimed over
twenty victims in 1898 and demolished scores of their jerry-built vessels.

By the time 150 boats and outfits had been lost on the White Horse
Rapids, Sam Steele laid down the law to boatmen: "There are many of
your countrymen who have said that the Mounted Police make the laws as
they go along, and I am going to do so now for your own good." Steele
prohibited boats from carrying women and children: "If they are strong
enough to come to the Klondike they can walk the five miles of grassy
bank to the foot of the White Horse."[9] No boats were allowed in the
rapids unless their freeboard was sufficient to ride the waves in safety. No
boats could pass unless steered by men who had demonstrated their competence to the Mounties.

Taken altogether, the Chilkoot–White Pass stampede was an incredible
occurrence. The mass movement was entirely without central direction; it
surged on in a mass comparable to that of a modern army, but without
leaders. It was an army composed of single individuals and small groups
bent upon rapidly crossing rugged country of which they were generally
ignorant, burdened with provisions, equipment, and menaced by a sometimes severe climate. That the vast majority of men, women, and children
reached the Yukon safely must be recognized as a tribute to their endurance
and resourcefulness. But much credit must go to the Mounties, too; their

efforts averted countless disasters. It seems remarkable that the distinguished work of the Mounties did not inspire the United States government to provide similar services on American territory. The response of the American government to the needs of law enforcement was meager during this stampede and equally deficient later when the Alaskan gold rush boomed.

9

Army Help and Arctic Fraud

To the Relief

The Klondike excitement stimulated much more military activity in the North. Four separate concerns directed the effort: relief of destitute miners, explorations, and the establishment of telegraph communication and roads. Far more was undertaken and accomplished in five years than in the previous three decades, the difference being due to the waves of gold seekers pouring into Alaska.

The overture to the military expeditions followed the lines of a comic opera. It was reported in 1897 that the miners at Dawson City, most of them Americans, faced a winter of starvation. Congress responded generously by appropriating $200,000 for their relief, and the Army was ordered to take on the task of their aid.

Some inspired official hit on a brilliant idea. Reindeer had earlier been imported from Siberia to Alaska's Seward Peninsula and had thrived there, so why not use the animals to haul provisions to the Klondike? If reindeer were suitable to the Seward Peninsula they could easily be driven over the trail to Dawson City. This kind of reasoning, mired firmly in ignorance of the varied regional geography of the North, has often plagued Alaskan endeavors.

Since navigation to the Bering Sea had already closed, Alaskan reindeer were unavailable. Sheldon Jackson, the missionary who had introduced reindeer to Alaska, was sent to Norway and Sweden in December, 1897. On February 27 the steamer *Manitoban* landed in New York with 538 head of reindeer, 113 drivers, 418 sleds, 411 sets of harness, and lots of reindeer moss for forage. By March 7, 1898, the animals, still in good condition, and the equipment reached Seattle. In Seattle the Army received word that food supplies at Dawson were adequate, not that the expedition could have arrived in time to be of help in any event. Mean-

while, curious Seattleites thronged the Woodland Park Zoo ogling the
exotic beasts while the military men pondered the situation.

It is not possible to learn from the military reports published in *Narratives of Explorations in Alaska* what happened to the relief project. Obviously, the Army wished it had never heard of reindeer, and the compiler
of *Narratives* discreetly dropped the story after explaining that the animals
"were to be turned over to Dr. Jackson as the agent of the Department of
the Interior."[1] By literally passing the buck to Jackson, the Army avoided
the embarrassment of subsequent events.

In May, the expedition disembarked at Haines, at the head of Lynn
Canal. Their destination was now Circle, on the Yukon, and they would
travel the Dalton Trail to the Klondike, enroute to the Alaskan town. It is
hard to imagine what the party had in mind. The supply of imported
forage was dwindling rapidly. Somebody *must* have known that the region
to be traversed did not support reindeer moss. Despite all, the trek commenced and proceeded to its futile end.

For nine months the expedition straggled along, beset by mosquitoes;
they pushed their way over mountains, glaciers, and snowfields, slowed by
swamps and hummocks. Wolves and Indians picked off a few reindeer,
but most were victims of starvation or the rigors of the trail. Finally,
in January, the party limped into Dawson, the drivers themselves half
starved and exhausted. Only 114 animals survived the adventure of the
year-long relief expedition.

On the Yukon

Another military relief effort consisted of the dispatch of two officers,
Capt. Patrick Henry Ray and Lt. Wilds Richardson from the state of
Washington, the nearest Army garrison, to investigate conditions on the
Yukon. They found a chaotic situation. In Dawson, stampeders without
adequate provisions were urged to try to get Outside before the 1897
freeze-up. Many headed downstream for St. Michael. Circle came to life
again as a couple of hundred miners who were unable to find rich Klondike ground returned to their old diggings. As the close of navigation
approached, hundreds of men in a wide variety of vessels were pushing
their way upriver, hoping to reach the Klondike before the ice barred
further progress.

At Circle the miners grew desperate as steamers of the two major
trading companies, the Alaska Commercial Company and the North
American Trading and Transportation Company, passed by, enroute to
Dawson. Provisions were short in Circle, and a starving winter loomed. A
miners' meeting resolved to take action and use force, if necessary. The
two last steamboats upriver were boarded by determined, armed men.

Thirty tons of food were unloaded from the *Weare*, 25 tons from the *Bella*. There was no violence. Company employees cheerfully helped the miners unload, while the captains fumed. Captain Ray was aboard the *Bella* and protested the holdup very mildly—he and Richardson were the sole representatives of United States military authority in the interior.

The miners explained their situation to the captain. Trading companies had ignored their appeals for provisions throughout the summer. "There is no law or any person in authority to whom we can appeal," the miners noted.[2] Money was not the question; the miners paid in gold dust for all that they took.

Ray sympathized with the Circle miners, who were orderly and posted guards over the newly acquired stores to prevent pilfering. At Fort Yukon, 75 miles downriver from Circle, the scene was more threatening. Lieutenant Richardson sent urgent word to Ray that a gang of 30 to 40 hard characters from Dawson intended to loot both company stores.

Ray started for Fort Yukon in a small boat. The river was still open, though it was running with ice. By night he heard the distant roar of ice in motion. An Indian told them this meant the river was freezing, and the eight men pulled for shore. Before they could make it, the ice piled up on either side in towering hummocks, leaving the boat in what Ray likened to a gorge. Night fell and the men sat it out, wondering how far they were from shore.

In the morning the party managed to creep over the ice to a nearby island and from there were ferried to shore. Ray and 150 other stranded men trekked 65 miles to Fort Yukon, where Richardson had thus far kept things in control. Richardson had ordered the storekeepers to supply destitute miners with food, in return for which the men would cut wood.

Enough of the lawless element was present, however, to make a camp a powder keg. A group of men demanded that Ray offer no interference; they meant to take what supplies they required for the winter. Ray faced them down by taking possession of both stores in the name of the government. He, Richardson, and a few miners stood guard, and the would-be looters desisted. Thwarted in their hopes, the same men got back at Ray by applying for supplies as destitutes—which they were not. Reluctantly, Ray let them have provisions and they thumbed their noses at the wood-chopping proviso and left the camp.

Experimentally, Ray caused a miner who had falsely claimed to be destitute and received a season's supplies to be arrested by the United States commissioner at Circle. After getting the supplies, the man hired a freighter to take them from Fort Yukon to Circle for 25 cents a pound. When the enterprising miner was jailed in Circle, the men of the camp demanded his release. When refused, they broke open the jail and gave the miscreant his freedom, whereupon he moved his supplies to a saloon and auctioned them off, gambled away the proceeds, and left for Dawson, "saying he had a good outfit there."[3] Ray learned the limitations of an authority that could not be enforced. He noted, however, that the old sourdoughs were not the lawless ones, but that the new men were running things.

Besides coping with the supply shortage, Ray was sending reports to his superiors advising the best course of action for the 1898 summer. He recommended that a speedy, shallow-draft steamer be commissioned to patrol the river to protect the trading companies, and also urged the establishment of several military posts, starting with one near the mouth of the Tanana. Ray also passed along geographic knowledge he had gleaned from veteran prospectors, urging the survey of a route from Cook Inlet to the Yukon via the Tanana. An "all American" route, either from Cook Inlet or Prince William Sound, would be shorter and could be kept open in winter. Most importantly, a foreign country would not have to be crossed in order to reach the rich goldfields of Alaska.

In 1898 two expeditions were launched by the Army. Captain William Abercrombie explored from Valdez to the Copper River; in 1899 he managed to slash a trail through the area. The other expedition, headed by Capt. Edwin Glenn, investigated potential routes from Prince William Sound and Cook Inlet into the interior. Both parties covered their ground and reported superficially on the region, its people, and resources. Luckily, the natives were invariably helpful; several soldiers owed their lives to Indian hospitality.

The exploration efforts of the Army were scarcely notable. Everywhere the explorers went they were preceded by stampeders who had not waited for the government trailblazing. The Army's explorations were too late to help much, even had they been conducted successfully—and they had not been. Perhaps the expeditions constituted a useful survival exercise for the soldiers; otherwise the results were minimal. A historian has described the military explorations as "a series of loops, stretching through the territory like a chain, rather than a solid line."[4] Delays plagued both parties, and the parties' provisioning always posed problems because of their ungainly size. Often backtracking was necessary. The Army's glory in the gold era, if any was earned, was to be generated by successful construction and operation of the telegraph line by Capt. Charles Farnsworth and others. Exploration required smaller, more capable parties with greater mobility, and, for lasting value, the results needed cartographic recording. It was the role of the United States Geological Survey (U.S.G.S.) to answer these needs in Alaska eventually.

Among the more positive contributions of the government were those

made by the U.S.G.S. in Alaska. Surveys of Alaska's mineral resources
were first undertaken in 1895 and in 1896. Both expeditions were modest
ventures limited by $5,000 budgets. With the Klondike excitement the
Geological Survey was better funded, so that more extensive field work
could be accomplished. Unlike the military explorers, the U.S.G.S. teams
traveled light, in small parties, and made meticulous observations, which
were published in the Bulletins of the U.S.G.S. Prospectors who consulted
the reports and maps could rely on their accuracy.

Alfred H. Brooks became head of the U.S.G.S. in Alaska during the
gold era and remained its leader for many years. Brooks and his men had
to be tough to do their job investigating a rugged country where they
sometimes had to cut their own trails.

In 1898, U.S.G.S. expeditions were intent upon providing guidance to
stampeders by mapping. The upper Yukon was mapped topographically
by one party. Another penetrated the interior of the Tanana River by way
of Cook Inlet and the Susitna River. J. E. Spurr led an expedition up the
Susitna, crossed to a tributary of the Kuskokwim, and descended that
great river to its mouth, some 1,300 miles. Brooks surveyed the Tanana
region, an area that would, a few years later, be the scene of another great
stampede. Thus, bit by bit, the vastness of the interior appeared on
U.S.G.S. maps.

Kotzebue Sound Fake

The expansive shores and waters of Kotzebue Sound straddle the Arctic
Circle. In 1898 the region was little known except to the Eskimo inhabitants. Russian circumnavigator Otto von Kotzebue had voyaged there
early in the century; British captains searching for the lost Sir John Franklin expedition had spent some time there; and an occasional whaling
vessel called. Missionaries were the only white residents. Rivers like the
Noatak, Kobuk, and Buckland spilled into the sound and built up imposing sand pits. Kotzebue Sound seemed an unlikely place to find gold, yet
thirty-three ships out of Seattle and San Francisco landed over 1,200 men
and women on its inhospitable beaches in July and August of '98.

Thomas R. Stewart was one of the Kotzebue Sound argonauts. A West
Coast shipping company's glowing circular caught his eye in Albany, New
York:

---

*Latest dispatches from Kotzebue Sound, by way of the United States
Revenue Cutter* Bear, *say 'The U. S. Government officials are staking
natives to work placer diggings.' Natives last year brought down a quantity of nuggets to trade. Captain Wagner, of the Schooner* Premier, *testi-
fies to receiving a nugget weighing one and seven-eighths ounces from a
native of Kotzebue Sound . . . Two prospectors have just arrived in Port-*

land with $15,000 in gold, taken from Kotzebue Sound . . . Gold fields
only four days' boating from ship's landing; only one day's towing; abso-
lutely no obstacles to the immediate working of mines.[5]

Stewart was out of work, so he packed up, entrained for San Francisco
and, once there, outfitted himself and took passage on the *Catherine Sud-*
den, a 400 ton, three-masted barkentine. After a two-month voyage the
old ship disembarked her passengers at Cape Blossom, north of the Arctic
Circle. The argonauts soon learned that they had been hoaxed. A resident
missionary, amazed at all the traffic to his remote station, asserted that no
gold had ever been found there. All the statements in the brochure had
been concocted out of thin air.

Two-thirds of the disappointed stampeders chose to prospect the region. Gold had not been found there—but they might yet be the discoverers! Their optimism was equaled only by their ignorance. Not one of the
group had any experience with survival in the North, and they would
suffer accordingly.

The party worked its way up the Kobuk River, one of the Arctic rivers
draining the Schwatka Mountains, and made camp for the winter. Scurvy
ravaged them over the long, cold months. Aching joints, receding gums,
and loss of teeth were general symptoms. Some of the men died of exposure; a few killed themselves. The quest for gold was forgotten; now it was
just a matter of survival until spring. When, at last, the weather softened,
Stewart recalled, "We stood and stared, blank-eyed, across the ice of the
Kobuk River. It was the one hope—the road back."[6]

Toiling back to the coast with the stronger men helping the weak was
an exhausting experience. Fortunately, the U. S. Revenue Service cutter
Bear was on hand to carry the most serious cases to the St. Michael hospital.
Other ships succored the rest of the weary argonauts who wanted to quit the
country. Hundreds of bitter men left, cursing the country and the greedy
shipping company whose deceits had caused them such travail.

The adventure had a happy ending for Stewart. After spending another
winter on the Kobuk without finding gold, he was getting ready to go
Outside, when word of the Nome strike reached Kotzebue Sound. Nome
was only 200 miles south, and so Stewart, although somewhat dubious
because of his recent experiences, took passage to the mushrooming Bering Sea camp. His luck changed and he struck it rich.

Another of the Kotzebue Sound stampeders fared even better. Among
the sailors manning the thirty-three sailing ships of the fraudulent
Kotzebue Sound stampede was one Erik Lindbloom, who deserted his
ship to become one of Nome's original discoverers and a millionaire.

10

Yukon Voyage

FOR THOSE who did not want any part of overland travel to the goldfields, there was an all-water route from Seattle and other Pacific coast cities. Ocean steamers carried passengers the 2,750 miles from Seattle to St. Michael, near the Yukon River delta, where they transferred to river steamers for the 1,700-mile course up the Yukon River to Dawson. The all-water route was more expensive than the route via the Chilkoot or White Passes and took longer—six weeks was the average time. Very few argonauts reached Dawson by way of St. Michael in 1897, most starting too late in the season. Freeze-up caught hundreds at various places along the river where they were forced to set up camp until navigation reopened. If they had adequate provisions, their lot was not hard physically; but their frustration was extreme as winter closed the passage before them. For weeks they whiled away the time in bitter boredom, plagued by their thwarted ambitions and the thought of the fortunes being reaped by others not imprisoned by the winter. A handful among the stranded secured dog teams and kept going, but both dogs and confidence in the ability to travel long distances with them were in short supply.

The great wave of Yukon-bound voyagers arrived in St. Michael in the spring of 1898, after the Bering Sea ice went out. Jeremiah Lynch, George Pilcher, and Will Ballou were among the thousands of ninety-eighters who traveled by this route, and each realized something of his aspirations.

Voyagers to Norton Sound passed through the Aleutian Islands and were sometimes landed at Dutch Harbor on Unalaska Island. Jeremiah Lynch and his fellow passengers were forced to spend three days in Dutch Harbor before continuing on to St. Michael. The delay was vexing, and none found his first Alaskan landfall very encouraging. Many of the 3,000 stampeders Lynch encountered there were short of money, lacked camping equipment, and were apprehensive of the travails ahead. "If this was the land and climate at Unalaska," reflected Lynch, "how much worse must it not be a thousand miles still further into the frozen north?"[1] Many wondered whether they had made a terrible mistake in joining the stampede.

When, having passed through miles of mud-colored sea stained by the silty water of the Yukon River, Lynch and the others reached St. Michael aboard the *St. Paul*, they found the island trading post equally unattractive, but at least they had completed the long ocean part of their journey. Passengers who were without through tickets to Dawson were lightered ashore and dumped on the beach, where thousands waited for the river steamboats. Others, like Lynch, were allowed to remain aboard the ocean steamers until their connecting river vessel arrived. Hundreds of tents clustered about the few buildings—stores, warehouses, barracks, and hotels. Saloons and gaming houses did a good business. Those uninterested in the pleasures they offered had few other options. Hiking for a view of the country was out of the question because of the waterlogged tundra in every direction. But at least there was time to write the last letters home before pushing on to the interior.

The first river steamers arriving from upriver brought plenty of excitement. Lynch and other passengers gaped from the rail of the *St. Paul* as a river boat dashed up to their ship and came alongside to permit boarding. Heavy boxes were transferred to the *St. Paul* from the river steamer; their contents were not hard to guess—Klondike gold! Now the men of '98 could hardly contain their impatience. With luck they could return to St. Michael in a few months with the same kind of precious cargo.

For the river voyage Lynch and others eagerly boarded the *Leah*, a steamer operated by the Alaska Commercial Company. More passengers were accommodated on a barge pushed before her than on the steamer itself. The barge was fitted out to carry 175 passengers: rows of crude berths lined the sides, and a long dining table ran its length. Its covered deck protected passengers from rain, but not from the mosquitoes. Despite its shallow, four-foot draft, the barge ran aground even before the *Leah* could nudge it through the silt-laden waters of Norton Sound into the Yukon's mouth. Soon, however, the experienced seamen got the vessel free from the sandbar, and the *Leah* reached one of the several river channels.

A boat such as this, pushing a barge up the Yukon against a four- to five-mile current, made about six miles per hour. Going downriver from Dawson, the boat could make about 15 miles per hour. Two hours were expended daily taking on wood provided by woodcutters who lived along the river. Each day the *Leah* had to take on about 30 cords of wood.

Wood prices varied from $14.00 per cord at Dawson to $7.00 on the
lower Yukon. Freight rates were understandably high because the boats
used 30 to 50 cords of fuel each day. Thus a larger boat's fuel for the
voyage from St. Michael to Dawson and return could cost $15,000.

All along the river the steamer passed small boats drifting down the
river to St. Michael. These carried men who had been in Dawson and were
now anxious to terminate their northern adventure. On one day Lynch
counted 111 boats carrying 500 disappointed men, all of whom shouted
the same doleful tidings to the *Leah* passengers: "Go back, cold winter,
poor grub, no work, and hundreds starving."[2] Such warnings hardly encouraged those aboard the *Leah*; clearly the Klondike gold had escaped
the grasp of these returnees. Still the fault was probably their own. Lynch
"contented himself with thinking them weaklings."[3] In a sense Lynch was
correct. Few aboard the steamboats rushing to Dawson in 1898 were
going to find rich placer ground that had not been staked, yet Lynch
would do well because he had the necessary capital to invest in mining
properities. Others not as amply prepared were likely to be disappointed.

The *Leah* stopped briefly at Rampart, which was by then a fairly prosperous little mining camp. Miners there were overjoyed to receive mail
carried upriver on the steamer, the first news from home many of them
had in over a year. Rampart had been a refuge during the 1897–98
winter for argonauts caught by the freeze-up enroute to Dawson. Rex
Beach, the novelist and short story writer, was one of these.

Beach worked as windlass man in a mine during the winter for $5 a
day, a bunk, and beans. When the river opened he took up woodcutting, in
hopes of making huge profits by supplying fuel to steamers like the *Leah*.
Unfortunately, competition kept the prices down. Offering their wood at
$40 per cord Beach and his partners were rebuffed by the river captains;
they dropped their price to $35, $30, $20. They finally moved their wood
at $10 a cord, but only after agreeing to load it as part of the bargain. By
then the woodchoppers had subsisted for some weeks on an unvarying diet
of grayling caught in the river, and they were desperate.

Beach decided not to bother going to Dawson with the '98 stampeders.
At Rampart he could find work, while too many men were leaving Dawson for lack of it. Without realizing it, he was gaining material for stories
that would provide him more gold than any mine he ever worked. Some of
the stories were told him by a Texan, Bill Joyce, "a lean hawk-faced
frontiersman," for whom he worked during the winter. Joyce's yarns were
"hilarious tales of adventures and prowess but underneath their humor,
lay a bitter resentment at the fact that time and ravages of life in the open
had severely sapped his early vigor."[4] Joyce was a septuagenarian who
walked the 24-mile round-trip from his mine to Rampart three times a
week to visit his lady love, this after 10 hours of digging.

Will Ballou and his Vermont party reached St. Michael about the same time as Jeremiah Lynch. Their goal was the Tanana River, but they could not get very reliable information on the prospects of that region. Indeed, the Tanana discoveries had not yet been made, though there were the usual optimistic reports in circulation. The Vermonters had already decided against Dawson, and the discouraging words of returning Klondikers were no incentive to change their minds. Rampart sounded like a better possibility; its mines had been producing steadily since 1896 and, reportedly, there was still unstaked ground available.

Ballou's party had a more adventurous river voyage than did Lynch on the *Leah*. It even included a mutiny. The mutiny ensued after the steamer and barge ran aground on a sandbar and seemed destined to remain there permanently. Despite the best efforts of the crew, the vessels could not clear the bar and the disgruntled passengers, ninety-nine in all, watched with increasing wrath as other boats steamed past. Finally, the passengers boiled over at the futile, sweating efforts of the crew to get free of the imprisoning shoal. An impressive document was drawn up and signed by all; the ship's officers were declared to be deposed and replaced by elected leaders, and all the passengers agreed to stand by their new leaders in any eventuality. For several days the passengers turned to and unloaded all the freight from both barge and river boat. Then the steamer's engine was fired once more and everyone pushed and heaved in the effort to clear the bar—to no effect. The bar continued to hold the vessels fast. With some chagrin the passengers dissolved their organization; authority was restored to the ship's officers who, at long last, managed to free the boats.

The rest of the voyage passing without incident, Ballou reached his destination at Rampart. Finding land prices were not extravagant, Ballou bought a town lot for $50. He and a partner wanted to have a log cabin built before they did any prospecting; its construction occupied their first weeks in Rampart. Timber of sufficient length had to be secured two miles upriver, floated down in a raft, then man-handled up the 30-foot-high bank upon which the town was situated. By mid-September their snug cabin was completed, a winter's supply of firewood was cut and stacked, and their cache was full of provisions. With equanimity Ballou watched the continuing parade of steamers passing by on the way to Dawson, and noted the first snowfall. Soon the winter would close the river, and the busy Yukon would become quiet again. Dawson's population was probably 40,000 or 50,000; Rampart had only 2,000 or 3,000 residents, yet the smaller Alaskan settlement was more stable than the big Canadian town upriver. Buying a claim from a miner who wanted to get Outside before winter, Ballou started to dig. Although he did not appreciate it at the time, Will Ballou was of a different stamp from the majority of stampeders. At Rampart he found a life, however arduous and poorly re-

warded, that suited him. Ballou numbered among that small class of men
who stayed put. Other waves of stampeders would surge by his cabin
without stirring him with their restless frenzy; Will Ballou put his roots
down at Rampart.

George M. Pilcher was another 1898 stampeder who arrived at St.
Michael the same summer as Ballou and Lynch. His goal had been Dawson, but he was dissuaded by the exodus from the Klondike camp. Pilcher
owned a river launch, made to his specifications in Seattle, and was well-
provisioned. To a reader of his notebook diary it is evident that the young
argonaut's love at first sight for the Yukon River could lead to a life-long
infatuation:

*Made a fine run to the mouth of the Yukon River across miles of shallow
water past great flats heaped with driftwood along a broad meadow of
grasses, moss and flowers. This evening presents a picture of posy dream-
land. As the sea is a perfect mirror while stretch(ing) from N.E. to S.W.
is a sky festooned and draped in the most soothing mellow hues that show
alike both sky and water completely obliterating the horizon. This can
only be surpassed by the floweriest pictures of the gateway to paradise or
soft low strains of music from heaven. Nothing in my sweetest dreams ever
compared to this scene.*[5]

Pilcher, 34 years old, had put everything he owned into the northern
venture. Pilcher could not give up and return to his wife and two young
daughters, who had been left behind in Ohio. If the Klondike held no
fortune for him, perhaps there were alternatives for a man willing to work
hard. An occupation was suggested by the size of the Yukon steamboat
fleet and its demand for fuel. Pilcher decided to find a camp site on the
lower Yukon, chop wood for a living, and perhaps trade with the natives.
In his spare time he could do a little prospecting. Too many men made
gold-finding an all-or-nothing pursuit; Pilcher saw no profit in such an
exclusive commitment. Like Will Ballou, George Pilcher settled down on
the Yukon, his restlessness lulled by the serenity of the great land. Let
others answer the siren call of each successive stampede, Pilcher heard a
different, less strident, drummer.

11

Glacier Madness

Valdez Glacier

Stampeders outfitted in Seattle or other American ports were required to pay duties on their goods at the Canadian border, whether they crossed the passes from Skagway and Dyea or voyaged to the Klondike on the Yukon River. Their interest in circumventing Canadian customs induced many stampeders to seek an "all American" route to the goldfields. Cook Inlet's deep penetration of Alaska seemed to offer one possibility, but no established trail or water route existed from Cook Inlet to the Yukon. Efforts to find one by the U.S. Army's 1898 expedition led by Capt. Edwin Glenn were not encouraging.

A better possibility appeared to be an entry from Prince William Sound, a huge bay on the Gulf of Alaska. The Gulf sweeps in a great arc from the panhandle of southeastern Alaska to the Kenai Peninsula, and though pierced by a few bays—Yakutat Bay, Icy Bay, and Prince William Sound —the massive ranges of St. Elias and Chugach form coastal barriers far more formidable than the approaches out of Skagway. Along the entire stretch of the Gulf vast glaciers move in their forbidding, ponderous way to the sea, feeding it with ice that calves from the glaciers with a terrifying roar.

Rumor got about in late 1897 that an old Russian trail led from Valdez at the head of Prince William Sound into the Copper River valley, and beyond to the Yukon River. Guidebooks to the goldfields dutifully reported the route's existence, and a shipping company, the Pacific Steam Whaling Company, announced its willingness to convey passengers and freight to Valdez. By spring 1898 between 3,000 and 4,000 rushers had disembarked at Valdez to try the new route. It is impossible to determine what percentage of the Valdez stampeders were actually bound for the Klondike. Many must have been lured by reports of gold discoveries in the

Copper River valley itself. Whatever their ultimate destination, they faced
an arduous journey that ended in tragedy and futility.

Captain W. R. Abercrombie's report on the U.S. Army's effort to blaze
a trail to the interior from Valdez is the best source of information on the
Valdez rush.[1] He arrived at Valdez in April, 1898, to find hundreds of
men strung out along the three and one-half mile trail from tidewater to
the lip of the Valdez Glacier. Like other military men who observed the
northern gold scene, Abercrombie was appalled at the lack of foresight the
argonauts displayed. Few had pack animals; for hauling baggage they
depended upon hand sleds that were useless after the snow melted. Miners
hauled a portion of their provisions from the shore to a cache near the
glacier, then returned for other loads. Inevitably the men's gear got mixed
up, requiring the soldiers to adjudicate conflicting claims of ownership.

Before the Army arrived there was no one to appeal to for help. When
a Montana cowboy, "Doc" Tanner, fell out with his two partners over a
division of their provisions, he resorted to murder. Very deliberately
Tanner shot and killed both his companions. The argonauts paused in
their furious flight long enough to remove this menace from their numbers. They assembled and deliberated briefly. Hanging seemed the only
answer. His arms bound, Tanner listened to the discussion and remained
cool: "Of course, it's hard, but do what's right," he advised. On the next
morning, a brilliant winter day, sunny and serene, a few of the boys dug a
trail through the deep snow to the base of a tall tree. Tanner's own rope
was prepared for the occasion—soaped so that it would run easily. Escorted to the tree, Tanner maintained his composure. He looked at the
rope and asked, "Don't you know you are stringing up the best man in all
Alaska with a six-shooter?" His subdued executioners did not reply but
put a flour sack over Tanner's head. "Boys, what are you going to do,"
cried the murderer, "pull me up straight and let me stay there? Pull
away."[2] Twenty-four men pulled. Later Tanner was buried at the foot of
the hanging tree. Justice, of a sort, had been done, and the argonauts
moved on.

Accustomed to orderly procedures and clearly fixed goals, soldiers
could not understand the vagueness of the gold seekers. "They had neither
the slightest idea regarding the topographical features of the country nor
any definite plan of campaign as to their future movements," observed
Abercrombie. Apparently the prospectors chose the most difficult trail
possible over the glacier; once the trail was marked none of those who
followed questioned it. Worse yet, "As to how they should supply themselves with the two most necessary articles for camping, wood and water,
they were utterly ignorant."[3]

Once on the glacier, parties of men stumbled forward along the 20-mile trail to the summit, hauling their laden sleds with extreme difficulty, sub-sisting, for lack of fuel, on uncooked food. The greatest menace of travel across glaciers—snow blindness caused by the sun's relentless glare reflected off the frozen surface—came as a complete surprise to most of the parties. Those afflicted suffered excruciating pain and, half-blinded, were incapa-ble of hauling. Their incapacity added to the labors of others and gener-ally led to the breakup of parties. Provisions were divided on the spot; Abercrombie's men were often called upon to supervise a fair division of the food and gear. Out of the hundreds of cooperative companies that had left Seattle, Abercrombie estimated that fewer than a dozen remained intact.

When the glacier was crossed, the argonauts reached the Klutina valley, where they found timber to whipsaw into material for building boats. All kinds of jerry-built boats carried men across Klutina Lake to the Klu-tina River, a tributary leading to the Copper River. For the first stretch, the Klutina waters are gentle enough, but the last 20 miles courses over swift rapids. Many of the boats were smashed before making it through to the Copper; provisions and clothing strewn all along the banks could not be recovered because of the current. By the time the mining parties reached Copper Center, they were only 100 miles from the coast, still hundreds of miles from the Yukon, with no easy route ahead. The journey for those heading for the Klondike involved tracking up the course of the Copper, crossing the Mentasta Pass to the Tok River, crossing the Tanana River, and reaching the headwaters of the Forty Mile River and following it to the Yukon River. It was a hard enough trail for those with pack animals; those without had to use the river and drag their laden boats up the swift-running current of the Copper. Winter closed the travel season before most travelers achieved their destination. Those who had not given up hope by this time halted and built log cabins for the season; small settlements sprang up along the entire route to Forty Mile.

The majority of the rushers who crossed the glacier decided a return to the coast was preferable to a winter in the interior. The exodus began in August and continued through the winter as half-starved, scurvy-ridden, bitter men turned away in defeat. Early in August the Army set up a relief station in Valdez and began issuing rations and providing medical treat-ment to destitute miners. Soldiers also rescued injured men from the gla-cier. A number of miners lost their lives crossing rivers; others fell into crevasses on the glacier or were crushed by avalanches.

Men who returned across the glacier cursed both the transportation companies and the government. They complained that shipping companies had misadvised them on the practicability of the glacial route and that the Army had not reached the scene early enough to cut and mark trails into the interior. Those who remained in the Copper River valley denounced the government for the irregularity of the mail service from the coast. Americans expected government services to keep pace with their pioneering efforts, and no excuse for failing to do so was acceptable to them.

Captain Abercrombie spent the 1898–99 winter Outside gathering pack animals and equipment necessary for the construction of a trail from Valdez to the interior. Reports of the dire plight of the miners in the Copper River valley and at Valdez having reached Washington, D.C., the Secretary of War ordered Abercrombie to carry provisions for the relief of the miners. In April he returned to Valdez on board the *Excelsior*, the same vessel that had transported the first successful Klondike miners to San Francisco in 1897. When the ship landed, crowds of disenchanted stampeders crowded aboard, their one thought to escape from the country they had flocked to with such high expectations a year or more previously. "A more motley-looking crowd it would be hard to imagine," observed Abercrombie; all "considered themselves full-fledged miners, although many of them had never handled either a pick or a shovel since their entry into the country."[4]

The miners were a sadly demoralized lot, and most had little or no money, although their boarding the *Excelsior* occasioned a spiritous binge that scandalized Abercrombie. Nor was the captain sympathetic to the miners' expectation that the government would furnish free transportation to Seattle: "It is not for some days that I could disabuse their minds of this fact."[5]

After landing, Abercrombie was greeted by Quartermaster's Agent Charles Brown, who had passed the winter in Valdez assisting the miners almost singlehandedly. "My God, Captain, it has been clear hell! I tell you the early days of Montana were not a marker to what I have gone through this winter! It was awful!"[6] In confirmation of this declaration, Abercrombie had only to look at the graveyard that had sprung up since he had departed Valdez. Victims of frostbite, exposure, and scurvy were buried there. A visit to the cabins housing the destitute miners exposed other evidence of hardship. Bedraggled groups of wretched men, up to twenty in each 12- by 15-foot cabin, sprawled listlessly. A horrible stench emanated from the scurvy-ridden and from the festering sores of frostbite sufferers. Through the dreary winter miners had struggled over the trail to Valdez, collapsing in these fetid cabins. Brown fed them and gave rudimentary medical treatment for frostbite, but there were no hospital facilities, nor even any means of bathing. The sickest died and were dragged to the cemetery; the others stared morosely at the stove, too miserable to care. Most were without adequate footwear and seldom moved from their cabins.

Although the limited care that Brown gave undoubtedly saved many lives, one can only wonder that the emergency did not inspire an earlier relief effort. It would have been difficult, but not beyond the capacity of a well-organized expedition, to help the Copper River valley miners over the winter. But in Valdez itself the relief that Abercrombie provided in late April could have been initiated much earlier. The harbor of Valdez was open to shipping throughout the winter, so nature presented no obstacle. Responsibility for the neglect must be attributed to the government officials in Washington, D.C., who were so dilatory in responding to the crisis. This and other similar incidents reveal the muddled consciousness of Alaska that prevailed in Washington. Where was the U.S. Army? Where was the U.S. Revenue Cutter Service?

Abercrombie improved the conditions at once. Cabins were acquired for a hospital and cookhouse, and staff were employed to operate them. From among the able-bodied miners, crews were hired to cut fuel wood for $1 per day and rations. Dog teams were dispatched to the interior with supplies and to carry back miners too weak to make it to Valdez on their own. Approximately 500 men in the interior were recipients of the Army's medicines and food.

In Valdez Abercrombie noticed that 70 percent of the miners were more or less mentally deranged. One big, raw-boned, wild-eyed Swede described the "glacial demon" who had strangled his son on the glacier. The demon first attacked the young man as they were hauling their sled towards the summit, but it was beaten off. Then as the Swede and his son were straining across a crevasse in a snow storm, the monster struck again. Despite the Swede's exertions he was not able to free his son from the demon's embrace before life was choked out. "When I heard this story there were ten or twelve men in the cabin," Abercrombie reported, "and at that time it would not have been safe to dispute the theory of the existence of this demon on the Valdez Glacier, as every man in there firmly believed it to be a reality."[7]

Abercrombie did not find any fault with his government. Rather, his official report stressed the ineptitude of the stampeders. Most of them "had probably never been out of sight of the smoke from a factory chimney" before voyaging to Alaska; three-fourths of them were wise enough to give up after encountering the glacier. Those who remained in the interior, "prompted rather by pride and a desire to face what was considered the rigors of an arctic winter," panicked when scurvy broke out. "A feeling of desertion and abandonment, not only by their comrades, but by the General Government, began to manifest itself," reported Abercrombie.[8] Hysteria was intensified when one party attempted a winter recrossing of the glacier and left two-thirds of its members frozen to death on the icy surface.

After his relief work Abercrombie began construction of a trail inland from Valdez, avoiding the glacier and passing through Keystone Canyon and Thompson Pass to Eagle on the upper Yukon. This trail eventually became a wagon road, not to Eagle but to Fairbanks, then the Richardson Highway. For many years it was the only overland route to the interior.[9]

Malaspina Glacier

The Valdez Glacier was not the only icy passage by which argonauts hoped to reach the goldfields. For reasons impossible to fathom, one party of eighteen men chose the Malaspina Glacier as an entry into the interior. Arthur Dietz, a Y.M.C.A. physical education director, initiated this 1897 expedition with an ad in the *New York Herald* announcing his interest in acquiring a partner or two to join him on a prospecting journey to the Klondike. Forty applicants replied, and Dietz picked seventeen from among them.

These New Yorkers made up a serious group. Throughout the 1896–97 winter they met every Sunday at Dietz's home to discuss arrangements. "Unlike many of the parties that had rushed away on the spur of the moment, our party," Dietz reported, "had a faint idea of the difficulties it was to encounter, and we attempted to take every preparatory precaution possible and to make the venture a success."[10] Background reading formed part of their preparation; works by polar explorers were perused for travel hints. The great flood of Klondike manuals had apparently not yet been generated, so the party made do with available books that seemed applicable to their needs, though their study of Arctic explorers must have been a minimal benefit.

The New York and Bridgeport Mining Company, as the party was called, planned to do most of its outfitting in Seattle, a "Sodom," as Dietz was to discover. Six dogs, four St. Bernards and two Newfoundlanders, were acquired in New York, as was their basic clothing: heavy, specially made sweaters, corduroy trousers, sombreros, heavy leather boots. Each man also armed himself with a Winchester rifle. Obviously the company had some flair. Newspapers reported on their intent and preparations. An immense crowd gathered at the Y.M.C.A. building to watch them start off, and several hundred spectators joined them on the elevated train to the railroad station. The expedition's personnel included a mineralogist, a physician, three toolmakers, two New York policemen, one tinsmith, one mail clerk, five office clerks, a factory superintendent, and Dietz. The men were confident that their varied talents would add up to success.

In Seattle the company joined with other groups to charter a boat, because the regular Alaskan steamers were fully booked. Their charter cost $5,000—no bargain, but they could not wait for a better opportunity. In late February the *Barkley*, an aged bark, weighed anchor and departed

Puget Sound. The voyage to Yakutat was a nightmare. Storms lashed the bark, knocking overboard dories and some of the crates housing the dogs; the cargo below deck had to be shifted and secured in the face of a gale; most of the passengers were too sick to leave the bunks to which they clung covered by their own vomit. After 25 miserable days Mount St. Elias came into view. This majestic, snowy peak heralded their destination. Soon the *Barkley* passengers sighted the huge Malaspina Glacier and heard the roar of its progress as great chunks of ice hurtled from its face into the sea.

Nowhere in Dietz's account of the expedition, *Mad Rush for Gold in Frozen North*, does he indicate his reasons for choosing a glacial route to the interior. His dates are confusing too. If the company organized early in 1897, it could not have been in response to the Klondike strike, nor would they have found shipping from Seattle so tied up by stampede traffic. It is more likely that his expedition left Seattle either in late 1897 or early in 1898. By some bizarre process of geographic reasoning, the party planned to travel to the lower Mackenzie River, where a gold strike had been reported. Why the Malaspina route was chosen for their purpose is most obscure.

Presumably the Malaspina Glacier looked, from a study of maps, as if it provided an entry to the continent. Though the glacier was the biggest in Alaska—dwarfing the Bering, Valdez, and others—a river, the Donjek, flowed from it to join the White River, which was a Yukon tributary. Obviously, the New York party had only the haziest idea of what travel over such a terrain would entail. Nor were they traveling light. Each man of the eighteen had 1,000 pounds of food and gear; in addition, the party transported heavy equipment, including a motor that weighed 800 pounds.

Considering the agony suffered by the members of the company and its tragic losses, it would perhaps be in poor taste to stress their abysmal ignorance of the North. What does invite censure are Dietz's own recriminations, not of himself and his guileless fellows, but of the government or "some inhuman brute [who] organized that mad gold-rush for selfish gain." It was Dietz's estimate that between 2,000 and 2,500 men perished during the rush. His sources are not given, though he claimed that a government report admitted 1,800 fatalities. All these casualty figures were gross exaggerations, which can be attributed to Dietz's bitterness. "Some measure should have been taken by the government to prevent that great loss of life," he felt.[11] One can sympathize with the tragic course of the New York expedition and still be at a loss to imagine what the most vigilant government might have done to forestall it.

The first stage of their journey took more than a week. All their supplies had to be relayed to the edge of the glacier over five miles of rough trail. They had no pack animals, and their sleds were useless over broken ground where snow existed only in patches. Hauling everything up onto the ice edge was still harder work, but by April 20 they were on the glacier where the sleds, each pulled by four dogs, could be put to use.

Soft, deep snow covered the glacier. The trail ahead of the sleds had to be broken by men on snowshoes and the ground tested for crevasses. Ten to 15 miles of progress each day exhausted the travelers, who were marching against the wind that swept continually down the glacier. All suffered from sore eyes and partial loss of vision because of the sun's reflection, though they wore smoked glasses. Sunburn was a painful irritant. Day after day they crept along, seldom speaking except to encourage the dogs. After two weeks of weary, silent slogging, the party still had not reached the summit. A blizzard struck with terrible fury. They had to halt altogether until its force abated, then dig all their gear out from under a two-foot layer of snow.

As they plodded on, disaster struck. Dietz's brother-in-law, the expedition's doctor, plunged into a deep crevasse; sled, dogs, and medicines disappeared with him. Near the summit another man and sled suffered the same fate; and just before reaching the end of the glacier a third man, with sled and dogs, was lost. It was the second of June, after a nightmare journey of nearly seven weeks, before *terra firma* was finally reached.

On into the interior the party wandered, following unmapped streams and avoiding the mountains. On July 29 the 800-pound motor was abandoned, and their rate of progress improved. Along the way they panned the stream beds. When one man died mysteriously of fever, fear of a typhoid plague spread gloom over the party. Weeks passed, and signs of winter appeared. They halted near what they thought was the Tanana River, built a log cabin and prospected the region in earnest until the cold confined their activities. Nine months had passed since they had set out optimistically from New York; now months of enforced idleness had to be endured. Three men set off to see if a native village could be discovered; they were never heard of again.

Over the winter the remaining eleven men lost track of time. They seldom left their sleeping bags and made no attempt to organize recreation. Talk was their only diversion. After reciting repeatedly all the poems and songs they knew, they turned to personal confessions, telling things that they would not otherwise have revealed even under torture. Always the cold bothered them.

With the coming of spring the men were rejuvenated and began sinking a shaft into the side of a nearby mountain. Bedrock gravel revealed only a few specks of gold and their enthusiasm diminished. Another man died, probably from scurvy. Three others set out on a prospecting trip and were killed by an avalanche. Summer passed and plans were laid for a dash to the coast once there was a snow cover for the sleds.

Their trip to the coast might have ended in the destruction of all the remaining seven, save for their luck in finding an Indian village. A white man living with the Indians, a "Squaw man" as such whites were termed, directed the New Yorkers to Orca on the coast. Somehow, after weeks of travel, the abandonment of all their equipment and sleds, crossing another glacier while subsisting on the flesh of their dogs, the survivors reached the coast, more dead than alive. Miraculously, their fires were seen by a U.S. Revenue Cutter Service vessel. A party from the ship found seven men lying in sleeping bags, four of them alive. On April 18, 1899, Dietz woke up in the hospital at Sitka and wondered how he had survived.

The final irony of the whole venture smote Dietz when he got back to Seattle. An article in the *Seattle Times* reported the arrival of his party with $500,000 in gold dust and nuggets. "Then the light began to dawn upon me and I began to realize why these wild stories were printed. To boom business! Yes, to make business for Seattle and the transportation companies!"[12] Dietz's bitterness was shared by many others who blamed entrepreneurial interests for causing hardship and disaster by publishing false information. Clearly false reports of gold strikes were distributed: the Kotzebue Sound fiasco was the result of one, and there were others. But it is not so easy to fix blame amidst the widespread hysteria and the innumerable flying rumors of stampede days. Dietz thought he knew whom to charge, yet did not reveal what kind of misinformation had sent him on such an improbable journey. Although he took pains to show the rationality of his company's preparations, Dietz never explained why the Mackenzie River had been his goal or why the Malaspina route was chosen. Perhaps he acquired a secret map of a legendary "lost mine." If so, he was certainly gulled, but not by shipping companies and not by the government. Information, from official as well as from commercial sources, existed in quantity concerning the Yukon River and Lynn Canal overland routes to the goldfields. This reliable data was disdained by the New Yorkers for reasons of their own. The price they paid was high: of the eighteen men who gathered before admiring throngs at the New York Y.M.C.A., four returned alive and of these, two were totally blind and the others' sight was permanently weakened.

12

Overland and River Routes

Dalton Trail

Among the less well-traveled routes to the Klondike was the Dalton Trail from Pyramid Harbor on Lynn Canal, 20 miles southwest of Skagway, to Fort Selkirk on the Yukon. This route was longer than those out of Skagway and Dyea but had the advantage of being the most suitable for pack animals and cattle. Jack Dalton, a veteran frontiersman, pioneered this entry and charged a toll to Klondikers using it. Others had tried to set up private claims to trails and collect passage money elsewhere with no success. A hopeful entrepreneur who cut a White Pass toll road was pushed aside by a wave of travelers, but not Dalton. To refuse toll on his trail was to court death. Dalton defended his right with armed force; his reputation as a gunfighter commanded respect, and the small number of Dalton Trail users paid $250 for the privilege. In Dawson Dalton was a hero because he brought 2,000 beef cattle over the 300-mile route in the summer of 1898 to alleviate the meat shortage.

The Edmonton Trail

The routes out of Edmonton were the longest of all those used to reach the Klondike in 1897–98. Distances varied, but the main water route covered some 2,600 miles via the Peace River, Athabasca River, Lane River, Great Slave Lake, Mackenzie and Porcupine rivers, before Fort Yukon was reached. The main overland route was 1,446 miles long and took stampeders across Peace River, to Fort St. John, along the Finlay and Kechika rivers to Watson Lake, thence along the Pelly River to Fort Selkirk.

Although stampeders on the all Canadian Edmonton routes were more successful than those who traveled through British Columbia, those who finally reached Dawson encountered incredible difficulties, and many were two years on the trail. One woman arrived in Dawson with a baby born on the trail, which was not as remarkable as the fact that the baby had also been conceived enroute from Edmonton. About one-half of the 1,500 who started out made it to the Klondike; the others turned back or decided to prospect other regions along the way. At least seventy deaths occurred on the trail, and perhaps twenty of the argonauts enjoyed some monetary reward for their labors once they got to Dawson.[1]

Edmonton was a sleepy prairie town of about 1,200 people when the Klondike was discovered and, like a smaller Seattle, it boomed with the influx of argonauts. The Alberta town was then the northernmost point of the Canadian Pacific Railroad with some tradition as an outfitting center for expeditions to Canada's North, thus it drew stampeders from the United States, Canada, and elsewhere.

On the map the route from Edmonton looked plausible enough. The pioneer Yukon prospectors, Jack McQuesten, Alfred Mayo, and others, had used the Mackenzie–Porcupine route to Alaska. What the 1897–98 stampeders overlooked was the difference between the methods of travel employed by such pioneers and themselves. Pioneers traveled light and fast, living off the land along the way; Klondikers, on the other hand, were encumbered by tons of provisions and hardware. After leaving Edmonton there was no opportunity to reprovision, which meant that everything necessary to sustain a two-year expedition had to be hauled overland or by boat.

It seems strange that the Edmonton routes lured argonauts in preference to the comparatively easy and well-known Yukon routes from Skagway and St. Michael. Probably the more obscure routes were taken because of the competitiveness of the entire venture. Rival stampeders could possibly be beaten by avoiding more familiar trails. Such hopes proved illusory for all those who started from Alberta.

Stikine River

Nearly 5,000 Klondikers steamed to Wrangell, a port halfway up the Alaskan Panhandle, to take the Stikine River route to the goldfields. Wrangell, formerly a post of the Russian–American Company, boomed in the 1870s during the rush to the Cassiar mining district of northern British Columbia. In 1897–98 Wrangell was a smaller version of Skagway, enjoying the attentions of some of the same rough crowd. Soapy Smith sent members of his gang to Wrangell to prey upon the Klondikers, and, as in similar American settlements, the criminals dominated the scene. John Underwood, an Alaskan newsman, described Wrangell as "one of the most lawless towns" he had ever seen on the frontier.[2] Colonel Sam Steele of the North-West Mounted Police touched there in February, 1898, and found little to praise, calling the place "a mean and squalid spot, with the usual number of gambling dens and other low dives, frequented by very tough-looking characters."³

Wrangell was ready-made for the parasites and thieves who livened the northern scene with their nefarious talents. Saloons and gambling palaces did not have to be erected to minister to the influx of stampeders; the buildings were there and waiting. After 15 years of slumber between gold rushes, it was only necessary to rip the boards from the windows and doors of main street dives, sweep out the cobwebs, and set up the faro layouts and roulette wheels once again. As other gold towns were being born, Wrangell was resurrected.

Underwood told of one young man who managed to get the drop on Soapy Smith's gang. The "Single O Kid" earned his nickname because of his proficiency with a revolver. In Wrangell he awed spectators in a shooting gallery by hitting the bull's-eye squarely with 125 consecutive shots. Wrangell's hoodlums honored the "Kid's" skill and kept clear of him, but made the mistake of fleecing his uncle in a poker game. After watching the gamblers cheat his uncle out of his entire bankroll, the Kid unlimbered his revolvers and picked up all the cash on the table. For once the Smith hoodlums were the victims; none dared to test the Kid before he made a quick departure from the unruly town.

Wrangell boomed because it received the blessing of the Canadian government as an excellent entry to the interior. Travelers could ascend the Stikine River from Wrangell to Telegraph Creek, then follow the trail to Teslin Lake 160 miles away. From Teslin the Hootlalinqua River led toward the Yukon headwaters. Plans were made for steamboat service on the Stikine and a railroad from Telegraph Creek to Teslin Lake, but, as with so many gold era transportation schemes, nothing was achieved.

Klondikers who slogged up the Stikine on the ice during the 1897–98 winter found this route to be an extremely miserable one and longer than any other except that from Edmonton. Alfred Brooks estimated that of the 5,000 men and women who reached Wrangell, about half made it up the Stikine, and of these only 200 to 300 fought their way over tundra and swamp finally to reach Dawson.⁴

Stratford Tollemache, a Canadian lured from his usual pursuit of trapping, was one of those who used the Stikine route in 1898. Tollemache was outfitted in Victoria, B.C., and chose the Stikine route as the most suitable one for reaching Dawson. From Wrangell he set off with dogs and sleds up the Stikine River. His pace was slow because spring rains turned the snow into a sticky slush. Other parties turned back, but Tollemache and his companions abandoned most of their supplies to lighten the sleds and kept on. Dogs and men suffered on the trail, and it got worse as the snow melted. Tollemache killed the weakened dogs and fed them to those still able to carry on. When the party reached the water course leading to the Yukon, only two of twelve dogs remained. Water transport was easier but involved a good bit of portaging. It was late summer, after months of strenuous labor, before Tollemache reached the end of the 1,200-mile trail from Wrangell—and he had nothing good to say about the route. It had been "considerably advertised as being the best, although it turned out to be about the worst."[5]

The Ashcroft River

The Ashcroft or "Long Trail" was in part the same as the Stikine River route, but it was entirely an overland route. Travelers commenced this weary journey after taking the railroad to Ashcroft, B.C., on the Thompson River 125 miles northeast of Vancouver, then followed the Cariboo Road and crossed the Skeena River before completing the first 1,000-mile leg to reach the Stikine and Telegraph Creek. Walter R. Hamilton, one of the stampeders, estimated that 1,500 men with 3,000 horses followed the Ashcroft Trail in 1898; of these, only a handful made it all the way to Dawson. The others gave up and turned back as their horses died. Dead horses littered the trail; reportedly, not a single animal reached the Klondike.

Because the route did not entail the expense of an ocean voyage to Skagway or St. Michael, it was known as the "Poor Man's Route." One could take a steamer to Vancouver, B.C., then a train to Ashcroft; neither trip was costly. After months of rugged plodding through the forests of British Columbia, the argonauts became bitter and blamed Seattle outfitters, shipping companies, and a Seattle newspaper, the *Post-Intelligencer* (P.I.), for deceiving them on the quality of the overland trail. One memorial of a disappointed gold seeker was blazed on a hemlock tree north of Hazelton in verses illustrated by crude sketches of the characters described. One verse gives the flavor of the whole poem:

> *This is the editor, false and cute,*
> *Who said it was proved beyond dispute,*
> *By evidence no one could refute,*
> *That the best way in was the Poor Man's Route.*[6]

Walter Hamilton was more fortunate than most Ashcroft stampeders in reaching Atlin near the Yukon headwaters in January, 1899. A gold discovery made there drew miners and construction workers who left their work on the White Pass Railroad to stake the new field. Through the winter Hamilton worked his claims and made good wages. By late summer he had a good grubstake and joined five other Atlin men to push on to

Dawson. The Atlin party reached Lake Bennett, then followed the water
route of the Chilkoot–White Pass stampeders to the Klondike.

It was the calamitous avalanche on the Chilkoot Pass in April, 1898,
that induced Hamilton and many others to take the long Ashcroft Trail.
From Ashcroft, the Klondikers followed the old Cariboo road to Quesnel.
This road had been built in the 1860s after the Cariboo gold finds were
made and was still in fairly good condition. After completing their first
150-mile stretch on the Cariboo road, stampeders crossed the Fraser
River and followed it to Quesnel. From Quesnel the men traveled north-
west over "a so-called trail" blazed through the country 30 years before
by the Western Union Telegraph Expedition.[7] Eventually they reached
Hazelton on the Skeena River after passing one of the notable landmarks
of the region, a suspension bridge near the mouth of the Bulkley River
built by Indians of materials abandoned by the telegraph builders. Hamilton observed other landmarks left by men who attempted the trail earlier
in the season. One was a mock grave with a headboard inscribed:

Sacred to the memory of [. . .] *may he rest in hell. He claimed to be a
guide, but he was a liar.*[8]

The lost and deluded men who raised this memorial had planned to
lynch their guide, who had falsely claimed to know the country. Somehow
the culprit escaped and the frustrated miners expressed their feelings with
an empty grave and epitaph.

After a terrible passage through the Skeena swamp, where numbers of
weakened horses had to be killed, Hamilton and his party finally got to the
Stikine where the Ashcroft Trail joined that out of Wrangell for the rest of
the long, hard journey to the Yukon. It was just after clearing the Skeena
swamp that Hamilton came on another message blazed on a tree beside
the trail. The Ashcroft seemed to inspire literary effort and this inscription
was more cheerful than the grave marker:

> *There is a land of pure delight,*
> *Where grass grows bell high,*
> *Where horses don't sink out of sight;*
> *We'll reach it by-and-by.*[9]

Hamilton still remembered this inscription 60 years later when he was in
his nineties. That last line "best expresses for me the spirit of those who
completed the trails of '98 to the Klondike, or died in the attempt."[10]

Another literary distinction of the Ashcroft trail was Hamlin Garland's
narrative, *Trail of the Gold-Seekers*. Garland was a writer who was "a
seeker after nature not gold." He wanted "to be a part of the adventure

and record its deeds," and he did a fine job of it.[11] Garland described the wilderness scenery with the felicity and care that harried fortune hunters could not match: the trees and plants, birds and blossoms, rivers and valleys of the awesome and lonely land. But even this contemplative author was worn down by the Ashcroft route. "As I now reread all the advance literature of this 'prairie route,' I perceived how every detail with regard to the last half of the trail had been slurred over. We had been led into a sort of sack, and the string was tied behind us."[12] Garland was shocked to discover that a well-marked trail did not exist and was sickened by the suffering of the argonauts' horses. Pack animals were forced to stagger along the torturous trail where forage was scarce, driven half wild by mosquitoes and black flies.

After reaching Telegraph Creek, Garland had had enough of the Ashcroft trail, so he took a steamer down the Stikine River to Wrangell, then another ship to Skagway. Skagway was quiet at the time—the stampede to Atlin had emptied the once exciting town. Garland traveled to Atlin and sensed the feeling of elation among the rushers, which reminded him of the Dakota land boom of 1883. "There is something fine and free and primitive in it all," he wrote.[13] Yet he described most rushers as "mechanisms drawn by some great magnet,"[14] weak rather than strong men—or men strong with one insane purpose. He grew weary of the "filth, greed, and foolishness of rushers."[15] The argonauts had been drawn to a hard country. Garland contrasted the rigorous northern mining with the "ease" of earlier stampedes to the Rocky Mountain and California districts.

13

Dawson City

THROUGHOUT THE AUTUMN of 1896 miners from Forty Mile and Circle staked claims on Bonanza Creek where George Carmack, Skookum Jim, and Tagish Charley had taken an incredible $4 in a single pan. Joe Ladue ignored the creeks and staked a town site on the muskeg along the Yukon near the mouth of the Klondike. After sending a messenger to Forty Mile to file his claim he rafted his sawmill and a load of lumber down from Ogilvie, a camp on Sixty Mile River that he had named after the Canadian government surveyor. Ladue built a warehouse and a log cabin that served as his residence and a saloon. This site, which he named after George Dawson, the Canadian geologist, was a bonanza in itself: soon the lots would be worth up to $5,000 a front foot. New arrivals did not take time to build, they simply pitched their tents near Ladue's cabin and hurried out to the creeks to find unstaked ground on Bonanza, Eldorado, and other creeks in the vicinity.

Gold was found in plenty through the winter and spring. Everything else—food, nails, tools, equipment, even writing paper—was desperately scarce. The miners were fortunate that William Ogilvie was near at hand. Ogilvie came up from Forty Mile to survey Ladue's town site and, more important, to survey Bonanza and Eldorado Creeks where the claims had been staked in rather haphazard fashion. Ogilvie's surveys spared confusion and anguish, eliminated overlapping claims, and established certain title to claims. Had he not acted, the Bonanza–Eldorado claims would have been the object of long legal disputes that would have profited no one but the lawyers. If an equivalent United States official had been on the scene in Nome a couple of years later, the early history of that chaotic camp would have followed a more orderly course.

Arthur Walden, after having precipitated the rush to Dawson from Circle with the letter he delivered to Harry Ash in January, was a busy man. During the winter he hauled food from Circle to Dawson, making three round trips before spring. All the Circle men knew enough about new camps to realize there would be a food scarcity; they realized that provision-laden steamboats from St. Michael could not be expected to reach the upper Yukon before mid-July. Thus they loaded their sleds with food, picks and shovels, indispensable rubber boots, gold pans, tents, and blankets. Those few who owned dog teams moved quickly to Dawson; those with only a dog or two were much slower; and those who pulled sleds by themselves were long on the trail. On his first trip back to Dawson, Walden passed the men without dogs, met them again on his second trip, and even encountered some on his third trip who were still slogging wearily along. By mid-May the last of the stragglers reached Dawson.

Walden and the other Dawson miners were down to a diet of flour by the time the thrilling whistle of the first arriving steamer brought all of the men from their tents and cabins to the river bank. It was July 18 when the *Bella*, loaded with food and liquor, tied up. Naturally enough the relieved miners went on a toot: "What few saloons there were opened up with free drinks: the ban was off and *everybody* got drunk. This included the temperance men."[1]

Dawson's tempo picked up in the summer of 1897 as stampeders came down from the upper Yukon and the coast. The town's population swelled to about 5,000; a year later the greater rush would bring it to more than 30,000. Although no one ever seemed to rest in the new town during the summer—what with building going on around the clock and the dance halls, gambling places, and saloons running full blast—all was orderly. A detachment of the North-West Mounted Police had been assigned to Dawson to keep order. The camp was lively but peaceful. In 1897 the number of Mounties on duty in the Yukon was increased from thirty to eighty. Just as Ogilvie's surveys prevented mining claim disputes from arising, the Mounties' presence assured that law and order would prevail. Thanks to the foresight of Canada's government and its willingness to spend nearly $400,000 on law enforcement, the Mounties were on hand to defend person and property.

One of the things that distinguished the Klondike diggings was the number of individual claims of prodigious wealth. On occasion miners scooped up a sparkling $600 in gold in a single pan, and the finding of $1,000 has been recorded. The most famous example of high yield was the fraction mined by Dick Lowe. Fractions were remainders between two staked claims existing because the prospectors had erred in determining their legal limit of 500 feet. Lowe was helping William Ogilvie survey the Bonanza Creek claims when their work revealed a small fraction, only 86 feet wide at its broadest point. Lowe reluctantly staked the tiny plot, then tried unsuccessfully to sell it for $900. Finally he sank a shaft without finding color, then another. On the second try he hit it big, cleaning up $46,000 in eight hours. Eventually a half million dollars came out of his fraction. Lowe's subsequent career was not atypical of Dawson miners. His obituary in a Fairbanks newspaper some years later noted that Lowe "got drunk and stayed drunk."[2]

Clarence J. Berry, an aptly named California fruit-farmer before he was lured to the Circle diggings, worked laboriously through the 1896–97 winter to reach bedrock. Once there, his Eldorado claim looked very good indeed. His first washup in the spring netted him $140,000, and there was more where that had come from. Others enjoyed equal returns. In two hours Jim Tweed panned $4,284 on Eldorado, and on Bonanza Frank Dinsmore took $24,480 in one day. The excitement mounted as claim after claim proved rich beyond any others ever discovered in the North.

Sensational discoveries on the Bonanza and Eldorado were followed by others on Dominion Creek, Sulphur Creek, and other tributaries of the Indian River. Soon the hillsides were staked as well: Gold Hill, French Hill, and Skookum Hills yielded high returns, and prospectors ranged over every stream, gulch, and hill in the region with high hopes. Hill claims required more digging than claims in the valley. Albert Lancaster sank a 79-foot shaft in Gold Hill before reaching bedrock, but for the next eight weeks the hole gave him an average of $2,000 a day. On the claim next to his a miner took out 30 pounds of gold in the first three days after hitting bedrock—and the price of gold was $17 an ounce.

By the time Arthur Walden mushed into Dawson to complete his third round trip from Circle, the new town showed tremendous changes. Along the riverfront for a half mile tiers of boats, scows, and rafts lined the bank. Many new arrivals lived on their boats; others set up their tents wherever space could be found. Dawson was not an attractive place in the spring of 1898. Mules, pack horses, and men floundered along the wretched main street, which was a sea of mud. Filth was strewn over the area. A friend of Walden's won a bet by traversing the course of the main street by jumping from one dead horse to another.

In these insanitary conditions an outbreak of typhoid was predictable. Scores succumbed to the disease, and the death toll mounted. This catastrophe spurred efforts to clean up the town site and the Mounties laid down strict sanitary regulations. By good fortune the new arrivals included men devoted to serving humanity rather than Mammon. "The Saint of Dawson," Father William Judge, was one of these. This frail, ascetic Jesuit mushed all the way from his native mission on the lower Yukon River, with a sledload of medicines. Knowing that the new camp would be in desperate need of hospital facilities, Father Judge strained his strength to fill this critical demand. With newly rich miners like Alex McDonald contributing generously to the cause, before long Judge realized his goal. Months of unselfish effort in organizing and building and in tending the sick wasted the 45-year-old missionary's physical resources until he too fell victim to typhoid. The priest's martyrdom to Dawson's cause was recognized by the grateful, sorrowful miners. Although caught up in the pursuit of wealth themselves, they venerated the man of God who put service before self.

A good two-thirds of the Dawson mines were owned by Americans. Canadian law did not discriminate against foreigners holding mining claims, but all operators were taxed 10 percent of their gross production, with an exemption for the first $5,000 yield. Needless to say, the considerable tax irked miners, particularly those accustomed to working in Alaska, where no taxes had been levied. At times, resentment against the Canadian government rose to mutinous proportions. Such discontent might have culminated in violence but for the effective control of the region by Canadian authorities. The tact of government officials and the presence of an experienced, incorruptible police agency soothed a potentially explosive situation.

At one point it looked as if the Americans might clash with the authorities. Rumors spread throughout the camp as the Fourth of July approached. It was said that the Mounties were planning to prohibit any celebration of the American national holiday. Although the report lacked basis in fact, it stirred the camp. "We swore we would celebrate in spite of everything," recalled Arthur Walden. Of course Col. Sam Steele had no intention of interfering with the traditional celebration and, according to Walden, issued a proclamation, "written almost in the language of a command," saying that the Americans and Canadians would celebrate the Fourth of July together.[3] Any malcontents in town who hoped for a confrontation were disappointed. The boys took their pleasures at the saloons, shot at each others' stovepipes and organized foot races and games.

Colonel Sam Steele had reason to be confident that the Mounties were providing adequate protection and efficient services to Dawson residents. With the flexibility that was a hallmark of their organization, the Mounties even took over the mail service when it faltered. Nothing disturbed miners more than poor mail service, and Steele realized this. A Seattle contractor, who was supposed to carry mail from the coast to Dawson, defaulted on his performance. Mail piled up in Skagway and in Dawson; so Steele assigned his men to the delivery job and all went well.

Still, some complained against the Mounties. Steele justly railed at the "considerable numbers of foreigners who, although doing well and given

the protection of the best laws in the world, had not the decency to abstain
from abusing the form of government of the country." Why should men
given the privilege of digging gold in Canada complain so vociferously,
wondered Steele, and why did they speak slightingly of our monarch? An
actor, whose criticisms of the queen offended Steele's sense of propriety,
was interviewed by the Mounties' leader. "He was given the opportunity to
say he would sin no more or take his ticket for the Outside. This had the
desired effect."[4] Perhaps Steele bruised the right of free speech on occasion, but even in the northern wilds there had to be a limit.

Steele kept a twelve-man police force on Dawson's streets day and
night. Pleasure resorts were permitted to run around the clock—except on
Sunday when every place of business closed—but were closely watched.
Cardsharpies and thieves had reason to fear the Mounties, whose demands
for stove wood were unlimited. Often fifty men labored busily on the
woodpile, chopping their sins away. A number of detectives checked on
the backgrounds of suspected criminals who were drawn to Dawson. Mur-
derers, train and stagecoach robbers, burglars, safe blowers, and diamond
thieves joined whores, pimps, and crooked gamblers in the gold town, but
Dawson did not resemble Skagway, and criminals maintained a low pos-
ture under the watchful eyes of the North-West Mounted Police.

For all this police vigilance, there was color and incident enough to
create a gaudy scene. How could it be otherwise where fortunes were
unearthed each day and squandered each night? Where such striking per-
sonalities as the Mizner brothers and Swiftwater Bill Gates competed for
the town's attention with a flamboyance that always reached dazzling
heights in gold camps?

Wilson Mizner was the liveliest of the Mizner brothers and the most
persistent stampeder. In Dawson, Wilson sang and played the piano in
saloons and watched for chances to turn a dishonest dollar. The ladies
loved Wilson, and he loved them. Nellie Lamore, Diamond Tooth Gertie,
Glass-Eyed Annie, and Myrtle Drummond were among the fortunate
whores and showgirls on the Dawson scene who joined Mizner in making
its night life memorable. Wilson even dared the wrath of the Mounties to
please Nellie Lamore. Nellie liked chocolate, and sweets were very rare,
so Wilson held up a restaurant in hope of getting a supply. The robbery
failed but Wilson evaded capture and thereafter concentrated on less risky
pursuits, cardsharping and badger games. Later Wilson carried his skills
and something of the Dawson entertainment atmosphere to Nome.

It was tough for any of Dawson's *bon vivants* to match Swiftwater Bill
Gates, about whom legends clustered like mosquitoes. His spending exploits, his amours, and his sartorial elegance stirred the town. Resplendent
in Prince Albert coat, top hat, diamond stickpin, and the only starched

collar in Dawson, Bill set out to spend his newly gained fortune in the manner of an oriental prince. All his life he had been a puny, grubby nonentity, but now he could parade his dash and raise some eyebrows. Drinks were on the house for all when Bill appeared in a saloon, and the cardsharps wrung their hands in anticipation of Bill's reckless gambling. But the girls were the chief beneficiaries of Gates' largesse. On occasion, he took a bunch to his mine to scramble about gathering nuggets.

On his hasty journeys Outside, Gates set the style for Eldorado kings of the North. Newspaper reporters following him everywhere were certain to get sensational copy, particularly on setbacks to his ardent pursuit of women. But more about Swiftwater Bill later; like Wilson Mizner and other Klondikers, Gates' storied career did not end with the decline of Dawson's placer fields. In Nome and in Fairbanks, Gates performed spectacularly and experienced a similar run of luck with mines and women.

Dawson's colorful history has been told many times in considerable detail, but too much emphasis on it in a book that is predominantly an account of the Alaskan gold era would distort the picture.[5] Excitement died down in the Klondike in 1899; its gaudy days passed swiftly; the scene of action shifted back to Alaska—but, happily, some of its liveliest actors moved with it.

14

Soldiers, Sailors, and Settlers
on the Yukon

IT IS IRONIC that Washington, D.C., began to concern itself with the Klondike stampede just when new gold discoveries were drawing miners from Canada to Alaska. Yet the activity in the Klondike did benefit the whole region because it spurred the United States government to give more attention to Alaska's requirements. Communication and law enforcement were obvious needs, but it was not until late summer in 1899 that concerted efforts were made to provide either along the Yukon River. Somewhat belatedly, the U.S. Revenue Cutter Service was assigned the task of patroling the river, and the U.S. Army dispatched soldiers to build garrisons near the mouth of the Tanana River and at Eagle, not far from the Canadian boundary.

The steamboat *Nunivak* was specially built for the Yukon patrol and assigned to the Revenue Cutter Service. Lieutenant J. C. Cantwell commanded her, with orders to enforce the customs and navigation laws from the river mouth to a distance of 1,000 miles upstream. Cantwell was also ordered to aid destitute miners, to assist civil and military authorities in law enforcement, to prepare charts of the river and its tributaries, to collect specimens of flora and fauna, and to compile statistics on traffic and mining.

It was mid-August before the *Nunivak*, after a sea voyage from San Francisco, reached St. Michael near the mouth of the Yukon River. The first patrol occupied the better part of a month as Cantwell worked his way upriver slowly, measuring and charting depths as he went. All steamers coming down from Dawson were boarded by customs officials for the examination of papers and safety measures. Early in September the *Nunivak* was moored on the Dall River, a northern tributary of the Yukon near Rampart, and readied for winter quarters.

All navigation on the river ended in October and the Revenue Cutter Service had little to do. Overland travel was not their concern, though it became obvious during the winter that miners were deserting Dawson in droves, lured by the Nome discoveries. The stampeders seldom stopped to visit the *Nunivak*; they were in too great a hurry, as Cantwell remarked, for "exchanging mere civilities."[1] Cantwell marveled that so few of them suffered serious injuries along the way; the ship's surgeon was called upon on only a few occasions.

The U.S. Army arrived in the interior about the same time as the *Nunivak*, but in greater force. Recommendations for military sites had been made as early as 1869, when Capt. Charles R. Raymond steamed up the Yukon to the Hudson's Bay Company's post of Fort Yukon. Raymond had recommended that a post be established where the Tanana River joined the mighty Yukon. Thirty years later his suggestion was finally acted upon. Civilian workers and two companies of infantry disembarked at the junction and set out to construct buildings. A similar party was sent farther upriver to Eagle.

The Army was not sent to Alaska to keep order—law enforcement was the province of civilian authorities—but to build and operate a telegraph system. Captain Charles S. Farnsworth commanded the Tanana garrison and supervised the building of Fort Gibbon. Fort Gibbon was 900 miles, or 103 steamer hours, upriver from the mouth of the Yukon and 700 miles downriver from Dawson City. Today Alaska's second city, Fairbanks, not yet founded in 1899, stands some 270 miles up the Tanana from the fort's site. The Yukon River is a good mile wide at Gibbon. Along the river beyond the site, wooded hills terminate in abrupt bluffs above the slowly moving waters. Most of the reservation area was thick in birch and spruce, the latter utilized for construction. The northern portion of the area being treeless tundra, it was chosen as the site of the various buildings.

By the time Farnsworth and his men arrived, the season was advanced, and livable winter quarters had to be readied at once. In pioneer days, as today, no one built in interior Alaska without the anxiety that arose from the perennial race against time. It was a tense and frustrating period. In January the work was still under way:

Our post is in poor shape, only half the barracks built and only one set of officers' quarters and no lumber or logs on hand to build more. Our force and material seems to be frittered away in doing small temporary jobs and contractors do not care whether they fill their contracts or not as they are not required to give any bonds. Our civilian employees are the most incompetent lot of men ever turned loose on a community, and it seems to be now evident that they only came here to spend the winter in idle-

*ness and then go hunting gold when warm weather comes. We are trying
to get in some logs now but it is slow work as all the animals except eight
mules are used in doing wood hauling.*[2]

Eventually, with all civilian and military hands working on construction,
the most needed quarters were completed. Fortunately, the winter was
comparatively mild.

The river freeze-up had come in November. This meant the end of the
navigation season and the end of communication with the outside world
since the nearest telegraph was 700 miles away, at Dawson. First class
mail came through occasionally in the winter via the United States postal
carrier, a man who must have received a tumultuous welcome everywhere
he called on the Yukon. All magazines and bulk mail directed to Alaska
were held up in Seattle until summer.

With the seasonal breakup, the *Nunivak* resumed her river patrol. Once
the ice went out, all kinds of boats were on the river, most heading down
to Nome. Cantwell was frequently solicited to settle quarrels among the
argonauts. Men who had been forced to winter somewhere along the river
grew heartily sick of one another's company. As often happened in the
gold rush, partnerships were dissolved and provisions divided, leading to further disputes. Even boats were divided. "It was not unusual to see, floating down the river side by side, the two ends of a boat which had been cut
into equal parts and patched up so as to afford transportation to both
portions of some disrupted party which had taken this novel and heroic
means of settling its differences."[3]

The stampeders floated downriver on crudely constructed boats or rafts
loaded heavily with provisions, mining tools, and dogs. These "restless
and hungry dogs gave vent to their discontent in lugubrious howls," wrote
Cantwell, who also observed among the traffic scow loads of horses "gazing
wistfully at the green shores, with now and then a lonely looking cow or
beef cattle, worried and stung night and day by clouds of vicious mosquitoes." Differences among the argonauts amused the Revenue Cutter
Service officer. Some floated down leisurely under improvised awnings that
offered protection from the sun, he commented, "while others of less
philosophical temperament would be pulling away at their oars as if life
itself depended upon the utmost speed."[4]

Cantwell's attitude towards stampeders was similar to that of Captain
Farnsworth, who during the same period was constructing the telegraph
line to the interior. Farnsworth had moved to Eagle in 1900 to survey and
build the first part of the telegraph line. These officers were immune to the
golden lure that propelled the men they observed. Both, however, were
sympathetic to any prospectors who suffered misfortune and sufficiently

sensitive to be aware that the spectacle was unique. "Taken altogether," Cantwell asserted, "this great stampede of gold seekers must be considered one of the most remarkable movements of the kind which has ever occurred in the world's history of the search for the yellow metal."[5] It was his estimate that from the first of the year through the summer of 1900, some 3,000 men and women made their way out of the interior enroute to Nome.

Lawkeeping had to be informal on the bustling Yukon. On one occasion the Revenue Cutter Service men boarded a trading steamer bound for the Koyukuk River, the northern tributary of the Yukon to which gold discoveries were diverting some of the Nome stampeders. Although the trading vessel lacked the required shipping documents, Cantwell allowed the captain to proceed to the new camp and discharge his cargo for the hungry miners before voyaging down to St. Michael and a commissioner's hearing. At Nulato, Indians complained that some white men had stolen their stock of driftwood. Cantwell made the miners replace the wood, then ordered them downriver to avert further conflicts.

Indian justice was observed at Nulato as well. A gathering of natives was considering the case of the accidental killing of a boy by his companion. For several hours the local shaman or medicine man harangued the meeting, advising the parents of the dead boy to seize the boy responsible for the death and enslave him. If the boy would not work, the parents had the right and duty to kill him, argued the shaman. Cantwell broke up the meeting by threatening punishment of anyone who harmed the boy, denounced the shaman as a liar, and offered to "take him on the *Nunivak* down to the ocean and send him away on a big ship"—if he did not mend his ways.[6]

A more alarming vicissitude for the Yukon natives was an epidemic of measles that assailed them. Every summer fishing camp along the river was affected. Pneumonia followed hard on the measles, and the natives died like flies. The crew of the *Nunivak* did all they could to relieve the sick, but the situation was a pitiful one. At one village, "we found that out of a population of 27 souls only 7 remained, and of these only 2 were strong enough to take care of the food and medicines we left for them," reported Cantwell. Dogs fed on unburied bodies, he said, and "everywhere was there the unmistakable evidence of terrible suffering, absolute neglect and grim despair." Natives living near trading posts or at missions like Holy Cross and Russian Mission were treated "with a tenderness and devotion which no words can adequately describe."[7] But even at Holy Cross, 57 of 200 natives had died prior to the *Nunivak*'s visit, and many were still ill. Few natives were healthy enough to undertake the seasonal fishing. Alerted to this by Cantwell, the Army averted general starvation by shipping supplies from St. Michael to all the villages.

The appearance of the U.S. Revenue Cutter Service and the U.S. Army on the Yukon did not affect settlers like George Pilcher and Will Ballou. In 1898 and in 1899 Pilcher continued to chop wood near Russian Mission on the lower Yukon, and Ballou mined at Rampart.

Nature dominated Pilcher's routine almost completely. Each spring he and his native neighbors watched anxiously for the Yukon's breakup. This was the signal for the renewal of activity along the river. It also ended the lean days natives faced some winters when food supplies dwindled. Honking geese overhead, savory fish in the river, and a plentitude of game raised the spirits of all. Snares were set for rabbits and other fur-bearing animals, while hunting parties set out to find game birds, caribou, and moose. Of course, mosquitoes appeared too, that feature of Yukon living was an inescapable harrassment.

Summer was always a delight. Pilcher had much work but also the diversions of berrying and excusions into the surrounding hills with a sharp eye out for gold traces. He would voyage down to St. Michael for provisions and a beneficial change of scene. By mid-August the foliage was already changing color and the first frosts came. It was time to prepare the cabin—which Pilcher liked to refer to as his castle—for the winter. Before freeze-up he had to haul his boat ashore and secure it.

With the first hard freeze and the first snow a quiet fell on the river. Not a complete quiet, however, because there was always the steady tapping of the woodcutter's axe. Wood must be readied for next year's navigation season. Except on the stormiest days, or when temperatures dropped below —20 degrees Fahrenheit, or when laid low by toothache or "bilious headache," Pilcher worked on his woodpile.

Ballou enjoyed his life at Rampart from his arrival there in the summer of 1898. There was much hard work, but this promoted a huge appetite, which he satisfied until freeze-up with the luscious salmon he netted. Each day his net yielded four or five 15-pounders, leaving him an excess to sell to the local restaurants. For variety, moose meat could be purchased for a dollar a pound. Ballou also appreciated the sense of freedom this life offered, recognizing that his contemporaries back home, working for big companies, experienced quite another atmosphere.

Soon the river froze; no tooting steamers disturbed the calm as the winter of the interior asserted its sway over the vast country. Ballou marveled at the display of the aurora borealis and wondered about the tales told of the coming season's severity.

But the winter weather offered no hardship. What really bothered Ballou was the absence of news from home. All the Yukon camps were served by the mail carriers coming by dog team down from Dawson, but they had nothing for the homesick young man until April—then all at once he received a bundle of sixteen letters that he devoured greedily.

In the spring of 1899, Ballou and his two partners hit paydirt on one of the claims they worked on a creek called Little Minook, Jr., getting up to $2 per pan. No wild dash to town to buy drinks for the house attended this discovery. They worked on, talked to no one, and bought up several more claims in the vicinity. Their very caginess and reticence was enough to spark a little stampede, and soon newcomers had staked the entire hillsides rising up from the creek. "The silent three," as the eastern boys were termed by the westerners in camp, burned fires day and night to sink their shafts down through the permafrost to bedrock, where they hoped substantial paydirt would be found. Feeling expansive, they hired six men to help out on their Little Minook, Jr., claims and two others to prospect for them on another reputedly promising stream. By the end of May they finished their cleanup, the sluicing down of the thawed muck hauled up their shaft through months of hard work. The gain heartened them. Though far from being millionaires, they had a good return for their winter's labors.

Then Ballou fell ill with scurvy. The winter's diet of bacon and beans left him prey to the disease that affected these northern miners just as it did sailors. Rampart's graveyeard had held only one occupant when Ballou and his party arrived the previous summer, now it contained a substantial population. Heart disease and scurvy were the chief killers, but, over the winter, there had also been one suicide and seven men frozen to death on the trail. Ballou's recovery fallowed rapidly on his return to town, where fresh foods were available.

He planted a garden and reflected upon his good fortune. Rampart's population had peaked somewhere between two and three thousand, but only a few miners had been successful. Hundreds left daily for Nome or for the Outside. Ballou's concern was that all those joining the exodus would give Rampart a bad name. The country "is all right for the right class of people—hustling and hard working. But there are too many kid glove lead pencil miners, and the sooner they get out the better."[8]

The results of the season's second washup almost crushed Ballou. His share amounted to a meager $100. Naturally his mood shifted abruptly from the euphoria expressed earlier in the spring. Now, he wrote his brother Walt, he felt disposed to jump the country for the Outside. "Don't be foolish and come here," he warned, "this country has been boomed and the work is too hard for this chicken to get nothing but a living out of it."[9] Ballou's lament expressed the situation for most miners in Alaska. Only a few men struck it rich, while the great majority of those who stayed on worked hard at their claims just to make expenses and subsistence. Eventually most sold out to large operators who came in with dredging equipment. From that point on, if they remained, they worked as employees of the mining companies. By 1899, dredges were being moved into the Klondike, and Dawson was losing its population and its glitter.

After such poor returns, Ballou took it easy for a time. He sat around the post office, showed samples of nuggets, boasted a little, and hoped the word of his success would spread. With spring, new arrivals would come and the young miner hoped to unload his claims upon them at a profit.

In September, 1899, Ballou's two partners left for the Outside but he decided to carry on. He hired fourteen men who were willing to risk waiting for their wages if and when bedrock proved rich, and he was able to get credit to purchase a steam thawer, winch, and the other necessary machinery. Only he knew how desperate a gamble was involved, but he counted upon eventually receiving financial aid from a backer in the East.

News of a new strike at Nome came up the river. Now gold had been found on the sandy beaches of the Bering Sea. It sounded ridiculously easy in the telling to make a fortune on the Seward Peninsula. All a man had to do was stand on the beach with a primitive rocker. No backbreaking shovel work, no thawing or shoring, no hauling of heavy muck up the shaft from bedrock. It was a dream to which Ballou did not succumb. Nome was overrated, he figured.

After a summer of leisure, fishing, hunting, and boating, Ballou felt relaxed. "After three such summers I think I would lose all desire to go back and would get me a squaw and have 18 children like Captain Mayo who has been here thirty-two years."[10] But this mood passed, and as fall approached he set to work. From the original fourteen men his crew jumped to twenty-two; in addition, he had two women cooks at work. "Working two dozen men for the winter without a dollar in my pocket and no cash credit is something you can't do back in careful old New England, eh?"[11] he kidded brother Walt.

Big or bust this year was his motto. If he went bust he would head for Nome in the summer. More and more good news from the beaches of the Seward Peninsula made him restless. Through the winter Ballou was occupied by his work and the successful sale of one claim, which enabled him to get out of debt. Legal matters occupied him as well. Twice he had to defend his claims in court against jumpers; the second time he defended his own case and won.

That winter saw the great exodus down the river to Nome. On one day more than 100 dog teams halted in Rampart for a rest before they pushed on. Men came on foot; they came by bicycle, and they came pulling their own sleds. Many chroniclers have recorded the journey from Dyea and

Skagway over the mountains to the Klondike country, but the 1,700-mile winter trek down the Yukon to Nome in the winter of 1899–1900 was even more arduous, especially for those without dogs. Ballou was astonished when a neighbor of his, 60 years old, insisted upon setting out downriver when the temperature hovered at 20° below. Such was the lure of Nome, where Tex Rickard's gambling saloon was already making a mint, and where Rex Beach, too, was to strike it rich.

With the opening of steamer traffic on the river in June, the young miner took passage for Nome, but just for a quick look. After three days in the booming camp he had had enough: "This is a hot camp but see no show for a *mining man* here. Everything is taken."[12] Also appalling to the veteran miner was the high incidence of violence and crime. Residents of Rampart were accustomed to a more harmonious atmosphere, and Rampart suited Will Ballou.

George Pilcher was not even tempted by what he heard of Nome. The *Susie, Sarah, Seattle, Jeff Davis*, and the scores of other freight- and passenger-carrying steamboats needed his wood. He would not join the restless mob dashing to the Seward Peninsula when his woodcutting provided a good living. Let others waste themselves in the futile pursuit of easy wealth; Pilcher had work enough and was content.

Part III

NOME,
FAIRBANKS, AND
OTHER ALASKAN
CAMPS

15

Nome—The American Klondike, 1899

Discovery

The Seward Peninsula is only 50 miles from Siberia. It is as if the two continents had been hacked apart at this point to create an unnatural division where nature had intended none. This, in a sense, is what happened ages ago when the land bridge that had tied the continents was flooded by the rising waters of the Bering Sea.

This northwestern tip of North America is a bleak and cold region most of the year. There is nothing of the spectacular beauty of the more southerly coast of Alaska, where awesome glaciers spew into the sea and heavily forested mountains tower above the shores. The Bering Sea coast is flat and monotonous: no timber, no contour, no striking physical attractions. In winter, snow blizzards slash the land; in all seasons searing storms rage in from the sea. Nature has been parsimonious in endowing the desolate Seward Peninsula.

No, there is nothing of commanding beauty and little of interest. The soggy tundra is a quagmire in the summer and an unmarked snow desert in the winter. Nobody except a few struggling Eskimos could or would live in such a region—unless, of course, there was an opportunity to get rich. Then never mind the cold and blizzards, the short winter days, the relentless light of summer. Forget, too, the inconvenience of being effectively cut off from the rest of the world for up to eight months of the year. Forget the high cost of dependence on shipping food, equipment, and everything else 3,000 miles from Seattle. No hardships deter men in quest of wealth. When the glad, frenzied cry of "GOLD" is heard, men will go anywhere.

Chance has always played a part in discovery of gold. Among the thousands of gold seekers who responded to the news of gold discoveries in the Klondike in 1897 were a number who had failed to secure transportation on the Yukon River prior to the autumn freeze-up. Rather than waste the winter in the dreary settlement of St. Michael, waiting to board a Yukon steamer, they made their way across Norton Sound to where the Fish River empties into Golovin Bay. There, on the southern side of the Seward Peninsula, which points like a finger to Siberia, they prospected the streams and found pretty good signs of gold. On such picturesquely named creeks as Sweetcake and Ophir they worked as best they could with their limited equipment; the clean-up that summer left them with a reasonable return for their efforts. The country looked promising, but no more than that. Nothing sensational.

In the autumn of 1898 chance, in the form of a fierce storm, again intervened. A party of prospectors, N. O. Hultberg, H. L. Blake, John Byrneson, and J. L. Haggalin sailed from Golovin Bay in a five-ton schooner to try their luck on the quartz ledges along the coast to the west.[1] The storm drove their ship into the mouth of the Snake River, a shallow stream that empties into the Bering Sea about 13 miles west of Cape Nome, soon to become site of the biggest, wildest, and lustiest of Alaskan gold camps. But for the storm they would not have prospected in that region, but having nothing else to do until the winds subsided the men investigated the possibilities along the streams for four or five miles from the beach. Finding some color but not enough to excite them, the party returned to Golovin Bay and disbanded. One member, Brynesen, not discouraged by what the Snake River country had revealed, confided his hopes to two fellow Scandanavians, Erik Lindblom and Jafet Lindeberg. The trio, soon to be legendary as "the three lucky Swedes" (though Lindeberg was a Norwegian), sailed to Cape Nome.

On a short tributary of the Snake, Anvil Creek, the three men found very promising signs. It was September 22, 1898, when they staked the discovery claim and panned $30 to $50. They realized they were on to something big, but needing provisions before winter set in, they returned to Golovin Bay. Increasing their party to seven, they got back to the Snake River on October 15 and proceeded to organize the Cape Nome Mining District. They fixed the boundaries of the district, adopted local mining law for governance, and elected A. N. Kittleson recorder.[2]

Mining law permitted each prospector to stake one claim of a maximum length of 1,320 feet per creek, in addition to the discovery claim made by the first locator. The law also permitted prospectors to stake claims by power of attorney for backers, friends, or relatives.

Natives were available to help with packing, and a camp was soon established on Anvil Creek. Their supplies included lumber from which they constructed crude rockers, and in a few days $1,800 was cleaned up by two such devices. Winter upon them, freeze-up of the streams prevented further work with the rockers. Agreeing upon the strictest secrecy the miners returned to Golovin Bay to winter. But such golden secrets are not easily kept. Somehow—through the slip of an elated word or the observance of a blissful smile—the news leaked out. It spread like fire, first to the nearby mission and reindeer station, then up the Yukon River, and finally to the Outside.

Once more the stampede was on! Down the Yukon poured the hopefuls by foot, dogsled, and bicycle. Gold-maddened men and women who did not enjoy ownership of sleds and dogs propelled themselves, their equipment, and supplies to the Snake River. Some slipped out of slumbering camps along the Yukon, Dawson, Forty Mile, Rampart, Circle, at night, so as not to disturb their neighbors, and drove hotly for the new Mecca.

King Mob Restrained

By the time word of the strike found its way to the Outside it was too late for anyone to reach Cape Nome from Pacific Coast ports. Not unless they were eager enough to voyage to Skagway, take the train to White-horse, the stage to Dawson, and the walk down the Yukon's 1,700-mile course to St. Michael and then along Norton Sound. Nonetheless, the camp grew steadily during the winter with stampeders who were already in the North. By mid-May, 1899, a tent town contained 250 souls; by early summer the population numbered a thousand and by late summer, a thriving, sprawling community of 2,000 lined the beach of the Bering Sea. A year later the population was to reach 20,000.

Many enterprising men spent their first season staking claims in preference to working them. Optimists believed that gold was to be found in every stream, and they staked from beach to skyline in their own names, and in the names their friends and relatives, as agents with power of attorney for others. The law required that a mineral discovery be made before a claim be staked and filed, but nobody had time to verify the presence of wealth. This random staking and the widespread abuse of the privileges of power of attorney to extend one's holdings fraudulently caused turmoil.[3] Abuses of mining law and custom in Nome ended the earlier northern tradition of restraint. These changes were perhaps inevitable following the Klondike excitement and in view of the vagueness of the law restricting power of attorney claims, but it was an unfortunate occurrence that was to result in almost interminable litigation.

As bleak as the town and its environs appeared, it was obvious that prospects of making money were very high indeed. Public-spirited citizens with a respect for private property demanded that law and order be maintained. The president of the chamber of commerce, the first organized body in the town, issued a decree against violence: "We will hang the first

man who unnecessarily spills human blood if we have to go to Council
City to get the tree to hang him on."[4] Council was a good distance to go
for a hanging tree, which gave his determination credibility.

Actually, disease posed an even greater threat than crime, since no
sanitation system existed and the area was full of refuse and offal. Eventually this debris was carried out onto the Bering Sea ice before the thaw,
but not before typhoid and other diseases took lives and excited alarm.

In remarkably short order, streets were laid out for a town site. A few
frame buildings, mostly saloons, were erected, but most people lived in
tents. Wood was exceedingly scarce. The wild claim-jumping taking place
all over the Peninsula extended to the town. Jumpers jumped jumpers in a
hectic struggle for ownership of valuable town lots. Even the construction
of a building did not effectively establish one's priorities, because jumpers
were not above dismantling structures.

During the short summer season, the camp bustled. Everyone was on
the move, building, prospecting on the creeks, or—after the beach gold
discovery—mining the sands.

The best ground of Anvil Creek had been staked by the three "lucky
Swedes," who were envied and resented. Why should a Laplander like
Jafet Lindeberg, who was brought to the country to herd reindeer, be
allowed to make millions when so many Americans were left in the cold?
And what about that Swede, Erik Lindblom? Maybe he should be returned to the ship from which he had fled? The grumbling in the camp led
to some plotting. A group of men banded together and launched a blatant
scheme. They determined to use the miners' meeting as a means of sanc-
tioning a new round of claim-jumping.

United States mining law held that only citizens or aliens expressing the
intent to become citizens could make valid mineral claims. However, it
stipulated that the alien issue could only be raised by federal authorities;
i.e., private citizens could not question another's right.

The Seward Peninsula stampeders of 1899 ignored this last stipulation.
Their greed and their envy of the "lucky Swedes" who were the discoverers, impelled them to take the law into their own hands. At a riotous
miners' meeting, they decided that aliens had no rights; thus those who
jumped discovery claims could prevail. Their resolution stated that the
discoverers were holding their claims illegally because they had not prop-
erly conformed to United States mining law. They believed the genius and
spirit, intent and meaning, of the American mining laws to have been
ruthlessly violated. The plotters who triggered this action were well-
prepared to benefit and dispatched some of their number to Anvil Creek.
When the resolution was carried a signal fire was to be lit in Nome, at
which signal the Anvil claims would be jumped and the Swedes thrown off
by force.

The miners' meeting was held in a saloon. Before a vote could be taken on a resolution to disallow all claims, Lieutenant Oliver Spaulding and a few of the soldiers garrisoned at Fort Davis near Nome marched in, bayonets fixed: "Gentlemen, withdraw that resolution!" Spaulding ordered. "What for?" they shouted. "We make our own laws. What do we care for you and your soldiers?"[5] Shouting and grumbling, the miners refused to act. At this, Spaulding took out his watch, announcing that the room would be cleared in two minutes unless the resolution was withdrawn. In two minutes the soldiers prodded the mob outside.

Lieutenant Spaulding had no more authority to break up the meeting than had the miners to take the law into their hands. The camp seethed with rage and discontent. Any spark might ignite the restless mob of disgruntled men. What saved the situation, and probably averted further tumult or even bloodshed, was another sensational discovery made a few days after the miners' meeting. Gold was found in the beach sands fronting the town! The narrow beach, between the tundra and the Bering Sea, contained gold in paying quantities.

Golden Sands

The rich beaches extended east and west of Nome, 40 miles each way. A 50-mile stretch, between Nome River on the east and Penny River on the west, proved the richest section. Near the low water mark, the bedrock was found 8 to 18 inches deep. Near the tundra, bedrock was 4 to 6 feet deep. Never had mining been easier. No slow burning of a shaft through 60 feet or more of permafrost to bedrock was necessary on the beach; a crude rocker set up on the beach would do the job. The rich sand was shoveled in and shaken down until the gold particles were trapped in the rocker. In the first season of the 1899 discovery of the beach gold, 2,000 men and women working shoulder to shoulder recovered over $2 million in gold by this simple process. At the same time, the creeks of the Nome district produced $1 million, though it was hard to keep miners working the creek placers so long as beach possibilities remained available.

A miners' meeting determined that no beach claims could be staked— each man could work a piece of ground measured by a shovel's length. Because much of the ground was between high and low water marks, when the tide came in to smooth off the digging, the miners withdrew. Once the tide had receded, the thick swarms of men would return to set up their rockers at one spot or another.

Now everyone was happy. Truly the beach was a poor man's diggings with enough for all. But harmony in Nome was ever a fleeting thing. Again and again greed provoked a storm. A mining company holding claims to tundra lots adjacent to the richest part of the beach insisted that its rights extended to the beach as well, and demanded that the military arrest trespassing miners. Dutifully the officer marched his troops to the beach and made a mass arrest. Now what? No civil authority existed to hear the case against the 268 "trespassers." No jail existed to house them pending trial. The military asked the complainant to pay for the maintenance of the miners. When this request was declined, there was nothing to do but to release the miners, who promptly went back to their rocking. Something in the mood of the camp had induced a change of attitude on the part of the mining company officials, who decided to ignore further trespassing.

By autumn of 1899, arrivals at Nome saw a tent city stretching 20 miles along the beach. The Rev. Hall Young arrived to hold the first church services. J. F. A. Strong launched the *Nome News*, the camp's first newspaper. The Creamerie Cafe served pork and beans for $1.50 in a handsomely and elegantly equipped establishment. According to the *News*, "What Delmonico is to New York or the Palace Hotel to San Francisco, the Creamerie is to Nome."[6] Such was the unblushing pride of the northern frontier.

Another item on the front page of the newspaper announced that Curly Carr and Ed Kelly, well-known middleweight boxers, were booked for a twenty-round glove contest. A warm fight was promised: Carr had recently beaten Billy Cooper, the Yukon champion, at Dawson, and Kelly was well known locally. But the place designated for the match is noteworthy—Wyatt Earp's saloon, the Dexter. The Dexter was jointly owned by Earp and Charles Hoxsie. Earp's reputation as a frontier gunslinger is better known today than are his talents as a boxing promoter, but the former buffalo-hunter, Dodge City deputy marshal, Tombstone hustler, Cour d'Alene miner, and saloon keeper had earlier ties with boxing. In 1896 he had refereed the Jack Sharkey–Bob Fitzsimmons fight. Earp seems to have rushed to Alaska in '98, but there is no record of his activity prior to his appearance at Nome. Apparently he left the North in 1901 or early 1902, joining the rush to Tonopah, Nevada, where he opened a tent saloon, The Northern. He moved on to Goldfield, Nevada, in 1903 until the boom burst there, then worked in Arizona, California, and elsewhere.[7]

A town government was organized. Something had to be done about a hospital and sanitation—several typhoid deaths occurred daily. In the absence of federal provisions for civil government in Alaska, the town government lacked authority. It had no means of raising revenue beyond requesting donations from businessmen. In spite of these difficulties, the most urgent tasks were accomplished, chief among them the establishment of mail service. The post office had not yet provided service and no help could be expected for a year. Private carriers were hired to mush a winter trail to Katmai on Cook Inlet—a distance of 1,200 miles through a trackless wilderness.

Some miners departed for the Outside with considerable pokes. Judge W. T. Hume, a former mayor of Seattle, left with $20,000 in gold, (He was to leave the new Fairbanks camp several years later under quite different circumstances; his frozen corpse, lashed to a dog sled, would be mushed to Valdez over the Valdez Trail.) Missouri Bill also steamed south with a big poke. Earlier he had made a fortune at Dawson. Some men were born lucky.

Robbery and plunder increased as the close of navigation neared. There was no timber within many miles of Nome. Coal was in short supply. Men of foresight gathered stockpiles of driftwood for winter fuel. Men of less ambition pilfered fuel as opportunity offered.

Familiar Dawson City rogues attempted to corner the market on lumber, food, and coal. "Steal now and sell later" was their basic entrepreneurial plan. "Let the grafters beware!" editorialized the *News*. "Sneak thieves should be banished to a more genial climate."[8] The Alaska Commercial Company hired a watchman to protect its wares. One Frank Gillis was shot while carrying off A.C.C.'s stack of canned goods.

A municipal police department tried to deal with the rising crime rate. In October, Chief Eddy made 74 arrests for drunkenness, fighting, and disorderly conduct; 46 for larceny and robbery; 12 for miscellaneous crimes. Six men were ordered out of the country without benefit of trial. Ten were deported after their conviction.[9]

Editor Strong of the *Nome News* always saw the bright side of things: "Nome has a criminal element but Skagway was much bloodier at the same point of time."[10] His comparison was just, if not entirely reassuring. The Skagway of Soapy Smith was one of the most lawless towns in the history of the American frontier, and Strong had been a newsman there, too.

Progress went on. Masons formed a club. The Nome Literary and Debating Society heard a debate on the legality of staking claims by power of attorney. Debater Button wowed the assembly. His "athletic imagination and geysher like flow of language, coupled with his Ciceronian eloquence and Byronic wit make him a great card to draw to," the *News* reported.[11] Poems were read. A tuneful duet closed the program.

Blue Tickets

Townspeople demanded action against the audacious looters, footpads, and thieves. Respectable folk feared for the safety of person and property —Nome had no jail and no street lights to alleviate the long winter's dark. Pressure built up for a general roundup and banishment of known and suspected crooks. Banishment from the country was the traditional punishment levied by miners' meetings in the Yukon camps. But the season was advanced. It was late October and only one ship, the U.S. Revenue Cutter Service's *Bear*, remained off Nome. Captain D. H. Jarvis was asked to carry Nome's "Forty Thieves" to Seattle. He agreed to oblige, and Chief Eddy gathered up a dozen men of the class that neither toils nor spins and ordered them aboard the *Bear*. No judicial proceedings sanctioned the event. No time!

Eventually freed in Seattle, none of the departees filed suit for false arrest and false imprisonment. An interesting legal case would have resulted if such a suit had been filed. How do you sue city officials whose offices were not legally established?

With the departure of the *Bear* and a good percentage of the town's unsavory characters, things grew somewhat quieter, though thieving was still prevalent. "No sentence can be too heavy for a sneak thief," raged the *News*; "no quarter for the sneak thief—to the wood pile."[12]

All but a few warm-blooded men gave up beach-rocking for the winter. On the creeks, miners toiled away at their diggings. It was hard work generally done with the knowledge that jumpers claimed the same ground. The uncertainty of the legal situation strained nerves. Even the *bon vivant*, notably amicable Wilson Mizner, leading light of the underworld, lost his calm over a civil suit brought before United States commissioner Rawson. His assault on Moses Rosencrantz got him a $25 fine with costs. And Wyatt Earp was fined $50 for assault on a policeman.

Over the winter, Nomeites wondered what the world thought of their camp. Clearly there would be a mass stampede from Outside in the spring. Occasional newcomers from Dawson over the Yukon ice reported that thousands were preparing to join the stampede. Estimates ranged from 20,000 to 30,000. "We will be IT next summer," chortled the *News*; but measures needed to be taken. "Let's plan wisely," cautioned the paper, "a little less attention to the work of grasping would do it."[13]

Judge Rawson's work attracted favorable notice. J. McGlade got 365 days on the woodpile for stealing coal. Prosecuting attorney in the case was City Attorney Key Pittman—later to be a United States senator from Nevada. Pittman was also the victim of McGlade's theft. Retribution came swiftly. McGlade was sentenced three hours after his arrest.

Rawson also acted to end speculation in driftwood. Without citing legal precedent for his interference with free enterprise, he ordered that no one may hold more wood than needed for his own use.

In November, Button's Circulating Library opened. Many saloons served the "choicest goods" and steam beer at two bits a glass. Jack

Mallon, imbibing too heavily while celebrating his mining successes, somehow shot another saloon lounger in the leg. A city policemen shot Mallon dead. The *News* accused the hospital manager of graft and mismanagement, but gave him equal space to reply.

What was it really like to be on the scene of these fast-paced events? To most it was an experience that marked the high point of their lives, and they recognized it as such. Even those who came to Nome rather reluctantly became immersed in the spirit of the place. Elizabeth Robins' situation illustrates this well. She went to Nome because her brother was a minister there and initially she was appalled at what was going on. "You see more, live more, in twenty-four hours of Nome than in a cycle of Cathay," her brother told her.[14] But she did not like what she saw, particularly the young preacher having to defend his lot and tent from jumpers at pistol point.

Miss Robins, later to become a celebrated actress especially noted for her Ibsen roles, was most maternal towards her brother. Nome was too hard on the 26-year-old preacher. The Robinses are too fine-grained, she argued; but he would not leave the hurly burly scene and, though disappointed, she was too sensitive to avoid responding to the town and its lure. "Nome is absorbing, devouring. She exacts such tribute as no mistress ever dared before, and she looses her hold only when the life is drained and done."[15]

Elizabeth Robins also understood the position of men who had been following the stampedes for years. She noted that they no longer wanted to return to their homes: "They are right. They have stayed away too long. The man who comes here young, and keeps putting off his home-going, letting the charm of his free undisciplined life get into his blood, does well to realize this is all."[16]

Exciting news spread of a gold discovery at distant Cape York. Surely, gold would be found all over the Seward Peninsula and the Arctic. Nome would be the trading center for the entire vast region, it was predicted. A reindeer express service between Nome and York came into being.

The Long Winter

Already, in the winter of 1899, the city boasted twenty saloons, six bakeries, five laundries, twelve general merchandise stores, three second-hand stores, four wholesale liquor stores, four hotels, six restaurants, six lodging houses, two paper hangers, two photographers, one brewer, three fruit, cigar, and confectionary stores, two tinsmiths, two sign painters, three watchmakers, two meat markets, one boat shop, a book store, three packers, two dentists, Congregational and Catholic services, eleven doctors, sixteen lawyers, four bath houses, a massage artist, a bank, two printing shops, a blacksmith, two construction firms, four barber shops, two clubs, a hospital, a water works and an undisclosed number of whores. All this in a community that did not even exist a few months previously. The population was about 3,000 souls.

Over the long, cold winter, town gossip and scandals described in the newspapers excited readers. Two robbers whose identities were disguised by mosquito bar masks held up a store. Joe Carroll, the mail carrier, collected money to deliver letters to Katmai, but mushed out of town without the letters. Thanksgiving, Nome's first holiday, was celebrated. On Christmas day George Murphy and Tex Rickard fed 400 guests free at the Northern Saloon, as they were to do each year they ran the Northern. Nome's first baby was born.

New Year's Day brought significant activity: the first, but by no means the last, claim-jumping stampede. The weather did not deter men from rushing to the creeks and restaking ground, then rushing back to the recorder's office. Some lawyers believed that jumpers could prevail over any original stakers who had not done the required location work before the old year expired. United States mining law required of a claim holder a specified amount of work each year. No one knew if this applied to the Nome situation, but the jumpers saw the gamble as worth the effort.

In January, the first blizzard of the season ripped and scattered tents. Frail canvas was no match for subarctic storms. Fortunately, the winter was overall a mild one. Men stood guard with guns over their woodpiles. Five prostitutes refused to pay an assessment of $17.50 levied against them by the municipal court. For a time, they were confined in a make-shift jail on the second floor of City Hall. They enjoyed themselves, singing French and American songs lustily, making the dogs howl.

Beer prices soared from $30 a barrel (six dozen bottles) to $60. Saloon keepers wanted $1 a bottle over the bar. This inflationary trend resulted from a shortage. Saloon keeper Jim Wilson controlled most of the beer in town and made a mint. Happily, whiskey was plentiful.

In March, school opened for twenty children. Prospecting went on. Rumor had it that one man, so discouraged at finding the whole country staked, cut a hole in the ice and claimed a section of the Bering Sea.

Peter Bernard tried to make it across the ice to Siberia, but failed. He did reach the Diomede Islands and reported rich prospects there. Ice conditions of the Bering Strait rarely permitted a winter crossing. Even during the coldest periods, the ice mass cracked and shifted ceaselessly, opening wide leads. Bernard and other traders were to make Nome the center of Alaskan–Siberian trade, an enterprise that brought the rich furs of the Russian North to market in exchange for rot gut whiskey and other goods.

Eight hundred thirty-seven people were fed up with the law enforcement agencies by March. They signed a petition calling for a military takeover. Be patient, cautioned editor Strong, Americans should not submit to military rule. Most miners agreed with Strong. They had complained long and hard against the semi-military government imposed by the Mounties in Dawson City—and wanted no more of that.

Any petitions were just one sign of the approach of long-awaited spring. One involved Mayor Cashel and Police Chief Eddy. The city council investigated reports that the officials had been seen "breaking a window and tumbling a female in the snow on the street."[17] Some people thought the officials should resign. They indignantly refused. By a three-to-two vote a tolerant council exonerated the exuberant men.

A mass meeting considered again the question of martial law. The majority still opposed. The ineffectuality of the municipal government occasioned many critical speeches. However, some pressing problems received attention. The chamber of commerce raised $7,000 for cleanup work; all the season's waste and debris was carried out onto the ice.

When would the first ship arrive from Outside, and how many stampeders could be expected? These were burning topics as the opening of navigation neared. "The scum of the United States will be spewed upon our shores," warned editor Strong.[18] He was right. Dawson City and other gold camps in their heyday got their share of the "sporting crowd" —whores, gamblers, and crooks—but none could compare to the size of the demimonde that flocked to Nome. Some travail attended a journey to the interior gold camps, but travelers from Seattle to Nome usually suffered no hardship or even the inconvenience of changing vessels.

Meanwhile, arrivals from Dawson City continued. H. B. Levy had left Dawson on February 12 and arrived March 24. He traversed the 1,348 miles by bicycle, putting in 22 actual travel days on the road. A honeymooning couple mushed in with fifteen dogs after 65 days on the trail. They reported that Dawson would be depopulated as all rushed to the Seward Peninsula. Five "ladies," whose sled driver was an 11-year-old boy, reached the city of gold. They brought few worldly possessions; one of them carried an extra hair pin as her only baggage. Surely their faith in the generosity of the men of Nome would be rewarded.

Letters coming in over the trail included numerous requests for information:

Will you be kind enough to answer this and advise me what outfit I want to go to Nome district, and about what time do I want to leave Seattle? How do they get the gold-bearing sand? Do they wade in the water or do they go in boats? What ocean is it and is the water cold all *summer? About how much money do you want to go there with? Please write me all the tools and what other things I want. Would you advise taking a boat? What is a rocker and where can you get one? Could you do better with a boat getting the sand than you could with a rocker? Wouldn't it be cheaper to take your provisions with you than to buy it there? Can you do as well alone or with a partner? Please answer as soon as convenient.*[19]

To old-timers, this must have sounded sweet and innocent indeed.

Overland arrivals were staggered to find the whole region staked and recorded. When one innocent pitched his tent on a vacant lot in town, a wrathful claimant pulled it down and threw it in the street. It could have been worse—jumper Billy Smith was shot dead. The mood in Nome was not growing more favorable towards claim-jumpers as the season advanced.

Everyone lamented the absence of government and the uncertainty of the land claim situation. Sam Dunham had expressed the anxiety poetically:

> *We've had some hard knocks on the Klondike*
> *From the Cub-lion's unpadded paws*
> *and suffered some shocks from high license*
> *And other innumerable laws;*
> *But they robbed us by regular schedule,*
> *So we knew just what to expect*
> *While at Nome we're scheduled to struggle*
> *Until we're financially wrecked.*[20]

Rumors plagued the community. How could it be otherwise with communication with the Outside so limited? Presumably the beach situation had been cleared up when the United States commissioner declared that tidal flats were federal lands, thus giving to all equal rights to work the sand. No one could legally stake a claim. Despite this, in April, miners stampeded to the beach, staking its entire length. This incident was triggered when the Alaska Commercial Company manager dug a ditch on or near the beach and recorded a claim. Just a precaution, he said. Observers succumbed to a rumor that the manager had news of congressional legislation opening the beach to claims. Off went the stampeders in a frenzy.

Another rumor proved factual. Someone reported that Congress had created three new judicial districts for Alaska. Nome would get a judge: order would be restored. This news cheered the camp. If the miners could have foreseen what was actually to result when Nome's federal judge assumed office, their mood would have been otherwise.

In April a booze famine threatened. The long thirsty winter nearly dried up the awesome reserves of the twenty saloons. Rather than impose rationing or stretching the goods with a tabasco sauce–water–molasses mixture, bartenders raised prices to four bits a shot. Drinkers moaned their anguish. When will those damned ships appear?

Milk drinkers were also dismayed. Nome's only cow gave up the ghost on May 19. A cafe proprietor bought the carcass of the popular jersey that had supplied the town's milk needs all winter. Evidently Nome required little milk. Several typhoid patients, including the Rev. Hall Young, believed they owed their recovery to the availability of milk.

The Cyclist

The first arrivals of 1900 did not come by steamer. They were men and women already in the North who decided that the Nome strike must be the real thing and contrived to get there before navigation opened. One such individual was Ed Jesson. He had been in the North since 1896, when he had rushed to Hope on Cook Inlet before joining the Klondike stampede. Luck eluded Jesson, and in the winter of 1900 he was occupied in hunting caribou along the Seventy Mile River, which he sold to the army at Fort Egbert.

The constant traffic of gold seekers stampeding downriver stirred him, too. First he mushed his dog team to Dawson City. Newspapers from Outside had just arrived. They announced American victories over the Spanish. But this did not interest Jesson so much. He heard that the messenger carrying the papers had arrived by bicycle. A bicycle, he figured, was just the thing for a Nome journey. At the A.C.C. store he bought the bike for $150. He also acquired a number of Outside newspapers.

On February 22, 1900, with the thermometer reading 20° below zero, Jesson pumped out of Dawson for Nome. For eight days he had practiced bike navigation, perfecting his skill at keeping the wheels from wandering from narrow sled tracks. He made good time the first day, but on the second day, the mercury fell to 48° below. The bike's wheel bearings froze and Jesson walked into Eagle carrying the bike. When the weather warmed up a bit, he was able to set out once more, making 50 miles before lunch the next day.

The bicycle created a sensation among the Fort Yukon Indians, who had never before seen such a vehicle. "Geasus Crist," one remarked, "White man he set down walk like hell."[21] But the bike was not the only unusual travel mode on the Nome stampede. Between Circle and Fort Yukon, Jesson passed a big Norwegian traveling on ice skates, making 40 miles a day.

Roadhouses were spaced at intervals of 25 miles or so, all along the trail. Each noon Jesson ate a hot lunch and at night bedded down on the floor of a crowded shack. He was grateful that his labors ended when he reached a roadhouse. Mushers had to provide for their dogs before they could rest.

In the Rampart narrows of the Yukon River a howling wind drove Jesson along until it skidded him into an ice dam. One of his handlebars broke and he twisted his knee. Still he hobbled on, joining some other men camping in a lean-to for the night. To the beans and hotcakes the men were cooking, Jesson contributed butter and bacon. They feasted and were happier than many millionaires, as they were on their way to Nome.

After emergency repair of the bike's handlebar, Jesson set out again. Despite the menace of the wind he forced his pace because of the condition of the trail. A horse-drawn sled had broken up the trail, and he wanted to get ahead of it. The weather varied from day to day. Days were warmer and longer, but on occasion a heavy snowfall obliterated the trail. When this happened Jesson remained at a roadhouse until other travelers broke the trail again. Roadhouse proprietors and guests read Jesson's newspapers gratefully, sometimes sitting up all night to get through them before his departure.

At Kaltag the trail to Nome left the Yukon River. It coursed westward to Unalakleet on Norton Sound. Roadhouses were fewer so Jesson loaded 25 pounds of provisions into a backpack and forged on. When he stayed overnight in native huts, he avoided lice infestation with a few precautions. Spidella seeds were sprinkled liberally in the bed to "keep the seam squirrels on the run."[22] He left his clothes outside.

Traveling grew more difficult after leaving the Yukon River. Hummocky terrain caused him many upsets, and snow and wind caused delays. He was fortunate that Eskimo families provided hospitality where there were no roadhouses. Jesson, like all veteran sourdoughs, made the best of his situation. Men who were new to the country had more adjusting to do. Jesson observed one young stampeder coughing up his breakfast after seeing an Eskimo mother lick her baby's face clean. Such sensitivity amazed Jesson.

After crossing Norton Sound on the ice, the cyclist had not far to go. The bicycle had proved a swift and safe means of transportation, though after a month on the trail, the weary cyclist's vision was affected by the glare from snow and ice. Most of Nome turned out on his arrival. It was the custom that spring to watch for mushers who might have the latest news from Outside, particularly news of the Spanish–American war.

Jesson's papers scored a hit. Editor Strong of the *Nome News* secured them and arranged a public reading in a dance hall. News from the *San*

Francisco Examiner and *Seattle Post-Intelligencer* cheered the crowd. Readers took turns—it was dry but exhilarating work. The isolated miners drank toasts to the battleship *Oregon* and its gunners, tossed their hats in the air and toasted Admiral Dewey. It was a wild night, but wilder days were coming, as the newspapers confirmed: Seattle's docks were humming with the thousands who were outfitting for the Bering Sea.

Breakup

Beer prices in Nome dropped from $60 to $35 a barrel—a sure sign that relief ships were due. At last, the steam whaler *Alexander* bruted her way through the disintegrating ice. On the next day the *Jeanie* and *Jeannette* joined her in the open roadstead. Jubilance reigned. Fresh vegetables, fruit, beef, ham, and eggs adorned tables once more. The long isolation had ended. News from Outside was devoured eagerly.

Soon passenger steamers arrived in a continuous stream. Thousands disembarked and marveled at the strange city of tents. In their turn the pioneers viewed with wonder the paraphernalia heaped on the beach. Most outstanding were the various mechanical monsters designed to gather up the beach sands for washing. Nome was on the way to becoming a city, and a very lively one. Its travails were only just starting.

16

The Turbulent Scene, 1900

Getting There

Eager argonauts flocking to Nome often experienced eventful voyages. Most were outfitted in Seattle, by then the firmly established jumping-off place to the North. All the Alaska-bound ships were overcrowded; some shipping companies sold the same berths twice. This disgruntled crew and passengers alike. Frances Ella Fitz, a stenographer whose services would be in much demand, voyaged on a ship whose passengers had had little use for the dining room. According to Fitz, the Chinese cooks deliberately tainted the food to reduce the numbers of diners. Other ships lacked adequate supplies of food. The steamer carrying L. H. French, an investor in mining claims, made good time, taking only 10 days to reach Nome. Still food ran out. Such penny-pinching imperiled passengers. If a ship got caught in the ice pack—a not uncommon happening—it could drift helplessly for weeks. Storms could also prolong a voyage by many days.

French did not like the looks of many of his fellow passengers. He divided them into three types: the "sporting class of both sexes; the idle, footloose men without definite plans; and the experienced miners, professionals and businessmen."[1] Early in the voyage the sporting class dominated the ship. Ship's officers became infected with the gala atmosphere pervading a crowd of soon-to-be millionaires. They boozed with the passengers, ignoring the tumult as the toughs diverted themselves with brawls. Only the captain tried to keep order. In attempting to break up a fight, he got his eyes blackened; at this the respectable segment of passengers grew alarmed. In the classic pattern of frontier "democracy," they formed a vigilante committee. French was elected chairman. The committee saw to it that the captain's rules were enforced. Patrols roamed the ship day and night to intimidate the unruly. These measures kept the lid on. What would Nome be like, wondered French, if the other ships racing there carried as many unsavory characters as the *Victoria*?

On other steamers the stewards tyrannized the passengers, doling out miserly portions of food and refusing service unless amply tipped. This kind of treatment provoked Rex Beach, a burly, young ex-football player, to take on the steward and pummel him soundly. Other entertainments aboard ships included voyage-long card games, exhortations delivered by preachers to the repentant and unrepentant alike, and the interminable quest for information on the best placer ground, new mining techniques, and the like. Promenading was impossible due to the crowds on deck.

Steamers to Nome did not navigate the famed, scenic inside passage to Alaska but kept well out to sea until reaching the Aleutian Islands, generally passing through the narrow Unimak Pass, unless planning to stop at Dutch Harbor when Akutan Pass was used. Usually there was little of scenic interest except birds and an occasional whale.

All the ships heading North early in the summer season had to halt at Dutch Harbor until the Bering Sea opened. Tent saloons and gambling places sprang up during the sojourn at Dutch Harbor. Adventurous women plied their ancient trade. Less sophisticated men played baseball. A group of lawyers, including Lanier McKee, occupied themselves in drawing up papers organizing a town site at Dutch Harbor. They suspected that their activities could not be legally consummated, but in doing so they kept their legal tools sharpened—one never knew when such a preparation might bring riches. After all, it was speculated that Dutch Harbor would become an important way station on the American–Asiatic–Philippine trade route.

Some ships were not permitted to land their frantic passengers. The *Ohio* was quarantined near St. Michael because smallpox was reported aboard. Among the grumbling and unhappy argonauts was one who voiced his complaints in print by publishing two issues of the *Egg Island Yellow Journal* aboard the anchored ship. There was not too much news in the little four-page paper produced by Joseph Lippman, self-styled "Editor-in-Chief, Manager and Devil," but he gave his readers a few laughs with his one liners: "Be it ever so bumfull, there's no place like Nome," and fulminations against the gentleman in room 236 who would confer a favor to his shipmates "by shutting down the dampers of the engine of his snoring apparatus . . . thereby enabling the Goddess of Sleep to bring sweet, soothing and refreshing slumber of repose to all inhabitants."[2] Attorney G. J. Lomen and his son Carl arrived off Nome on the *Garonne* on the afternoon of June 23, 1900. Passengers had to remain aboard until the next day when lighterage would be available. But the *Garonne* passengers were in high spirits: "Many of them revelled until

long after midnight—a midnight almost as light as day." G. J. Lomen did
not join the revelers, but mused on the gold rush scene, "On the morrow
the ways of 800 people would part, each seeking to grasp, in his own way,
the elusive and winged wheel of fortune."[3]

Nature had not blessed Nome's Bering Sea location with many endow-
ments beyond its gold-laden soil. Not only were there no trees, there was
not even a harbor to shelter the ships that carried the thousands of hopefuls with all their supplies and their equipment. At one time in the summer
of 1900, seventy ships rolled at anchor in the roadstead, where they were
highly vulnerable to the frequent, fierce storms common to the vicinity. If
the seas were rough, the landing operation could be uncomfortable and
dangerous. Small craft ferried passengers and stores two miles or so from
ship to shore. The beach was littered with the debris of unsuccessful
passages, as well as the innumerable heaps of stores that had landed
without mishap.

Once safely ashore, the scene either dismayed or exhilarated the new-
comer, depending upon one's outlook. Peacefully inclined women like
Sara Fell were appalled:

> *We reached Nome, that human maelstrom, at night. We could see from
> afar the twinkling of the lights and their reflections dancing in the waters
> of the sea. We proceeded through the main street, and if ever pandemo-
> nium raged, it raged there. The streets fairly swarmed with a hetero-
> genous mass of people. Drunken gamblers grovelled in the dust; women,
> shameless, scarlet women, clad in garments of velvet, silks, laces, of
> exceedingly grotesque character but universally decolette, revelled as
> recklessly as any of their tipsy companions. From the rough dance halls
> the scraping of a fiddle rose above the noisy clattering of heavy boots
> that sounded like a chariot race in an empty garret. Dust settled around
> about us like a heavy fog. We waded through rivers of it before we
> reached our hotel. There were thirty thousand inhabitants in Nome at
> that time, of nondescript character. Cultured, intelligent men hobnobbed
> with the uncultured and ignorant. The one touch of nature that made
> them all akin was the greed for gold.*[4]

Yet if the observer was a young man of the quality of Jack "Doc"
Kearns, the lively scene presented a different aura. Surely it was not
lovely. Years after his northern experience, Kearns recalled that Front
Street "staggered through this assemblage of hovels as if it had been
surveyed by one of the hordes of drunken miners."[5] But still it was a
fabulous place despite being a bedlam of sounds: howling dogs, drunken
voices raised in argument, the banging of rinky-tink pianos, and the shrilling of whores to potential customers. The place smelled of beer, whiskey,

unwashed bodies, and cheap perfume; to young Kearns this was a heady mixture. He enjoyed watching men fight in the streets, gamble, drink, and debauch with the showgirls and wished himself in no other place in the world. Of course, Kearns had come to Nome to enjoy just such adventures and to escape the dullness of more sedate surroundings. He had no money to invest in mining properties and no concern for the orderly development of the camp. Neither was he much concerned about his immediate future. Nome brawled and glittered without restraint and offered all the excitement he craved: "I thought it was marvelous."[6]

Crime and Chaos

In 1900, the thirsty citizens of Nome City had a choice of no fewer than fifty saloons. Thirty-three of these watering places lined Front Street, the narrow main thoroughfare, which was thronged night and day with men, dogs, and horses. The list included the Baldwin, Behrin, Belmont, Blanche's, Bohemia, Cabinet, Columbia, Dexter, Elite, Exchange, Gold Belt, Grotto, Thomas Hogan, Hub, Hunter, International, Frank Johnson, Kelly and Holland, Luckie and Moore, Madden House, Nevada, New Eldorado, Nome Liquor Co., Northern, J. T. Obrien, Ocean, Pioneer, Portland, Reception, Sideboard, Southern, Treasury, and the Warwick. The most popular of these was the Northern.

In 1900 and 1901, when the fever of the stampeding thousands was at its peak, Nome was as lawless a community as ever existed in the West. It was crowded with gamblers, con men, whores, pimps, trigger-happy ne'er-do-wells, and honest adventurers. Regardless of background and intent, criminal and solid citizen alike voyaged to the Seward Peninsula for one reason only—to make a quick fortune. Nome was as wild and turbulent as the Skagway of 1898 and even gaudier.

Needless to say, the population's combustible elements flared often into violence. Shoot-outs, muggings, and saloon brawls made peaceable citizens insecure. A veteran of all the northern mining camps, the geologist Alfred H. Brooks, found it necessary for the first time to carry a weapon for self-protection. In his years in the North he had never experienced a tougher town. The first sound Dr. John Hewitt heard as he landed at Nome was a pistol shot. A gambler at the Northern Saloon fired on someone from the doorway, ignoring the hazard to crowds on Front Street. Will Ballou, down from Rampart to investigate the scene, stayed for three days. Each day there was a killing. "We had a dead man for breakfast most every morning," said Will.[7]

With the town growing rapidly, municipal government broke down. One scandal followed another. Some officials resigned; others were fired. Corruption seemed endemic. Accusations, counteraccusations, denials, and vilification raged in public circles. Little work was accomplished. James H. Murray came to look for his son, not knowing the boy had been a typhoid victim; at the grave, Murray shot himself. Another suicide left a note: "Sick, destitute and a long way from home. What else could I do?"[8] Petitions calling for military control failed several times. A newspaper editorial bemoaned the fact that arrivals included so many men of questionable pursuits, as well as many traders; miners were wanted and needed. Once, when a sudden storm swept in, wrecking the ships that were unable to shelter behind Sledge Island, tents, provisions, and equipment were strewn along the beach. Several men were drowned, and beachcombers fought each other for the salvage from shipwrecks.

The *News* commented upon all the "jackass machinery" lining the beach. Each piece of equipment was "just the thing." Editor Strong correctly predicted that most would lie useless on the beach until it rotted away. "Pumps of many kinds there are; and windmills too in charge of modern Don Quixotes; steam engines of varying horse power; pipe of diverse colors, and assorted sizes; rockers of every conceivable pattern, all warranted the very best, grizzlies, patent sluice boxes— in fact the greatest assortment of mining machinery that has ever been seen in a mining camp. Owners will call sands barren because contraptions won't do the job."[9]

Rex Beach, a veteran of the Rampart mining fields, was one of many owners of such "jackass machinery." He was in Chicago when he heard about Nome's rich shores and decided to return North. Borrowing money, Beach hired an engineer to build something that would gather and mine the beach sands, then set out for Nome. In Seattle he secured passage to the goldfields on one of the overaged scows that had been taken from the boneyard to meet the demands of the Nome traffic. Nome he described as a thin row of saloons, dugouts, and canvas shelters lying like a wagon track between the surf and the treeless, spongy tundra that ran back to a low range of inhospitable hills. There were those who could find beauty in the tundra, but not Beach, as he sloshed through the wet moss and mud up to his knees, "Aside from the sandy beach there was not a dry place to stand; of course, nobody had time to sit down."[10]

The scene was exciting to Beach despite the discomforts. There was no law to speak of, and with all the bickering and quarreling going on incident to recovery of baggage heaped up on the beach and the quarrels arising from claim-jumping, a man could pick the sort of fight he preferred. Beach was young and tough enough to enjoy the sense of insecurity one felt in a town that had jumped from 3,000 to 20,000 population in a couple of weeks. Though he witnessed a few shootings, bystanders were generally unaffected by such individual duels. Besides he had much work to do.

The mechanical monster commissioned by Beach had to be assembled to join hundreds of other strange machines that inventors had devised to work the beach sands. Beach's behemoth was to reach out into the surf with its dredges and sand suckers to gather the yet unexploited gold that must be found beyond the low tide mark. Many machines had been designed to suck up the sand in some mechanical way, but as Beach ruefully remarked, the only suckers that worked were the owners "of these hapless monsters."[11] None of the machines fulfilled expectations.

Beach's hired hands lost faith in the contraption before he did. They had to try to keep the hoses and moving parts of the machine free from clogging sand. Since this entailed braving the cold Bering Sea water, "They shrieked like Vassar girls when the surf engulfed them so for weeks I battled it alone," Beach recalled.[12] Constant immersion in the icy water turned Beach the color of a tuna, and he feared he was adopting some of the fish's mannerisms as well.

Happily for his health, a crowning disaster terminated his laborious efforts. A three-day gale smashed across the beaches and littered the beach with wreckage of the costly dredging devices that had been shipped so far at tremendous expense and with such budding hopes. The dredge of the Mongollon Exploration Company had cost $74,000 and produced $350 in gold. Beach's work had left him with the grand sum of $25 in dust. After paying off his crew he had nothing except an oil burner, pump, hose, and a case of canned cherries.

Such assets put him on a par with thousands of others. Winter was near. No jobs, no money. Thousands thronged aboard the last steamers of the season; hundreds robbed and pilfered; and a handful—like Beach—struck it rich. Beach's success did not entail any great effort.

A claim was offered him for purchase and, by good fortune, he found a partner who had some cash to close the deal. With a few weeks' work the mine showed great potential and Beach was offered $30,000 for his interest. For a few of fortune's favorites it was just as easy as that.

The same issue of the News that complained of the "jackass machinery" reported a "real Western shoot-out" in a dispute over a town lot. Things were livening up. Lucius Golden and Frank Simons opened a no-limit faro game at the Hub Saloon. When Jimmie the Goat raked in $14,000, a free-for-all broke out. Someone started shooting, then fled out the back door. By this time the crowd was so great that the game was transferred to the Northern Saloon.

The Nome Chronicle, devoted to "conscientious and truthful reporting," began publishing; its editor pledged "fearless and just criticism of whatever may demand the restraining influence of exposure"—and attacked Judge Arthur Noyes' inactivity. He also called for a vagrancy law. "There are any number of criminals, confidence men and dissolute characters who shrink from the suggestion of honest work as the devil shrinks from holy water."[13]

A grizzled boozer at the Hunter Saloon regaled the bartender with his method of judging economic activity:

You can tell a camp's development by the price of drinks. Four bits means recent occupation, unsettled conditions and presence of one half barrel which has come over trail. Two bits means a regulation boom is on, that tenderfeet are plenty and that regular communication with outside is established. Next drop is to three for a half. Not a sign of slump, but shows first excitement passed—the town is getting down to business basis. Fifteen cents means the business basis reached, court and school are going, claim jumping has become bad form, plug hats are tolerated and faro banks have moved upstairs. Any further decline, however, is a danger signal. Two for a quarter whiskey is a sure sign of deterioration and five cent beer means the stampede has started for the next diggings.[14]

Police arrested French Joe, who had been tempted by a staggering miner flourishing a heavy poke of gold dust at the Madden Saloon. Joe grabbed the poke and ran out the back door with the miner and others at his heels. To divert the chasers, Joe threw the poke aside and got away temporarily. The bag contained sand. The miner had been robbed at the Madden previously and had played drunk in hope of entrapping the culprit. One sport named Hall made $4,000 in a faro game at the Northern Saloon. He bought three rounds of drinks for the house. "I'm from the Klondike where you have to show me," he said and settled the $200 tab.[15] In the Tenderloin district, marshals arrested the girls who would not fork over $10 on the spot.

Two partners in the drug business fell out. Albert Hoepner claimed that Isaac Abramson had hypnotized him into giving him one-half interest in Hoepner's drugstore. That only contented Abramson for a short time. He wanted the other half interest and kept putting his persuasive eye on Hoepner, who now had built up some powers of resistance. Abramson followed Hoepner around trying to engage his eyes. The latter averted his gaze from the burning orbs of the hypnotist. Finally, in desperation, Abramson pulled a gun and ordered his partner off the premises.

By August, Nome held 100 saloons, of which only twenty-two bothered to pay the $1,500 annual license fee. As their numbers grew, life in the saloons became more and more unruly and troubled. The United States marshal announced a crackdown on "sure-thing" games and arrested a gambler wielding loaded dice. On three consecutive days, unknown persons tried to set Dick Dawson's Second Class Saloon afire. Saloons were important social centers, where miners met and talked, discussing their big and little affairs, argued, and fought.

C. A. S. Frost of the United States Department of Justice had been sent to Nome to investigate that infamous conspiracy which was to trouble the gold camp seriously. At first, Frost stood firm, observing Nome with a neutral eye, and he justly warned the press that here lived "the largest number of vicious men and women that ever infested a pioneer mining camp."[16] But soon, it was just one of those vicious and corrupt men, who bought off Frost for a handsome fee. It was Alexander McKenzie, leader of the "Spoilers," who corrupted Frost. But more on this later.

The noise level on Front Street compared to that of an oriental bazaar. Professional spielers earned $1 an hour for shouting out the virtues of particular services or products, making a sizable contribution to the din. When their pay was cut to 50 cents, they did not shut up but roared their protests. Fortunately, newspapers were silent—but their editorial tone grew shrill. The *Chronicle* attacked its rival for opposing city incorporation. The Spoilers also opposed incorporation, because the chaos served their purpose.

The *Chronicle* snarled at the street loungers, too. Two prostitutes drew a large gathering of spectators as they fought in the street on Second Avenue. They clawed, bit, pounded, and rolled around for 10 minutes before police intervened. That none of the gaping men attempted to halt the violent spectacle was evidence of the "growing refinement" of the camp, reported the *Chronicle* sarcastically.[17]

When thieves could not get a store's safe open, they carried it away despite its great weight. Deputy marshals did not see this. They seldom noted the frequent robberies, burglaries, and assaults that enlivened Nome's streets every night. Most of their duty hours were logged at the Northern Saloon, where harmony and good fellowship prevailed. Perhaps the tender officers already felt too cold to patrol the streets. Towards the end of September, frosty nights heralded the approaching winter and continuous preying on coal supplies. A group of thieves tried to corral the coal, and tons were stolen. Another gang hauled off coal belonging to two poor washerwomen providing for a sick brother. For the *Chronicle*, this kind of crime was "almost beyond belief." The thieves could not have used dogs for hauling, said the report, as the "majority of malemutes in the camp would howl curses on the master who forced them to such a dastardly offense."[18]

The grand jury recommended that women be banned from saloons and that something be done about ribaldry in the streets. On Second Avenue "a colony of painted French women hang out their windows and shout across the street to each other in strident tones that can be heard a block away." The editor of the *Gold Digger* knew no French but could scarcely believe the women were discussing the "management of well regulated households or singing odes to the moon."[19] The brazen effrontery of their manner spoke for itself.

The crime wave continued into October. Something must be done, editorialized the *Chronicle*—either hire more deputies or replace those who are not doing the job now—"The point is that there is lots of talk and no work accomplished." Nome had more felonies than cities of half a million population. "While all the officials talk the burglar and footpad ply their vocations and honest pedestrians mush home with their hands on large sized guns they carry in outside pockets . . . Nothing is done to discourage crime."[20] The *Chronicle* called for a military takeover. Once again, as during the 1899 troubles, a military foot patrol of six men patrolled the streets nightly to help the deputy marshals keep order.

Arrangements were made in October to ship the destitute out on the *Lawton*, an army transport. In August the *Lawton* had carried 220 men to Seattle, only sixty of whom had actually been without money. Captain Charles French announced that he would investigate the finances of applicants.

November brought no relief from crime, even though dropping temperatures should have helped to keep predators indoors. "The organized gang of crooks which is preying on this community has reached the limit," wrote an irate editor.[21] Men had forced their way into L. Daglow's Front Street home, chloroformed him while he slept, and robbed him of $1,300. One gang of thieves stored their loot in several shacks on the sand spit at the mouth of Snake River. Neighbors reported that sleds were busy all night freighting in stolen goods. Police raided the shacks and found cases of butter and eggs—but no evidence they had been stolen.

The editor of the *Gold Digger* complained at the lack of space to record all the crimes perpetrated. The *Digger* could only offer a sampling of incidents over one bustling weekend: John Butcher was held up in the Tenderloin, knocked down, and robbed of $140. Three masked footpads entered Jones' Front Street cabin, ransacked it, and took $300. Miss Ross' lodging tent was robbed of everything—clothes, nuggets, blankets, and stove. Men with a two-horse team took most of Mrs. Ohahal's forty-three sacks of coal despite her protest. One hour later they came back for the rest! A store owner caught James Smith cutting through a tent wall and he was sentenced to 60 days. The proprietor of the Golden Gate Hotel bought two valuable sled dogs and sent them to the dog stable for boarding. The dogs had been stolen from the same stable just before the sale. On the sand spit, Charles Wooy's tent was robbed of a massive bedstead, 10 feet high and very bulky: the next night thieves returned for his sleigh. Curnet shot up the Northern Saloon and fought the arresting officers like a wildcat. Thieves dashed into a cabin, grabbed a stove that contained a burning fire, threw it on a dog sled and ripped off—all in 60 seconds. A soldier ran amuck, threatening Front Street pedestrians with a fixed bayonet, while two others held a shoot-out in the street after being thrown out of a saloon.

The *Digger* warned darkly that things had deteriorated far enough. People were arming to protect their property and the thugs "may get surprised." Leading citizens laid plans for a vigilante committee.[22]

Still, life went on. Captain Banks, a miner, needed the assistance of deputy marshals to win his bride. His rival for the girl's affections had locked himself and the girl in her room. Banks and the marshals broke down the door, and the reunited lovers went to the preacher for knot tying. The couple moved into a room above the Nevada Saloon, where they billed, cooed, and ran up a $500 wine bill. Suddenly it was all over. Mrs. Banks, "whose wings were not clipped by the storms and passions of some thirty years," flew the coop.[23] She had discovered that Banks had exaggerated his wealth during their courting days. Discussion of this marital disharmony made the men lining the bars of the Second Class, Nevada, Northern, and the Dexter reflective. Women sure could cause a fellow trouble. Banks lost his bride and a lot of money—next he lost his freedom. He had sought out his wife in an effort at reconciliation. She remained adamant; she needed a monied man. He pleaded to no avail. Growing angry, he flourished a revolver—and ended up in jail. Confirmed bachelors among the miners felt vindicated by the Banks' case.

From 4,000 to 6,000 people had remained in Nome for the town's second winter of existence, and an editor mused: "We are prisoners in a jail of ice and snow, a little group of adventurers acting as outposts for a civilization."[24] This feeling of being imprisoned by winter certainly promoted restlessness, unruly conduct, and crime. The cold simply could not eliminate these.

A. F. Raynor was very busy serving meals at the Nome Cafe. He had salvaged a range and kitchenware left at St. Michael and had the only eggs in town. Prices were steep: beans, $1 per plate; ham and eggs, $2.50; black coffee, 25¢ per cup; evaporated spuds, 50¢ per order. Sometimes Eskimos brought him fresh grayling from the streams and ptarmigan from the tundra. These were snapped up at any price he put on them.

Two weeks after Raynor opened his restaurant a man with a cow arrived on the *Centennial*, and arranged the delivery of fresh milk at $1 a quart to anyone interested. To fulfill all his milk contracts the cow would have to produce 50 gallons a day. Something was delivered, but it obviously was not fresh milk. Later, Raynor joyously bought the overworked cow and posted the cheering news that steaks could be eaten at the Nome Cafe. He did not believe that the cow met her death at the hands of a butcher; probably it died from malnutrition. Raynor had never before seen such a scrawny array of bones. Nonetheless, Raynor displayed his steaks to stimulate appetites. One miner insisted on ordering a huge porterhouse and dove at it mercilessly with knife and fork. What he needed was dynamite. Finally he carried platter and meat to the door and threw it to the dogs that were always hanging around by the restaurant door.

In Judge Stevens' court, the ownership of a good sled dog was disputed by two claimants. Before the case could be settled, the dog was stolen from the courtroom by a third party. Coal thieves were once again caught in the act. They dropped their sacks and dashed off, with bystanders in hot pursuit. While the chase went on, someone else carried off the coal.

Strident measures against criminals were called for by the editor of the *News*. Now robberies even took place during the day, which was short and dark enough, and few arrests followed. The *News* warned, "We are at the mercy of a gang of thieves. A reign of terror exists. None dare testify against the crooks for fear of vengeance. If correction does not come lynching will, and that will hurt our reputation."[25] Things were no better at the creeks, where, the *News* reported, "Thieves are so thick that miners have to keep their grub down the shaft."[26]

A "family" quarrel ended in a shooting. Stevens and Larson, two miners in their 50s, had been partners and friends for many years. Peacefully they shared the same cabin until a 26-year-old woman came along. She was fleeing from a lover who had beaten her. Larson took her in, and the pair launched a big spree. Subsequently Larson woke Stevens up and ordered him to cook some grub. This seemed out of line to Stevens, who then proceeded to beat Larson. Larson grabbed the axe. Stevens shot his partner. When the law arrived Larson was in bad shape, but he asked that his partner not be punished. "It was only a family quarrel anyway."[27]

The *News* considered whether vigilante committees should attempt to restore order and advised against it. Vigilante committees have not been successful in Alaska, argued editor Strong, who had reason to know. He had been a newsman in Skagway during Soapy Smith's reign and had labored hard to organize a group to overthrow the rogue.

At the Grotto Saloon, a benefit for Frank O'Connor was given. O'Connor sold newspapers for a living. The year before, on the stampede down the Yukon River from Dawson City, he had traveled alone and had almost frozen to death. He had lain helplessly in the snow for five days before being discovered. At Tanana the U. S. Army surgeon amputated both legs.

Miners admired his pluck and wanted to raise enough money to buy O'Connor a better-fitting pair of artificial legs.

Just before the close of navigation, thirty thugs, sneak thieves, stickup men, and prizefighters were rounded up in the saloons and shipped out aboard the *Centennial*. Merchants raised the passage money of $773.50 and called on the United States marshal and military to make the roundup. Judge Noyes sanctioned this somewhat irregular proceeding. Precedent existed for it. The previous year a group had been sent out on the U. S. Revenue Cutter Service *Bear*. One of the deportees asked for a writ of *habeas corpus*. Noyes refused to consider it. There was not adequate time before the freeze-up. It was some relief to have the "Forty Thieves" bagged.

Miners stampeded to the Kuskokwim and Koyukuk Rivers, but found nothing there to detain them. Things quieted a bit as the winter wore on. At the Christmas civic banquet, toasts were given to the judiciary, law, and order. These were answered with eloquence by Judge Noyes. No one laughed. A saloon was held up that night. Tex Rickard and George Murphy of the Northern Saloon served free meals to 800 men on Christmas Day, 1900. Editor Strong did not quite like the style of Nome social life that winter: "The Phillistines are upon us," deplored the *Nome News*, "earlier we danced in mukluks and mackinaw, ate pork and beans, now it's swallow tail coats and low neck dresses. Tenderfoots brought their own climate with them—all that makes life undesirable."[28] Newspapers now paid less attention to public officials and more to abusing rival editors. President William McKinley's re-election was the biggest story of the winter. It was February 5, 1901, before a mail carrier mushed in with this news.

17

Lawless Camp: Nome in 1900–1901

The Spoilers

Frontier America could boast of many imaginative swindles, but the conspiracy concocted in Washington, D.C., to control Nome's goldfields tops them all for audacity. Among the 1900 arrivals in Nome was the much needed federal judge of Alaska's newly created Second Judicial District, Arthur H. Noyes. It seemed fortunate to the miners that Nome would now have a court and law enforcement officers. Because of successive waves of claim-jumping, all property titles were clouded. Thievery and gun play endangered property and life. At last Nome's snarled affairs could be untangled. But, alas! As it turned out, the situation worsened, for Judge Noyes was a crook, and his appointment as the first judge of the new federal judicial district had been concocted by Alexander McKenzie and others like him. Their scheme, an audacious example of bare-faced impudence, involved men in high places. In the McKinley era, roguery flourished.

If ever a town needed honest law enforcement, it was Nome in 1900. Instead, it got Noyes, the pliant tool of a group of swindlers, including several of Nome's lawyers who were active claim-jumpers. One had jumped discoverer Jafet Lindeberg's most valuable ground and aimed to hold it.

In no other northern mining camp was claim-jumping so prevalent. One could only hold his property by being physically present—and armed! Ejections by force were not uncommon. Shoot-outs over claims to town lots as well as mining properties occurred. At Circle and other early Yukon camps, claim-jumping had been rare; the miners respected one another's rights. But anarchy reigned in Nome. A total breakdown of order ensued. Veteran miners, accustomed to complaining about Canadian authorities in Dawson City, now longed for the stability imposed by the Mounties. With disgust, Walter A. Starr, a veteran prospector, observed shootings on Front Street and the manipulation of the judiciary: "Conditions at Nome made you blush for your country."[1]

And rascally lawyers who jumped claims had an easy time of it. In 1900, attorney O. P. Hubbard went to Washington, D.C., to see what could be done. Plenty, as it turned out. At the time, the Senate was considering the bill providing civil government for Alaska. Senator Henry Hansbrough of North Dakota proposed a modest exception, that it be illegal for aliens to hold claims in Alaska—and that such provision be made retroactive. Hansbrough's inspiration originated with Alexander McKenzie, who had been contacted by Hubbard. Hubbard could not have picked a better man. McKenzie, a giant fellow in physical stature, was the political boss of North Dakota, and as a leading Republican an intimate of President William McKinley. A skilled and powerful lobbyist, he served the Northern Pacific and Great Northern railroads for years. Earlier, when he had been a frontier sheriff, he had had the reputation of being a fearless defender of the law. Apparently, aging brought corruption.

McKenzie, Nome attorney Robert Chipps, and Hubbard incorporated the Alaska Gold Mining Company with a capital stock of $15 million. Forty-nine percent of the stock was reserved to pay for jumpers' titles, while the balance went to friends in Congress and to investors.

The "Spoilers"—so dubbed by Rex Beach in his famed novel—would mine the jumped properties, exhibit the gold, and sell the capital stock. All parties would make a fabulous profit. One beauty of the overall plan, aside from its essential audacity, was the time element. Even if eventual court decisions favored claim discoverers over jumpers, the former would still lose out. The wheels of justice grind slowly; most of the gold would be mined before the courts could act.

Debate on the Hansbrough amendment occupied the Senate for a month.[2] Senator Thomas H. Carter of Montana, a McKenzie man, was a leading supporter. Both senators spoke feelingly of the virtue of Americanism and seemed to disparage aliens. But in the end, the amendment was defeated. Not that this finished the Spoilers. The cooperative Senator Carter had chaired the committee drafting Alaska's laws. He saw to it that the federal judges received immense authority in their far flung districts. Arthur H. Noyes of Minneapolis was selected by McKenzie as the ideal judge for the Second Judicial District.

Senator Carter's choice for United States district attorney was Joseph K. Wood, and for United States marshal, C. L. Vawter, both of Montana. Carter's brother-in-law would serve as United States commissioner and watch over Carter's interest in the Alaska Gold Mining Company. These men, with McKenzie and Noyes, entrained for Seattle, and reached Nome on July 19, 1900, bringing beach mining equipment with them. Twenty thousand people awaited the benefits of federal law and order.

Within four days, McKenzie controlled all the disputed mining claims. It was simply done. Customary practice in similar situations was followed. The court appointed a receiver to administer the properties until the ownership tangle could be resolved. Noyes appointed McKenzie—a friend who had been good enough to pay off Noyes' home mortgage back in Minneapolis. McKenzie demanded of the legal firm of Hubbard, Beaman, and Hume one-half interest in jumpers' titles they held, offering stock in exchange. He insisted that Wood get one-quarter interest in the law firm's business, and that he receive one-quarter himself.

One witness to McKenzie's dealings with the attorneys was Hubbard's stenographer, Frances Ella Fitz. She owned one of the few typewriters in Nome and commanded high wages. Working 15 hours daily with bleeding fingers, she typed the documents appointing McKenzie receiver over all claims jumped by Hubbard. Noyes signed them immediately without bothering to read them. McKenzie posted a modest bond of $5,000 for each mine. Some of the mines were then producing $15,000 daily. Receiver McKenzie did not shut down the mines; instead he hired all the idle miners available. Gold poured into the depository bank.

Meanwhile the discoverers, the so-called "lucky Swedes," with Charles D. Lane, a California mining veteran and the purchaser of a number of claims, were not idle. Their attorneys attempted unsuccessfully to get Noyes to rescind McKenzie's appointment. He refused. Later the Circuit Court of Appeals in San Francisco wondered why a receivership was necessary in the case of mines: "The order was so arbitrary and unwarranted in law as to baffle the mind in its effort to comprehend how it could have issued from a court of justice."[3]

Court of justice indeed!

This was in reference to Noyes' seizure of all the property found at the mines under litigation: supplies, tools, tents, sluices, boilers, horses, personal property of the miners, and even gold dust that had been mined elsewhere. Truly McKenzie and Noyes had vociferous appetites. McKenzie bragged a lot in Nome. His position seemed invulnerable. His looting went forward without a hitch. The judge, he informed others, was his appointee: "To hell with them all! Nobody can hurt me! I am too strong at headquarters!" Headquarters was Washington, where indeed McKenzie had many friends. The big Scotch-Irishman was contemptuous of the opposition of the discoverers: "Give me a barnyard of Swedes and I'll drive them like sheep."[4] San Francisco, seat of the Circuit Court of Appeals, was 3,000 miles away, and there was no telegraph connection.

But there was time before the close of the navigation season for the beleagured, defrauded pioneers to appeal to San Francisco. A special examiner of the United States Department of Justice, C.A.S. Frost hurried to Nome for an investigation. The Spoilers bought him off with an appointment as assistant district attorney.

But McKenzie did not intimidate all the Nome miners. While the legal battle was going on in San Francisco, William H. Metson, the attorney who was directing the discoverers' case, sent some men to the Anvil claims to oust McKenzie's hirelings. "McKenzie's men were a little slow," according to Metson, "and a gun went off. Instantly they made great speed."[5] When McKenzie heard about the action taken at the mines he appealed to the Fort Davis military commander, Major Van Arsdale, who summoned Metson and McKenzie for a meeting. Tempers were inflamed. Metson and McKenzie exchanged charges of gold stealing.

"Wait till I get you outside," threatened the receiver.

"Now, let's understand it," replied Metson. "Does that mean that the first time we get outside it is a case of 'turn her loose'?"

"You can cut loose right now," shouted McKenzie.[6]

Both men went for their guns. Metson had a small caliber pistol and figured it would take a shot in the head to stop the big receiver. Before either man could fire, soldiers jumped them. Tempers calmed somewhat and McKenzie offered a $1 million bribe to Metson—which was indignantly rejected.

Before the summer was over, the pioneers' attorneys secured a writ from Circuit Court Judge William Morrow. McKenzie was ousted. All mining properties were to be turned back to the pioneers. All court proceedings would be suspended. Judge Morrow smashed the blatant looters in one fell swoop.

McKenzie tried to get away with the gold, but the authorities prevented it. The particular incidents are disputed. Some old-timers remembered a fierce mob racing McKenzie to the bank vault that housed the gold and storming the building. But for the timely appearance of the soldiers, McKenzie would have been lynched. Miner Dan Sutherland's account rings truer: "I joined the hostile crowd watching him walk from Stedman Avenue to General Randall's tent. He was an imposing figure, calm, powerfully built, piercing eyes, and determined. None dared attack him."[7] McKenzie's reputation as the "quickest draw in Dakota" deterred the aroused miners. The former sheriff awed the miners, but he kept to the company of the soldiers for the brief duration of his stay.

When Noyes received the Circuit Court writs, he responded in character by ignoring them. Instead of returning the gold to the pioneers he ordered the military to guard the bank vault. McKenzie still controlled his puppet, but Noyes grew fearful and anxious. Again the pioneers' lawyers were dispatched to San Francisco. The Spoilers had another month's reprieve.

Finally, two deputy marshals arrived from San Francisco. It was October 15, 1900. They arrested McKenzie and ordered him to open the vault. The master rogue refused, whereupon the deputies pried the vault open with crowbars and returned the gold to the pioneers. McKenzie was finished. Noyes hid in his chambers until McKenzie was taken aboard ship—though he did send his boss a note of sympathy.

In California, Judge Morrow sentenced McKenzie to one year in prison. Considerable pressure was put on President McKinley by McKenzie's cronies, who demanded a pardon. Despite the opposition of Judge Morrow, McKinley's old friend was pardoned.

Nome still had to put up with Noyes. The judge drank heavily. In court, his vacillations outraged all parties. It was probably just as well that court was seldom in session. Newspaper editorials urged him to get moving on the clogged calendar of cases. In time, they called for his resignation, as did the bar association. It was a long winter; crime was rampant and justice slumbered.

With the opening of navigation came an order to Noyes to answer a contempt of court citation in San Francisco. Nome buzzed with glee. At last, release from fraud and ineptitude loomed on the horizon! But Noyes informed the press of his intent to stay. At this the community outrage burst its bounds. Merchants, lawyers, and miners formed vigilante groups. The time had come to hang Noyes, Wood, and any others of the old gang. Just in time, keeping in character, the judge changed his mind and decided to face the music in San Francisco.

His last official order brought vigilante action. A claim on Glacier Creek had been jumped by Noyes' friends, who held it by force. Noyes ordered it returned to the true owners, but rescinded the order aboard ship in the course of a boozy farewell party with his friends.

A vigilante group determined to restore by force what could not be restored legally. Sixty-three well-armed men commandeered the railroad connecting town and mines, surrounded the mine, and rushed the guards. One guard was wounded; the others were threatened with death if they dared return. Settling this illegal affair was left to Judge James Wickersham, who had been ordered from the Yukon to Nome by the Department of Justice.

In San Francisco, Noyes received a $1,000 fine, while District Attorney Wood was sentenced to four months' imprisonment. Such light penalties indicated that Washington, D.C., was still looking after the Spoilers.

Certainly the Spoilers retained their influence in the U.S. Senate. In February, 1901, Senator William Stewart of Nevada referred to Nome: "There is a worse condition of things there than ever occurred in the Phillipines or Cuba under Spanish rule . . . for the want of a proper judiciary."[8] Senator Hansbrough could not overlook this reflection on Judge Noyes—who was still on the job in Nome at that time. Hansbrough read into the record a letter from Noyes defending himself and McKenzie from accusations of corruption. According to Noyes the only bribes offered in Nome were those offered him by McKenzie's enemies. A four-page brief, detailing the alleged bribes, was also placed in the record. Hansbrough blithely ignored the fact that the Circuit Court of Appeals in the McKenzie case had considered these bribery charges and found them without substance.

Senator Richard Pettigrew of South Dakota also defended Noyes as "a capable and honest man," and McKenzie as "a man of character, ability, and wealth."[9] In Pettigrew's view, a number of California grafters tried to grab the mines from the discoverers. McKenzie and Noyes prevented this and the grafters were spending millions to blacken the characters of the defenders of justice. Pettigrew then had the audacity to attack the circuit court: "It is a proceeding that ought to bring the court in San Francisco into contempt on the part of every honest man everywhere."[10] The Supreme Court did not agree with Pettigrew. A month after this speech the high court upheld McKenzie's conviction.

Even in 1902, after the conviction of Noyes, his friends in the Senate still defended him, but the scandal was brought into general public view for the first time through the vigilance of the *Washington Post*. Senator Ben Tillman of South Carolina read an article from the *Post* into the record, and its subject opened a debate. The *Post* had noted that both Noyes and District Attorney Joseph Wood, who was sentenced to four months in jail, were still on the federal payroll. "An influential coterie of politicians is wielding an influence that is amazing. All these men come from the West, and by quiet but forceful means have been able to block progress at every turn in this most remarkable judicial incident."[11]

Hansbrough responded "that the record in this transaction will fully vindicate Mr. McKenzie and acquit him of the miserable charges against his character and integrity."[12] He then attacked the Circuit Court for hearing evidence of the conspiracy rather than restricting itself solely to the charge of contempt of court. Since Noyes did not choose to appeal the Circuit Court decision, he apparently did not share Hansbrough's belief in its irregularity.

In February, 1902, the people of Nome heard about Noyes' conviction. In the *Nugget* editor Strong recalled "the most amazing conspiracies to obtain gold by legalized robbery that has ever been known in the history of the jurisprudence of this or any other country." Now the conspirators will have "plenty of time to chew the cud of bitter reflection within prison walls." They thought that on the extreme confines of civilization they could exercise absolute control. "Cheechakos themselves, yet schooled in all the wiles and subterfuges taught in a depraved school of politics, they no doubt reasoned that the gold miners and gold hunters of these frozen regions were all 'brothers to the ox.' " But the freebooters had met men as astute and resourceful as themselves. "Their names will be anathematized so long as warm blood runs through the veins of the people of Alaska."[13]

Years after the events of 1900, Nome pioneers were still thinking about them. In meeting old friends they would discuss whether Rex Beach's model for the hero of *The Spoilers* was Jafet Lindeberg or Gabe Price, a California miner who joined the "lucky Swedes' " party shortly after the Anvil discovery. Or they reflected in more general terms. William H. Metson recollected his contribution with some pride: "Of course, it was all in a day's work. I went to Nome with some standing and I figured I might just as well come out in a box as show the white feather." Metson had been raised on the frontier—"Where we were taught never to entrench on anybody's rights and at the same time allow no man to entrench on ours."[14]

18

Judge Wickersham in Eagle and Nome

First Court in the Interior

Judge James Wickersham had been appointed judge of the Third Judicial District at the same time as Arthur Noyes was assigned the Second Judicial District; in fact, they steamed North from Seattle on the same ship in 1900. Wickersham's destination was Eagle, a gold camp on the Yukon near the Canadian border. The district assigned to Wickersham did not seem as important as that of Nome. Nothing much was doing in the interior while Nome was the center of excitement. However, Wickersham resolved to do his best, little anticipating that circumstances would cause him to replace Noyes in Nome.

When Wickersham reached Eagle via Skagway and Dawson, he established the first federal district court in the interior of Alaska. After building his own log cabin in Eagle, he took up the duties of his extensive judicial district. Nobody knew how many natives it contained but the 1900 census indicated there were only some 1,500 whites—a number that would soar dramatically beginning with the 1903–04 rush to the Tanana valley. Boundaries of the district extended from the Arctic Ocean on the north to Attu Island of the Aleutian chain to the west, a distance of 2,000 miles. Approximately half of Alaska, some 300,000 square miles, including the great Yukon valley, was encompassed. In the entire district there was not a courthouse, a regular jail, school, nor any other public building. There was not a mile of public wagon road or trail. No money had been appropriated or promised by Congress for any of these purposes, except that the district judge had been authorized to reserve two town lots and build a courthouse and a jail out of license funds.

In those years interior Alaska was in many ways more an appendage of the Canadian Yukon than a substantially founded United States territory. In fact, it was not until some five years after Wickersham's arrival in

Alaska that United States currency was available in the quantity needed to transact business. The media of exchange until then were gold dust and Canadian currency.

Wickersham's first law enforcement effort in Eagle was to compel gamblers and prostitutes to recognize that the law had arrived. Keepers of bawdy houses and gambling places were arrested. Wickersham planned to fine them "a reasonable amount each quarter in vindication of the laws and as an aid to the fund to maintain the police."[1] An effort to accomplish this practical means of subsidizing law enforcement had failed the year before because the jury's sympathies were with the defendants.

First the judge presided over two jury trials in which the defendants were prostitutes. To his dismay the juries found no wrong in the girls "doing their thing." In a petulant diary entry the judge raged against the "weakness and cowardice of the men of Eagle . . . Men who should stand by the courts abuse them and acquit flagrant law violators."[2] It looked like a sharply drawn battle between the saloons and the court, with the saloons taking the initial victories.

Rather suddenly, however, the girls and the gamblers realized that the good, free-wheeling old days were over and, as each was tried in turn, they followed the hallowed ritual of pleading guilty and accepting a small fine as the price for remaining in public service. Thus ended the last defiance of judicial authority by whores along the Yukon.

Other Yukon camps were in need of law enforcement, so the judge arranged for court sessions in Circle and Rampart. Circle had been the most active camp on the American Yukon in the pre-Klondike days, but by 1900 it was virtually deserted. Rampart had somewhat more activity, enjoyed some prosperity, and even had two weekly newspapers.

Rampart, where Will Ballou, the young Vermonter resided, was somewhat unruly. The editor of the *Alaska Forum* looked forward to the court session. He had been assaulted on the street and hit on the head with a revolver "for daring to publish the news; which a certain element states, it only did when it failed to levy hush-money. Hush-money was offered— and refused. *Forum* policy is independent and fearless."[3]

Another lament came from one John Morgan, who had rented his cabin "to a blonde representative of the *demi-monde*." She soon moved out, taking the contents of the cabin along and forgetting to pay the rent. When John called at her new domicile requesting his furnishings, she indicated that she was protected by "a certain ex-official" and John had better clear out before he was perforated. John fled "sans stove, sans bed clothes, sans everything."[4]

But the petty crimes of Rampart were readily taken care of. Much more of the court's time was used in the adjudication of mining claim disputes.

Among successful litigants was Will Ballou, who noted his approval of the judge. In considering reasons for the animosity later directed against Judge Wickersham, the outcome of court cases weighs heavily; the losing claimant sometimes became an unrelenting enemy. The editor of the *Forum* cheered the judge's arrival and when, a couple of years later, the Department of Justice sent an investigator to look into the court's operation, a *Forum* editorial questioned the necessity of this action. Then, suddenly, the *Forum* opened fire on Wickersham, roasting the judge until the paper folded.

A court session was held at Circle as well. There was not much now to occupy the court in the camp that had supported eleven saloons in 1896. Wickersham discovered that the United States marshal in charge had posted a notice on the jail door the previous winter calling for all prisoners to report by 9 P.M. or be locked out for the night. During winter, when it was 200 miles to a point of escape, and the temperature might range from 20 to 60 degrees below zero, there was no danger of any prisoner's violating jail rules or attempting escape.

Wickersham had to do a good deal of traveling in order to conduct court sessions at three different towns on the Yukon. In summer, steamboats provided a pleasant trip, but it was other than pleasant in winter, when dog sleds provided the only means of conveyance. If one pictures a traveler snugged up in fur robes and nestling in the sled as the eager canines flew down the trail, some correction of the image is necessary. Actually the sled was utilized chiefly for provisions, while the men walked. Wickersham was often on the trail for a week or more at a time, averaging 20 to 30 miles a day. Such walking was pretty fair exercise and uncomfortable only during storms or extreme low temperatures. But if fresh snow had fallen, men had to break trail ahead of the dogs and the going was then very slow. In the North, people did not make idle excursions.

Wickersham described a sled expedition in *Old Yukon*. "Our long, Indian-made, spruce-basket sled was filled with dunnage bags, and dog feed, generally rice and bacon, sometimes dried fish; with blankets, dry sacks and warm clothing." Also packed were a well-stuffed grub box, extra dog harness, and soft caribou skin moccasins for trail-sore dog feet. The load was well wrapped in waterproof tarpaulin and lashed down with ropes. "On the right side of the front end of the sled the gee-pole extended forward; the driver ran astride the low hanging rope which attached the dogs to the sled." He guided the team with his whip and voice, and the sled with the gee-pole. "At the rear of the sled a pair of handle bars, similar to those of a common plow, enabled the rear guide to manage the sled and to keep it in an upright position on sloping ice ways."[5]

Soon, disturbing rumors of the McKenzie–Noyes machinations at

Nome reached Wickersham on the upper Yukon, but events there were none of his official business. However, as the Seward Peninsula situation deteriorated and the "Spoilers" were exposed, the entire mess was thrown to Wickersham. The United States attorney general ordered him to Nome to temporarily take over the court there. Judge Noyes had been ordered to Washington.

Authority Restored

The crooked and inept Judge Noyes had left Nome in August, 1901. Judge Wickersham reached the city in September. In the interim, the violence over the Glacier Creek claims induced the military to post guards over the properties. Effectively, if informally, martial law was established at the mines. Once again the military exceeded its authority, but probably prevented further shootings by its action.

A poem by Sam Dunham, poet laureate of Nome, appeared in the *Nugget*. The advice rendered poetically was certainly heeded by embattled miners:

> Now, I advise you men who mush—you men who dig for gold:
> When you have found and staked a claim you feel inclined to hold,
> Don't mush to town and tell your friends, nor let the lawyers know,
> But camp there with your loaded guns and give yourselves a show.[6]

If Wickersham had been either lethargic or corrupt, the seething citizens of the Seward Peninsula probably would have exploded. For three years they had been suffering from the lack of an effective judiciary. First they had waited impatiently for a dawdling Congress to recognize their needs and establish a court, then, when Congress had acted, the post had been filled by a corrupt judge.

The docket was jammed with hundreds of claim disputes that Noyes had never got around to hearing. Wickersham went right to work. Summoning the bar, he advised them never to call at his chambers, for there would be no secret discussions. He also told them that cases would not be postponed until the next summer. In the month remaining before the close of navigation, the attorneys were to prepare depositions from litigants and witnesses who planned to winter Outside.

The judge and his clerks worked night and day, and so did the Nome lawyers. Among them were men destined for future fame. Key Pittman later became a United States senator from Nevada. Albert Fink gained an outstanding reputation in Alaska as a trial lawyer and defended Al Capone in the '20s. G. L. Lomen would eventually become a judge in Nome. Certainly there must have been a fair number of rogues as well. Claims were often jumped on the advice of lawyers. Some prospectors found it more convenient to add a lawyer's name when staking claims to save the cost of hiring one later.

While the mining claims cases were being prepared, Wickersham turned to the peculiarities of Nome's law enforcement officials—holdovers from the days of McKenzie. They were a corrupt lot: R. N. Stevens, formerly of North Dakota, was United States commissioner, *ex officio* justice of the peace, recorder, probate judge, and coroner. The year before, he had arranged to have himself appointed municipal judge as well.

Wickersham forced Stevens to show his reports of official receipts and expenditures. These proved that the commissioner had fared well. His receipts totaled $22,895.65; by coincidence, his expenses ran to $22,-700.45. He turned in $483. Stevens padded his expense account by billing the government for his house rent, coal, food, and salaries for his wife and daughter, among others. He also earned an extra salary as municipal judge. Wickersham removed Stevens from all of his offices. He had authority to do so. Not only did Stevens lose his commission, but, by declaring Nome's municipal court illegal, Wickersham also liquidated that judgeship. He had, however, no evidence to support a criminal prosecution. This pained him because he was convinced that Stevens had shared leadership with McKenzie and Noyes in the mine claim conspiracy. Stevens slandered Wickersham in Nome and assured his cronies that friends in Washington would remove Wickersham, once Stevens could reach them.

Next, United States Marshal Frank Richards—another McKenzie appointee—was investigated. Like Wickersham, Richards lived at the Golden Gate Hotel, but the marshal's expense record showed that he paid twice the rate the judge paid. Wickersham conferred with the hotel owner who admitted that this padding for public officials was the local custom. The officials kept the difference between the actual and recorded costs. The judge could not remove Richards from office but could only harass him for inflated expense accounts.[7] Wickersham realized that honest law enforcement would be impossible as long as Richards remained marshal in Nome.

Richards fixed juries regularly. Whenever a jury was called for in cases involving his friends, Richards would go next door to Joe Jourdan's saloon. Accommodating loungers were rounded up and brought to court. Their verdicts supported Richards' friends.[8] Finally, Wickersham was able to bring contempt of court proceedings against Marshal Richards and Jourdan. Richards did all he could to win the case. Witnesses were bullied and intimidated by his friends and the police, but it was to no avail—the evidence was clearly against him.

A packed house attended the trial. Albert Fink, the lawyer who would be resourceful and clever enough to catch the attention of Al Capone one day, defended the fixers. District Attorney John McGinn had blood in his eye—all too often he had lost cases because of Richard's manipulations. Wickersham found both defendants guilty but, surprisingly, fined them only $300 each. The conviction, he thought, "will hurt me in Washington where Nome matters have been a stench anyway."[9] But Washington backed the judge in this case. Later, a Department of Justice investigator journeyed to Nome, looked into Richard's office, and fired him.

In routing the "dastardly cowardly and corrupt" officials, Wickersham was taking some chances. He was fully aware that the Spoilers still had good friends in Washington. President McKinley's pardon of McKenzie and the light punishment of Noyes made that clear. For all the judge knew, the Justice Department might have preferred to remove him rather than Marshal Richards.

The grand jury had wanted to indict Judge Noyes, but Wickersham had dissuaded them, pointing out that Noyes had been tried and convicted in San Francisco. Noyes had been fined $1,000 for contempt of court, a light penance, yet disgraceful enough for a judge. A few months later he died. Wickersham wanted the judicial disgrace forgotten. "We should hide this blot on American judiciary—put it behind us."[10] Wickersham extended charity to Noyes, whom he considered misled rather than corrupt. For the pioneer miners and their attorneys he had high praise for "fighting the most astounding, vigorous and treacherous attack known to American jurisprudence."[11]

As the winter wore on the judge found time to join Nome's social activities. He attended a dinner given by Jafet Lindeberg. A china platter filled with gold nuggets worth $3,800 served as a centerpiece for the table. Guests were encouraged to choose a nugget as a party favor. When news of President McKinley's assassination belatedly reached the town, Wickersham delivered a eulogy. The first mail of the winter brought Wickersham news of a personal tragedy. The judge's eight-year-old boy had died in Tacoma, Washington. Grief stricken but unbowed, Wickersham carried on. Nome's attorneys presented a resolution of sympathy.

By January, Wickersham had cleared a good portion of the court calendar, often holding court from 9 A.M. to 10:30 P.M. The satisfaction among the townspeople was general, although some losing claimants sulked. The judge had conducted himself with poise and calm purpose. His reputation was assured. Members of the bar petitioned the attorney general, requesting that Wickersham be named as Noyes' successor. For the next quarter century he was to be the leading political figure of the Alaska. Faith in the judiciary was restored.

In February, he called a month's recess and enjoyed a rugged dog team journey to Cape Prince of Wales. After a spring session, he was ready to return to his own judicial district and his home at Eagle. When the judge had been called from the interior to Nome the year before, his district was a dull one. Now, just as the Seward Peninsula was cooling down a bit, things were happening in the interior. Soon after he reached Eagle, another great stampede took place. This time the scene of the frenzy was the Tanana valley, where Fairbanks would be established.

19

The Founding of Fairbanks

ENROUTE TO NOME, Judge Wickersham met E. T. Barnette at St. Michael. Barnette had been grubstaked by a customs officer there and had hired a steamboat, the *Lavelle Young*. This was the beginning of a long association between the two men—the one dedicated to law enforcement, the other dedicated to swindling and jury fixing. Barnette's plan being to establish a trading post on the upper Tanana River, he loaded the steamboat with provisions and steamed up the Yukon River.

As the *Lavelle Young* churned her way up the great river in 1901, stopping only for two hours daily at woodcutting stations such as George Pilcher's, there was already some activity in the vicinity of her destination. Several prospectors searching the Tanana valley found very good placer prospects. One Felix Pedro, or Pedroni, an Italian-American who had been prospecting in the North for years, had long anticipated the riches of the Tanana. Pedro had discovered indications of gold along one of the then unnamed tributaries of the Tanana some years earlier. Carefully marking the spot and noting his location as well as he could, he journeyed to Circle for provisions. Once resupplied, he went back in quest of his original find, but to his dismay could not find the place again.

Pedro would not be thwarted. His determination and skill finally led him and his partner, Tom Gilmore, to several potentially rich deposits along Fish Creek and Goldstream. Just as the prospector was preparing to make the long, hard trek to Circle for provisioning, he spotted smoke on the horizon. Standing on the hill overlooking the valley, later named Ester Dome, he watched with great delight as the *Lavelle Young* moved slowly up the Chena River and docked along the bank. Today it is only a drive of several miles from Ester Dome to the point where E. T. Barnette decided to end his voyage, but Pedro and Gilmore had three days of hard going through the swampy flats with their pack horses. They were overjoyed to

Gold Fever North

NOME MINERS AT THE NORTHERN SALOON CELEBRATING THE NEWS OF
DEWEY'S VICTORY DURING THE SPANISH-AMERICAN WAR.
(Dr. Charles Bunnell Collection.)

BEACH DIGGING FOR GOLD IN NOME, 1900.
(Ralph MacKay Collection.)

SEATTLE ADVERTISES THE ALASKA-
YUKON EXPOSITION.
(Dr. Charles Bunnell Collection.)

1909

ALASKA · YUKON · PACIFIC
EXPOSITION
SEATTLE
WASHINGTON.

JEFFERSON "SOAPY" SMITH IN THE DOORWAY OF HIS SALOON, SKAGWAY, 1898.
(Ralph MacKay Collection.)

THE NOME BEACH WRECKER AT WORK

An industry that has almost been made to assume an air of legitimacy is shown up in its true hideousness by the accompanying allegorical caricature. Like wolves feeding on the body of one that has fallen by the trail, wreckers have been greedily patrolling the beach during Nome's two recent storms, watching for such stores as may drift ashore and claiming as a right all they rescue from the surf. Hundreds of men have engaged in this ghoul-like occupation, many no doubt hardly realizing the criminal nature of their employment. It has been a case of "an ill wind that blows nobody good" and it is a lamentable fact that more people have rejoiced in the coming of a storm and the destruction it wreaks than have lamented.

Hundreds of men lined the water front on the wild nights of August 2nd. and 7th, everything of apparent value that came ashore being seized upon and carried off as spoils. A box of canned goods or even a piece of lumber were many times responsible for fights among the wreckers and it is probable that many of them worked harder in the surf than they had ever done before at a legitimate employment. Many amusing incidents occured as well, such as the violent "ducking" of some venturesome spirit who was tempted too far into the breakers by a fat looking box, or the disappointment of another who worked like a Trojan for a cask that proved when gotten ashore to be empty.

New Suits Filed. | COMMISSIONERS APPOINTED.

THE NOME CHRONICLE, 1900.

THE NOME NEWS.

VOL. 1 No. 6   NOME, ALASKA, MONDAY, NOVEMBER 13, 1899.   PRICE 25 CENTS

EXTRA EDITION.

JACK MALLON DIES A TRAGIC DEATH

After Attempting to Kill Geo. Stewart Meets His Own End.

FATAL SHOT FIRED BY OFFICER EDWARDS.

Mallon Shot Through the Face as He Turned and Fired Upon the Officer.

Stewart Shot Through the Left Thigh in the Little Blanche Saloon, But Will Recover—Affray Took Place About 4:30 O'Clock This Morning—An Inquest Now Being Held on Mallon's Body.

John F. Mallon, commonly called "Jack" Mallon, lies dead in the city hall. Geo. Stewart, known as "Scotty," is in St. Bernard's hospital shot through the left thigh. Stewart will recover.

Mallon was attempting to escape

witnesses, including J. S. Stack-house, Geo. Harbach, Blanche Lamont and E. H. Zanders, Mallon pulled up his parka and whipped out a revolver. Stewart caught the gun by the muzzle, deflecting the bullet which entered his left

and Flaherty earlier in the night. After the shots were fired and while Edwards was taking Fish rty to the city jail, Capt. Holmberg stumbled over Mallon's body, it being very dark at the time. Mallon fell on his face, the snow where he fell being deeply crimsoned with his life blood. A minute or two after he was taken to the City hall he breathed his last. The body lay on its back with a fur parka on it and a fur cap on the head. The face was covered with blood and was much swollen.

It is claimed by some that Mallon had a poke containing some $800 or $900 and that efforts were being made to deprive him of it. He had been in the Little Blanche two or three times during the night and the last time he went in and bought a drink one of the men in the saloon said "Ain't 1 in this?" Mallon replied, "This is all the money I have but you can have a part of my drink."

Stewart, who was shot in the leg, was taken to the hospital after Dr. J. H. Koons had been summoned to attend him. At the hospital Drs. Koons and Pohl rendered the necessary surgical assistance. Stewart had lost considerable blood but is not considered to be in danger.

Some of the men who were on the

THE NOME NEWS, EDITED BY J.F.A. STRONG.

TUG-OF-WAR, FAIRBANKS, 4TH OF JULY.
(Lulu Fairbanks Collection.)

A HUMAN CHAIN ON THE CHILKOOT PASS, 1898.
(Dr. Charles Bunnell Collection.)

FAIRBANKS IN FLAMES, 1906.
(Dr. Charles Bunnell Collection.)

SEATTLE WATERFRONT DURING THE 1898 RUSH.

(Lulu Fairbanks Collection.)

DAWSON WATERFRONT, 1899.

(Bassoc Collection.)

MINERS' MEETING AT ATLIN.

(Bassoc Collection.)

MINERS LEAVING DAWSON FOR THE NOME STAMPEDE.

(Bassoc Collection.)

A LITTLE POKER WITH A NATIVE.
(Ralph MacKay Collection.)

NOME, 1900.
(Lynn C. Denny Collection.)

WILL BALLOU'S CABIN NEAR RAMPART.
(William B. Ballou Collection.)

MINING ON ANVIL CREEK, NOME.
(Charles Hamlin Collection.)

POST OFFICE NOTICE.
(Lulu Fairbanks Collection.)

FRONT STREET, NOME, 1900.
(Dr. Charles Bunnell Collection.)

MINERS UNDERGROUND.
(Lulu Fairbanks Collection.)

PROTECTING THE GOLD DUST.
(Clara Rust Collection.)

CIRCLE CITY, 1895.

DRINKING UP IN NOME.
(Lulu Fairbanks Collection.)

CROSSING THE VALDEZ GLACIER.
(Guy F. Cameron Collection.)

find the steamboat still moored in the Chena. This meeting of Pedro and Barnette established the location of Fairbanks on the Chena River, about five miles from its junction with the Tanana River. The trader thus became the founding father of the future town, though he had actually intended to establish his post farther up the Tanana at Tanana Crossing. Barnette's quest for a way around shallow waters of the Tanana brought him to the Chena, and when Pedro revealed his hopes for the region, Barnette agreed to set up a post there.

The *Lavelle Young* was the only steamboat available at St. Michael when Barnette prepared to establish a trading post on the Tanana River. Its skipper was a young man, C. W. Adams, who agreed to haul Barnette, his trade goods, and six members of Barnette's party, including his wife Isabelle and a cook, Jujuira Wada. Before Pedro reached Barnette the trading party were disgruntled about the Chena site. Adams argued that he could not get the boat any farther up the Tanana and that Barnette had better give up his original plan and choose a site. Barnette wanted to keep trying, but Adams refused to consider it. Mrs. Barnette was hysterical and crying over the prospect of putting in for the winter at such a remote place. The region was seemingly empty; there were no Indians within miles and, apparently, no prospectors either. Adams helped Barnette pitch tents and said goodbye. Barnette refused to shake hands. A couple of years later Adams met Barnette in Dawson City and found him much happier. By chance the trader had struck a golden opportunity—and had known how to make it work to his advantage (*see* Chapter 21).

Particular note should be taken of men like Pedro. Two stereotypes of the prospector are most commonly accepted. One is of the lucky, wildly successful, free-spending wastrel who squanders his nuggets and dust on women and booze, like Dick Lowe or Swiftwater Bill Gates. The other is the essence of persistence and failure, the grizzled character always in pursuit of the will-o'-the-wisp, incapable of recognizing his own futility.

But Felix Pedro, and others like him, did not fit either of these descriptions. Felix was a rather slightly built man in his early forties who had spent most of his life digging, not for gold, but for coal. As a boy in Bologna, Italy, he had followed his father and brothers into the coal mines, then followed the same pursuit in France before emigrating to America to labor in the coal mines of Illinois, Oklahoma, and Carbonado, Washington. Once on the west coast he had not far to travel to join the stampede to the goldfields of Caribou, British Columbia, in 1893. From there he headed north to the first rushes at Forty Mile in the Yukon Territory and, though near at hand when the Klondike finds were made, he was not among those who hit paydirt.

The techniques learned by coal miners were no handicap to those who had to sink shafts through many feet of frozen muck to the potentially gold-bearing bedrock, but it was not that experience which alerted a prospector to the possibilities of any particular region. Rather it was the knowledge gained through years of observation in the field, month after month of patient plodding over hill, across valleys, along likely looking streams where the battered gold pan would be dipped again and again while keen eyes watched for a flake of the elusive yellow stuff.

It would not do to romanticize a man like Pedro. There was little glamor in his profession. It offered lots of hard work, a very poor diet, interminable discomfort due to wet clothes, frigid temperatures, foot soreness, back aches, and the not inconsiderable danger of encountering an aggressive bear, stumbling over a cliff, or spraining or breaking a leg miles from any source of help. It goes without saying that experienced prospectors were hearty and determined men. Other prospectors followed Pedro and his friends to the vicinity. None of the men owned any equipment beyond pick and spade. Consequently, it took many months of backbreaking labor to sink mining shafts and months more to hoist the bedrock.

Even by the spring of 1903 there were no boilers operating on the creeks; yet there were enough indications of ample paydirt to trigger a stampede. Most of the stampeders came from the upper Yukon River and Dawson. They were not impressed by what they saw. Miners were still using the primitive means of slow-burning fires to penetrate the permafrost. A large majority of the new arrivals were entrepreneurial types rather than miners. Their interest was in the camp's potential as a commercial center, and its conditions were not prosperous by any means. Hurriedly the speculators decamped, spreading the word that the Tanana country had little to offer. Their reaction embittered the working miners because much depended upon attracting capital investment in mining equipment.

The boom's collapse did not last long. Despite the laments of those who were disappointed, word of impressive finds spread again in the fall of 1904. Again a stampede was triggered. This time the earliest arrivals came overland on the winter trail from the little coastal town of Valdez, 370 miles distant on Prince William Sound.

On Thanksgiving Day, 1903, miner George Preston left Valdez with seven other men and six dog teams. Worn out and very cold they reached the new camp of Fairbanks on January 4. The place did not look like much of a town, and the rushers having left Valdez because of disappointed prospects there, Preston felt they had jumped from the pan to the fire. It was not a cheerful camp until the spring cleanup proved the wealth of the diggings. Lighting was provided by kerosene lamps and candles.

Men who had no better place to go found cheer only in the warm saloons lining the river.

Among early arrivals from Dawson was George Butler, who brought a welcome 50 tons of whiskey. George affirmed his pleasure at being across the line again, especially since the Canadian authorities had not renewed his liquor license. The whiskey was soon dispensed among thirsty miners. Twenty-five cents, the smallest coin in circulation, bought the patron any drink at any bar in town.

Preston took a job at the local Northern Commercial Company Store, where he was ordered to sell the few sacks of frosted spuds on hand in limited quantities and only to those suffering from scurvy. The camp had to endure an extreme shortage of provisions that winter. Gold dust was the main medium of exchange then, though it was company policy to make credit available. The Northern Commercial Company further benefited the community by building a power plant and providing electricity to the whole town. Electric light helped a great deal to make life easier in an area where the shortest day of the winter lasts a mere four hours.

Reminiscing in later years Preston recalled that the old sourdoughs in the Fairbanks of '04 found the town much wilder than Dawson, where the "yellow legs"—the Mounties—were not permissive in law enforcement. Fairbanks saloons had no locks; the bars lining First Avenue were always open, thirty-three of them in four blocks, and the "booze much better than it is now."[1] Gambling competed with boozing as the miners' chief recreation.

The men of Fairbanks were impressed when Chee-chaco Lil, a well-known prostitute from Dawson, deserted that town to set up an establishment on Second Avenue. Lil's presence indicated her staunch faith in the future of the camp. Her arrival brought the number of prostitutes to four—not early enough for the fast-increasing population. She was followed by dozens of whores who hoped to share in the new gold strike by proffering their services. As the town grew, lonely men had no trouble finding women, either in the hastily erected dance halls or the cribs forming "the Row" where prostitutes offered their charms. The cribs were small, one-room structures, hardly large enough to contain more than a table, chair, and bed; yet these were the temples of pleasure for hard-working miners of the North.

Without much supporting evidence, one might suspect that the girls of the Fairbanks' Row might not have had the beauty and charm of their frail sisters of Seattle, San Francisco, and other temperate climes; yet they shared the experience of rigorous northern living with their men and reflected just as surely the camaraderie of the northern mining camp. Women of the North, whether wives or whores, tended to be more hearty, easy-going, and less spoiled than those elsewhere. Women led a pioneer existence in Alaska for decades after the historian Frederick Jackson Turner announced that the American frontier was closed.

It did not take long for Fairbanks to begin to take on the appearance of a town. Plenty of timber grew near at hand and a busy lumber mill was soon providing materials for construction. Virtually all the structures in the camp were built of logs, and soon proud residents were referring to the "largest log cabin town in the world," the same boast Circle people had made some years earlier. Everyone was busy in the young town. Some were whipsawing lumber for construction and getting $200 to $250 per thousand board feet for it. Others were dragging in spruce logs for their cabins. Spruce trees of 6 to 24 inches in diameter covered the whole region. The price of town lots climbed steeply and in the shift from tent city to wooden city, everyone seemed to be jumping, staking, recording, and building.

The Court Moves to Fairbanks

It was in March, 1903, that Wickersham heard about the rich strikes in the Tanana valley. The center of activity, Fairbanks, had been named by the jurist, although he had not yet seen the camp. Earlier Wickersham had suggested the name of the senator from Indiana for the location of E. T. Barnette's trading post while Barnette was making preparations at St. Michael for his founding voyage. In view of the lawlessness threatening Nome during its first season, Wickersham considered ordering soldiers from Fort Gibbon to Fairbanks, but decided to have a look at the camp himself before doing so.

In April he set out from Circle with a six-dog team and a driver. The route he traveled being fairly well populated, he found a cabin to stay at each night. One stormy night he found himself one of eight people crowded into a cabin measuring 12 by 12. It was as dirty as it was stuffy, but the lady of the house provided good sourdough pancakes for breakfast, and that compensated.

Wickersham fell in love with the Tanana valley at first sight; its vastness and verdant grandeur moved him as no other scene yet encountered in the North. Standing on the brow of a hill overlooking the valley, he took in its 50-mile expanse, a prospect of unrivaled beauty that made the blood race in one's veins. Scattered about the valley were abundant stretches of evergreen forests and the "rising waters of the Tanana, in lake-like spaces, sparkling in the midday sun;" in the distant east and west "as far as the eye can reach, and to the base of the snowy range along its southern bounds, the unfretted valley is carpeted with evergreen." Beyond what he liked to call the Ohio-of-the-North stood the colossal Alaskan range capped by many peaks: "To the eastward they descend, one behind another, until the distant horizon limits the vision but not the range." He recognized Mount Hayes, Mount Deborah, and Mount Hess and, to the west, Mount McKinley, "This mountain is to the Tena, what it must always remain to all tribes of men in this region, Denali, the high one."[2]

The Tanana is the greatest tributary of the Yukon. Rising near the Canadian border, it winds its way northwest for hundreds of miles before joining the Yukon. The few Indians dwelling along its banks had called the imposing waterway the Tanana, "river of the mountain," and found it rich in life-giving salmon, not knowing or caring about its hidden treasures. Rivers flow on like time, seeming to have no past. Yesterday and tomorrow resemble today. For hundreds of miles the river churns its way through a valley of surpassing beauty.

But the Tanana does have a history, a most ancient one that explains why, among all the rivers of the interior, its tributaries had become so rich in gold. To the geologist, the presence of gold is no mystery. Placer deposits, streaks of gold, are found at bedrock in the gravel of old stream beds. Perhaps as long as 150 million years ago the bedrock surface of the valley was pierced by hot, molten rocks forced up from below by some raging turmoil in the bowels of the earth. This intrusion lifted and cracked the bedrock in many places, leaving small veins into which the fiery mixture of rock and mineral flowed. Ages passed, and the fissured bedrock was uplifted and eroded. The lighter rocks and minerals were broken down and removed by the streams, but the gold accumulated in the creek bottoms, to be covered by later erosion products. A permanently frozen crust as deep as 70 feet, and often more, obscured and protected the precious metal that lay beneath. The gold was there and, though hard to reach, men would have it despite all.

On reaching Pedro Creek, site of the first strikes, Wickersham talked with a successful Italian prospector, Jack Costa. He described Costa's "happy, smiling face like the full moon over the Ketchumstock hills [as he] emerges from his pit, he remarked—probably for the thousandth time—'By Godde, I gotte de gold.' "[3] After their meal at Jujuira Wada's restaurant the judge appointed J. Tod Cowles justice of peace and accepted Frank Cleary's offer of a corner lot for the jail. A representative from Chena called on the judge to petition him to locate the court there rather than Fairbanks. Chena seemed a more logical center than Fairbanks for the principal town of the region. It was located at the head of steamer navigation on the Tanana, whereas in order to reach Fairbanks it was necessary to ascend the Chena slough a few miles. Fairbanks' big advantage, apart from Barnette's original location there, was its greater proximity to the neighboring creeks where the mining was being done.

This proximity and the fact that the Judge Wickersham threw in with Fairbanks—the town he had named—thwarted the development of Chena, which faded away after a few years. Today virtually nothing remains of the Chena town site, which has long since been washed away by the Tanana River.

The day following the judge's arrival was cold and clear. Though the temperature the night before had fallen to 20 degrees below zero, the afternoon sunshine bathed everything in warm sunshine. It was spring, and spring promotes optimism. The judge felt that the Tanana valley would one day be the garden of Alaska, where as many as one million people might reside. Wickersham observed unfolding pussy willows and cattails and gathered a bouquet of birch limbs with swollen buds. Overhead appeared other harbingers of spring, great flocks of geese heading for their summer nesting in the Yukon flats. These lovely fowl always rested for a time in the Tanana valley before winging onward. Before long the judge observed the most significant sign of spring, when, with a roar, the rivers opened. The Tanana opened first, then the Chena; soon the streams of the entire valley were flooding down towards the parent river, the Yukon.

Much to the pleasure of the reader the very script of an original diary reveals the writer's mood. In recording his sensations on a beautiful morning that first May in Fairbanks, Wickersham betrayed joy and ebullience in his oversize, looping, exuberant penmanship as he anticipated warmer weather. Nature abounded. "Ducks, geese, robins, birds, squirrels—the woods are vocal with animal and bird song." And, again he rhapsodized, "the Tanana Valley is the garden spot of Alaska."[5]

The judge recorded his impressions, too, of the people of the Fairbanks camp. The crowd was a motley one, thought the judge, "sourdoughs and cheechacos, miners, gamblers, Indians, Negroes, Japanese, digs, prostitutes, music, drinking! It's rough but healthy—the beginning—I *hope*, of an American Dawson."[4]

The first newspaper published in the valley was written entirely by the judge. Entitled the *Fairbanks Miner*, it was filled with local news and ads and sold for $5 a copy. Only one issue appeared; its primary reason for being was to provide Wickersham and a party the money they would need to outfit themselves for a Mount McKinley climbing excursion. Three copies were given away to be read in the saloons; one went Outside to Senator Fairbanks.

Publication day turned out to be breakup day as well. Wickersham marveled once more at this "wonderful manifestation of the natural force of water and ice. It came down suddenly without warning and in five minutes the ice was pushing into the woods breaking into great sections, pushing, grinding, rolling and tearing, an irresistible flood of ice, mud and water."6 Then soon, all flags flying and whistle shrilling, came the first steamboat of the season, loaded with friends, relatives, and fresh provisions.

Gold fever did not leave Wickersham untouched. He freely gave his power of attorney to prospectors—successful ones—so that they could stake claims for him. Yet he did not preoccupy himself exclusively with either gold or his official duties. He seized the opportunity of learning something of the Indian culture that was so swiftly being disrupted by the intrusions of thousands of white men. He spent whole days visiting old Koonah, the local Tanana medicine man, making notes of his conversations with Koonah and other natives. In the midst of the haste and squalor of the boom, he showed the scholarly curiosity of a cultured man. Soon he had compiled a good vocabulary of the native language of the Tanana district; he even found time to lecture townsfolk on the customs of the aborigines of the valley.

The Presbyterian preacher Hall Young was one of the first resident ministers of Fairbanks. The Reverend Young met hundreds of old friends from the Klondike and other mining camps where he had served. It was the presence of so many experienced miners that made Tanana different from earlier northern stampedes. People in the Tanana valley, it was evident, had learned how to live in Alaskan country. No epidemic ever threatened; the water supply in the area was excellent. The prospect of a scarce food supply was faced with great endurance and courage on the part of the people.

Young praised the Fairbanks climate as "the most healthy and comfortable I have experienced; disease seems to shun the climate."7 The weather of the interior of Alaska has always excited attention. Newcomers have ever been amazed that the dry air of the semi-arid region and the usual lack of wind mitigate the severity of sub-zero temperatures that prevail from November through March.

The minister remarked favorably on the large proportion of women in the community and welcomed the arrival of more. Greater family stability was needed, and the presence of women undoubtedly pleased him, but Young also had the practical consideration of gaining an income, and found his principal support in wedding fees. One nuptial in particular gave him a windfall. The bride knew Young from Dawson and refused to have any other minister perform the ceremony. She and her intended lived on the Koyukuk River, some 600 miles from Fairbanks, but undertook the winter trip lightly enough. Young's fee from the grateful groom was a lump of gold worth $96.

Stampeders on the Koyukuk trail did not always have the leisure to seek out a preacher. In the 1898 rush to that remote region a man and woman fell in love and called on "French Joe" Durrant, another miner, to tie a marital knot. A lovely contract was recorded:

———————

Ten miles from the Yukon, on the banks of this lake,
For a partner to Koyukuk, McGillis I take;
We have no preacher, and we have no ring,
It makes no difference, it's all the same thing.
                                        —Aggie Dalton

I swear by my gee-pole, under this tree,
A devoted husband to Aggie I always will be;
I'll love and protect her, this maiden so frail,
From those sour-dough bums, on the Koyukuk trail.
                                        —Frank McGillis

For two dollars apiece, in Cheechaco money,
I unite this couple in matrimony;
He be a rancher, she be a teacher,
I do the job up, just as well as a preacher.
                                        —French Joe[8]

———————

At that time, 387 log houses and 1,000 residents were counted in the town proper, and perhaps another 500 to 1,000 were dwelling along the tributary creeks of the Chena and Tanana on the various claims. Boosters of the camp naturally looked forward to the next step in development—in the North, with its vast reaches, this was always a call for transportation facilities. Now for the railroad, urged the editor of the *Fairbanks News*, and it would not be too long before there was a partial fulfillment of the rail dream.

Wickersham's newspaper warned miners against indiscriminate slaughter of moose. "Kill what you need, use what you kill, because hundreds more hungry men are coming."[9] Hunters were running down cows laden with their unborn in the deep snows in order to gather dog feed. Most miners' diet consisted of moose meat and beans, and sometimes just moose.

Although 200 men left the camp for Nome on the last steamer because of the threat of hunger, available food supplies were still inadequate for the increased population, and the early closing of the rivers made reprovisioning by steamer shipment impossible. Fort Gibbon's commander secured permission from the War Department in Washington to sell the fort's extra provisions in case of need. Meanwhile prices soared. A 100-pound sack of flour went for $35. As it turned out, nobody went hungry in the valley during the winter of 1903–1904. Moose hunters had great success, so there was plenty of meat available.

During the winter Fairbanks promoters were not idle. George Hill, editor of the *Fairbanks News*, reached Seattle in January to boost the Tanana. In February a number of Seattleites began their journey to the interior, and by spring Dawson people were ready to try again.

Soon there were several tent and cabin towns in the Valley: Golden City at the head of Pedro Creek, Cleary City near the first discovery on Cleary Creek, Meehan on Fairbanks Creek. Each "city" supported its own saloons, stores, whores, and roadhouses—though none of these approached the standards of Fairbanks.

In Fairbanks the recreation of residents was no longer restricted to drinking, gambling, and the girls of the Row. Amenities included family concerts performed every evening at the Fairbanks Hotel. One could go in style. At the Comet Tonsorial Parlors ladies' hairdressing was a specialty. Fairbanks built up its population of women and children more rapidly than any of the earlier camps along the Yukon River because it drew from the established communities of Nome and Dawson. This no doubt contributed heavily to the rapid transformation from camp to town and the speedy establishment of a school. A first-year term for nine pupils ran 70 days and closed on May 6, 1904.

The first banquet in the Tanana Valley took place at the Tokyo Restaurant. What bore this grand name was just another one-room log cabin. Judge Wickersham invited all the members of the bar and the camp's leading citizens. Lawyers always had much work in mining camps, what with the stimulus of claim-jumping and the general confusion resulting from imprecise locating of claims. Seven members of the bar were already on hand by the spring of 1903, and more were on their way. Drinks were served from the old gold pan with which Felix Pedro had made his original discovery. The pan was presented to Wickersham, who promised to send it on to Senator Charles Fairbanks along with a bottle of gold dust. Food and drink were important where severe winters permitted indoor entertainment and amusement only; dice and cards were the leading participatory pursuits. But in summer, miners would be able to enjoy a baseball game, a popular sport.

The pace of a mining camp was sure to quicken with the opening of the navigation season each spring, when breakup brought back outdoor life and activity. The simple pleasure of seeing newcomers arrive on the latest steamboat added a measure to life much missed during the tedium of winter days. Everyone regarded all riverboats as a precious link to the outside world. Residents would greet and praise the new steamer *Tanana*, a swift and finely built craft designed especially for the Fairbanks trade after the model of Columbia River steamers. Citizens admired her fixtures and commented upon her 150-foot length, 30-foot beam, 5-foot depth of hold, and 225-ton freight capacity, as well as on her spaciousness, which allowed room for 150 passengers. While not the biggest boat on the Yukon River system, she was the one of which Fairbanks was fondest, particularly as she repeatedly broke distance records throughout her career. On her maiden voyage the ship ran from St. Mary's on the lower Yukon to Fairbanks in five days and 17 hours.

Among the stampeders who left Dawson for Fairbanks in 1904 was an extraordinary Venezuelan soldier of fortune, Rafael De Nogales. Nogales came into the Yukon country on a game-hunting excursion and to rest from his martial adventures in China and Korea. Prompted more by curiosity than gold fever, Nogales decided to join the Dawson men waiting impatiently for the Yukon River to break up so that they could rush to Fairbanks. On a June night the whole town was aroused by the thundering roar of the straining ice, a "noise that was sweet music in our ears as it grew louder and louder. Suddenly, with a roar like that of an exploding shell, the frozen Yukon burst in front of us into countless fragments and the onrushing flood wave." Enormous masses of drift ice flowed past Dawson's waterfront "with a crash that made the earth tremble under our feet," and Nogales heard a shout of joy ring from one end of the camp to another: "A mighty, savage prayer of thanksgiving addressed by the stampeders to Mother Nature for opening the road to their land of fondest dreams, where they would be able to dig for gold."[10]

Nogales and a partner launched a little boat on the Yukon River and floated down to Fort Gibbon, where the Tanana joined its parent. There they secured a Peterboro canoe and began their ascent of the Tanana. Nogales soon discovered that interior travel was no lark. He and other stampeders poled and pulled their vessels against the current day after day, dodging the rushing chunks of river ice and sometimes struggling along, up to their necks in the icy water. If one had the leisure to look, there were interesting sights along the way: bleached bones of ancient mammoths lay among the sands of higher portions of the river bank; occasional moose and other animals were encountered. The moose stopped their browsing in the muddy waters of the river's sloughs long enough to stare at the passing men, taking a "critical look at fools going through so much for useless gold and bucking against nature instead of eating grass."[11]

Camping on the bank one night, Nogales and his partner were joined by a boatload of bitter and angry stampeders. These were passengers who had paid $200 for first class tickets in order to travel in comfort from Dawson to Fairbanks. Instead, they found the little steamer *Diogenes* virtually unprovisioned and lacking not just staterooms but bunks. Passengers included a group of infuriated dance hall girls who did not take to sleeping on deck and providing their own food. The steamer's captain, an acquaintance of Nogales, appealed to the young adventurer for help in pacifying his mutinous passengers. Nogales soothed everyone by scrounging up all the liquor and canned delicacies aboard and throwing a party. After this wilderness debauch the *Diogenes* moved on, Nogales aboard, a happier ship.

In Fairbanks Nogales took a job helping the mining claims recorder sort the confused records. "In that manner I became by chance one of the fathers and patriarchs of the city of Fairbanks."[12] Rumors concerning the shady side of the life of the town's true father were current even at that time. Nogales heard that trader E. T. Barnette had served time in a Montana penitentiary (actually Oregon). Another current rumor reported by Nogales showed the distrust among miners of an unidentified "bank president," probably Barnette, who had moved from storekeeping to banking. According to this story, a bandit had been hired by the banker to harass mine operators so that they would be more inclined to deposit their dust in the bank. The prevalence of such rumors makes it hard to understand how Barnette was ever able to gain such a prominent position for his bank and later cause so much woe to depositors.

Nogales' account of Fairbanks, like the accounts of many stampeders, is a mixture of fact and fiction that has to be read with caution. The details he gives of Fairbanks seem valid enough for the most part, but the credibility of his memoirs degenerates in a description of a stampede out of Fairbanks that involves some peregrinations of improbable compass and a too generous dose of romantic trail incidents—hungry wolves, starving prospectors, interminable blizzards, and the like. An anecdote that does not ring true was based on a murder trial at which the judge's exhortations to the "Gentlemen of the jury, pride of the nation," were greeted with laughter and catcalls from the "pride of the nation."[13] Although an Alaskan jury might include a few of the "swarms of speculators and commercial parasites" Nogales observed in Fairbanks, its members would be unlikely to resent the judge's description of them. What Nogales missed in assessing the character of the mixed populace of northern mining centers was the firm conviction of residents that they did indeed represent the "pride of the nation."

Although Fairbanks developed in a tranquil fashion compared to early Skagway and Nome, the rumors concerning the jailbird founder, "Cap" E. T. Barnette seem to have stigmatized the town's reputation somewhat. Nogales' impressions gain some credence from the memories of a 1907–1908 visitor, the polar explorer Ejnar Mikkelsen. Mikkelsen was entertained royally by the social leaders of Fairbanks and was amused by their pride in the "Paris of the North." At a civic banquet given in his honor he sat among bejewelled, ostentatious women and, rather more unlikely, among men "sweating in skins," which could not be removed because of the tattered shirts worn beneath. All, according to Mikkelsen's later memories, spoke expertly and cheerfully of the treatment they had received in various Outside prisons. A banker present (Barnette?) observed the explorer's amazement and called the table to order by rapping his glass: "Friends, don't talk so loud about prisons, remember our guest of honor, who is perhaps the only one of us who has not made personal acquaintance with one!"[14] This announcement stilled the conversation—but only for a moment.

Mikkelsen's presence in Fairbanks provided an occasion for entertaining celebrities that did not occur as frequently in the interior as in Nome. Nome's Bering Sea location made it the destination or outfitting center for several of the greatest Arctic explorers. Roald Amundsen, the indomitable Norwegian, was honored there after navigating his tiny *Gjoa* through the Northwest Passage in 1906 and on other occasions as well. Knud Rasmussen and Vilhjalmur Stefansson were other explorers entertained in Nome. Mikkelsen, the city's guest after his Beaufort Sea travels, found that Nome's hospitality was all inclusive—even the drinks he ordered in the saloons for himself and his friends went on the civic tab, and a gift of $500 was raised for him. Mikkelsen mushed to Fairbanks after leaving Nome and found the Tanana valley residents eager to match the generosity proffered him on the Seward Peninsula. Although he had dogs and sled Fairbanksans arranged his transportation to Valdez on the post sledge.

Mikkelsen was not impressed by the women he met in Fairbanks, but had interesting recollections of women he encountered in roadhouses along the trails. Traveling to Fairbanks he observed two kinds of trail woman. One variety carried a revolver strapped to her thigh, had a hard sharp gaze and a tight clamped mouth. These tough, strong-willed women were out for gold and ready to sacrifice to get it. Everything about them said "touch me if you dare." A hush fell on the roadhouse when one came. Men became softer spoken, looked for a chink in her armor and found none. "She minded her own business and by sheer force of character curbed those who were usually so unbridled."[15] The other, more merry type, arrived to the jingle of sled bells, emerged smiling from a fur-covered sled, lissome and soft. She greeted all joyfully, ate and drank, accepted the men's homage, and directed her attentions to the richest among them. Eventually she left on the arm of a fortunate man. Watching either type of trail woman leave the roadhouse the men would spit on the stove and agree "she was a hell of a woman." But for the more rugged, independent woman, their admiration was not mixed with contempt.

There were other women who did not fit either of these stereotypes, women who were not golddiggers of either class. Mikkelsen and other men were resting in a roadhouse on the Valdez Trail, exchanging information and exaggerations, when this was brought home to them. Among the interior-bound travelers was a woman going to join her husband in Fairbanks. She listened anxiously as the men competed with horror tales detailing the hardships of northern life. As the anecdotes became more and more terrible she broke down and cried out her wish to return home. This sobered the raconteurs, who then denounced their stories as lies and inventions. Of course, women like these conquered their apprehensions and joined the other mining camp pioneers to help build stable communities.

The Great Fire

On May 22, 1906, the largest log town in the world suffered a disastrous fire that virtually wiped out its central area. Fortunately, the fire's occurrence in the spring lessened the hardship on those dispossessed and rebuilding could be commenced immediately. Had the fire struck in winter on an extremely cold day none of the buildings would have been saved because the fire-fighting equipment would have frozen. That might have finished Fairbanks if the businessmen had decided to begin again in Chena or at some other site. As it was, the holocaust did not stifle the optimism of the people. Businessmen quickly put up signs heralding "a genuine fire sale," and started building new quarters.

Any fear of a shortage of provisions was snuffed out by the Northern Commercial Company's ad in the newspaper the day after the fire: "There are supplies in town enough for everybody. Prices will not be raised."[16] Saloons never closed for long in Fairbanks. The popular Fraction Bar had been burned out, but by the next day was ready as a garden cafe, advertising "fresh bar, fresh air and good treatment."[17] Within a month most of the town had been rebuilt. Such an accomplishment over so short a time is both a tribute to the energy of the people and a reflection on the quality of building.

The builders of Fairbanks were energetic—and they were generous. One of them, Al McLeod, related one example of such generosity. In 1908 a miner working for the Berry brothers at Ester Creek was killed in an accident. No one knew much about him as he had only been in the area a month, but his wife's address was found among his belongings and she was notified. Also found was a baby's blue stocking, a memento of his young daughter that the miner had carried along when he departed for Alaska. This story touched the heart of Fairbanks and the hat was passed. Within three weeks the miner's widow was sent $7,500 for the baby's maintenance and an eventual college education.

John P. Clum was appointed postmaster at Fairbanks in 1906. Giving the job to Clum must have pleased the old-timers because it assured that the vital mail services would be supervised by one who knew the North intimately. In March of 1898 Clum had been appointed Post Office Inspector for Alaska and, in the course of his duties, traveled 8,000 miles through Alaska and the Yukon and established new post offices at Haines, Sheep Camp, Eagle, Fort Yukon, Rampart, and other places. After completing a circuit of the Yukon River, the inspector voyaged to Cook Inlet to equip post offices at Tyonek, Sunrise, and Homer. Clum left Alaska after that frantic summer, but in 1900, with the Nome stampede, he was sent North again as a special agent, and spent his summers in Nome for the next five years. Among his achievements in Nome was the establishment of free mail delivery on Front Street, with Fred Lockley as carrier. It was Alaska's first free mail delivery service.

Clum took his family with him to Fairbanks and secured a five-room log cabin for a home. Winter was slow in arriving in 1906, but when it came it was memorable. "The sun rose gloriously about 11:30 A.M., described a small arc above the southern horizon—and disappeared at 1:30 P.M. Two hours of sunshine—but no warmth in the brilliant rays. The demon COLD pursued us—silent, persistent, relentless."[18] The postmaster had to rise each morning, pull on his coonskin coat, fur cap, and felt shoes, and start up the kitchen fire. Fighting the cold was fun for a while but grew tiresome over an 18-day stretch when the temperature ranged from 35° to 60° below.

Despite the frigid weather the mail came through more or less regularly. Horses were used on the Valdez–Fairbanks trail in all seasons, just as they were on the run from White Horse to Dawson. Handling the mail upon its arrival in Fairbanks by the winter trail could be painful. "The instant you touched one of those packages, your fingers ached and you dropped the package."[19] Mail had to be warmed up before it could be sorted.

Like many other Alaskans, Clum had earlier blazed other frontier trails. In 1880 he had started the *Tombstone Epitaph* with a hand press and a few fonts of type. Yet, as remote as Fairbanks seemed on Clum's first visit there in 1905, he found its newspaper plant "the best the market afforded."[20] Clum was one of three prominent Arizona pioneers who played a part in Alaska's gold era. Ed Scheifflin, the founder of Tombstone, prospected along the Yukon River in 1882 and Wyatt Earp was a Nome stampeder. Clum had become famous in Arizona after negotiating with Geronimo and his Apache warrior band and securing their surrender to the government.

Fairbanks, in common with the rest of America, had money troubles because of the 1907–1908 depression. Currency was in short supply. "Fairbanks was an isolated, shut-in community—financially embarrassed."[21] The solution was provided by the issuance of "homemade" currency by the banks. Clum was one of three signers of all the bills, and the improvisation worked. All of the bills were redeemed in the spring. To Clum this example of northern ingenuity and honesty was meaningful. Pioneer traditions, as the Arizona veteran knew, included both the meritorious and the outrageous.

20
Tanana Valley Style

Crime Wave

The "blue parka bandit" was the most celebrated individual criminal in the early days of the Tanana valley. He was a road agent named Charles Hendrickson who worked the roads leading out of Fairbanks to the creeks. His escapes from custody allowed him to menace the community again and again. Once he broke out of the Fairbanks log cabin jail before he could be tried; later he jumped into the Yukon River to escape the steamboat carrying him to the federal prison on McNeil Island near Tacoma, Washington. Each time he returned to his haunts and recommenced robbing travelers.

His frequent appearances before Judge Wickersham became practiced routines, as the *Times* noted: "The promptness with which the accused . . . said 'not guilty' and Judge Wickersham said 'remanded for trial' made it appear as if these little seances were getting monotonous to both the court and the prisoner."[1]

Such good humor was not evident when Hendrickson was loose. During one period in the summer of 1905 the wave of robberies so excited the town that, at the instigation of the *News*, a vigilante meeting was called. Cooler heads prevailed, and the men disbanded; yet the *News* continued to berate local authorities.

Seattle newspapers even got into the act. The *Seattle Times* picked up the story when Al White, local president of the Prospectors and Pioneer Association, wired Washington, D.C., requesting the dispatch of United States troops from Fort Gibbon to help keep order in Fairbanks. Marshal George Perry, his pride somewhat injured by this hysterical reflection on his ability to deal with the situation, promptly telegraphed the *Seattle Post-Intelligencer*, to rebut White's statistics and to assure the Outside that Fairbanks was an orderly town.

The *Times* backed White and insisted that from January to mid-August 1905, there had been fourteen holdups in Fairbanks rather than the five Perry reported. "Perry's office did not seem to know about the hold-ups."[2] The chronology of events in the *News* was impressive:

Jan. 7 — Masked man gets $479 from Pioneer Saloon.

May 3 — Cabin on Cleary Creek entered. Three men held up and $20,000 in gold taken. Thief drops loot during pursuit but escapes.

May 15 — Two men held up on Creek road.

May 18 — Vigilante Committee organized and is supported by Archdeacon Hudson Stuck because it is realized that the law cannot handle the situation. Marshal objects so movement is dropped.

May 21 — Another cabin entered.

May 26 — Hold-up on Creek road.

May 31 — Alaska Express Co. hires armed guards to bring the gold in.

June 1 — Two new deputies transferred here. Gambling stopped to rid town of undesirables.

June 15 — Freighters held up on road.

June 20 — A tent, mine and miner are robbed.

June 21 — Freighter held up by man in blue parka. Two other men held up by blue parka man.

June 24 — Four different men held up by blue parka man. Two other different hold-ups occur.

June 25 — Sunday. Manhunt organized.

June 26 — Hold-up near Sister's roadhouse. Stage held up same day. Hold-up on road. Bandit gets $3.50 and gives victim back fifty cents "for a drink."

June 27 — Lee St. James disobeys roadman's order to halt and is shot and wounded. Reward of $1,100 set. Hendrickson arrested then escapes with use of iron hoop saw while awaiting trial.[3]

The Great Gold Heist

The greatest robbery in the annals of Tanana valley crime involved a shipment of gold that was enroute to Seattle by steamboat—some $179,000 in gold bricks. Robert E. Miller, mastermind of the theft, was a watchman on the *Tanana*, on which the gold traveled the first leg of its voyage. In preparation for the heist, Miller had carried heavy lead birdshot aboard the steamer and hidden it in his stateroom, making several trips to get it aboard without exciting suspicion. While the *Tanana* was underway to its rendezvous with the *Ida May*, the steamer that would carry the *Tanana*'s passengers and cargo on from Fort Gibbon, Miller broke open one of the cases containing the gold bricks, removed thirty-eight of them, leaving two in the case. He then refilled it with birdshot and carried the bricks to his stateroom. The robbery was discovered because of a second robbery that took place at Fort Gibbon, where the case with two gold bricks and birdshot was taken off the *Ida May*.

These events were the sensation of July, 1906, in the Tanana valley, and the newspapers called for a swift solution to the case. Police got some help when one of Miller's accomplices was seen stumbling along with an extremely heavy suitcase and avoiding the obvious route to his destination, which would have led him along the boardwalk of Cushman Street. Sure enough, he had some of the gold that had arrived back in Fairbanks on the *Tanana*.

When Miller and several others were arrested, most of the loot was found buried under the floorboards of Miller's cabin. The trial was well attended and the conviction of Miller was assured, since one of his accomplices avoided prosecution by testifying against him. One flaw in Miller's planning might have been his lack of generosity in dividing the loot. The two men who assisted him were to receive $1,000 each when they finally managed to get the gold to Seattle for him. Most certainly Miller is a "Napoleon of finance," remarked the *Times*.[4]

Drifters

Little tolerance was shown to men who drifted into Fairbanks without visible means of support. If they seemed indifferent to gainful employment, their presence was an offense to the business community and a potential threat to security and public order. Drifters were highly visible in so small a community, and the Chief of Police would soon confront an idle new arrival with some queries on his immediate plans. An evasive or unsatisfactory reply meant the issuance of a "blue ticket," which, as one wag explained it, entitled the recipient to pay his own passage to the Outside.

Occasionally the rumor arose that all the criminal element from Dawson was moving on Fairbanks *en masse*. This was enough to panic some businessmen and prompt newspaper editorials calling upon the townspeople to back the local police against the invaders.

Jailbreaks occurred with some regularity. It did not take much force or ingenuity to get free from the stuffy little log house that served as the town's first lockup. Escapees enjoyed only brief freedom. Limited transporation restricted their chances of getting far.

A daring robbery caused consternation at all the mines in the fall of 1905. Two masked thugs went right to the source of the area's wealth, the mine shaft on 9 Below Cleary. The fireman tending the steam boiler was forced down the shaft at gunpoint and the robbers gathered up the day's gain from the cleanup, $3,000 worth of gold.

In Seattle sharp-eyed con men were as quick to prey on the Tanana valley argonauts as they had been earlier on Klondikers. An unsuspecting hopeful from Idaho met three men in Seattle eager to hire him to work in a mine they allegedly owned near Fairbanks. On the pretense of some banking problem, the victim was induced to exchange his draft for $340 for a draft his partners had drawn on the First National Bank of Fairbanks. All looked fine to the dupe because one of the Seattle men planned to voyage with him to Alaska on the *Ohio*. Unfortunately, before the ship left the dock, the Seattle man had disappeared. The steamer carried the disillusioned miner to Valdez, where he arrived dead broke save for the draft, which, of course, proved to be worthless.

Municipal Court

While Alaska's federal court entertained weighty matters like claim-jumping and homicide, the municipal court treated various minor frailties of mankind. One of the most colorful of early municipal judges was Lewis T. Erwin of Fairbanks. Journalists enjoyed the judge's approach to his business, and the court no doubt played up a little to the press. When Dr. Joseph Weyerhorst, who was to appear in other courts later on different charges, rather vigorously assaulted his wife, he gave occasion for the judge to review the history of western civilization. The judge began by remarking upon the model life of Cicero, "whose oration on morality and love of home was the basis of the present love and respect in which women are held," then according to the *Fairbanks Times*, Erwin traced the progress of Christianity and the higher civilization along the path of time until he got back to city hall. The journalist warmed to his task in much the way the judge had to his, "Had he been addressing 10,000 people they would have risen up as a man and cried three times three '*le bas* Weyerhorst.' "

Judge Erwin was in no hurry. "I regret, sah, that your wife was not heah to testify against you, sah. But, Sah, I understand she is afraid that you will kill her . . . I will give you, Sah, the benefit of the limit." Here the judge hesitated before meting out a modest $100 fine, to the visible relief of the defendant. But there was more to come: "The doctor swung his arm over the chair as if he was about to spring the old gag about having that much in his hip pocket" when the judge, after a pause, added a 50-day sentence to the fine. "It was at this announcement that the doctor showed symptoms of paralysis." Many Americans were recent immigrants in those days, but there seemed to be no sensitivity—in the press at any rate—in reporting on imperfect or heavily accented English. In Weyerhorst's case, for example, the press relished its chance to quote his testimony precisely as it sounded: "I lofe my wife and hev lofed her for—let me see—joost twelve years and six months day before yesterday."[5]

Judge Erwin's 50-day prescription did not suit Weyerhorst, who fled downriver to St. Michael but was taken into custody and returned. Dr. Weyerhorst left Fairbanks shortly after he served his time, but he did not leave the North. In 1911, Alaskan newspapers reported upon his current problems with the law. This time he was convicted in Douglas for "masquerading as a physician and practicing medicine without a license." The particular incident that led to his arrest was an operation on a woman for the removal of a gland infected with tuberculosis. Weyerhorst asserted that he was the only surgeon in town capable of "this act of mercy."[6] Besides being a wife beater, Weyerhorst was a quack in the tradition of Cagliostro and John Brinkley of goat gland transplantation fame. Between his stints in Fairbanks and Douglas, the inventive doctor had practiced in Nome, where at first he was well received. Newspapers reported with respect on an amazing operation in which he had transplanted the tendon of a living rabbit to the wrist of an injured miner. The doctor loved to operate. Trouble came to him in Nome when a woman who did not want an operation and, apparently, did not need one, was cajoled or coerced onto the table by Weyerhorst. She died and relatives complained. This and similar incidents aroused the medical fraternity. They demanded that the doctor appear before an examining board, but Weyerhorst, who knew the law, refused indignantly. Charges brought against the spurious physician by the medical association were dismissed in court. Congress had made no provision for setting up standards of medical practice for Alaska. The court in Douglas had remedied this congressional neglect by ignoring it.

Most of Judge Erwin's cases dealt with men less exotic than Dr. Weyerhorst. On the ordinary day, Judge Erwin might greet a man like Spence Koonce who would put in a hard season of work and then come to town to see the boys and have a good time. If he accomplished his recreation with a surplus, as often happened, the judge would extract a $20 fee for drunk and disorderly conduct. It once occurred that Spence did not have the $20 on hand, but had no inclination to chop wood for the city to work off his fine. Judicial business was held up while the defendant tried to borrow the fine money. Since Spence had no luck in the courtroom, the judge let him make a quick run down to Front Street, where he met success and hurried back to prolong his liberty in exchange for the $20.

Erwin was a good moneymaker for the town. He had been a miner in the Klondike and felt he understood men of the North. "Make the boys remember their punishment or it does no good."[7] Rarely did he fine anyone less than $100. In November, 1906, he reported revenues of

$37,688 in court fines for the previous six months, no small pickings for a community the size of Fairbanks.[8] One can only respect the civic consciousness of men and women who so consistently supported public institutions in this way.

One Arthur Davis was once summoned by Judge Erwin to explain his disorderly conduct of the previous night. Davis began by affirming that he was an American and proceeded with great patriotic eloquence to develop the theme of Americanism. This, the press tells us, "made the judge sit up and take notice." In fact, the judge, finding himself enjoying the recital too much, had to interrupt and fine Davis $10. "Someone said that if Davis had been allowed to speak longer, he would have gotten the best of the court and he would have been fined the minimum, the judge paying the fine."[9]

Occasionally the law had to intervene when good drinking companions fell out over trifles. One night one William Rudolph told ex-Seattle fireman Herman Graw that the "Seattle Fire Department are a lot of Swedes and other unmentionable things." Big Herman soon put a hammerlock on Bill that made the latter anxious to declare that no fire department ever got to a fire as fast as Seattle's. When a cop intervened, Bill grew confused and swung on his protector. Also confused was the testimony Bill gave the next day in municipal court. He was broke and couldn't remember how long he had been in town. The judge, "in a fatherly talk," offered some advice on where to go ofter he had worked out his fine by cleaning the strects.[10]

Some townspeople found the municipal judge pompous and were annoyed by his flowery language. Erwin's eloquence reflected his concern that the high standards of Old Southern oratory be maintained even on the crude mining frontier. Then, too, his moralizing aggravated those who knew that he customarily beat his wife for fancied offenses. Once a man charged with striking his wife with an axe appeared in court. As was his wont, the judge began delivering a denunciation of one who would dare to hit a woman, ignoring the defendant's plea that his action had been strictly disciplinary in nature. "No gentlemen would beat his wife," cried the judge, and at that point caught the amused eye of a friend of his, attorney John Clark, and hastily added, "with an ax."[11]

Erwin drank mint juleps at the various saloons, usually taking in more than was good for him. On his return home from such visitations his humor was uncertain. If his wife remonstrated with him, she was likely to suffer for it. Once, preparing to attend a ladies' social evening, she inquired how he might react if she reeled home in an intoxicated state. "Mah deah," responded the judge, "I would show you how a gentleman should be treated."[12]

In May 1923, the *Alaska Weekly*, a newspaper published in Seattle, had an obituary on the pioneer municipal judge, who was known "from Skagway to Nome." Erwin's last will and testament was reported on with some relish. Erwin left $3,500 to a daughter "in appreciation of a kind, sympathetic letter written me when her mother had me arrested and taken from a train at Topenish, Washington when enroute as national delegate to the Baltimore Convention." The will specified Erwin's aversion to any attempts of disappointed heirs to litigate and directed his executor to make any contest as "expensive as possible." Any contestant who lost his suit would lose any gift provided by the will. "While I was baring my bosom to the storm of sleet and snow and almost suffered death many times in the early pioneer days," Erwin wrote, "my beneficiaries have enjoyed modern conveniences."[13]

Soiled Doves

In Fairbanks and other Alaskan towns the men who mined gold were, in turn, mined by prostitutes and showgirls. Known variously as hookers, floozies, sports, or chippies, the girls of the Row in Nome and Fairbanks practiced the same skills as such women elsewhere, for similar rewards. No novelties unknown to other frontier communities distinguished the whoring commerce of the North. However, the northern prostitute had to be hearty to withstand the rigors of the climate. Alfred H. Brooks, head of the United States Geological Survey in Alaska, was convinced that women who had faced the hardships of the trail developed some "elemental good qualities" unknown to their class in happier climes.[14]

Another distinction of prostitutes on the northern frontier was owed to its remoteness. In the early years of every town's development, women were few. Prostitutes dutifully joined every stampede along with miners, lawyers, and saloon keepers. These sturdy camp followers established themselves in small cabins and got to work. Miners labored hard and played hard. The soothing attention granted by the prostitutes was grate-fully received. Still the men liked to make a little ribald fun of the women whose services they enjoyed:

> *Lottie went to the diggings;*
> *With Lottie we must be just.*
> *If she didn't shovel tailings—*
> *Where did Lottie get her dust?*[15]

It is difficult to determine the numbers of whores in any one town at a given time. Presumably, supply met demand. There was always a time, though, when their numbers became offensive to city officials. Then, the so-called tenderloin district, where the tiny log or frame shacks housing the women were located, would be surrounded by a high board fence. Children were warned away from the district, and respectable women never dared to pass along that particular street. Although polite society ostracized the women, the transition from the *demimonde* to respectability by way of marriage occurred often enough. Pioneer John Wallace told of a former dance hall queen who married a Nome miner, then objected to the presence of whores at municipal baseball games.

Judge Wickersham, in his wisdom, did not worry whores and gamblers in the interior or at Nome, except for revenue-raising purposes. His successor at Nome, Judge Alfred S. Moore, was more puritanical. Unlike Wickersham, he would not leave such matters to the jurisdiction of municipal government. Thus, in 1907, to the dismay of many, Judge Moore ordered the closing and demolishment of the "Stockade." Newspaper editorials praised the judge's decisiveness and called for a park on the site. Within a day or two of the closing, the women were back in business. Now they were scattered about town in whatever quarters they could find. The glee of the reformers shifted to gloom. It was discovered that the dispersal worsened the nuisance. Doc Ed Hill, Nome's health officer, complained "they have taken a boil and scattered it, and now the body politic, instead of having one big boil that can be lanced when necessary, has fifty little boils to be treated."[16]

Nome's mayor and chief of police allegedly decided to remedy the situation and turn a tidy profit at the same time. According to the *Nome Gold Digger* they hired a front man to build cribs for the ladies on the sand spit at the edge of town. The officials vigorously denied any involvement and the mayor engaged the *Digger* editor in a punch-out. In any event, the project was abandoned, and the wild fillies of Nome remained uncorraled.

Iditarod also had trouble with its restricted district. The majority of the city council voted to move the district out of the center of town where its activity might cause less scandal. This decision outraged one councilman because he owned the cribs. He had worked hard to make money on his property and now his right of free enterprise was being trampled. His protests were to no avail, and some more fortunate property holder benefited in his stead.

Police court could be a sordid and depressing place, but its officers in Fairbanks had a way of lightening the proceedings. On the northern frontier human frailty was less shameful than in, say, middle America, and evidence of it was reported by the press with some gusto. Townsfolk appreciated this since they usually knew all the participants quite well.

On the judicial consideration of a fight between two of the girls on the Row, for example, the defendant was asked to describe her style of fisticuffs before the court. Gabriel, the Frenchwoman, admitted that she knew something of the art of prizefighting and "punched holes in the air to show

how different blows could be delivered with force." Gabriel was clearly a hard-hitting and determined antagonist. Even though a doctor was needed to patch up her opponent, Irene Wallace, after the fray, Gabriel wasn't satisfied "with the terrible execution she had done on her opponent" and tried to get at her again. Gabriel suffered a $50 fine. Irene, fearing for her life, departed on the next boat for Nome, "and left Gabriel the victor, as well as the terror, of the Row."[17]

Police protected prostitutes too, as the *Fairbanks Times* reported when Dutch Lil, also known as German Lilly, was robbed by Elmer Hauser. He had opened the window of her little Fourth Avenue cabin and removed $100 from Lil's purse as it hung behind her bureau. After he had hustled down the boardwalk to cache his loot, he went back to Lil's place. When Lil appeared on the scene she noticed her loss at once, spotted Elmer, who was somewhat the worse for drink, and threw him down. The altercation attracted the chief of police, who arrived to find Lil very much ascendant over Elmer, who had already been moved to return $10 to his conqueror. The chief helped the robber find another $55, but the balance never did turn up. Anyway, Elmer stoutly insisted that his sole motivation for the larceny had been to teach Lil a lesson on her carelessness in leaving money about.

Prostitutes by temperament and calling were sociable and capable of sponsoring their own diversions. In Iditarod, the girls gave the "Pretzle Ball" every year and invited the men who, presumably, had been faithful customers. Photographs indicate these were gala affairs. The big bosomed hostesses of the event appear pleased to be sponsoring this legitimate recreation. Sometimes the girls grubstaked miners and thereby shared directly in mining profits. In Nome, such lucky strikes were celebrated by picnics. The women and their guests took the railroad out to one of the roadhouses for a wild party. Such events were welcome diversions. But life of northern whores should not be painted in rosy tones. Newspapers frequently carried grim news items like the following:

Mabel Dixon, woman of the underworld, swallows bottle of carbolic acid. "Australian Mabel" had been drinking and was despondent. A note was pinned to her dress, "Good bye, girls; I am tired of it all."[18]

There is more than one way to measure the prosperity of a gold camp. Robert Marshall's examination of Wiseman, a camp on the upper Koyukuk River, compares numbers of working whores with annual gold production. With Marshall's census as our guide, it would perhaps be reasonable to date the end of the golden era—not just for the Koyukuk but for all Alaska—as 1918.

A Mining Camp's Measure of Prosperity[19]

Year	Permanent White Population	Gold Production in Thousand Dollars	Prostitutes
1898	200		0
1899	120		0
1900	270	107	2
1901	320	173	6
1902	350	200	10
1903	300	301	7
1904	210	200	0
1905	220	165	1
1906	160	165	0
1907	120	100	0
1908	240	220	6
1909	230	420	5
1910	190	160	8
1911	160	130	5
1912	230	216	9
1913	250	368	8
1914	270	260	13
1915	300	290	14
1916	250	320	12
1917	200	250	7
1918	150	150	2
1919	130	110	2
1920	119	90	0
1921	107	78	0
1922	101	132	0
1923	97	37	0
1924	92	54	0
1925	88	50	0
1926	93	68	0
1927	98	78	0
1928	90	46	0
1929	83	32	0
1930	77	31	0
1931	71	27	0
Total		5,028	

Diversions and Recreations

Cheers and groans mingled as Henry Bloom and his men pulled their opponents off their feet. Once more the dauntless Swedes had proved invincible, and the spectators scattered to the saloons to pay off their bets or collect their winnings—depending on their luck. Henry Bloom picked up a well-filled poke from the judges and passed out, as he always did after a tough tug-of-war match.

It was the Fourth of July, the one holiday besides Christmas that everybody observed in Alaska. Saloons did a roaring trade; there were baseball games to watch, boxing matches, foot races; but the trump event was the tug-of-war. This test of endurance was once the leading amusement at lumber camps and mining towns all over the West. It developed to the point of supporting semiprofessional teams, like Bloom's, which made seasonal tours to take on the local boys in other towns. These exhibitions of brute strength have since gone out of fashion, and little wonder—they were killers!

Henry Bloom was the anchor man and at 225 pounds smaller than the average. Anchor men were encased in heavy leather and steel belts weighing up to 60 pounds, harnessed to the Manila hemp rope 120 feet long. Their job was to brace themselves securely and hope that their brawny teammates, usually ten in number, could out-pull their opponents. The man just in front of the anchor man was the knot man; he strained to keep the rope down to reduce the leverage on the anchor man. The other eight men moored their feet into cleats spaced every six inches on wooden planking and pulled on the rope for dear life, trying to force the other team to step over the line that designated the goal. The point man, lead man on the rope, was chosen for his ability to wage psychological warfare with his opposite number and his strategical ability; he was the quarterback. It was customary elsewhere to halt the matches after 30 minutes; but in Alaska contests were fought to the bitter end.

Sometimes there were horse races on the Fourth, but these were always disrupted by dogs who enjoyed agitating the nervous horses. Although town officials threatened to shoot dogs bothering the horses, loose dogs always presented a problem, and no one really dared to kill the valuable malemutes. There were many of them, and during the summer they were underemployed, although in the winter they earned their keep. "Tie up your dogs," warned posters announcing the holiday program, and the townspeople generally complied. Outdoor holiday events would otherwise be impossible in Alaskan towns where population of dogs sometimes exceeded that of people.

Other summer diversions available to Alaskan miners included water excursions. From Nome one could take a short Bering Sea voyage to

Siberia; Fairbanksans liked to take a barge down the Chena into the Tanana to visit an Indian village and picnic. Rail excursions over the short line roads serving the outlying mines were popular, too. Picnic parties were not, however, undertaken during the peak mosquito season.

The highlight of Nome's winter season was the All Alaska Sweepstakes, a dog sled race that was run 408 miles from Nome to Candle and return. For a purse of from $4,000 to $10,000 and whatever they cared to bet on the side drivers undertook this marathon with superbly conditioned teams. In 1910 "Iron Man" Johnson took the race after running the distance with his eleven dogs in 72 hours. One 5-hour rest was the only breather of any length taken by Johnson.

A driver could hitch up as many dogs as he pleased, but no relays were permitted, and all dogs had to return to Nome either in harness or on the sled. The Sweepstakes did a great deal for the improvement of the quality and care of dogs. Men could see the difference in endurance between a team that was well looked after and one that was neglected. As a result, dogs began to live a better life.

Since a telephone line existed along the route of the race, news of the contestants' progress was received in Nome throughout the race. Saloons posted the positions of all drivers, and patrons rooted for their favorites and covered bets. When the exhausted winner eventually stumbled over the finish line, he became one of the most famed men in the North.

Another test of endurance that amused gold town dwellers was the indoor marathon race. In March, 1907, the winner of two out of three races held within a three-week period in Nome was a famous musher. Newspapers featured the story: "Carrying an American flag in his hand for the last two laps, James Wada, the Japanese representative, won the big 50 mile race on Saturday last, in the fast time 7 hours, 49 minutes, 10 seconds."[20] James Wada was actually Jujuira Wada, the phantom prospector of the North, the man who sparked the first stampede from Dawson City to Fairbanks in 1903 and was threatened with lynching by the disappointed rushers.

In Nome the races took place in the Eagles Hall. Round and round the racers ran; thirty-two laps made a mile. "The excitement for the last two hours was intense and the spectators went wild as the men struggled around the track in their desperate efforts to win the big prize and the money for which their friends had backed them."[21] Musher Scotty Allen, who had won the All Alaska Sweepstakes dog-team races several times, finished behind Wada. Allen was quite a character. He claimed to have taken a dog team across the Bering Strait to Siberia on the drifting ice pack during the Nome stampede, but we have only his word that the feat was actually accomplished. During World War I, Allen was called upon to take 440 sled dogs to France, where he supervised hauling of ammunition for French forces in the Vosges Mountains. The employment of Alaskan talent had another parallel during the Great War in the assignment of Alfred Brooks. Brooks, in charge of the United States Geological Survey in Alaska, knew about gold ditches and diggings and, in France, advised on the technology of trench warfare.

But to return to Wada. Little is known about this small, stalwart man, but he deserves recognition as one of the fabulous figures of the gold era. He was in on most of the big stampedes and many of the less important ones. As late as 1923 the *Alaska Weekly* reported that Wada was "still on the mush."[22] He had recently reached Winnipeg with his five-dog team after a 2,500-mile journey along the Arctic Coast to Herschel Island and up the Mackenzie River. Wada gave a newsman a summary of his career highlights. He had been born in Japan, had shipped on a sealing schooner to the Bering Sea around the time of the Dawson rush, and joined the stampede. In 1920 he rushed to Fort Norman oil fields to prospect for petroleum. Now he was looking for backing so that he could return to his Herschel Island diggings.

Wada had a little trouble with the law in early days, but his difficulty probably grew out of his dealings with E. T. Barnette, the founder of Fairbanks. After escaping the lynching at Fairbanks, Wada was directed to move on. He did so, and took along a bundle of forty mink furs Barnette claimed as his own. Barnette's honesty never matched his business acumen; it is likely that Wada had not been paid for his services as cook and had to help himself. At any rate, Wada appeared at Nome in July, 1903, and the police were eager to talk to him. The *Nome Gold Digger* reported on the arrest of the "festive young Japanese, a sourdough of years' standing in Alaska, the boomer of the Tanana strike, whom it will be remembered [sic] came near being lynched."[23] Friends of Wada posted bond for him but he shipped out before his hearing came up. The *Aztec* carried Wada to safety in Seattle; yet he must have cleared himself in some way later to have restored his standing in Nome.

In 1908 Wada rushed to Katalla. In the period between his Nome marathon victories in 1907 and the mush to Katalla, he had prospected around the Mackenzie River delta. The 1910 Iditarod strike drew Wada there for a short time, but he had visions of rich prospects in the Kuskokwim River country and had to mush on. Never shy with newsmen, Wada told a Seattle reporter in 1912 that he had $1 million backing for his Kuskokwim claims. This glad word was flashed all over Alaska, and soon Wada charged through Iditarod again enroute to his diggings.

How many miles did this veteran mush? How much gold did he win from the ground? What of his family? A woman, claiming to be his daughter, arrived in Fairbanks in 1914, looking for him; she was vaguely directed to the Kuskokwim. These and other questions may never be answered. But his image is fairly clear despite the blur of his speed afoot as he mushed on—and on: he was a giant pioneer. (*See also* Chapter 21).

Johnny Wallace, a Nome sourdough, remembered Wada's races in Nome for one social effect of his victory. It seems that a whore bet $5,000 on the Japanese at five to one odds. When she received her winnings she quit Nome for the Outside and for respectability.

Clubs

Much of the legitimate social life of northern towns was sponsored by such familiar fraternal groups as the Eagles, Moose, and Odd Fellows. It was never very long after the founding of a sizable camp before one or the other of these organizations put up a meeting hall for dances and other entertainments. In Fairbanks the Eagles Hall was a commodious building rented to others when not being utilized by the fraternal order.

Peculiar to the North was the Arctic Brotherhood, which had its origin aboard the steamer *City of Seattle* enroute to Skagway in February, 1899. The fraternal spirit aboard the ship suggested "the formation of a great social brotherhood of the North where men from all parts of the world going to the fields might meet and know each other."[24] Skagway was designated Camp No. 1, and as successive stampedes created other towns, a new chapter of the Brotherhood was established in each one. Men took great pride in membership in the A.B. and wore its badge, a tiny gold pan with three nuggets at its base, at all times. "Never," wrote a historian of the A.B., "has the brotherhood of man been exemplified to such a re- markable degree. Our Northern spirit is as manifest as the Aurora Bo- realis."[25] Eventually there were thirty camps and thousands of members of the A.B.; its activities were primarily social; some charity was extended to members in need and ceremonious attendance at the funerals of mem- bers was customary.

A similar group was the Pioneers of Alaska, organized into "igloos" rather than "camps." The Pioneers were an offshoot of the Yukon Order of Pioneers founded in Dawson. Nome formed Igloo No. 1 of the Pioneers of Alaska. Both groups flourished outside of Alaska, notably in Seattle, San Francisco, and other Pacific coast cities where former sourdoughs were numerous. The long existence of these brotherhoods Outside is evi- dence of the persistence of the "northern spirit" among stampeders. Even men who had only spent one season in the North were deeply impressed by the experience—it was *something* to be a sourdough.

21

Founder–Swindler Barnette of Fairbanks

The Canny Trader

Ebenezer T. Barnette, the founder of Fairbanks and its first mayor, was a rogue of the first water. He came to Alaska from Ohio to start a store in Circle in 1897. Some traders were famed for their liberality in grubstaking prospectors and extending credit to down-and-out miners, but not Barnette.

In fact, Barnette was a tightfisted opportunist. There is some evidence that a miners' meeting tried him for theft in 1897 or 1898 and acquitted him. This experience did not daunt him. In the winter of 1900, he gained control of all of Circle's flour and jacked up prices.[1] By then the miners' meetings had given way to more conventional law enforcement. The camp seethed at Barnette's gouging but did not act as they would have formerly.

When the Alaska Commercial Company broke Barnette's flour monopoly, he decided to relocate. First he went Outside for financial backing. In an interview published by the *Seattle Post-Intelligencer*, the wily trader described the Tanana country and its prospects, omitting to mention that he had never been there. Twelve to fifteen men were getting up to $3 a pan, he asserted. Actually, in 1901, there was no camp in the Tanana region. Gold had not yet been discovered there. By the time Barnette got back to Alaska, settled his affairs in Circle, and outfitted himself at St. Michael, prospectors had invaded the Tanana. Barnette borrowed money from J. H. Causten, Deputy Customs Collector at St. Michael, and leased the *Lavelle Young* for his enterprise. Then he was off for the Tanana and fortune. (*See* Chapter 19, page 136.) The business arrangement with Collector Causten soon slipped his mind. Years later Causten had to sue for recovery of his investment.

Naturally, the prospectors were delighted to see the trader. They could buy Barnette's bacon, flour, beans, and tea and save themselves the long trek to Rampart or Circle for reprovisioning. But Barnette wanted more customers than were then present in the area—and knew just what to do.

One member of Barnette's party was a Japanese named Jujuira Wada. (*See also* Chapter 20, p. 163.) He worked for Barnette as a cook initially but did not remain in Fairbanks long. Wada was to kick off many stampedes, but the one to Fairbanks was his first. Barnette's scheme utilized Wada, whom he sent to Dawson City to sell furs and boost the new camp. His exaggerated reports sparked a stampede of about 1,000 men. Barnette's store did a thriving trade.

No one actually knew whether the Fairbanks region held significant gold deposits or not. None of the first miners on the scene were equipped to mine during the 1902–1903 winter; no one had enough capital to bring in a boiler for thawing. Thus "Cap" Barnette felt compelled to anticipate a bit. His confidence in the area was boundless, but it was not shared by the Dawson stampeders, who did not stay around long. The men from Dawson were annoyed at Wada, whose report of paydirt nine feet deep had stampeded them. Wada had returned to the new camp at Fairbanks with them, and some miners proposed making an example of him. A miners' meeting was called to consider punishment. Henry Badger chaired the session, which developed into a mock trial to scare the wits out of Wada. Actually, the men probably realized that the true culprit of the affair was Barnette, but the trial of the Japanese cook gave them a chance to blow off some steam.

Even before Wada was sent to Dawson, Barnette had triggered a minor stampede from Rampart. He had been sending letters to Dawson, Nome, and Seattle, lying about the local mineral wealth, but without getting any immediate response. Then fortune smiled. A U.S. Army officer from Fort Gibbon turned up to look things over. Barnette led the guileless Lieutenant Gibbs to one of his claims. Gibbs instantly spotted the gleaming nuggets that the trader had planted for the purpose. As soon as he could, Gibbs telegraphed the glad news to Fort Gibbon; fifty men rushed down from Rampart when the word reached there.

Conditions were somewhat grim in the early spring of 1903. Provisions were short. Barnette wanted the camp to prosper but could not overlook a heaven-sent opportunity to increase his profit margin. According to one story he raised the price of flour from 25 to 40 cents per pound. This occurred before Judge Wickersham and his deputy marshal appeared on the scene, so the miners took their traditional recourse. A miners' meeting was held, and it was agreed that a representative should be sent to give

Barnette a solemn warning. This was done and though the words were not
recorded, it is not hard to imagine the tenor of the remarks. The trader
was a tough man and not easily intimidated. His rejoinder was to build a
wall around the trading post. Presumably, he intended to defend his property by armed force.[2] Once more the miners met to consider action.
Reports on their deliberations struck the trader as too ominous for comfort. He backed down, lowered prices, and prepared to journey Outside
for a spell. Sudden departures to avoid irate citizens of Fairbanks were a
feature of Barnette's career.

Stories of the early days of gold camps always have variants. Henry
Badger, later to be known as the "strawberry king" of the Tanana valley,
recalled that Barnette had 17 tons of flour and a stock of canned goods
"that were no good."[3] Barnette naturally wanted to push his tainted
canned goods, so he refused to sell flour unless every purchaser of a 50-
pound sack took three cases of the tinned food. A miners' meeting pondered the situation, then passed a resolution that every man could buy a
sack of flour alone. This resolution was posted and "inside of a half hour
a string of men were lining up to buy," passing into the front door of
Barnette's store and out the back with a sack of flour on their shoulders.[4]
Private enterprise had to give way before the miners' determination.

Barnette's history of swindling and gouging did not hinder his business
success. He made money hand over fist. Judge Wickersham had agreed to
appoint him claim recorder for the district in exchange for naming the
town after Senator Fairbanks of Indiana. To fees received as recorder, he
added store receipts, rents from town lots, profits from the *Fairbanks
News*, which he backed, and rich returns from miners he had staked. He
also acted as postmaster and, surprisingly, as town banker. That miners
would entrust their money to the cunning trader seems odd. Obviously the
man possessed qualities of personality that do not shine through the historical record. Whatever the circumstances, Barnette advanced from an
informal holder of miners' pokes to the presidency of the Washington–
Alaska Bank, which he founded with the backing of Seattle financial
interests.

With all his business activities Barnette still found time to serve his
community in political office. Whether civic-mindedness or the desire to
protect his interests prompted him cannot be determined, but Barnette
entered the first city council election and won a seat. Customarily in such
elections, the council members would raise to the mayor's office the member who had received the highest number of votes. The precedent was not
followed in the first election held in Fairbanks. Perhaps a deal was made.
Barnette received only sixty-seven votes to the leader's seventy-three; yet
he got the mayor's job. Rampart's newspaper, the *Alaska Forum*, grum-

bled about this outcome, but acknowledged that it was "no different from what is to be expected from the average city council of an Alaskan town."[5]

Barnette and Wickersham

Judge James Wickersham assured the growth of Fairbanks when he moved his federal court there from Eagle. His court calendar included a number of contests over mining claims in which Barnette had an interest. The mayor hinted that an interest in a valuable mine would be given Wickersham when the judge left office.[6] On the second hint, Wickersham indignantly walked away. Wickersham tolerated these bribery attempts because he considered Barnette miserly rather than dishonest. Later on, he would know the banker better. Wickersham had invested in mining claims and town lots—operators of the popular California Saloon paid him $3,600 annual rent—but luckily for his reputation, he apparently had no business connections with Barnette, although he did lend the banker money on one occasion.

Wickersham did, however, see a lot of Barnette both in Fairbanks and in Washington, D.C. As a politician he needed support, and Barnette must have offered it. There is no record of the banker giving direct financial aid, but the editorials of the *Fairbanks News* resounded with praise of Judge Wickersham until he resigned his judgeship in 1908.

Alaskan politics was as rabid as politics anywhere else in the country. What marked the political scene as singular was the territorial status of the region. All important decisions were made in Washington, and all judges, marshals, district attorneys, and the governor were appointed by the federal government. Wickersham earned enemies every time he decided a mining claim case. The jury fixers he convicted in Nome did him every disservice possible in Washington. Still he maintained office as judge for seven strife-ridden years. For the last three years the Senate refused to confirm his appointment. Teddy Roosevelt kept him on the bench with interim appointments each time. As Alaska's delegate to Congress he was re-elected time after time, serving a total of 14 years, but with increasing turmoil and difficulty. One needed to be a very tough and persistent battler to survive in Alaskan politics—and such was "Flickering Wick," as his enemies called him.

A friendly newspaper in Fairbanks was a particular necessity because of the town's size and importance. Furthermore, the *Fairbanks Times* was dedicated to Wickersham's destruction. The *Times* was not alone in this. Rampart's *Alaska Forum* began denouncing the judge in 1904 and shrilled on for years against him. But the virulent *Times* had more readers. Gleeful editorials greeted the Senate's refusal to approve Wickersham's reappointment in 1906. When Roosevelt appointed him anyway, the *Times* complained that the President opposed the will of Alaskan miners. "Everybody is unhappy and some fear his knowing of their opposition."[7] Opponents of the judge had good reason to fear him. He held a good portion of the patronage power and never missed a chance to punish political enemies.

The *Times* tried to point up the close relationship between Barnette and the judge. Its editor argued that another federal judge should be transferred to Fairbanks temporarily to hear cases in which the banker was a party. "Wickersham won't hear cases of Barnette's interest since he was accused of being in his influence."[8]

On the other hand, the *News*, Barnette's paper, supported Wickersham. The editor could not understand the Senate's rejection of the much loved judge. On occasion the entire editorial page was devoted to fulsome praise of the judge and acerbic attacks on his enemies. Civic consciousness probably did not motivate the editorial policies of either newspaper. Personal convictions and animosities played a much stronger part.

In November, 1906, Barnette was sued in Seattle by former Customs Collector J. H. Causten, who had grubstaked the trader's founding voyage to the Tanana. Causten had long known that his "partner" Barnette had made a fortune, but he had been patient. Rumors of a close relationship between Judge Wickersham and Barnette dissuaded him from bringing suit against the latter in Fairbanks. Causten initiated his civil suit in Seattle by securing a levy on $200,000 in gold shipped there from Barnette's bank. In the course of the trial, Causten's lawyer revealed a juicy bit of scandal concerning the defendant. Barnette was an ex-convict.

Jail Bird

Barnette's indiscretion occurred in 1886 in Oregon. One George De-Wolf entrusted him with $2,000—perhaps the transaction was Barnette's first experience as a banker. When DeWolf wanted his money back, he heard a sad story: an Indian had taken the money away from Barnette. Barnette was damn sorry about it, too. DeWolf complained to the law, and Barnette was convicted of larceny and sentenced to four years. After 18 months he either had been pardoned by the governor (his story) or had had his sentence reduced (Causten's story).

Seattleites were stirred by this news of the founder of Fairbanks and its leading banker. In Fairbanks the story created a sensation, yet no run on the deposits of the Washington–Alaska Bank was reported. The *Fairbanks Times* published the first account of the exposure without editorial comment. Apparently the *Fairbanks News* did not receive the telegraphed story initially, because it lambasted the *Times* for publishing such lies and recalled that *Times* publisher, "Cap" Anderson, had been a "Barnette shouter." Yes, admitted the *Times*, Anderson supported Barnette for mayor in 1905, "but double dealing ended that."[9] While Anderson campaigned, Barnette jumped his claim on Dome Creek. A few days later a *Times* editorial noted that "it would be criminal to suppress the most important news since the fire about Alaska's most prominent citizen," implying that the *News* favored suppression.[10]

Judge Wickersham's reaction was somewhat curious. His diary records his spleen against "Cap" Anderson: "Two years ago Cap Anderson . . . was a tramp and Barnette aided him." Barnette had even used his influence with the judge to get Anderson appointed road commissioner. "Anderson is a beggar on horseback! A Blackguard and blackmailer!" Anderson is a "dirty cowardly assassin."[11] Obviously Wickersham's principal concern was his own reputation. His Washington enemies had accused him of too cozy relations with the banker, and now they would have more dangerous charges to bring.

President Roosevelt had not yet reappointed Wickersham, so he had reason for concern. W. F. (Wrong Font) Thompson, editor of the *News*, telegraphed Roosevelt, urging Wickersham's reappointment. Some Fairbanks businessmen did the same. Percy H. Palmer told the President that critics of the judge were motivated by vindictiveness. The *Times* called on citizens to boycott Palmer's business. This worried several businessmen who then withdrew their support from Wickersham. Wickersham's diary records his outrage: "The most pronounced characteristic of a businessman is cowardice. He calls it conservatism."[12]

The effect of the Barnette exposure cannot be definitely determined, Roosevelt reappointed the judge for another year, but, to placate the opposition, ordered an investigation of Alaska's legal system. This would be the third such investigation. Angered by this, Wickersham resolved to resign his post.

Barnette was presented with a golden opportunity to avenge himself on "Cap" Anderson of the *Times*. A grand jury indicted the publisher for forgery in a mine dispute. But somehow the two antagonists must have reconciled their differences. Trial evidence pointed to Anderson's obvious guilt; yet the jury was hung and charges were dropped. Wickersham believed that Barnette had fixed the jury by arranging that his father-in-law serve.[13] Former Judge Wickersham was annoyed at this, but not to the extent of confronting the foxy banker.

Fairbanksans continued to deposit their money at the Washington–Alaska Bank. In newspaper ads Barnette's name was no longer listed among the bank's officers. People still thought of it as Barnette's bank— and indeed it was, as subsequent events proved. A one-week closure that occurred as a result of the 1907 Causten suit in Seattle should have forewarned depositors. Yet the bank seemed prosperous. So did Barnette, who paid $65,000 for a Kentucky horse ranch and gathered extensive properties in Mexico. Fairbanksans must have forgotten or forgiven the swindler.

Bank Failure

A rude shock came in January, 1911. The Washington–Alaska Bank closed its doors. Much panic ensued in Fairbanks as depositors bemoaned their position. Where was the money? cried one and all. Barnette was Outside at the time and could not be immediately consulted.

Barnette was interviewed in Los Angeles. Don't worry about the failure, he advised. Everything will be all right. In Fairbanks, none were reassured by this calm message. The *Times* reported that the ex-convict first transferred all his property to his wife, then offered his personal guarantee in support of the bank.

Anxious depositors were not too relieved by a court order requiring bank directors to pay them 16 cents on the dollar. About $1 million in deposits was involved. Eventually half of that was returned to depositors. A grand jury met to consider the matter. The *Times* urged it to do its duty: "On numerous occasions in the past, this paper has done its best to show up Barnette in his true light."[14] No one denied that.

To the surprise of many, Barnette and his wife made a winter sailing from Seattle to Valdez. They would journey to Fairbanks over the Valdez Trail. He announced before leaving Seattle that he would stay in Fairbanks until everyone had been paid. "I won't quit there until that has been accomplished." A *Times* editorial greeted this welcome news, and advised readers to get the money first. "There will be plenty of time afterwards to ask questions and attend to the other details."[15]

The steamer *Victoria* carried the wayward banker to Alaska. Fairbanksans were eager to hear news of the ship's safe arrival at Valdez. Instead, alarming word of a grounding reached the town. Friends of "Cap" Barnette called on the local press to assure them that the banker was not in any way responsible for the *Victoria*'s grounding.

Finally, the great day dawned. Barnette arrived and, after a time, issued a statement to the press. This long, vague discourse purported to explain a previous bank merger, the bank's connection with a lumber company, the withdrawals made by Barnette, and troublesome overdrafts. The banker asked the larger depositors to remain patient until bank assets were disposed of and offered to pay the smaller depositors at once. Depositors rejected this proposal, so Barnette promised to liquidate his private property to satisfy all that was owed. A few days later, he signed over all his American and Mexican real estate. Even the *Times* was impressed by this action—though its editor was not quite ready to abandon his suspicions. "When we have been convinced that all of his dealings with the people of this camp have been open and above board, we will not hesitate to admit that we have done him an injustice."[16]

But the situation worsened. Lawyers advised the depositors that Barnette's contract with them was not binding, and that no binding agreement could be drafted. Depositors demanded an immediate cash payment of $50,000. The banker refused to pay, claiming he had to travel to New York and London to get financial aid. Barnette petitioned the court to require the bank receivers to accept the contract even though the depositors had rejected it.

All these negotiations kept Fairbanks buzzing for months. During the same period, the grand jury had been sifting through the bank's affairs. Alaskan newspapers seldom waited for the conclusion of legal proceedings before declaring the guilt of the accused, particularly when the latter was unpopular. The *Times* interpreted the grand jury report: "All the officials of the bank . . . stand convicted, by inference, of having obtained deposits through misrepresentation and of having disposed of the money in a way that would not be safe outside Alaska."[17] At this point the women depositors banded together and called for a mass meeting to examine the issue. They reacted against the grand jury report which the *Times* seemed to have misinterpreted. Now the newspaper applauded them for having enough spunk to try getting back their money, implying that the grand jury had erred. Contrary to the *Times'* editorial, the grand jury at this time did not find clear evidence of misrepresentation by bank officials.

Barnette found it prudent at this point to slip out of town. Under cover of darkness he sledded off in pursuit of the Valdez-bound stage. He knew better than to attempt to board the stage at the Fairbanks terminal. His friends—and he still had some—concealed his departure.

Embezzlement Trial

A *Times* editorial called on depositors to petition the court for another grand jury. "The fact that one Grand Jury has failed to do its duty to the people should discourage no one."[18] Two hundred twenty-five depositors agreed and petitioned the court, charging Barnette with embezzlement. Ignore the obstructionists, the paid Barnette sympathizers, who should be thankful their man was not handled with violence. The banker cannot get beyond the reach of the law, cried the editor.

Barnette, who left Fairbanks hurriedly in March, returned in June to look over some of his mining properties. He was not harassed on this visit. Bank affairs were in the hands of the court and a receiver. By November all the bank's remaining assets, including its building, had been sold, but depositors had recovered only 50 percent of their money. There was no one to blame but Barnette. The grand jury indicted the banker and he was arrested in San Francisco. Barnette maintained his bluff. Calling his arrest a stab in the back, he asserted his innocence. Although he was not legally responsible for the bank's debts, he would pay them. Currently, he claimed, a London syndicate was negotiating to buy his 12,000 acres in Mexico. This sale would yield more than enough to pay depositors.

The trial of Barnette and all the other bank officials on charges of embezzlement was set for June, 1912. Attorneys for the accused felt—reasonably—that the mood of Fairbanks would make a fair trial there impossible. The court agreed; a change of venue to Valdez was ordered. The United States attorney general assigned Robert Gibson to assist in the preparation of the prosecution's case. Gibson had successfully prosecuted some crooked Pittsburgh bankers.

When the prosecution subpoenaed witnesses, there was another uproar. Most of the business community were among those served. They asked for a postponement of the trial until fall. Leaving Fairbanks in June would be a disaster to their business interests. The Alaska Bureau of the Seattle Chamber of Commerce wired the attorney general to the same effect and the trial was reset for December.

Judge Thomas R. Lyons presided over the trial, which was one of the most extensive ever conducted in Alaska. Barnette's legal staff included some able men: Albert Fink of Nome, Leroy Tozier of Fairbanks, T. C. West of San Francisco, and the members of the Valdez firm of Donohue, Ritchie, Brown, Lyons and Ostrander. Fairbanks newsmen telegraphed reports of each day's proceedings to their papers. Their stories dismayed all but Barnette sympathizers. The banker was acquitted on all embezzlement charges and found guilty only of the misdemeanor of making false reports. "A tragedy," moaned the *Times*, "it kills the hopes of those who expected that Barnette would be punished for his wrong doing."[19] The *Times* raged against two Fairbanks attorneys whose testimony favored the banker's cause and called for their disbarment.

One-time district attorney of Nome, John McGinn, whose libel suit against newsman Strong has been discussed elsewhere (see page 268), was one of the attorneys attacked by the *Times*. His testimony was a great help to the defense. McGinn forgot to put Barnette under oath when bank reports containing false statements were drawn up.

In fining Barnette $1,000 without costs, Judge Lyons was most apologetic. He doubted the banker's guilt but would go along with the jury's finding. No cry was raised by the federal prosecuting attorneys, nor was there an appeal. Obviously the prosecution simply lacked the evidence to sustain an embezzlement conviction. But in Fairbanks the general mood was bitter towards the court. With the usual Alaskan journalist's disregard of due process, the *Fairbanks News Miner* labeled the trial the "rottenest judicial farce the North has ever witnessed."[20]

Other Alaskan newspapers did not view the outcome in the same light. The *Cordova Daily Alaskan* grumbled at the "fiasco" of the government's waste of time and money.[21] The prosecution did not have either the facts or the law with them, yet insisted upon bringing the case to trial.

For some years Fairbanks residents kept their memories of their founding father green. Mention of his name never failed to raise bile and invoke strong language. But in time he was almost forgotten. Old-timers died off or retired Outside; younger people replaced them. Thus it was that the Fairbanks school board, in searching for a name for a new primary school, had the happy thought of commemorating the city founder. The Ebenezer T. Barnette school was dedicated in 1960. Its current principal would like a portrait of the founder displayed in the school, but, for some reason, the great man avoided photographers. The only extant photo is a group shot and Barnette looks glum before the camera lens.

Barnette wound up his Fairbanks affairs after his trial and had little inclination to revisit the town he had founded. He did not skip to Mexico and drop out of sight, although that is one of the local legends, but spent most of his time in Los Angeles. In 1920 the *Alaska Dispatch* reported that Isabelle Cleary Barnette had been granted a divorce.[22] The *Alaska Weekly* made a brief reference to Barnette's current activities in April, 1923.[23] What happened to him after this is not clear. "Cap" was never one for yarning about old times with newsmen.

22
Restless Camps and Busy Trails

A JITTERY ATMOSPHERE prevailed in mining towns, where men were opportunists to the bone. That's what the game was all about. Alert and restless, listening to all rumors, comparing notes, they were ready to stampede at any time. They were as tense as bird dogs sniffing the wind, as nervous as a runner threatening to steal second base.

Newspapers coyly reported the abrupt departure of prospectors, especially those with a reputation for success. Why, the editor would ask, did not the taciturn prospector take time to say goodbye to his friends? Much speculation and discussion would enliven proceedings at the saloons that day. Then, perhaps, another of the boys would pack and harness his sled and depart as quietly as eight howling dogs would permit. By the following day, everyone would be edgy. Merchants had mixed feelings; they wanted no sudden depopulation of the town—yet a new strike in the vicinity would insure continued prosperity. And if the strike was *not* nearby, perhaps they too should try to get into the action early.

Suddenly, the town stampeded. In a few days or weeks, perhaps, most of the stampeders would be back, exhausted and chagrined. If the distant strike proved fortunate, the demise of older communities could result.

Miners stampeded readily to undeveloped regions. Most such rushes were in vain. Only a handful of high-yield areas were ever discovered in the North, yet there were hundreds of stampedes involving countless miles of travel and incomprehensible hardship. Why did they endure the dangers and the travails of the trail on the strength of rumor? It is easy to see, given the prospector's psychology and the history of the gold-mining frontier. After all, the men first on the ground in the Klondike rushed in response to a rumor—and they became millionaires.

The lore of stampeders to California in '49 is rich in stories of overland treks and clipper voyages to the goldfields. California argonauts suffered enough from weariness and exposure, yet there were few major disasters, the most notable being the loss of the Donner party. If the California-bound men had left wives, children, livestock, furniture, and pianos be-hind, the rigors of the trip would have been much reduced. Prospectors sometimes wandered into savage desert country and died there, but such occurrences were relatively rare.

In Alaska, by contrast, death on the trail was commonplace. Even the experienced, well-equipped musher was imperiled when a sudden blizzard wiped out his trail. If a traveler had to wait out a blow in an exposed condition in frigid temperatures, his chances of survival, especially if alone and in an exhausted condition, were virtually nil. Those who experi-enced winter travel on the less-traveled trails never felt the need to exag-gerate the hardship and danger.

Rex Beach described one of his trail expeditions in response to jour-nalist Westbrook Pegler's assertion that the hardship stories related by the northern gold rushers needed discounting. Beach was in Nome when news reached town of a strike on Candle Creek, near Kotzebue Sound on the Arctic coast. He tried to resist the temptation to make the winter trip because he had already profitable workings quite close to Nome. Further-more, he was enjoying the good life—good at least for those with his youthful stamina—dancing all night and working all day, sleeping alter-nate nights only. However, his partner persuaded him.

On Thanksgiving Day he and a companion set off with dogs and sled. The trip was one of 300 miles. Driving a dog team meant running after the dogs. Only when the sled was pulled across bare ice could the driver catch a free ride, and there was small opportunity for that. Journey plans called for making 30 miles each day. The travelers soon established a routine. The first business, at the end of each day's run, was to burrow into the snow for fire fuel, sickly brush that was extremely hard to ignite yet burned up in seconds once it caught fire. It took a good two hours to prepare supper for themselves; the task of feeding the dogs remained. It took as long to cook food over such sprigs as to cook it by body heat. One man unharnessed the dogs; the other put up the tent. A pan of snow was put over the fire, which had to be constantly fed. It takes longer to do ordinary tasks when it is very cold. One can't move freely in bulky clothes. Mittened fingers can not strike matches very well; nor can frozen fingers working without protection. The dogs' meal had to be con-siderable, providing enough energy to keep the ten dogs going throughout the next day. Yukon mushers fed their dogs fish, but having no convenient supply available Beach cooked the alternative, cornmeal and salt pork.

It was no picnic. "Always there was the cold to contend with." It was like a constant weight pressing in from all sides, and from it there was no escape. There was no exhilaration to it, no deep and grateful inhaling of breath or pounding of the chest. Nobody ever professed to be glad he was alive on such a glorious morning. In the first place, the mornings weren't glorious, wrote Beach; "if the weather wasn't bad it promised to become so and we talked about little else except that, and our indigestion."[1]

Beach was never romantic about the North. His experiences inspired no rhapsodies. Winter travel was a grueling effort demanding the limit of a man's energies, and this on a meager and restricted diet of baking-powder bread, underdone beans, and fat pork. The real call of the wild, Beach declared, was not the howl of the timber wolf, the maniacal laughter of the Arctic loon, nor yet the mating cry of the moose; it was the dyspeptic belch of a tired miner's sour stomach.

The trip was monotonous. On the fourth day the cold was bitter and the men were forced to follow a meandering river bed that added miles to their journey but assured that they would not become lost. "We did not meet a soul on the trail, nor pass a human habitation, not a sound except the complaint of our steel-shod sled and our occasional profanities broke the silence."[2] Finally they reached their destination at Candle. A roadhouse, virtually buried in the snow, offered welcome comforts after the long trip. As so often, the journey had been made for nothing. The fraction between established claims that had drawn them to Candle proved to be too minute to work. So once more they packed up and harnessed the dogs for the long trip back to Nome.

Frauds and Hoaxes

It was galling to join an unprofitable rush triggered by someone's bragging, ignorance, or unmitigated hopes. It was even more embarrassing to be deliberately duped. Salted diggings and outright frauds occurred regularly. An enterprising roadhouse operator on the Seward Peninsula once devised a scheme for building up his trade. An Eskimo he hired was sent to Council with some gold nuggets, supposedly found at the headwaters of the Koyukuk River. Council quickly emptied as 200 excited men mushed away. After a trip of 200 miles and much unsuccessful searching, the men gave up and returned to Council. Shortly thereafter, the Eskimo reached town again. With the angry men threatening his life, he revealed the hoax. Tom Welch, the culprit who hoped to improve his business, could not be found at his Norton Bay roadhouse. Whether he got out of the country before any of the irate miners encountered him is not recorded.

Some frauds were more elaborate. The Midas Creek case was a celebrated example, whose perpetrators, George W. Duncan and Charles R. Griggs, were prospectors who reported rich findings in the autumn of 1902. Their discoveries were on a tributary of the Koyukuk River—

according to rumor. Much excitement attended their revelations in Nome, where opinions on their veracity were divided equally. Undeniably though, they showed nuggets of size impressive enough to spread gold fever.

Laughing off the disbelievers, the two rogues embarked on the last ship for the Outside, promising to return in the spring. If they could raise enough money Outside, they would lead a major party to Midas Creek. Backing by Nomites, they stated, would not be refused. But resourceful prospectors did not always wait for the best travel season. A couple of men attempted to find Midas Creek during the winter, without any luck. Natives in the region had not heard of any discoveries. The prospectors smelled a rat.

Nevertheless, the buoyant "discoverers" returned to Nome in June, having formed the Treasure and Midas Creeks Gold Mining Association of Alaska, incorporated under the laws of Oregon. The company's assets included four claims of 20 acres each. Issuance of 174 to 240 shares per stockholder was provided, each share representing 20 square feet of a claim. How could supporters lose with ground that had yielded $449.50 per cubic yard to Duncan and Griggs?

Opinion remained divided in Nome. A lampoon of the affair appeared in the *Nugget* that purported to be an interview with a company man, Mr. Othmer, who could "never think of Midas without associating it with the figure of $300,000,000." Mr. Othmer asserted that such an amount of money could be used "to free Ireland or to convert the United States to socialism," while he did not promise to devote his profits to either cause.[3]

As the company's party made its preparations for departure, other prospectors were ahead of them in the field. Speculation placed the Midas, perhaps, as a stream about 200 miles from the mouth of the Koyukuk. Men looked in vain for gold-bearing gravel—but then they were not in the confidence of Messrs. Duncan and Griggs. Duncan and Griggs embarked on the *Louise*, the other company members on the *Research*. Freelance prospectors took what vessels were available—the stampede was on!

The bubbling optimism of the company argonauts faded somewhat when their leaders failed to rendezvous with them at St. Michael. They cursed the lost leaders for the delay, but continued their Yukon–Koyukuk voyage anyway. After all, they had a map showing Midas Creek as a tributary of the Hogikakat River. Although by this time suspicion of fraud ran high, they would not return to Nome without making a search for the sparkling wealth of Midas Creek. But first—where *was* Midas Creek?

While the company party of fifty men, including Judge F. T. Merritt, who had been appointed commissioner for the new mining district, pushed on, some word of Duncan and Griggs, now familiarly known as the Midas Prophets, reached Nome. Reportedly they had landed 40 miles up the

Koyukuk River. Their stores were meager enough—a mere $80 worth of
food, hardly the provisions for men intending to spend the season in a
remote country. At the Northern Saloon and other refreshment centers of
Nome, opinions crystallized. Undoubtedly, Duncan and Griggs had
headed Outside. Saloon miners congratulated themselves for their sagacity
in avoiding the Midas snare.

Duncan and Griggs had been landed on the Koyukuk River, a northern
tributary of the Yukon, but only to confuse pursuers. A year earlier they
had cached a riverboat there, and now they recovered it and voyaged
down the Koyukuk River to its confluence with the mighty Yukon River.
Warily they watched for the *Research*, concealing themselves in the brush
along the river bank. Once the *Research* had passed them and begun its
ascent of the Koyukuk, they floated on down the Yukon on the first leg
of their journey to the Outside.

Meanwhile, in Nome, they were reported to have been seen elsewhere.
One rumor located them at Fort Yukon, where they were said to be
boasting of a $50,000 take on the swindle. Another indicated they took a
Yukon steamer for Dawson enroute to the Outside. Estimates of the swag
varied, but most gossip favored $50,000—$20,000 of which had been
raised in Nome and $30,000 Outside.

The Midas argonauts had a hard time of it. Much swampy and rough
country was traversed. Mosquitoes and gnats plagued them. Game proved
to be very scarce and provisions dwindled. They started eating their
horses. From July through September they sought the elusive Midas. Finally they gave up. On the return journey to Nome, the weary stampeders
did not talk too much. They wore the preoccupied air of men grappling
with weighty decisions. By what means, each must have reflected, would I
dispatch Duncan and Griggs if I ever encounter them again?

A grand jury investigation of the whole affair revealed more information. The $1,500 in gold dust, shown by the Midas Prophets in Nome, had
been purchased by them in Bettles. They had staked a claim at the mouth
of Koyukuk Creek, but had found no gold there. From the outset the
whole scheme had been a deliberate swindle. Nome's newspapers encouraged the grand jury in its deliberations: "If ever men deserved punishment
for crime committed, these two are they."[4] As usual, frontier editors did
not wait for a court conviction to determine guilt, especially since the
grievance outraged popular opinion. Nome, abetted by newspaper editors
like J. F. A. Strong, thirsted for revenge.

Feelings ran high against prominent men who had backed the swindlers.
Among those endorsing the project had been Judge Alfred Moore, Judge
F. T. Merritt, and City Clerk George Borchsenius. Their support had been
important to the success of the scheme, and their reputations suffered

accordingly. Only the more charitable noted that the distinguished trio had been duped as thoroughly as the others.

Glad news made headlines in October: "DUNCAN AND GRIGGS PICKED UP IN PORTLAND."[5] Swiftly, the grand jury issued indictments; arrest warrants were prepared, and U. S. Deputy Marshal Al Cody left for Portland on the steamer *St. Paul*. The close of navigation stranded Cody in Portland until spring, but he had Griggs safely lodged in jail. Duncan was never found.

Time and distance raised the costs of criminal prosecution in Alaska. For the sake of trying Griggs, a deputy remained Outside for most of the year. Transportation charges for the accused, officers, and witnesses were to be borne by the government. Alaskans, in their unending complaints of federal neglect, did not dwell on matters like this. In July, Griggs was brought back to Nome, arraigned in the district court on a charge of obtaining money under false pretenses, and jailed. Though disappointed at Duncan's escape, all Nome looked forward to Griggs' trial and conviction. Deputy Cody's winter-long chase proved fruitless. From Oregon he trailed Duncan to Vancouver, B.C., and from there to Provo, Utah, where the trail grew cold.

Defense counsel included James Fenton and O. D. Cochran. Fenton requested a change of venue, supported by six affidavits of prominent businessmen stating that the defendant had no chance of getting a fair trial in Nome. The judge decided otherwise, to the applause of editorial opinion: "So Mr. Griggs will have justice meted out to him in Nome—as it should be met."[6]

Fifteen witnesses presented evidence for the prosecution. The jury needed very little time for reflection. The Midas Prophet was convicted and sentenced to five years at McNeil Island. Newspapers applauded the result but wondered where all the money went. So did the company backers.

Other Departures

Other reasons occasioned sudden departures. If one could board a steamer undetected in late October, a long winter of creditors' harassment could be avoided. It wasn't easy in communities like Nome and Fairbanks where residents knew each other too well and the dock never seemed unobserved.

But, often enough, a man whose expectations had not been met disappointed those of his creditors as well—and slyly slipped away. Whether aboard the *Victoria* in Nome's open roadstead or the river steamer *Lavelle Young* at Fairbanks, the furtive voyager watched debarkation routines with considerable anxiety. His spirits soared when the steam whistle shrilled farewell. Back in town, gloomy merchants commiserated. They cursed the memory of the absconder and questioned the legitimacy of his birth. Live and Learn! Another bad debt written off.

If the absconder was prominent enough, his untimely departure stimulated newspaper comment in an ironic vein: "George Corbett who achieved considerable fame as a moral reformer departed without notice, waiting until evening shadows fell." He will be missed, the reporter asserted, by his numerous creditors. Corbett's cautious leave-taking was prompted by his fear that "a public demonstration would be made in his behalf."[7] If the hasty traveler's roguery warranted criminal prosecution, pursuit sometimes ensued. Every summer the marshals of the larger towns toured the saloons of Seattle and Tacoma looking for men deemed worth the trouble of arrest. An apprehended culprit faced considerable travel. He unwillingly voyaged back to Alaska. Then, if convicted of a serious felony, he faced transportation to McNeil Island in Washington state—the nearest long-term federal lockup.

Men found insane also had to leave. Insanity and suicide were common in the North—men snapped under the pressure of frustration, discomfort, malnutrition, and loneliness. Because Alaska lacked institutions for the care of the insane, each person committed had to be taken Outside in the charge of an officer. Although time necessary for this duty taxed the manpower of the police, there was no alternative.

Of course, there were conventional departures. The exodus for the Outside in October was a fixed feature of northern life. Some of those packed aboard the last boats were leaving the North for good, having made their fortunes or given up trying. Most, however, would be back in the spring. These were miners going Outside for a deserved rest or to raise money for equipment, wives and children avoiding the rigors of winter, and merchants whose business dwindled during the cold months.

Tears mingled with cheers at the dock. Despite the mixed emotions, the pervading spirit was festive. There had been time for a few drinks while awaiting the boarding. The scene was familiar throughout the North. On the Yukon, steamers whistled impatiently to get visitors ashore and begin the long voyage from Rampart or Ruby. Lining the Chena River embankment, Fairbanksans waved their last farewells to departing friends and relatives. None of the riverboats went beyond St. Michael at the mouth of the Yukon, where passengers waited for an oceangoing ship; travelers from the Seward Peninsula, Valdez, or other coastal towns did not have to change vessels, however.

After the last vessel churned off, the town settled into its winter cycle. Nowhere in America was seasonal change noted with such intensity. Signs of fall heralded winter. And winter meant a complete transformation of life-style. Preparations must be made, fuel and provisions laid in. The first snowfall, the first ice in the river, raised speculation on weather prospects. How severe would this winter be?

Customarily, the local newspaper's editor tried to cheer his readers. Well, yes, he would admit, it is sad to see our friends and loved ones go Outside and, admittedly, we face eight months of separation and cold. On the other hand, mining prospects remain good (to say otherwise was the unforgivable sin) and conditions should be prosperous. Then, too, winter is more restful and we have time to enjoy the many fine social events planned: musicals at the Arctic Brotherhood Hall, smokers at the Eagles Hall, and boxing matches at the Pioneer Lodge. And the big iron stoves will glow cheerfully at the Eldorado, Bonanza, Board of Trade, and other saloons.

J. F. A. Strong, editor of the *Nome Nugget*, liked to warn his readers of the perils of isolation: narrow prejudices could be the result. Consider how hermits become narrow. To be undisturbed by the hurly-burly of the Outside would hold drawbacks. "We bristle, we live and we think that we think. In reality we vegetate; cobwebs are apt to grow on the brain; we are cribbed, cabined and confined by the wall of isolation . . . a bar to mental progress."[8] Perhaps Strong's little lecture encouraged the boys to gather 'round the saloon stove, there to chase off mind-numbing cobwebs with shots of whiskey and good talk.

Valdez Trail

Established trails along which roadhouses were spaced to provide some comforts were much less hazardous than those used on stampedes to remote places. The most important overland route into the interior was the Valdez Trail. Originally surveyed and built by the government, the "all American" route was intended to reach Eagle, on the upper Yukon. After the discovery of the Tanana valley goldfields, the trail was directed to Fairbanks rather than to Eagle. This route was open summer and winter; it closed only in late spring when thawing streams and mud made passage virtually impossible.

Travelers who did not care to walk the 376-mile trail but did not own dogs or horses had the option of going on one of the stage coaches of the Ed. S. Orr Stage Company. Orr began his service in 1906 with 150 horses and 50 drivers. He carried passengers, mail, and freight. Freight cost 75 cents per pound for small parcels and 50 cents per pound for large ones.

Passengers, who were charged $150, left Valdez early in the morning, enjoying some of the North's finest scenery. A glimpse of the Valdez glacier and a passage through a forest containing one of the finest stands of timber in Alaska made the first leg of the journey pleasurable. Soon out of Valdez the road commenced an uphill grade towards Keystone Canyon. The view of the canyon was spectacular as the road followed the gorge, which was towered over by huge blocks of slate and granite, and cascading narrow waterfalls (or frozen columns, depending upon the season), to heights of 1,000 feet. Before a road wide enough for double teams was blasted through the gorge in 1908, this part of the trip gave more chills than pleasure; only smaller stage coaches pulled by one team could make the narrow trail along the gorge. Rather than traverse the river ice, which might at any time be undercut by the swift water running beneath, travelers often preferred to attempt passage over the rocks that overhung the canyon. Much labor was involved in this, as the steeper places could only be surmounted by hauling the vehicles over them by block and tackle.

The summit of the Coastal Range was traversed by way of Thompson Pass. Deep winter snow prohibited the use of the pass by any but single-horse or dog sleds. The ascent is a sharp one; in the last four miles to the summit the road climbs more than 2,000 feet. From the summit, the view was superb, but the weather rarely permitted enjoyment of it. More frequently the wind roared through the exposed travelers; those fortunate enough to be Orr passengers burrowed into their fur robes. About 100 miles out of Valdez, travelers reached Copper Center, the most important point between the two terminals.

Orr's sleighs carried ten passangers on its four double seats and another on the driver's box. Horse relays were available every 20 to 25 miles; usually the journey took nine days. A nightly halt was made at one of the roadhouses to be found every 10 to 15 miles of the way. The better roadhouses had heated stables for travelers' horses and dogs in addition to standard amenities of hot food, liquor, and bunks. In the early days of the Tanana rush, the roadhouses were not distinguished for the quality of their service. One critic writing to the *Fairbanks Times* in 1906, complained that the roadhouses offered only "blankets, beans, and biscuits." The editor promptly defended the innkeepers as "good samaritans" who performed for the public weal in providing shelter on the trail.[9] It was all in one's point of view, but certainly the establishment of the Orr stage service did lead to a substantial upgrading of roadhouse service.

Promotional literature made light of the hardships and stressed the comforts of roadhouses at such places as Dry Creek, "one of the smaller home-like places along the trail," where fresh milk, eggs, and butter were available: "What more could a hungry traveler demand in an 'ice and snow bound wilderness'?"[10] What, indeed?

Twenty-four miles farther on from Dry Creek was Sourdough, where "Mrs. Yager's reputation for fine cooking is heralded up and down the length of the trail."[11] Much closer to Fairbanks was the Salchaket Post, the electric lights of which greeted the traveler from a distance as he crossed the river in the evening. On reaching the Post, "a helping hand is extended to assist him to alight. Inside all is warm, bright and comfortable."[12] Proprietors of the Salchaket Post advertised it as "the greatest roadhouse in Alaska," and insisted that "you're sorry to leave after an overnight stop."[13] One may suspect that travelers often felt this way, particularly on stormy days or when the temperature was minus 40°.

Living was not cheap at the roadhouses; the traveler had to figure on $8 to $10 a day expenses. Not unnaturally, considering the expense of freighting, costs were cheaper near the terminals of Valdez and Fairbanks than along the midsections of the trail, where prices of both food and lodging doubled. Meals, for example, jumped to $2 some 100 miles out of Valdez.

Much less used was the Fairbanks–Nome trail that followed the Tanana River to the Yukon River and the Yukon until the village of Kaltag, where the trail branched over to Unalakleet on Norton Sound. This was a much better route than could be found by following the southwestern course of the Yukon River to its mouth. The 800-mile journey was best made by dog sled during the winter. Roadhouses could be found along this trail too, and in a pinch one could find shelter with natives, woodchoppers, or in mail cabins along the way.

Providers of Beans and Bacon

The Alaska Commercial Company had twelve steamers plying the Yukon River and its tributaries—the *Alice, Bella, Hannah, Leah, Louise, Margaret, Sadie, Sarah, Susie, Victoria, W. H. Seward*, and *Yukon*—and four oceangoing ships carrying passengers and trade goods between San Francisco and St. Michael. The A.C.C. river fleet was the biggest and best in the North. Vessels like the powerful 185-ton *Bella* cruised up the river from St. Michael to Dawson in 20 days. Passenger fares from St. Michael to Circle City were $65, to Dawson, $90. Dogs went at one-third the passenger rate. Freight rates were high: 53 cents per ton per running hour with the minimum charge of $136 per ton to Dawson City. Steamers covered a 4,000-mile route on the Yukon and its principal tributaries—the Koyukuk, Tanana, and Kuskokwim rivers.

In the big towns, Nome and Fairbanks, the A.C.C., known after 1901 as the Northern Commercial Company, was well entrenched, extending its activities into providing electric power to the community. In Fairbanks Volney Richmond, company manager, became a folk hero for his part in stemming the disastrous fire that swept through the town in 1906. Fire fighters called for ever greater water pressure in their efforts to contain the blaze, but the wood-fed power plant boilers were not up to the task.

Richmond, in an inspired moment, called for the bacon stored in the company warehouse. Wagons raced to the power plant with bacon chunks to be fed into the boilers. This fuel turned the trick; pressure went up and a large part of Fairbanks was saved. It took a ton of bacon, a staple commodity retailing at 50 cents per pound, but Richmond thought it a good investment!

The difficulty involved in provisioning small towns can be illustrated by looking at the trading post of Sunrise located on Turnagain Arm, a northern branch of Cook Inlet. Sunrise and Hope, a nearby camp, were rushed in 1896, then again by the Klondike overflow in 1898. Miners wanted and needed a store to save themselves the inconvenience and extra costs of shipping in their own provisions. Thus the general manager of the A.C.C., whose headquarters was on Kodiak Island, received an early invitation to set up a Sunrise outlet. A businessman engaged in building a hotel offered to secure a lot for the company and assured the manager, "the miners want you."[14]

Since there were about 400 men in the Sunrise district it seemed a good possibility to the manager, who sent out an agent with a stock of goods. Keeping the station supplied was not easy. Upper Cook Inlet froze in the winter, closing the most direct water route from Kodiak. The best alternative route was via Prince William Sound. Shipping could readily reach Prince William Sound in winter, but moving freight on to Cook Inlet involved a difficult overland passage—a climb of 1,000 feet from the location of today's town of Whittier and a hazardous passing of the five-mile breadth of a glacier. The miners themselves made a trail to the Pacific Ocean along the Kenai Peninsula, roughly the same as that over which the Alaska Railroad was built, but costs of shipping over it were high. Practically speaking, then, Sunrise was cut off for the winter and storekeepers had to anticipate their demands in stocking up.

Well before the last boat left with the miners who wanted to winter Outside, the trader had to guess what the winter population of the camp would be. If he was too far off on either side of his estimate, trouble ensued. Fewer residents meant an unwelcome stockpiling of goods; more miners meant a scarcity of some items. The Sunrise district was not a great goldfield. From 1895 to 1900 it produced $780,000; from 1901 to 1906 the output totaled only $543,000. Thus, the digging could only support 100 or 200 miners. As low as these numbers seem, this population assured that a store would be a profitable enterprise, particularly because the supplementary activity of fur trading added to profits. *One* store but not three! Yet in 1897–98 the A.C.C. faced two rivals in Sunrise, which meant slim pickings for all.

The A.C.C. agent, L. B. Smith, was pleased that he could maintain an edge over the other stores during this period even though a rival store-keeper who doubled as deputy collector of customs was able to influence some residents. This official closed his eyes so that the proprietors of the four saloons and two hotels could bring in whiskey. In return for this favor, the proprietors of those establishments encouraged their patrons to trade with the deputy collector.

Smith's business correspondence indicates the array of talents expected of a trader in a remote mining camp. He had to have an expert's eye for quality in furs and gold dust; impurities in the gold sharply decreased its value. He had to assess shrewdly the honesty and future prospects of customers to whom he extended credit. Not uncommonly, stores carried patrons throughout the winter in anticipation of their profitable cleanup come spring.

In 1900 the A.C.C. store had only one competitor; by 1901, as the population dwindled, it was left the only trading post in Sunrise. Now when trade goods were not delivered on time the situation became more serious. Smith reported to Kodiak in June of 1901 that he was entirely out of staples. "This is a hardship on people with money, especially the lack of rubber boots for men standing in cold water. Send coal, oil, tomatoes, bacon, ham, corn, cream, lard and etc."[15] It was the same each year as the store repeatedly ran out of stock before the opening of navigation allowed the company provision vessel to reach Turnagain Arm.

But the complaints did not flow in just one direction. The general manager at Kodiak often cautioned Smith and other field agents on their management. When Kodiak complained that the Sunrise gold dust contained too much foreign matter, Smith offered an ingenious explanation: the great quantity of empty tin cans in the creeks contaminated the gold with lead. If some stock items moved too slowly Kodiak would approve their sale at San Francisco prices. Outstanding accounts bothered Kodiak very much; if an agent had too many customers in arrears, he was in trouble. Bringing solvent defaulters to justice was more than inconvenient; on one occasion Smith had to take a long sea voyage to Juneau to bring a collection suit before the court.

The company necessarily followed the fortunes of the miners. By 1910 Sunrise could no longer support a store—the N.C.C. red flag was hauled down. New goldfields attracted attention; the rush was on to Iditarod, a new camp 400 miles into the interior from Cook Inlet. Of course the Iditarod stampeders needed a store. Thus, the death of Sunrise and birth of Iditarod—long live the N.C.C.!

23

Soldier on the Yukon

EARLIER, MENTION was made of the work of Capt. Charles Farnsworth in the establishment of military posts at Fort Gibbon (Tanana) and Fort Egbert (Eagle) in 1899–1901. The U.S. Army was assigned the job of building and operating a telegraph communication system, a most useful service to the mining communities. Using soldiers as construction workers bothered Farnsworth and other Alaskan commanders because it was not their men's "proper" work. Even in the far interior of the North, military units had to face the rigors of the inspector general's examination, which required them to keep up their drill and marksmanship. Farnsworth's successor at Fort Gibbon in 1901 did not fare well in the report of the inspector general because the barracks square was not well policed and the men were sloppy at drill. Although the post was under construction and the soldiers had been kept busy as builders, their performance was measured according to conventional military standards. Such rigidity galled the Yukon soldiers. Servicemen were likely to protest work assignments. In the same period, the commander of the U.S. Revenue Cutter Service's steamboat *Nunivak* faced an incipient mutiny among sailors who resented orders to construct winter quarters. Captain Farnsworth reported no such difficulties during his first year, but re-enlistment by soldiers on telegraph duty was unheard of. Another factor in the soldiers' discontent was the attraction of high wages to poorly paid soldiers—up to $10 daily—whenever there was a stampede in the vicinity. Farnsworth's command lost seven deserters on this account during the Nome stampede.

For the men at Fort Gibbon who did not have families with them, the long, cold winter months of 1899–1900 were tedious. When spring came and the river ice broke up, the steamers charging upriver carried eager prospectors desperate to reach the latest strike. Farnsworth suspected that the transportation companies "who make a good thing of all rushes to out-of-the-way places" spread false reports of gold strikes.[1]

Warmer weather ended the inactivity and all the men went to work again on building. On July 4, 1900, festivities included raising a flag pole, canoe races, shooting matches, and field sports. Indians participated in all these events and in the grand ball that culminated the holiday celebration.

Before the end of the summer, upsetting orders reached Farnsworth: he was to take his company and move up the Yukon 600 miles to another post established at the same time as Fort Gibbon. This was Fort Egbert, located near Eagle, Alaska, about 20 miles from the Canadian boundary and 90 miles from Dawson.

Eagle was a pretty tough place at the time. Some of its citizens pilfered lumber from the camp, while others tempted the soldiers into their friendly saloons. In handling the situation, Captain Farnsworth demonstrated the ability that would eventually raise him to the grade of major general. He urged his superiors to authorize the building of a post exchange, where his men could enjoy beer in the comparatively sedate surroundings of their base. This was far preferable to the only alternative for the man who wanted to drink—the boisterous saloons of Eagle. Besides, as Farnsworth pointed out, men who earned as little as $25 per month could not afford much beer at 25 cents a glass.

Some members of the Eagle community resented the federal troops, seeing in their presence a threat to their liberty. Certainly the old, free-swinging days were drawing to a close as both the U.S. Army and the U.S. Revenue Cutter Service patrolled the Yukon. A third source of law and order appeared in the person of Judge James Wickersham, who arrived in 1900.

Wickersham and Farnsworth got on well together. The captain took the judge to the Army's hunting camp for a sporting excursion, after which Wickersham posed with his kill for Farnsworth's camera and happily reported shooting four caribou.

By plunging into the more edifying community life of Eagle, Farnsworth brought about better relations between military personnel and civilians. Permission from Washington allowed the town the use of the Army's sawmill for lumber for the courthouse and jail. Eagle residents were not eager to support a town government. As the captain ruefully remarked, "It is amusing to see how the zeal for freedom from military oppression is smothered by the discovery that the alternative is taxation."[2] Farnsworth also joined the local clubs and made a speech at the opening of the town's reading room. The social interdependence of the two communities was reflected in his scheduling twice-monthly dances at the post. Some frontier pomp and elegance attended these affairs as two officers, smartly attired in green livery, swept around in a sled pulled by four mules to gather up the town's seventeen ladies.

The military ball could be the occasion of disharmony in the small community. A Presbyterian minister, James Kirk, established a mission in Eagle just prior to the Army's arrival. Although the Kirks were invited to the ball, it was understood that they would not come. Unfortunately, however, the first ball had been scheduled for a Friday night. Farnsworth had not realized that Mrs. Kirk gave her musicale each Friday. A confrontation of grave social import was avoided when the ball was postponed.

With spring, the infantry company commenced their principal tasks: they were to build a telegraph line to the Canadian border, which would give the post communication with the Outside via the Dawson line. At the same time, Farnsworth was ordered to survey and build an all-American line that would more or less follow the Yukon River. The first job was soon accomplished, but the second was to occupy the company for two years. A 250-mile portion of the line had to be started in the spring of 1901.

A busy season of survey and construction followed the breakup. The skilled explorer, William Abercrombie of the U.S. Army Corps of Engineers, was supposed to locate the overland portion of the telegraph route from Eagle, but work on the wharf in Wrangell delayed him, so Farnsworth set out on a long reconnaissance of the unknown country. That being done, the men could begin the line.

When the military telegraph line—and a wireless as well—was in operation, the responsibility of the military was to maintain service on it. Small repair stations were established at 25-mile intervals along the line, every second one manned by a three-man crew; the extra cabins existed to provide a nearer refuge to repairmen surprised by storms or severe cold. It would be difficult to imagine harder duty than that of the crews sent out to distant stations: They received a year's food supply, clothing, boats, dog sleds, dogs, and repair material, and then were almost wholly isolated until their 12-month stint ended. For the provisioning of the stations, the Army's equipment included two small steamboats and two gasoline launches, besides mules, horses, dogs, wagons, and sleds.

Captain Farnsworth's record of his Yukon experiences reflects the interests and travails of a commanding officer, but we do have some documentation of the enlisted man's view. Henry David McCary served at Fort Egbert from 1908 to 1910 as a company bugler. Today he does not recall his tour as being either difficult or monotonous. All of the post buildings and the telegraph line were completed before his arrival, so the troops had "almost total leisure." His youth—he turned 16 at Fort Egbert—protected him from many of the temptations that imperiled older men: "I lived in a world of pure fantasy," a fantasy compounded of musical expression and northern atmosphere. In the evening he would sound taps and noted that many men would open their windows to listen. The bugle's notes bounced off the walls of the granite bluffs 1,000 yards distant and then seemed to circle over the frozen Yukon creating a five-fold echo. "I thought I was communicating with angels, or with soldiers who had died in battle," McCary mused. Of special pleasure to the men was the arrival of steamboats, bedecked with flags, "appearing as graceful swans." They watched anxiously, too, the desperate effort of the last boat to go downriver before the freeze-up, its paddle wheel hitting chunks of floating ice as it made for St. Michael and the sea.[3]

Gambling went on regardless of regulations in a bunk house maintained a mile from the post. For the length of McCary's two-year northern sojourn the poker game never stopped. Players waited for others to quit, then took their places. McCary spent virtually all of his time in the post's large gymnasium. An excellent sports program not only occupied the young soldier fully, but determined his subsequent career as a physical education instructor. Besides the gym programs, classes were given in the basic academic courses, and informal discussions on all topics were arranged.

One is not surprised to discover that career military men did not identify closely with the permanent residents of the region. Farnsworth's pessimism concerning the economic potential of Alaska was constant. In 1899 he wrote:

This is a desolate country and I would advise a man to keep out of it. There are just as many chances to make money in Pennsylvania as there are here and there is not half the hardship or risk attending it. I have not yet seen a man who has gotten rich digging gold. There is gold in the country but it is only about one man in five thousand who finds it and it is not because the other 4,999 are lazy or fools either. The other day, in dipping a bucket of water out of the river in front of our house, we found a speck of gold in the bucket. It is an easy thing to find gold here, but it is another thing to find it in paying quantities.[4]

And in 1900, gold seekers seemed a "gambling, incompetent lot of men," to him, albeit hard-working: "I have never seen men or animals work so hard as the men work up here for a bare living on bacon, beans and coffee . . . Men are slaving their lives out all over this wilderness prospecting."[5] Not even during his last Alaskan stay in 1910, when the Tanana valley, like Nome, was a well-established gold-mining region and the stampede to Iditarod was underway, would Farnsworth mention the riches of the great land's earth or acknowledge the fortunes made. Skeptical of all news of gold strikes, and viewing all rushing activities conservatively, Farnsworth's mentality differed greatly from that of a gold seeker. An officer's work was not to take chances, but to receive definite orders, lay out a concrete plan and see that it be carried out and finished exactly according to expectations. He and other soldiers certainly accomplished that. In good time they provided and maintained for interior Alaska—and its gold seekers—communications with the outside world.

24

High Rollers and Their Recreations

Tex Rickard, Gambler and Fight Promoter

The Northern Saloon was the biggest, grandest drinking and gambling place in Nome. George Lewis Rickard, better known as Tex, and George Murphy opened it in 1899 and prospered. Rickard, later to be famed as a fight promoter and builder of Madison Square Garden, went to Alaska in 1896. At Circle, the former Texas marshal worked in Sam Bonnifield's gambling joint. Bonnifield liked the young man, who was only 24 years old, and when he built a new, glamorous gambling emporium, he let Rickard have his old place. Rickard promptly lost it in a card game with a customer and went back to work for Bonnifield.

The young man rushed to Dawson City in 1897 and bought an interest in valuable mining properties. After selling his claims for $60,000 he opened the Northern Saloon. Within four months he and his partner were worth $400,000 until Rickard lost his entire interest in one night of high stake play. All together he had quite a year.

Rumors of rich pay on the Seward Peninsula coincided with his loss of the Northern, so he decided to try his luck at Nome. Before he got to Rampart, winter had gripped the Yukon River, so the gambler decided to winter over in the lively American camp. At Rampart, Rickard met Rex Beach, who was later to use the town as a setting for a novel, *The Barrier*. Both men took part in a miners' meeting that considered a divorce request. An Indian woman asked the miners to grant her a divorce from her sourdough husband because of his loud, persistent snoring. Although the offending husband promised to sleep on his stomach, she had had enough of him. The miners voted in her favor—not out of gallantry, Beach noted, but sympathy: most of them had partners who slept with their mouths open.

With spring, Rickard left for the new diggings. His slender poke was down to $21—but that was enough. In St. Michael he bought a barrel of whiskey that he took to bustling Nome. In no time he was dispensing drinks from a tent and, with the proceeds, building a new Northern Saloon.

Adversity must have tempered the high roller's spirit. The record reveals no further vicissitudes in Rickard's career like his early setbacks. In Nome he was notable for his reserve and honesty and he commanded great respect and popularity. When the first municipal election took place, Tex led the voting for city council. According to frontier practice, the leading vote-getter became the mayor, but the young man declined the honor. Nome's reputation, he argued, would be tarnished if it were known that a gambler held the mayor's office.

By coincidence the Nome populace included a number of men later to be famed in the world of prizefighting. Wilson Mizner, Jack "Doc" Kearns, Tommy Burns—a future heavyweight champion—and Rickard head the list. Rickard staged fights at the Northern; Wyatt Earp at the Dexter; and Mizner handled some of the boxers, including young "Doc" Kearns. Although the windswept shore of the Bering Sea was far from Madison Square Garden, the future shrine of professional boxing, its cornerstone was laid in Nome—at least in Rickard's imagination.

At that time boxing was a disreputable sport banned in most states. Pugs battled in dingy clubs or saloons with no fanfare and for thin purses. They traveled from town to town, picking up a handler as needed at each stop, and considered themselves fortunate if they got their three squares a day. Training camps, press conferences, and the spotlight of glamor and fame were unheard of. In later years, Tex Rickard, promoter of the first million dollar gate, and "Doc" Kearns, manager of Jack Dempsey, would be instrumental in elevating the fight game to the big time.

Fights followed the stage show in the theaters of Nome on Saturday nights. The purse in the catch-as-catch-can bouts consisted of a shower of coins from the spectators after the bout. Rex Beach recalled an occasion in which one of the scheduled combatants failed to show. His opponent, a hairy longshoreman, stepped into the ring to declare: "I came here to fight and fight I will. I'll meet any man in the house but there's one dirty dog I'd like to lay my hands on." The crowd's interest quicked at this. "Is Paddy Ryan present?" shouted the longshoreman. "If so, I'll dare him to show his cowardly length." With a savage yell from the back of the auditorium, Paddy started for the stage, shedding his clothing as he came. Both men were held as they shouted abuse at each other. Once bets were made the fight was on.[1]

Mike Mahoney, one of the greatest of the North's mushers, caught Rickard's eye when he decked another man in a brawl at the Northern.

Mahoney's forte was free-style fighting in which he employed his feet in devastating fashion; a swift and well-delivered kick to the solar plexus took the starch out of any opponents. Rickard wanted to hire the husky lad as a bouncer, but Mahoney demurred, saying his mother would be shamed if he were associated with a saloon.

In one formal match at the Northern, Mahoney took on Tommy Burns in a free-style tussle. They sparred for a few rounds until Mahoney saw an opening for a savage kick. Down went Burns for the full count, the first knockout for a pugilist who, a few months later, was to become the World Heavyweight Champion. Burns later acknowledged this defeat, graciously sending the victor a signed photograph.

Some years later, Rickard remembered Mahoney's talents when seeking opponents for champion Jack Johnson. He offered the young musher $50,000 for a fight—with no kicking. Mahoney countered with an offer of the same purse to Johnson if rough and tumble rules could apply. No chance. Alaska lost the opportunity to produce a champion. By that time Mahoney was making $10,000 a week from his Fairbanks mine, so he had no strong inclination to take up prizefighting.

Rickard was successful with the Northern but not all owners of saloons and game rooms made a profit—especially if they boozed with the customers. A case in point concerned McGinley, the landlord of the Fairbanks Hotel, and successful prospector, Frank Cleary, a fellow Irishman. The Fairbanks Hotel was not a splendid establishment by conventional standards; yet in 1904, it was Fairbanks' finest hostelry and the two-story log house occupied a good location on lot No. 1, Front Street. In season patrons of the bar could watch the arrival and departure of the busy steamboats on the little Chena River. In the winter, however, there was not much to see. Customers drank and, to be friendly, the landlord drank along with them. So it was on a November morning that Mr. Cleary gained a half interest in the Fairbanks Hotel in exchange for gambling losses suffered by the landlord during the night.

McGinley petitioned the court to void the transaction. "It is currently believed that the Lord cares for and protects idiots and drunken men," stated the court in dealing with the vexing question of whether the landlord was in his right mind at the time of parting with his property.[2] McGinley sold whiskey to the miners of Tanana for four bits a drink and was regular "in taking his own medicine and playing dice with the customers for a consideration. Who shall guide the court in determining how drunk he was at 3 o'clock in the morning?"[3]

Judge James Wickersham felt it necessary to clarify the background circumstances: "The opening scene discovers him, McGinley, drunk, but engaged on his regular night shift as barkeeper . . . to those of his customers who had not been able, through undesire or the benumbing influence of the liquor, to retire to their cabins." The judge went on, "At about 3 o'clock in the morning . . . they were mutually enjoying the hardships of Alaska by pouring into their respectable interiors unnumbered four-bit drinks, recklessly expending undug pokes, and blowing in the next spring clean-up." While thus employed, "between sticking tabs on the rail and catching their breath for the next glass," the dicebox appeared and the alleged wager took place. Cleary claimed he laid a $5 bill on the bar "and that it constituted the visible means of support to the game and transfer of property which followed. That the defendant had a $5 bill so late in the evening may excite remark among his acquaintances." The question was whether the players "then formed a mental design to gamble around the storm center of this bill." McGinley argued that at the moment "his brains were so benumbed by the fumes or the force of his own whiskey that he was actually *non compos mentis*; that his mental facilities were so far paralyzed thereby that they failed to register or record impressions." Cleary stoutly swore that McGinley's vigor and strength of constitution enabled him to retain his memory. At any rate, the game went on "and as aces and sixes alternated or blurringly trooped athwart their vision, the silent upthrust of the index finger served to mark the balance of trade." The testimony of a witness to the transaction received judicial notice. Tupper Thompson, asleep behind the oil tank stove, had been aroused to sign the bill of sale that led to the dispute. Judge Wickersham mistrusted Thompson: "Whether his mental receiver was likewise so hardened by inebriation as to be incapable of catching impressions could never be certainly known to the Court." But Thompson thought McGinley the drunker of the two contestants since he hung limply and vine-like to the bar. Cleary, on the other hand, could stand without holding on to the bar. Another witness, O'Neil, was not much help. All he remembered was that at the conclusion of the dice game, he noted the "defendant's arm around the plaintiff's neck in maudlin embrace." Cleary finished $1,800 to the good.[4]

Most cases presented in the federal court of the Third Judicial District lacked the color of McGinley versus Cleary. Judge Wickersham knew the participants intimately and his published decision reveals his enjoyment of the occasion, although there is some evidence that his clerk, Richard Geoghegan, a scholarly Irishman, may have written the opinion. "Above the mists of inebriety which befogged the mental landscape of the principals . . . rise a few jagged peaks of fact,"[5] reported the judge, who, after reviewing these at some length, reached the following decision: McGinley had indeed conveyed an interest in his property to pay a gambling debt and "equity will not assist a gambler to recover losses at his own game."[6]

In December, 1900, Tex Rickard and other Nome gamblers were arrested for—of all things—gambling. Federal law prohibited gambling, but it was customary in the North to ignore such puritanical restrictions. Nome's businessmen favored an open policy: gambling kept money circulating freely and benefited the whole economy. Although municipal government tolerated the games, the federal officials occasionally felt compelled to enforce the law.

Sometimes their compulsion derived from other motivation, however. After Rickard left Nome for good, he told Judge Wickersham what it had cost him to remain open in Nome—a mere 15 percent of the take. Each month, U.S. Marshal Frank Richards and Deputy Marshal Al Cody arranged for their split. It was just as bad elsewhere. In 1902 Rickard sold his half interest in the Northern Saloon to his partner for $50,000. In three years he had earned a half million dollars but held on to only $15,000. The gambler opened a swell place on Seattle's First Avenue called the Totem and decorated in Alaskan style. Because Seattle's hoods had demanded 20 percent of the take and Rickard had refused to comply, two cops were stationed at the door opening night and the few remaining nights of the Totem's existence. A disgusted Rickard soon returned to Nome and the Northern, remaining there until 1904 when he left the North for good.

Judge Wickersham did not believe that gamblers should be prosecuted. He liked the games to be open and observable, considering that there would be less fraud and crime thereby. During his tenure in Nome everybody was content with the gambling situation, but his replacement, Judge Alfred Moore, harassed gamblers and whores, and finally put the lid on for keeps in 1907. It was well that high rollers of the Rickard–Mizner variety had by then found other fields of action.

In Fairbanks, the same pattern was followed. As long as the Third Judicial District was Wickersham's concern, the games went on merrily. The judge did ban gambling in the small mining centers on the creeks, as he wanted to concentrate the sporting crowd in Fairbanks, where the marshal could keep his eye on them. When Wickersham stepped down, the new judge closed everything up. This signaled the passing of an era.

Unfortunately, Tex Rickard recorded neither his northern experiences nor subsequent incidents of his crowded life. He lived in high style and was always in the news. In 1929 he died in Miami. Encased in a $15,000 solid bronze casket weighing 2,200 pounds, his remains were shipped to New York in a private railroad car. Mourners waited at each stopping place along the route, and in New York people lined the sixteen blocks between the station and Madison Square Garden where the great promoter was to lie in state. If Rickard had seen the spectacle he might have resorted to a favorite expression: "I never seed nothing like it."

Why did the gambler-promoter enjoy the same popularity throughout the country as earlier in Nome? Charles Samuels, who wrote *The Magnificant Rube*, Rickard's biography, answers this question. Rickard, a country boy who rose to the top in Horatio Alger fashion, had remained honest in two of the most crooked professions existing—gambling and prizefighting.

Wilson Mizner, Prince of Nome

The Mizner brothers, Wilson, Edgar, and Addison, stampeded to the Klondike, but only Wilson endured in the North after the initial excitement. After his brothers went back Outside, he joined the rush to Nome and found there the perfect setting for his remarkable and varied talents. In Nome there were no Mounties to close saloons and gambling places on Sunday, or to otherwise interfere with the operations of a slick con man and prodigal gambler. Wilson Mizner was "Prince of Nome" according to his biographer, Alva Johnston, and, if uncrowned, he was no less meritorious. He was the kind of rogue everyone—except recent victims—loved. Big, hearty, handsome, and debonair, this Mizner was the life of every party. His razor sharp wit and prodigious abilities as a raconteur made him an ever-popular drinking and gaming companion.

Accounts differ on the origin of Mizner's sobriquet, "Yellow Kid." He was either dubbed after a comic strip character of the day, after he lost his front tooth, or, more colorfully, earned it by his habit of mining gold from his hair. According to the latter version, which appears often enough in northern annals to merit respect, Mizner labored as a saloon cashier in Dawson and Nome. Mizner was always thinking, and it struck him that he might increase his fringe benefits by a simple trick. Each day he poured syrup in his hair, so that after weighing out gold from a miner's poke in his job as cashier, he could brush his hand through his hair, leaving fine particles of the gold trapped by the syrup. At day's end he managed a fair cleanup from his hair sluicings!

All his life, the Yellow Kid had his ups and downs as he made and lost fortunes with equal ease. He set the pattern in the North, where fleecing amateur card players and running badger games provided capital for successful speculation in mining stock. Then, exuberantly, he would convey his gains to the Northern Saloon where the young, hard-eyed, honest professional, Tex Rickard, would relieve him of the burden of affluence.

Ready cash was not a must for the merry Mizner. Merchants found it painful to refuse credit to one with his open and genial nature. Every summer during his Nome years Mizner voyaged down to San Francisco to consult his tailor, Bullock and Jones, then returned as the best-dressed man in Alaska. Years later the tailor got his money after suing Mizner.

An expert at the badger game could combine pleasure with business. The idea was to pose as an irate husband and crash into a hotel room to catch a loving couple in *flagrante delicto*. Of course, the embarrassed "wife" was a part of the act. Once, in Nome Mizner almost overslept such an appointment and could not locate the revolver needed to make his "outraged husband" look imposing. Instead, he grabbed a tomato can, tore off the label, and crashed into the lovers' room, swearing to blow all three to hell with his can of dynamite. His victim bought Mizner off with a full belt of gold dust.

Although generous to a fault, Mizner did not invariably assume obligations. When his feminine lead in the dynamite drama demanded her share of the take, she received instead the empty tomato can. What, she wondered, could the can be good for? "It just got me ten thousand dollars," said Mizner.[7]

The Yellow Kid once related to Jack Hines the true events surrounding the sudden death of big Jim Wilson. Wilson ran the Anvil Bar and made a lot of money. It was the custom in the North for saloon proprietors to throw a Christmas party for steady patrons—all drinks on the house. At the Anvil, Jim Wilson seated his 300-pound bulk among his friends and urged them to drink up. The big man's booze capacity awed everyone in Nome. Though his ruddy face glowed purple as the evening advanced, he liked to think he could outdrink the whole town. After long hours of celebrating the Christmas of 1900, Wilson, his girlfriend Ione, Mizner, the Hobo Kid, the In-and-Out Kid, and others toured the other saloons, where Wilson bought drinks for the house. Eventually the party sat down to a big meal at a restaurant, then returned to the Anvil. By then it was morning and some of the gang thought it might be best to wind up the party, particularly in view of Wilson's condition—he was conscious but unable to hoist his leaden body out of a chair without help, and his puffy face appeared ready to explode. But Ione encouraged further tippling. Earlier that day she and Wilson had quarreled and now she had a plan.

Mizner possessed the best baritone in Alaska, and Wilson called for his favorite ballads. The Yellow Kid responded with "Tom and Ned," a war ballad that aroused tears. Wilson raised a tumbler of whiskey to Mizner and toasted "my oldest friend—and the best damned songbird in Alaska!"[8] Then he downed his last drink in a gulp before falling forward on his face. He was out cold but still breathing, and Ione assured the others that Wilson's condition was normal and that a doctor was not needed. Very shortly, Wilson gave up the ghost. Mizner and Wilson's other friends were saddened by the tragic end of the magnificent Christmas party but felt better when Ione distributed the saloon keeper's jewels among them. Mizner got a big diamond-studded gold watch with a heavy gold chain and a bejewelled watch charm worth a fortune. This handsome gift triggered the Yellow Kid's memory. Now he recalled that big Wilson had often said that Ione would get the Anvil at his death. Ione's plan had worked perfectly.

When the scrawny Jack "Doc" Kearns met Mizner in Nome, he was impressed: "Mizner dazzled me and had a lifelong effect on me." Mizner stood six feet, three inches tall and weighed about 220 pounds. "To a wide-eyed kid like me, Mizner was a fabulous personage, though to others he was flamboyant, overly aggressive, and bombastic," said Kearns, who became Mizner's protégé and all-'round flunky, which gave him immediate status with the sporting society of the town.[9] In later years Kearns followed Mizner's career with constant admiration as the amiable con man went on to manage boxers (both men managed the great Stanley Ketchel briefly), write Broadway plays and movie scripts, and promote Florida real estate. Mizner "had a mousetrap mind and a scalpel tongue which contributed a number of phrases to the language."[10] Kearns noted several that became familiar, such as "the first hundred years are the hardest." And a tribute to Hollywood, "It's like a trip through a sewer in a glass-bottomed boat." On social climbing, "Be nice to people on your way up because you'll pass them on the way down."

Wilson Mizner held no brief for honest toil. Although it is hard to imagine him spending much time at it, he did do some reporting for one of Nome's newspapers. As unofficial greeter of Nome, he was kept busy meeting the shiploads of new arrivals, which activity gave him a chance to lavish his charm on fair young ladies and watch for suckers among the men.

Throughout his life, Mizner remained good copy for Alaskan newspapers. Some years after departing from Nome, Mizner married a widow of fabulous wealth. Mrs. Myra Yerkes' antiquity and vicious temper were offset, in Mizner's eyes, by the millions she inherited from her industrialist husband. New York cronies teased him unendingly about his rags-to-riches success through this marriage, and newspapers hinted that Mizner was a fortune hunter.

Such reports pained the former sourdough. Finally he wrote his own account of the match for the *New York American*, which was picked up and featured in the *Nome Nugget* and other Alaskan papers. Mizner summarized his career in the North in modest terms. He did not claim to have made a fortune there; in fact, though he owned some property in Alaska, he left the North with less money than he took in, he asserted. Mizner confessed to some puzzlement at the public's response to his marriage to Mrs. Yerkes. After all, though he was not rich, he had enough for his needs—"which, by the way, are not small." Alaskans, remembering Mizner's spending and gambling habits were able to confirm the expansiveness of his needs. It would take all the gold of the North or all the Yerkes' millions to maintain the boisterous Mizner in the style in which he was capable of living.[11]

The Million Dollar Gate, Doc Kearns' autobiography, is interesting for more than his memories of Wilson Mizner in Nome. It is a revelation of the uncertainty of one's reminiscences of events that occurred 60 years past and a warning to historians. In Kearns' memory all the northern gold rushes were one. Stories heard and actual experiences are lumped; geography is confused; time sequences are distorted. Kearns constantly refers to the Klondike, though he did not get within 1,500 miles of that legendary stream. He recalls meeting Soapy Smith in Nome, although the fabled King of Skagway was killed before there *was* a Nome. This particular mixup of fact and legend is instructive because it points up the truth that, in a sense, Soapy Smith was at Nome in spirit. In his reminiscences Scotty Allen, the famous dog musher, places Smith in Nome too. Undoubtedly Soapy was at Rampart, Fairbanks, Flat, and Ruby as well. As time passed every sourdough shared in one of the great legends of the North. Consider all those dull winter days in stuffy log cabins, or more cheerfully, in rowdy saloons. Conversation invariably turned to the tricks of Smith and his ilk. Stories proliferated, and who, in this convivial group sharing fine whiskey, would admit that he had not been at Skagway during Smith's regime? Surely Smith was a genuine part of the scene in every northern camp. Memory of his colorful infamy kept his image bright. He was the predominant folk anti-hero and in the saloons and in crowded roadhouses on the trail, wherever men gathered to divert themselves, Soapy Smith lived again.

Jack Hines, Nome's Merry Minstrel

Jack Hines was a man in his twenties who thrived on the Nome scene as prospector, newsman, and mining company executive. He got to the booming town in 1900 with $300 in his pocket and a very definite expectation, the determination that his life would not be ordinary. A visit to Tex Rickard's Northern Saloon seemed in order. There, six bartenders poured whiskey with beer chasers for the crowd of patrons while painters were still at work on the building. After a drink or two Jack sang a sentimental ballad. This stimulated business, and Rickard offered him free drinks any time he cared to call at the Northern Saloon.

That first summer Hines bought a lease on a claim near Anvil Creek and made pretty good money, averaging $160 for each 12-hour day. With the freeze-up, he was ready to relax and devote himself to social affairs and musical performances at the Standard Theater and the Northern Saloon. There was not a dry eye in the house after he warbled through:

> *Once in a purple twilight*
> *Long and long ago*
> *I stood outside your window*
> *Where the roses blush and blow*
> *And heard you sing a love song*
> *Tender and sweet and free,*
> *But I did not know that in singing*
> *You were thinking of me—of me.*

Hines discovered a special spirit in Nome. Of Nome's spirit he later wrote, "It derived from the Gay Nineties in New York and San Francisco; yet it had something very much its own."[12] Part of this was owed to the winter isolation, which created an atmosphere Hines likened to that of an ocean liner vacation cruise, "The whole winter was one big celebration." Certainly the young minstrel contributed to the festivities for all he was worth. Cheers greeted his appearances at the Northern. Sturdy miners called for a song and Hines would respond with an unfailing tearjerker like:

> *Why don't you write a letter home?*
> *Why do you tarry?*
> *Do not wait.*
> *Why don't you send them just a line?*
> *Why don't you write before too late?*
> *You know they know not where you are,*
> *Or else some word to you would surely come.*
> *But you know just where a line would reach them,*
> *So why don't you write a letter home?*

This song had special meaning for many. Inquiries concerning the whereabouts of individuals were often directed to Nome's postmaster from anxious relatives Outside. A considerable percentage of stampeders severed all but sentimental ties with their families.

Fate held some earnest innings for the merry minstrel. He married a comely girl, daughter of a member of Nome's legal fraternity, and settled down somewhat. The couple enjoyed Nome's society, particularly the international set, which revolved around Count Constantine Podhorski, who was often in Nome on business matters. He was a partner in John Rosene's Northeastern Siberian Company, which held a Siberian mining concession from the Czar's government. For Northeastern Siberian entrepreneurs Nome was the supply and transportation center as well as the glittering mecca of social life. The Russian side of the Bering Strait boasted no such metropolitan center.

The Count, a Pole by birth, gave splendid parties aboard the Russian gunboat that ferried him between Asia and America. Russian ships called at Nome often in those days. Diners invited aboard were served lavish food and drinks by a dozen waiters while the ship orchestra entertained them with music. Newcomers to Nome marveled that such civility could be found in as unlikely a place as the open roadstead off Nome. Podhorski played the perfect host, flattering the ladies—of whom he was very fond—and, conversing with charm in one of his six languages, depending upon need. Near the close of the navigation season, Mary, Hines' wife, had to go Outside to attend to family matters. By coincidence or design, Count Podhorski, who had on occasion flirted with Mary, took passage on the same ship. The count wooed Mary ardently throughout the voyage, but she resisted his seductive charms or, at least, claimed she had. Finally the count grew impatient, and, according to her story, forced her stateroom door and raped her.

It was a long winter for Hines in Nome. Something had gone wrong, he knew, but precisely what was not clear. At long last, navigation opened and Mary arrived on one of the first steamers. Mary's story determined Hines to avenge Podhorski's assault. He would run the count down and kill him. Hines hired Al Cody, notable private detective of Portland, Oregon, who had once been United States deputy marshal in Nome. Cody sent word that Podhorski was in New York, so Hines made the long trip there. Friends of Podhorski warned the count of Hines' presence in time to avoid a confrontation. Podhorski disappeared once more. Eventually Cody wired that the count was in Goldfield, Nevada, the scene then of the development of a new mining field. Hines headed west.

In a restaurant the young miner found his man, strode up to his table, and fired three shots into the stocky nobleman's body. After the count pitched forward on his face, Hines calmly pumped a fourth bullet into the Pole's head. Hines' calm might have undone him. The law recognizes the extenuating circumstances of a violent act committed in the heat of a justified passion, but this incident did not quite fit the bill. Hines killed Podhorski months after the provocative act, after announcing his intent publicly, and traveling several thousand miles to find his victim. To top this cool performance, he calmed the restaurant, where pandemonium raged, by explaining his motivation—pocketed his gun and turned himself in to the sheriff.

Friends of Hines in Nome were much concerned. Reports reached the Seward Peninsula indicating that public feeling in Nevada ran high against

Hines. Attorney O. D. Cochrane, Mary's father, journeyed to Nevada to conduct the defense. A plea of temporary insanity was entered.

In the period before the trial, Hines' charm worked wonders. Preferential treatment was given him at the state penitentiary, and public opinion turned in his favor. No less a personage than Nevada's governor visited, to advise that "everybody in the State is in sympathy with you."[13] The trial lasted two weeks. Twenty-five character witnesses testified for the defendant. To Hines' indignation, the prosecutor implied that Mary was a willing victim. Cochrane had to explain away Hines' calm assertion to the restaurant patrons that he had come thousands of miles to shoot Podhorski. Hines did not know what he was saying at the time, asserted Cochrane. Despite the evidence pointing towards a premeditated crime, the jury decided that the amorous count probably got his just deserts, and acquitted Hines. All Goldfield cheered the result and so—when the news arrived there—did Nome.

Jafet Lindeberg

Prosperous miners did not defer their spending sprees until they could go out to Seattle or San Francisco. Jafet Lindeberg, one of the original discoverers of Nome's Anvil Creek, loved to take friends on sumptuous picnics. Cost was no consideration to the fortunate Norwegian who had hit it big and did not mind spreading his wealth around to awe his neighbors.

A New Yorker on a visit to Nome was invited to one of the Lindeberg picnics and was suitably impressed by the ostentatious display. The party journeyed out of town for a few miles on the Wild Goose Railroad, then left the train to travel farther over the tundra with a train of pack horses. So numerous were the heavily packed animals that the guest figured they were carrying supplies to one of Lindeberg's mines. Not so. When the party reached a favorable picnic spot, Lindeberg's servants unloaded carpets, an elaborate dining service, chairs, tables, and spirits and foods of all kinds.

All this amazed the New Yorker, who then committed an outrageous *faux pas*. Spotting a sparkling brook, he decided to taste the water. Noting his guest's approach to the brook, Lindeberg asked him where in hell he thought he was going. The guest explained and the mine owner blew up. No guest of an Alaskan frontiersman had to drink from any mountain brook. Did he think that Lindeberg ran some kind of a piker outfit? Suitably abashed, the guest resigned himself to drinking beer or champagne—but instead, was given a bottle of water imported from Europe. Each of Lindeberg's picnics cost him in the neighborhood of $10,000, and he gave them often. Lindeberg was no booster of Alaskan products; no reindeer or Bering Sea fish graced his picnic tables—all edibles were imported and out-of-season.

Lindeberg's rich mines were among those jumped by henchmen of Nome's "Spoilers," the McKenzie–Noyes gang that seized disputed claims under the shadow of the law. He proved a tough antagonist for the gang. Lawyers hired by Lindeberg and Charles D. Lane, a California miner who had bought some of the valuable Anvil properties, were those who managed to bring their dilemma before the circuit court of appeals.

The young Norwegian took the law into his own hands on occasion. He led the group of armed miners who drove McKenzie's jumpers from one disputed mine. In the course of the fracas, one of the jumpers was wounded. The shooting resulted in a grand jury indictment against Lindeberg and others involved. Judge James Wickersham was in the process of restoring order in Nome and felt that some punishment should be meted out. Lindeberg disagreed. When he learned of the indictment he grabbed his coat, took a poke of gold from his safe, and raced for the beach. The steamer *Queen*, the last ship to leave Nome before freeze-up, had already hoisted anchor, but the wily miner hired a boat crew and managed to reach the steamer in time. Prudently he wintered in San Francisco. By the next spring, the affair was forgotten.

Lindeberg was wintering in San Francisco again in 1903 when Cupid struck him with a fatal blow. One Miss Metson caught his eye and a lively courtship ensued. Unluckily, a reporter for the *San Francisco Examiner* got wind of the romance and reported on it. According to his story in the *Examiner*, the rough-hewn, youthful millionaire was illiterate and was being schooled in the ways of society by Miss Metson. The mine owner did not care for the story—in fact, he was outraged by this journalistic intrusion on his privacy. Lindeberg, who always stayed at the luxurious Palace Hotel, one fine day found the *Examiner* reporter snooping around the lobby. The reporter was invited outside, where Lindeberg pounded him to the sidewalk. Lindeberg's millions had not made him soft, as the indiscreet newsman discovered.

Photographs reveal Lindeberg as small, slender, but dynamic. Nome's millionaire worked hard and moved fast. Much of the money he earned from Anvil Creek he invested in banking and other enterprises. He also founded the commercial reindeer industry on the Seward Peninsula, an enterprise that was later developed to its peak by Carl Lomen. Rex Beach drew on Lindeberg's role for the depiction of the leading hero of *The Spoilers*. Lindeberg was, of course, something of a hero to Alaskans—not because of any fictionalized exploits, but because he was respected as a progressive businessman. And also because he had leaped from reindeer herdsman to millionaire in the best tradition of the gold legend.

The Pursuit of Swiftwater Bill Gates

If no man is likely to be a hero to his valet, he is much less likely to retain the esteem of his mother-in-law. Imagine, then, the distinction of having your mother-in-law become your biographer. This honor befell the grand plunger, Swiftwater Bill Gates. Mrs. Iola Beebe does not eulogize Bill or laud her subject beyond reality—she shows him "warts and all." Swiftwater left no similar memorial to Mrs. Beebe. Whether he felt affection for her cannot be said. All we know is that he was able to charm her again and again.

In *The True Life Story of Swiftwater Bill Gates*, the biographer unfolds the saga of the millionaire miner. Prior to the Klondike strike Bill was not much to boast about, a scraggly, whiskered, ordinary man of 35 years, five feet, five inches tall, a dishwasher in a roadhouse at Circle. There he heard about the riches of the Klondike where he rushed to stake the fabulous No. 13 Eldorado.

It pained Mrs. Beebe to recount Bill's indiscretions once he filled his poke from the easily reached bedrock of Eldorado Creek. "Had he exercised the most common, ordinary business ability," he could have cut himself in on other claims and, with little strain, made $1 million the first season.[14] Instead, he dragged his heavy poke into Dawson, set up drinks in a saloon, shouted his discovery to the world, and announced his intent to buy the finest gambling hall in town.

Dressed in a black Prince Albert coat and black silk top hat, Bill soon opened the Monte Carlo, a gambling emporium that knew no limit on its games. Then Bill revealed his fatal weakness. Among the dance hall girls who flocked to Dawson City to share the fortunes of the miners were the comely Lamore sisters, young hustlers in a good position to make their fortune.

Bill craved Gussie Lamore with a burning passion. Enough to proffer Gussie her weight in gold—$30,000 by his estimate—if she would marry him. No, said the lady, let's just be friends. So they became friends, until a trifling lovers' quarrel separated them. The quarrel and Bill's jealousy were preludes to the legendary egg episode.

None of the famous incidents associated with Bill has been more often and variously repeated than the romantic episode of Gussie and the eggs. It seems that Gussie entered a restaurant one day on the arm of Bill's rival and the couple ordered fried eggs, the highest priced item on the menu. Bill, observing this and knowing how much Gussie loved eggs, bought up all the eggs in Dawson and either: (1) presented them all to Gussie; (2) had them fried and flipped them out the window to hungry dogs; (3) treated the dance hall girls with them; (4) or something else. All the facts of the case are in dispute, including the price paid for the eggs. Pierre

Berton's admirable *Klondike* tries to run them down, but even witnesses' reports conflict.[15] The weight of authority supports the opinion that Bill turned over two coffee cans full of gold for two cases of eggs. In Mrs. Beebe's version of the egg story Bill bought up all the eggs in Dawson for $2,280 in gold dust and tempted Gussie back to his own breakfast table because she could not otherwise get eggs. Mrs. Beebe did not believe this means of regaining a lover represented much of a victory for Bill. "We all figured the laugh was on Swiftwater, and I think every woman who reads this story will agree with me."[16] She did not understand that earning the sobriquet "Knight of the Golden Omelette" might have been a suitable enough return on Bill's investment.

No one in Dawson was surprised when Bill gave Gussie two coffee cans filled with gold dust, but the following episode in this tumultuous courtship staggered the camp. Even men who regarded Swiftwater as a fool wondered at the extent of a woman's treachery. It seems that Bill sent Gussie to San Francisco with the understanding he would follow later. Nuptial bliss would then commence. Gussie departed. Bill wound up his affairs and joined her in the Bay City, but the obstinate girl still refused his hand.

Bill countered by marrying Gussie's sister Grace to make Gussie jealous. While a splendid house in Oakland was readied for the couple, they bedded down in the luxurious bridal suite of the Baldwin Hotel. There Bill displayed his wealth to the world. If a mother-in-law and others can be believed, he tipped bellhops to point him out to other guests as the "King of the Klondike," as indeed he was.

But the "King of the Klondike" made little headway with the Lamore sisters despite his lavishness towards them. Grace left him even before their palatial home was ready and commenced divorce proceedings. In a rage, Bill swore off the Lamores—and, one would think, all other women as well, and went back to work.

After his partner secured a mining concession from the Canadian government on Quartz Creek, in the Klondike, the plunging miner was ready to restore his diminished fortunes. First he voyaged to London, got financial backing and bought the most modern hydraulic mining machinery available. When the machinery reached Seattle, Bill prepared to convey it to Dawson. In Seattle's Hotel Butler, a mutual friend introduced Mrs. Beebe to Swiftwater Bill Gates. "When I think of what happened to me and my daughters, Blanche and Bera," wrote Mrs. Beebe, "and of the years of wretchedness . . . that came after, I am tempted to wonder what curious form of an unseen fate shapes our destinies."[17]

Mrs. Beebe claimed to have been wary of Bill despite his "low musical voice, the kind of voice that instantly wins the confidence of nine women out of ten."[18] She knew the Lamore stories from the newspapers and was traveling north with two young, lovely daughters who caught Bill's eye at once. Yet she needed help. She hoped to establish a hotel at Dawson, and Swiftwater pledged his assistance.

Bera Beebe, 15 years old, deliciously plump, pink cheeked and blue eyed, spun Swiftwater into spasms of longing. She liked him, too, so he spirited her aboard the *Humboldt* just before the steamer's scheduled departure for the North. Unfortunately for their longed-for tryst, mother caught them before the steamboat cast off. But love will have its way despite the vigilance of the most conscientious parent. A month later the two parties encountered each other once again in Skagway, at the frenzied height of the '98 stampede. This time Bill and Bera got away, up over the Chilkoot Pass to the Klondike, before Mrs. Beebe could obstruct them.

Mrs. Beebe followed. It was the second stage of her odyssey, her epic, unrelenting pursuit of Swiftwater over trails marked with disappointment, frustration, woe and, unaccountably, sudden bursts of sympathetic understanding. How could the dastardly Swiftwater, Bera's abductor, get around Mrs. Beebe, eluding her after solemn promises, even managing to swindle her out of her entire fortune? Pierre Berton, chronicler of the Klondike, has speculated that despite all the wounds inflicted, Iola Beebe shared her daughter's desire for the wily Gates. Bill treated Bera handsomely for a time. No treat was too costly for her, even melons at $40 each. Mrs. Beebe joined the newlyweds and swallowed her resentment of Bera's paramour. In time she became a grandmother.

Meanwhile Gates' affairs floundered. Creditors pressed him hard. More money was needed to develop Quartz Creek. After pouring in all the capital he amassed from Outside and Dawson, he tapped Mrs. Beebe for $35,000. When his partner did not come through with a promised $100,000, Swiftwater was through. To avoid embarrassing his creditors, he departed suddenly for Nome, the scene of the freshest gold discoveries. He took Bera but left the baby with grandmother. Mrs. Beebe was abandoned and broke. Soon she was dispossessed as well. One of Bill's partners turned her out of Bill's cabin because she refused to permit him to share a bunk.

Indirect news concerning Gates reached Mrs. Beebe. With his usual luck, the miner had taken a lay on Dexter Creek and struck it rich. Gates and Bera wintered Outside in their usual splendid style. The anguished mother-in-law, meanwhile, subsisted on public charity through her second winter in Dawson.

Finally a letter from Chicago reached Mrs. Beebe in the spring. All was well. Gates had more than enough money to pay back her loan. She was to meet the family in Nome. Bill and Bera would steam there in the first ship out of Seattle when navigation opened. "Isn't it curious how a woman will forget all the injustice she suffers at the hands of a man," Mrs. Beebe reflected, "when it seems to her that he is trying to do and is doing the right thing?"[19]

After waiting for three weeks in Nome, fruitlessly calling at the post office for mail each day, Mrs. Beebe began to suspect trouble. She was right. A Seattle newspaper caught her attention. A front-page story recounted a new romance for Swiftwater Bill Gates. This time his inamorata was Kitty Brandon, another 15-year-old. Bera, who by this time had delivered a second child, had been left in Washington, D.C. Gates was on his way to Alaska when Kitty, a convent girl, attracted him. A swift elopement and marriage followed.

Now Gates was in for some anxiety. Another mother-in-law joined the chase. Kitty's mother found Gates at a Seattle hotel but found it hard to corner him. As Mrs. Beebe put it, "then it was that Swiftwater evinced that capacity for resource and tact which, as all his friends know, is one of his most distinguished characteristics."[20] Gates and his bride scurried out the back door of the hotel to a waiting hack and lit out for Tacoma.

Mrs. Beebe and her deserted daughter set up housekeeping in Seattle and watched for the reappearance of the bigamist. Since Gates was good newspaper copy, the press kept track of his arrivals, and before long the women read that the miner was in town. Mrs. Beebe prowled all the hotels searching for the elusive miner and discovered him, after forcing a door, lurking in a bed. At the moment Gates was down and out. His wardrobe, usually the height of fashion, consisted of a few cast-off garments and shoes through which his toes could be observed. Yet he knew a man in San Francisco who would back a prospecting venture in the Tanana country. Penniless as he was, how could he get to San Francisco?

Mrs. Beebe maintained her record for being the softest of touches. After putting the miner up for the night, giving him breakfast, and washing his clothes, she pawned her jewels and loaned the proceeds to Gates. Off Gates went to San Francisco. With a replenished wardrobe and his dazzling verbosity, he soon gathered thousands of dollars from investors and returned to Seattle. Carelessly, he forgot to call upon Mrs. Beebe, who again depended upon the newspapers to alert her. Before she could confront him, the miner took ship for the North.

Gates quickly made another fortune on Number 6 Cleary Creek, near Fairbanks. Mrs. Beebe got wind of this and set out on the long journey to the interior via Skagway, Dawson, and the Yukon. In Fairbanks she cornered the famous miner and Don Juan. All would be well, he assured her, once he made the spring cleanup on Number 6. Enough gold for all creditors and wives would be washed up.

Kitty's mother was in Fairbanks too, living in a tent on Bill's property and waiting for the cleanup. The presence of his two mothers-in-law did not fluster Bill, whose luck was running, and the cleanup netted $75,000. Bill and Mrs. Beebe then embarked for the Outside. The newly prosperous miner shocked his mother-in-law on the voyage down the Tanana and Yukon rivers. Two of the passengers were young women he had induced to join him. By the time the steamer reached St. Michael, at the mouth of the Yukon, Mrs. Beebe's patience was exhausted. She telegraphed Seattle, warning Bera to meet the *Ohio* if she hoped to get any money, and she made up her mind that there would have to be a showdown of some kind. The Seattle showdown followed the tradition of previous Beebe–Gates encounters. The police were looking for Gates; Bera had charged him with bigamy. After some furtive negotiations, which not surprisingly, ended in Mrs. Beebe's efforts to help Bill escape the law's net, the miner was arrested in the Beebes' hotel room.

Then began an extraordinary proceeding. Gates summoned the superior court judge, a battery of lawyers, and the wine waiter. Bottle after bottle enlivened the legal discussions. Because he was short on cash, Mrs. Beebe paid for the wine. In time, agreement was reached. The judge would postpone the bigamy case if Gates would deposit $2,250 with the court. This money would be used for maintenance of Bera and attorney's fees. Mrs. Beebe loaned Swiftwater $1,250. Eventually Bera received $750.

Gates' troubles were not over. Kitty Gates appeared and demanded money, threatening to press the bigamy prosecution. Gates pleaded desperately with Bera. Unless she divorced him, all of his Alaskan property would be taken. Their children would get nothing. Bera complied. Now he had to contend with his other wife, Kitty.

The *Fairbanks News*, like other Alaskan newspapers reported zealously on Swiftwater's matrimonial woes. Joyously the *News* recounted the squaring of the Beebe conflict and Kitty's filing of criminal charges just when Bill began to enjoy the Outside.[21] Fortunately for Bill's good name, the police just then arrested Kitty for running a disorderly house in the fashionable Cherry Street district of the city. Police accused her of blackmailing Gates and indicated they had arrested Kitty repeatedly during the time the miner was slaving away in the North.

Kitty insisted that the police were out to get her. Earlier she had told the press that "these cops here would pinch me for larceny if I stuck my hand into a vacant lot." It also came out that Kitty was Gates' niece and that he had silenced outraged family members by making wedding presents to the clan from "a bankroll that a horse couldn't kick apart." Soon after their elopement Gates had returned to the North and Kitty had determined to make a place for herself in society. She had been "the star performer in several of the best known police courts between Seattle and San Francisco. Her specialty, according to the *Fairbanks Times*, had been "a clever demonstration of the art of removing the works from a telephone without kicking it more than once, and she has never failed to draw a full and appreciative audience."[22]

Back in Fairbanks the next season Swiftwater made another big cleanup. He also took time to socialize a bit. Dan Sutherland, a Fairbanks miner who later served as Alaska's congressional delegate, worked a mine adjoining Bill's on Cleary Creek. When the miners on the creek pitched in to raise a tent as a social hall, Bill offended all at the opening ball by appearing with a "lady who did not meet all the moral requirements of the fraternal elite." The irate and righteous miners threw the couple out, in spite of the fact that Bill had contributed the planks for the dance floor. Sutherland thought the Cleary people made a mistake "in bouncing the best woman dancer in the whole town."[23] Swiftwater Bill Gates had enemies as well as friends; his success inspired envy in some, but awe and admiration in others.

Meanwhile Mrs. Beebe was still left without compensation, so she set out once more on the arduous trip to the North. The journey's events included two shipwrecks on the Yukon. Once more the familiar scenario took place. "I will square everything up," insisted Bill.[24] She believed him for the last time. The rascal skipped town for Seattle with Mrs. Beebe in hot pursuit.

In Seattle Mrs. Beebe ended her physical pursuit and had recourse to the law. Gates threw all his creditors into confusion by assigning his mining properties to a partner and declaring bankruptcy. Mrs. Beebe got nothing. Thus it was in 1908 that the frustrated woman sought to make a few dollars and vent her spleen in one of the oddest of biographies, *The True Life Story of Swiftwater Bill Gates*, hoping to resolve the question of "what manner of man, in Heaven's name," is this Swiftwater Bill Gates? "Perhaps some people will say that when Swiftwater Bill, down deep in his prospect hole on Eldorado, looked upon the glittering drift of gold that covered the bedrock, the glamor of that shining mass gave him a sort of moral blindness, from which he never recovered."[25]

However negligent Swiftwater was in marital and money matters he hardly deserved the jolt given him by Superior Court Judge Griffin in the course of one trial in Seattle. In the lowest of blows the judge attempted to destroy the legend of Swiftwater's famed extravagance in the matter of Gussie Lamore and the Dawson eggs. The egg question arose again when Bill's lawyer contended that his client's reputation as a millionaire was undeserved. Bill's great wealth was a myth developed from his alleged purchase of a crate of eggs at an exorbitant price to please his sweetheart.

Judge Griffin smiled at his opportunity to strike a blow for truth—and perhaps make a few headlines. "I know the story is false. I was in Dawson at the time." Then the judge went on to relate that he had looked with envious eyes upon the first crate of eggs to arrive, as did Gates, and how the owner's hopes of exacting a fortune for the precious items were dashed by the arrival of several other boats with enough eggs to flood the market. "Eggs at once dropped to $7 a dozen, and that was the price at which Gates bought them."[26] But legends of '98 were not so readily snuffed out by judicial dictum of 1906. The Gates eggs, whatever they had cost—$2 each, $7 each, or their weight in gold—will always be remembered and so will the little man who, perhaps, tendered them to his lady love.

25

Settling Down: George Pilcher, Will Ballou, and the Lomens

Lower Yukon

Earlier, the experiences of two 1898 stampeders as they settled on the Yukon River were described—George Pilcher on the lower river and Will Ballou in Rampart (*see* Chapter 10, pages 58–62, and Chapter 14, pages 88–91). Remaining in Alaska for many years, each avoided the larger gold towns and the lure of repeated stampedes, yet both represent pioneers whose lives were altered by the great Klondike gold rush.

Pilcher's relations with his native neighbors were interesting. Although he reflected his day's prevailing white attitude of superiority to the natives, he was much more involved in their community life than were frontiersmen who lived in white communities. Although contemptuous and sometimes violent when natives failed to measure up to his personal work ethic, his was basically a spirit of live and let live. Their community, such as it was, and Pilcher were mutually dependent. He was buyer and seller to them. He occasionally employed a man to chop wood and a woman to sew.

As a vigorous man in the prime of life, Pilcher had sensual needs that could not be satisfied by a yearly trip to Nome; thus he often entertained "native daughters" in his cabin. Such occasional liaisons worked out better for him than one attempt to form a more permanent arrangement. His "marriage" to a native widow terminated when her relatives encouraged her to sulk during the "honeymoon." Then, in an effort literally to bring him to the altar, she left the launch on which they had been cruising. This ended Pilcher's patience; he put her baggage ashore and remained adamant to her pleas to be taken back. With great relief he moved back "into [his] happy old cabin," alone once more.[1]

Pilcher's phonograph was the delight of the area. Night after night he entertained whole native families with its music while dispensing tea. These "tea parties" seemed as important to him as to his guests. They helped dispell winter boredom, though Pilcher complained at times of the monotony of the parties as well.

When the government first established a school in a nearby village, Pilcher tried to advise the teacher on his handling of the natives. He frequently acted to bring about mutual understanding between the white and native cultures. Schoolteachers and their families, new to the area, sometimes could not cope with the natives.

The woodcutter occasionally visited his white neighbors, especially when he found a convenient house where he could stay overnight on an extended trip. Such infrequent meetings among old friends usually included all-night talk sessions in which news of the latest gold strikes figured prominently. Pilcher, in turn, was a generous host when visitors called at his cabin; they were always sent away happy. There, on the Yukon, where ships and people traveled towards the Tanana valley, the upper Yukon, and elsewhere, Pilcher had his place, a home in his cabin, a role to fulfill. There, he never had to face the corruption and crime that plagued larger communities. On his trips to St. Michael and Nome he would carouse with the best but soon became disgusted with town life. After a visit to Nome in 1901, he lamented over "doing the rottenest town I was ever in. Poverty. Extravagance. Murder. Robbery. Wreck and ruin. Am sick of Nome in two hours."[2] Of course, he also had an awesome hangover.

Yet violence intruded even into Pilcher's cabin one winter's day. A stranger calling himself Harry Bates stopped there and asked for a meal. Bates was a desperate man, whose real name was Loper, a deserter from the U.S. Army post at St. Michael. After Loper finished eating, he began preparations for leaving. The woodchopper made small talk: "That's a tough proposition mushing to St. Michael this frosty weather." Loper growled a reply: "There are lots of tough propositions in this world."[3] Philosophies exchanged, Pilcher turned away from the door. At that moment Loper pulled out a revolver and fired at the back of Pilcher's head. Somehow the bullet missed its mark. The woodcutter whirled around, catching his assailant's arm just in time to divert a second shot. Loper tore from his grasp and fled the cabin. Pilcher grabbed his shotgun, useless because Loper had surreptitiously emptied it while his meal was being prepared.

What followed tells something about the spirit of the more stalwart Alaskan pioneers. There were no police within hundreds of miles, but Pilcher was determined to see justice done. The effort cost him months of time but seemed worthwhile to him. He sent off native messengers to spread the word up and down the river. Two days later he set off in pursuit. After two days' searching he discovered his man at a native village. To avoid risking the lives of natives, Pilcher did not confront Loper there, and the rogue got away again. Relentless in pursuit, Pilcher kept on for three days without sleep until he caught up with Loper once more. Within 200 yards Pilcher threw back his parka hood so that he could be recognized, and called to Loper to stop. Loper had no intention of being detained, so Pilcher fired on him with his shotgun, hoping to wound rather than kill. The wounded man was unable to travel, so Pilcher hired a man to guard him and went alone to St. Michael, where he turned himself in to the United States marshal and languished in jail until he and Loper could be tried in Nome. Loper was convicted and Pilcher freed. Of course, the woodcutter received no compensation for all his efforts at law enforcement or months of time lost.

The experience did not break the woodcutter psychologically or physically. Upon being released he found himself 550 miles from home and flat broke. Not wanting to wait for the opening of navigation for the short steamer cruise to St. Michael, he decided to return on the trail. By borrowing a few dollars he was able to purchase a bicycle. He struck off April 7 on the trip that must have been as difficult a bike journey as has ever been undertaken. No roads linked Nome and the lower Yukon; the trails of sorts were partly awash in slushy snow. Despite the ruggedness of the way and the snow blindness that afflicted him along the way, Pilcher rode into his camp on May 8. By then his bike's much punctured tires had been stuffed with rope, but he had made it and was surpassingly glad to be home at last.

Founders of civilization in that part of the world, both native and white, had to have great practical skills, courage and endurance, good health, and beyond that, enough creativity to entertain themselves during the long winter cold, darkness, and isolation. They were not only able to accept the extreme winter's hardship, but they seemed to love it and be proud of their accomplishments. Pilcher's self-sufficiency was characteristic of pioneers. Besides providing for himself and to some extent for his family back home in the 'States', he built his own cabins and stores, made much of the equipment he needed, kept his boats and mining gear in repair, and even made his own mukluks and snowshoes. In addition, he wrote poetry—doggerel, in the Robert Service vein—short stories, articles on Yukon life for the Buckeye Press Association, and a book-length manuscript *Life Along the Yukon*, which, unfortunately, has been lost. Often he worked at portraits of his family, drawing them in crayon from memory or photographs. Pilcher did mechanical work on what he called a

skigo—a motorcycle that he adapted for skis. It may be that he was one
of the first inventors of the snow machine that has supplanted the dog sled
in native villages and has become a popular sporting vehicle for Alaskan
town dwellers.

Pilcher's world did not keep him in close touch with current events.
Once, at St. Michael, he read a political account in a magazine already
two years old and was startled to learn of events of which he had heard
nothing. "Verily, I am a trifle out of the way," he remarked, we may
suspect, without too much disappointment.[4] Communication was better
after radio reached the region, and Pilcher even traveled to Marshall from
his camp on Elephant Creek on an autumn day in 1932 to hear news of
Franklin Roosevelt's election. World War I is referred to in only one diary
entry describing a speech someone made at a dance concerning the importance of conserving materials. The trenches of France must have seemed
far away from the peaceful Yukon.

No portrait of Pilcher is available, but he must have been a hearty
character. Throughout his life he complained of headaches, pleurisy,
neuralgia, colds, flu, and, worst of all, severe toothaches that had to be
tolerated until his summer visits to the dentist at St. Michael. If this were
not enough, there were the various bruises caused by flying wood, frequent
bouts with snow blindness, frostbite, and monumental hangovers. Yet his
constitution weathered all this, perhaps because of his vigorous approach
—when a swig of Dr. Wyley's Cureall did not bring relief, he would take
up his axe and dash out to chop wood.

Pilcher did not begin mining until 1913, when he turned from his
trader's and woodcutter's life to a new life working claims with several
others near Marshall, not far distant from his other lower Yukon River
residences. That he was much respected by his neighbors is indicated by
his election to the office of recorder.

George Pilcher never struck it rich through gold mining, from which he
retired in 1940 at the age of 77, but he earned a living. In 1935 he sent
his notebooks to the University of Alaska with an apology for the brief-
ness of his daily entries. "They were never intended for anyone to read,"
but were kept as a means of recording dates "because I was a lone dweller
on the lower Yukon."[5] Pilcher thought in his modest way that the university might find the notebooks of some interest and pointed out that one
entry noted a sale of wood to the *Lavelle Young*, which was carrying E. T.
Barnette's party upriver to its eventual founding of Fairbanks. George
Pilcher is gone now. He was taken Outside a short time before his death
and, sadly, could not be buried by the Yukon River as he had wished. But
his notebooks are full of life and comprise precious documents on the
pioneer world of the lower Yukon.

Will Ballou at Rampart

Will Ballou put in two winters mining in Rampart and made enough money to go Outside in 1900 for a visit with his family. After a winter back in Vermont, Ballou returned to Rampart in the spring of 1901. His zest for the community had not faded. He regaled Walt with the local gossip:

My friend, Tommy McGraw, went to Short and Dirty instead of Scar Face Ellen as was his habit in reaching town. Passing Ellen's cabin later she took three shots at him with a 44 Colt, carefully missing but getting him to beg for his life. He spent the night with her. Moral: Don't play with the affections of a squaw. He is trying to keep it quiet.[6]

Though clearly an earnest and hard-working young man, Ballou did have fun sometimes. In September, 1901, he took a holiday in Dawson. The town was less lively in 1901 than earlier when it had been the center of the original Klondike rush in 1898, but it was still the metropolis of the Yukon and offered more amenities of life than the much smaller towns along the river. Three dance halls entertained the stomping miners, who bought four chips for $1: one for the dance hall girl, one to the house, and two redeemed in drinks at the bar. "One has no idea what excesses a man will go to until seeing a western dance hall," wrote Ballou, who could not imagine why miners threw away a hard-earned $20 to gain one little kiss from a showgirl.[7]

The young man found romance on this Dawson trip. It all began with a tear in the eye of Miss Corrine Gray, caused by the harassment of the Mounties. The Mounties had it in for Miss Gray for whose unrequited love one of their officers had committed suicide. Her professional interests were suffering through this police interference and she was sinking into debt. Jail threatened. Would Ballou save her? Indeed he would, and just before his steamer was to embark for the voyage downriver to Rampart, he smuggled the girl into his cabin. Clearing Dawson was no problem, but by the time the steamer got to Forty Mile, the last stop before the United States border, the Mounties on duty there received a telegram notifying them of Miss Gray's departure. A boarding party searched the ship from stem to stern. In Ballou's cabin they found a sleeper they could not rouse; an empty whiskey bottle protruding from under his pillow told the story. They gave up, and the girl, who had been secreted under the blankets, came up for air. Sheer delight attended the balance of the cruise, as Ballou enjoyed the affections of the grateful Miss Gray. He would have been "perfectly willing to sail on like that for ages." They discussed the future. She decided to open a sporting house in Rampart where he could "go for a home whenever he wished." Despite the risks of running afoul of the Mounties, or perhaps because of them, Ballou enjoyed the little adventure.[8]

Gossip attended the arrival of the steamer at Rampart, where the small community watched the proud man disembark with his attractive young lady. But Ballou was outmaneuvered. After establishing the girl in his town cabin, he had to spend some time at his mine. On his return to town the girl was betrothed to another young man in town, Luther Durfee, a friend of Ballou's and the wastrel son of a big Wisconsin lumber tycoon. With some reluctance Ballou gave the couple his blessing. For a time the town's 400, as Ballou liked to term the social leaders, ostracized him, blaming him for the match between a woman of dubious reputation and the wayward young man. The displaced lover assuaged his disappointment with work, of which there was always plenty on his various claims.

Ballou wrote to his Vermont family often, unnecessarily apologizing to his brother Walt sometimes for the lack of literary talent in his letters. It wasn't easy to write gracefully while living in a 16- by 18-foot cabin with six or eight other men—yet such company also added a measure to life. These were men who called the world their home; their stories revealed a rich variety of experiences. Ballou admired all their characteristics save one, "that everlasting craving for change, travel and excitement which keeps them always on the go and always broke." But, he asked his brother, "Do you wonder why I like this life with these free and careless people, any one of whom . . . will take their winter wages next spring and buck the first gambling table until not a dollar is left, and move up or down the river to another camp."[9]

In the summer of 1902 Ballou took a temporary job with the Northern Commercial Company, which was closing down a store at Fort Hamlin, a little Yukon station 40 miles northeast of Rampart. Ballou figured his bookkeeping was up to the task since all the records were encompassed in a single cash book. He found it "restful to be out of the whirl of big Rampart," which by that time might have had a population of 500 or so.[10]

A little romantic musing enlivens a correspondence and Ballou enjoyed titillating his brother at times with alluring images of the free and untrammeled life along the Yukon. Although his experience had never included observation of Turkish harems, except possibly through the pages of the Sunday newspaper supplements, he could make comparisons:

We see a fair maiden with black, sparkling eyes, her red lips and row of white teeth shining through the everlasting smile, dressed in her bright calico dress without corset or underclothes and seated in the doorway of her tent on a pile of luxurious fur robes and blankets doing bead work and making a picture similar to what you see of the harem in Turkey and those eastern countries. The maidens have such a pleasant, although rather bold (at least it would be bold . . . in Boston), way of blushing very coy like . . .[11]

In the winter of 1903 Ballou liked the Yukon country less. "I'm getting to hate this desolate waste of a country pretty fierce and long for even a quiet little humble home out in god's beautiful country."[12] The rheumatism common to miners affected his mood that winter; he could do no more than hobble about. Word reached him that his friend and rival Durfee had died, leaving a lonely widow. The widow, his erstwhile love, took charge of nursing Ballou's rheumatism, and for a time all was blissful in the couple's town cabin. Unfortunately, it was not to remain so. The young woman was pregnant by her late husband and badly addicted to opium. Ballou tried without much success to keep her off the dope and to ration her formidable booze consumption. Her baby lived only a short time. When money was sent her from her in-laws in Wisconsin, Ballou submitted a bill for her use of his cabin. "My deed was horrible and disgusting and against the rules of the underworld," he admitted, but he blamed the hard life in the North for his cold-blooded attitude.[13] In response, the widow put him out of his house. After a few weeks she demanded that he find some drugs for her; at his refusal she brandished a revolver and threatened both their lives. Her threat came from her dramatic flair, Ballou figured, but soon after, she shot herself to death. The incident may have been what made Ballou decide to abandon the life of Rampart's leading gallant. That fall he visited his family in Vermont, coming back to Rampart in the spring with a bride.

For the next few years Ballou continued to work in the Rampart region. Occasionally he would go farther afield for prospecting but he always returned to his mines at Rampart. He enjoyed the pleasures of family life but became more and more disenchanted with mining. "I have little to show for years of hard work," he reported in 1906.[14] Other times things looked somewhat better, and he was able to invest his earnings in his brother's business in Vermont. His appointment to the office of United States commissioner in 1906 indicated his respectability in the community. Now he was Judge Ballou and responsible for minor law infractions. In the declining town his duties were not arduous. Still, each year he considered whether he should leave Alaska for good. "Hope to leave mining and go Outside," he wrote in 1909.[15] Then in 1910 he thought he might move instead to the new mining center at Iditarod. In 1911 he had "been studying rather to go on working and handing profits to the Northern Commercial Co."[16] That fall he did go to San Francisco for the winter, but he was not content there either: "San Francisco is a lonesome town. Wish I was back on the Yukon. No good red hot stove in the Post Office as at Rampart where a fellow can start a good argument on most any subject. People are too busy here."[17] After looking for some investment property the Ballou family returned to Rampart.

In 1915, efforts were made by the citizens of Rampart to get the town school reopened. The decline of population had forced its closure a few years earlier. The attempt failing, Ballou was concerned about his son: "The boy is seven and by the time he is nine we will have to rope and tie him to get him to school unless we go Outside."[18] This was probably one reason that, at long last, Ballou sold out his Rampart interests and moved to Seattle in 1917 after almost 20 years in the Yukon. He tried to enlist in the Army but at 40 was over the age limit. For a time he had an auto sales business; then he traded it for a 60-acre farm outside Seattle. Next he obtained a "soft job" as a supervisor with an auditing firm. The aging sourdough settled into his new life—the lure of Alaska's gold no longer moved him. Judge Ballou, for so many years one of Rampart's leading citizens, never returned to the North.

The Lomens of Nome

Among the 1900 rushers to Nome had been attorney G. J. Lomen and his son, Carl. The senior Lomen started a law practice while his son took up mining. Adjusting to the camp was not difficult, as both men had plenty to do. Their housing was poor the first winter, a single room above the law office, but when summer came, G. J.'s wife and the other children voyaged to Nome and a new family home was built. The Lomens took to Nome, where they were to remain for many years. Although not a part of the saloon crowd, they enjoyed the color and style of the unusual Bering Sea community. One character who impressed them was Mother Woods, alias Dawson Kate, alias Stampede Woods—a formidable mining woman. Mother Woods was about 50 years old in 1900, somewhat weatherbeaten and wrinkled, but tall and slim. She wore a skirt and jacket of wool trimmed in leather, a cowboy hat, and high wading boots and she drove one of the finest dog teams in town. In her mannerisms and speech Mother Woods resembled a man and was known to use coarse language when excited.

Gus Boltz was another celebrated character. When he landed at Nome in 1900 his ambitions were prodigious. Gold was in the ground, and all one needed to do was stake claims. Boltz staked and staked, jumping about 100 claims already spoken for, but this proceeding did not win Boltz' fortune. Next he turned to a surer thing, delivering Nome newspapers outside of town; miners wanted the news and paid 50 cents for papers that sold for 25 cents in Nome. Conspicuous because of his flaming red beard, stocky build, and contentious manner, Boltz loved to talk and argue to the point of nonsense. People like the Lomens thought him a little crazy; whenever this opinion was expressed to Boltz, he had the perfect rebuttal: "How can I be nuts when I'm Boltz?"[19] When Boltz lost a lawsuit over ownership of a Front Street lot, he lost his trust in the Nome judiciary. Judge Alfred Moore became the target of his vengeful humor. Boltz named his dog team leader "Judge Moore," and whenever he mushed through town for his hauling business, he found reason to upbraid the leader with cries of crookedness and incompetence, using the kind of language favored by dog drivers and mule skinners.

Carl Lomen kept a diary all his life. During his first years in Nome he noted occurrences important to a young, healthy man. When he was not working—either at mining, legal clerking, or in any of the family enterprises that developed over the years (clothing store, photo studio, drugstore, lighterage service, and reindeer meat industry)—he was active in sports, church choral singing, arranging dances and other social events, Bering Sea excursions to hunt walrus, and getting to know his Eskimo neighbors a little better. Carl showed more interest in Eskimos than did most mining men. He jotted down a vocabulary as he learned new Eskimo words and enjoyed conversing with the natives. Lomen remarked on the Eskimos' response to the turbulence of the 1900 stampede and the rusher's tendencies to steal everything within reach. "White man plenty steal."[20] Eskimos could not understand why. People like the Lomens gave Nome a refinement and social stability that caused its transition from a brawling camp to a genteel—though unique—community. In their special ways they contributed to the development of frontier life.

26
The Guggenheims Come to Alaska

Another Metal

Gold opened Alaska to development and brought the waves of stampeders to the great land, but other minerals were mined as well. Tin was produced on the Seward Peninsula during Nome's early boom years; galena was mined in the '80s on Golovnin Bay; gypsum deposits were exploited in southeastern Alaska. But aside from gold, the only mineral strike of sensational proportions was copper. One of the richest copper lodes ever known to the world was developed in the Chitina River valley, a rugged region lying between the Chugach and Wrangell ranges in south-central Alaska.

The first explorations of this region were made by U. S. Army personnel, the Abercrombie 1884 expedition and the 1885 party led by Lt. Henry Allen. Lieutenant William Abercrombie and his men spent two months trying to ascend the Copper River, of which the Chitina is a tributary, before giving up the attempt. The Copper is a large river swelled by glacier-fed tributaries. It spills into the Pacific through many channels that shift across a 15-mile stretch of delta, spewing blocks of glacial ice and boulders, and is virtually unnavigable. Allen succeeded where Abercrombie failed by alternately canoeing and portaging up the river with the aid of local Indians. Chitina Indians showed Allen samples of the metal they customarily shaped into utensils. Information regarding the copper was published but did not cause any great excitement at the time.

Subsequent exploration of the region came as a result of the Klondike gold rush. Some stampeders chose Valdez on Prince William Sound as a port of entry for an all-American route to the interior. As a result of their activity, the Army assigned Abercrombie the task of making a military reconnaissance of the Valdez–Copper River areas. In 1898–99, his men surveyed and pushed through a military road from Valdez to Copper

Center, 50 miles up the Copper River from the point where the Chitina joins the main branch. One member of the party was civilian mining engineer Stephen Birch, who was anxious to investigate copper prospects. Influential backers had grubstaked Birch and arranged for his attachment to the Abercrombie party.

Other prospectors also were in the field. One party, climbing to the 4,000-foot level above Bonanza Creek, spotted great, green cliffs of copper. This discovery was made in August, 1900, and a mile-long claim was staked. The prospectors were stunned by their own success when a sample of the ore was tested, revealing a 70 percent copper content, substantial amounts of silver, and a trace of gold. Stephen Birch bought out the discoverers, paying $25,000 to each of the eleven partners, and formed the Alaska Copper and Coal Company to continue exploration of the region's prospects. In 1908, a Morgan–Guggenheim combination bought the mines, retaining Birch as manager.

The Syndicate

The entry into Alaska mining by the Morgan–Guggenheim interests, usually referred to in Alaska as the "Alaska Syndicate" or, more casually, as "the Guggs" was of momentous importance for the territory. Until 1908, Alaskans had only one whipping boy, one institution to which all woes could be attributed—the federal government. The Northern Commercial Company, of course, drew some fire, but its villainy could not compare to that of the Washington pols. Now a monster of similar strength and one with a voracious appetite appeared to complicate the northern scene.

The story of the Alaska Syndicate is an integral part of the gold era's history. Its interests were not confined to what became known as the Kennecott copper mines; it bought out the largest shipping company serving the North and formed the Alaskan Steamship Company, which called at all Alaskan ports from Ketchikan to Nome with a fleet of seventeen ships. The Syndicate operated fish canneries and mined gold as well, carrying on many of the large-scale dredging operations in the Klondike, the Iditarod district, and elsewhere in Alaska.

Reasons for the unpopularity of the Syndicate in certain quarters surface clearly. Some were real, some imaginary. It was true that the Alaska Steamship Company gave preferential rates to subsidiaries of the Syndicate. It was true that the Syndicate lobbied effectively in Washington for a reduction of the fish pack taxes that were passed on to Alaska. It does not appear, however, that the "octopus" had the capability—even if it had the desire—to strangle all Alaskan enterprise it did not control, as was so often asserted by the northern press. Readers of the *Nome Gold*

Digger, for example, learned in 1907 that the "vampire which has already started its blood sucking operation is laying its plans for the complete subjection of the country to its will."[1]

The Irish Prince

To exploit their rich copper mines the Syndicate needed a railroad to penetrate the interior over some of the most forbidding country in the North. The approaches to the Chitina valley were an engineer's nightmare. Over miles of Copper River flats, full of mud and quicksand, a roadbed supported by thousands of tons of rock had to be laid. Then the road had to traverse several icy miles across a glacier, and bridge the river between two other towering glaciers; thence the grade was forced through the mountains to reach at last the mines 200 miles from the coast.

The 5,000 men who labored from 1906 to 1911 through rain, snow, sleet, and mud were headed by Michael J. Heney. Heney was one of the best known and loved men in Alaska. A handsome, two-fisted, articulate, superlative leader of men, the "Irish Prince" had earlier built the only other long-distance line of the gold era, the White Pass and Yukon Railway connecting Skagway and Whitehorse. Heney was notable for his determination and his firm belief in his own judgment. His assessment that the route from Cordova (then Eyak) was the only practical one gained him a victory over rival builders and eventually forced the Syndicate to buy him out, while retaining him as construction boss. The Syndicate initially chose Valdez as a terminal because of its fine harbor. But the possibility of developing extensive coal lands along the route provided incentive to run the railroad from Katalla instead. Katalla's vulnerability to storms necessitated the construction of a breakwater to protect shipping in the unsheltered roadstead. At a cost of over $1 million, the breakwater was built.

Heney gambled that the Katalla breakwater could not survive the fierce storms of Controller Bay. He also gambled that he could best another construction rival, H. B. Reynolds, a plunger who saw moneymaking possibilities in Valdez after the Syndicate pulled out for Katalla. Valdez people were, of course, bitterly disappointed when their economic bubble burst, and this left them ripe for Reynold's picking. He organized the Alaskan Home Railroad to build a line from Valdez. "Alaska for Alaskans" was his cry. Keep "the Guggs" from exploiting us, he urged. With the backing of a misguided former governor of the territory, John Brady, he sold thousands of dollars of railroad stock in Alaska and Outside.

Newsman Strong of Katalla

The survival of three boom towns depended upon the results of the railroad race. Katalla's position was critical; its only economic reason for existence was as a terminal to the copper mines and coal fields. J. F. A. Strong (also known as Major Strong), a newsman who has appeared in this mining frontier story on several other occasions, established the *Katalla Herald*. Why Strong sold out his interests in the *Nome Nugget* and rushed to Katalla is not clear. From 1899 to 1907 he kept Seward Peninsula readers enlightened and amused with his causes and feuds. Probably Nome had become too sedate for the fiery editor who had taken part in most of the major northern stampedes. Once in Katalla with his press intact, Strong felt right at home. His boosting of the camp began at once. At Katalla, "where the Rails meet the Sails," as the *Herald* legend had it, the future shone bright. But once the Syndicate halted construction of the railroad there, the end was in sight.

During the 1907–1908 winter no work was done on the railroad but editor Strong tried his best to assure *Herald* readers that all would be well: "Persons interested in other points, and paid knockers and piebiters may pound and hammer until their auditors are deafened but the unimpeachable fact remains that Katalla, with its immediate coal and oil resources and a practically level grade to the copper fields, holds the key to the rail situation."[2]

Strong had much to fret about and recalled that he was well experienced in the news business, where "vicissitudes and trials have been found," but that Katalla was a new low. "No mail, no telegraph . . . even the grapevine route is threatened." The "imbecile" post office had cut Katalla from the mail route. "Katalla has received an unexpected bump. It has been slugged and knocked, kicked, cuffed and buffeted on all sides."[3] Perhaps, suggested one *Herald* reader, the post office has joined the Guggs to kill the young, promising town.[4]

On top of these woes the Seattle and Cordova newspapers were gloating over Katalla's demise: "The yellow *Seattle Times* and its equally saffron-hued proto-type published at Cordova, dwell much on the 'porcupine diet' which Katalla people subsisted on for two months." Nonsense, huffed Strong, in fact we even had to support a crippled man here who was abandoned by his Cordova friends.[5] The *Herald* took to running in each issue the headline:

ANYWAY WE HAVE THE COAL AND OIL

This did not bring the Syndicate back, so Strong replaced it with another:

THEY WILL NEED THE COAL TO GET THE COPPER

Unfortunately for these arguments, the coal fields near Katalla no longer served as an attraction. In 1906, President Roosevelt had withdrawn all Alaskan coal fields from public entry, calling for legislation that would extend the 160-acre ownership limit. A long political battle focusing on conservation policies prevented any resolution of the situation. It was not until 1915 that the coal fields were reopened for entry. What really doomed Katalla's hopes and caused the Syndicate to move to Cordova was the wrath of nature Mike Heney had gambled on. A devastating autumn storm smashed the town's breakwater to bits in 1907. Clearly there was no way to protect shipping at Katalla.

Keystone Canyon "Massacre"

Before the Syndicate succumbed to Mike Heney's judgment that Cordova afforded the best entry for the railroad, the Keystone Canyon affray occurred. The incident multiplied hostility towards the Syndicate in Alaska, seeming to indicate it would stop at nothing—including murder and jury fixing—to crush opposition to its stranglehold on Alaska's resources.

Keystone Canyon, a narrow defile, offered the only passage through the mountains for the Valdez route. Construction crews of the Syndicate had built a grade through the canyon before switching to the Katalla route. Because Reynolds' Alaska Home Railroad could not be built unless the Keystone Canyon was utilized, a confrontation was precipitated.

When 200 of Reynolds' workers marched into the canyon armed with tools (Reynolds' story) or weapons, including short-fused dynamite (the Syndicate's story), they were expected. About forty "Gugg" workers awaited them. According to Reynolds, who later swore out warrants for a weapon search, many of the men packed revolvers. But apparently the only shooting was done by Ed Hasey, who scattered the Reynolds' gang with rifle fire, wounding five men, one of whom later died.

As an aftermath, Valdez teetered on the brink of lynch law and rioting. Only the quick action of the military headed off chaos. A speedy trial was ordered for Hasey with the venue transferred to Juneau. According to Syndicate supporters, including the historian who most recently has examined what evidence is available, Ed Hasey was a deputized United States marshal who acted in his official capacity to avert a battle by firing on an armed mob after ordering its dispersal. The anti-Syndicate view is that Hasey was an employee of the Syndicate who was deputized for the particular purpose of coloring use of armed force with legal authority.[6]

Bribery?

Efforts to arrive at the truth of the matter are muddied by the conduct of the trial. To the glee of former district court judge James Wickersham, recently elected delegate to Congress on an anti-Syndicate platform, evidence surfaced indicating the possibility of bribery of witnesses and jurors.[7] A Syndicate employee who had lost his job provided the former judge with an expense billing submitted by one of the attorneys retained by the Syndicate to defend Hasey. Among the expenditures were listed the costs of entertaining prosecution witnesses and jurors. Hasey was acquitted at his first trial on the charge of second degree murder. Subsequently, he was tried for assault with a deadly weapon, convicted, and sentenced to an 18-month sentence. That two juries considering the same evidence should differ on the essential facts in dispute raised the suspicions of many Alaskans.

Whether bribery was actually involved in the outcome of the first Hasey trial cannot be absolutely determined. Syndicate representatives had easy answers to the expense accounts in question: the witnesses had been called by the government prosecutor, then rejected as hostile to the government case, and subsequently used by the defense; as for the jurors, their entertainment by the winning attorneys was customary practice in Alaska. Some Alaskans felt the government witnesses in question had been "got to" by the Syndicate and had accordingly changed their stories, but no certain evidence exists.

27

Other Camps

OUT OF THE MOSS AND NIGGER HEADS AROSE AN INLAND EMPIRE. Thus cried the banner headline of the *Iditarod Nugget*. Most readers of the *Nugget* were familiar with its style because it was edited by an old hand on the northern scene, J.F.A. Strong of Skagway, Dawson, Nome, and Katalla. Strong's arrival in Iditarod in the fall of 1910 to start the town's second newspaper indicated the growth of the booming camp that had developed over the 1909–1910 winter.

Goldfields were sparsely located in the great area of the lower reaches of the Yukon–Kuskokwim basin. Iditarod, named after a tributary of the Innoku River, which flows into the Yukon from the south, and Ruby, somewhat higher on the Yukon, were the only sizable towns and they flourished at about the same period. Of course, other smaller camps developed, settlements like Ophir and Marshall produced fairly well for a number of years, as did numerous other camps scattered over the North. But the distinctions between a camp and a town are the population and the amenities that accompany greater numbers. One of these amenities is a newspaper, which takes us back to editor Strong. Undaunted by his failure in Katalla, the town that collapsed with its hopes of becoming the Copper River railroad terminal, Strong was once more on the lively scene of a stampede, marveling at the "embryo city abuilding these ten days," noting that "one year ago you could not find Iditarod on the map."[1] This year the gold output would be about $500,000, reported Strong, but next year it could be as much as $5 million.

Rushers reached Iditarod by two routes, neither of them easy. The longer but less difficult in navigation season was from Valdez to Fairbanks over the trail, thence by steamboat down the Tanana to the Yukon, and finally to Iditarod by way of the Innoku River. The alternate route, used primarily in the winter, was a trail blazed all the way from Seward on the Gulf of Alaska, a proper test for men and dogs stretching 489 miles.

As in most new towns, some food shortages existed at Iditarod during its first winter. Transport routes developed rapidly wherever the need arose in the North—thanks to the work of the U.S. Army—but a season's lag was normal. As always the *Nugget* editor saw the bright side: "Iditarod may be somewhat shy of solids, but there is a large promise of no shortage of liquids. If one really needs something to be thankful for, how about this?"[2]

Strong was struck by the familiarity of the townspeople. By his calculation, fully 90 percent of them had been in the North since Klondike days:

> The number of old timers in Iditarod is rather large. Some of the newcomers are Chechakos or tenderfeet and are few. This is essentially a community of sourdoughs, pioneers who have blazed many a hard trail and whose residence dates back to 1898 or before.
>
> Here is a record that probably cannot be duplicated by any other section of Alaska — a camp composed almost exclusively of pioneers, the seasoned kind, that know conditions in a new mining camp will be hard and try to meet them with smiling faces and courageous hearts. So unfailing is the spirit of the pioneer that he might well be numbered in that class of whom it may be said, "Blessed are they that expect nothing, for verily they shall not be disappointed." But they keep hustling just the same.[3]

Such a camp resembled a family reunion. Charles Hoxsie, once Wyatt Earp's partner in the Dexter Saloon, came down from Nome to open a saloon; Dan Sutherland mushed in from Fairbanks with his bride; Jujuira Wada, associated with "Cap" E. T. Barnette in the founding of Fairbanks, appeared. Two other old-timers bumped into each other on the street, "What in hell did you come here for?" asked one. "Hell, I had to go somewhere, hadn't I?"[4] So it was with the veterans who could not resist a new stampede. Even before the town was fairly launched, a stampede to the Kuskokwim River took several hundred men on a fruitless winter journey.

Iditarod's remoteness from the principal routes of transportation made it harder to reach than any other gold town of similar or larger size. It would have no reason for being once the shallow bedrock was mined, which would take only a few years. Yet, according to booster Strong, Iditarod was "the Hub" of Alaska. His argument in support of this designation was logical though not practical. Seward was 489 miles away, Fairbanks 499 miles away, and one had to travel 484 miles to Nome. One would think these mileage figures could only support a contention that Iditarod was about 500 hard traveling miles from *anywhere* in whatever direction, but Strong contended that its location made it an important terminus for the railroad! Naturally the railroad builders would see the wisdom of routing their line from Seward to Iditarod before continuing on to Fairbanks and Nome! That would have been *some* railroad, but unfortunately by the time the most obvious route was chosen—Seward to Fairbanks—Iditarod was well on its way to becoming a ghost town.

Most of the gold diggings were located near Flat, a town nine miles away connected to Iditarod by a narrow-gauge tramway. Mules pulled wagons along wooden rails laid none too securely across the sodden tundra. In later years a few automobiles with iron flanged wheels were used. Only one romantic episode is associated with the tramway: a robbery of gold that was being freighted into town. In no time at all the thieves were apprehended and the gold was found on the tundra where they had abandoned it in their flight.

Donald McDonald, later to become Alaska's foremost road builder, was raised in Iditarod. His mother ran a hotel and he sold newspapers. He remembered selling papers to girls living in the little row of bungalows that made up the pleasure quarter of the town. A sign displayed on the front door of each bungalow indicated whether "Fannie," "Annie," "Sally" or another held court. At the back of each dwelling rose a mound of empty beer bottles, the size of which was a sure guide to the girl's popularity. Young McDonald was amazed by the attitude of the town's respectable women who, before they would chance a face-to-face encounter with a whore on the boardwalk, would cross the street, even if it meant wading through a foot or two of mud. Despite this reaction, the girls comported themselves with ease in the male-dominated society; each spring they gave a ball that was always the well-attended highlight of the social season.

The churchgoing folk of Alaskan towns were better known to the Rev. S. Hall Young, the Presbyterian minister who had already served 20 years in the Panhandle before the gold era opened. For eastern readers of a church publication, Young described his journey to Iditarod, trying to convey some idea of the distance involved: 1,000 miles from Seattle to Skagway; 110 miles over the White Pass railroad to Whitehorse, where a two-week delay occurred because the ice had not yet gone out on the Yukon River; then 450 miles to Dawson; 975 miles down the Yukon and up the Tanana for a visit to Fairbanks; a return trip of 275 miles down the Tanana to Fort Gibbon on the Yukon; then 543 miles down the Yukon to Holy Cross; finally the "most tedious" part of the journey on the sluggish Innoko and Iditarod rivers "both indescribably crooked, absurdly crooked, resembling the convolutions of an Elizabethan ruff more than anything else I can think of."[5] For the first 320 miles his steamer pushed a huge barge ahead of it, and often either the steamer, the barge, or both were grounded on sandbars in the river. At Dikeman, passengers had to transfer to small gasoline launches for the final lap of 80 miles.

Iditarod's site did not charm the veteran preacher; it had been hastily built in a hummocky, swampy area where the mosquito infestation was notorious—even for Alaska. But cheered at least by meeting many friends he had known at other camps, Young went right to work. For $40 a month he rented a cabin for a reading room; for preaching he secured the largest building in town, the Arctic Brotherhood Hall. Besides providing newspapers and magazines for a town reading room the preacher placed reading material in the roadhouses and mining camps. This was vital service; more than one miner lauded Young for having "saved us from insanity" over long winter months.[6] The heartiness of pioneers like the Reverend Young is evident. At the time he established his mission in Iditarod he was 65 years old. Yet that winter he mushed to Seward on the coast to attend a meeting of the Presbytery of the Yukon.

Because the bedrock of the local creeks was very shallow, open-cut mining was more practical than sinking shafts and drifting from them. Open-cut mining called for heavy equipment and the means to secure it. Many claim holders sold out to agents of the Morgan–Guggenheim Syndicate. Editor Strong had noted the appearance of representatives of his old Katalla nemesis in town but crowed, "We're not afraid."[7] By 1912 the Syndicate had the region's first dredge in operation.

Strong decided in 1912 that the town could no longer support two newspapers. He shut down his plant and went Outside, taking his wife on a tour of Europe. Ralph Lomen, who had come down from Nome to start a stationery and photography business, closed down after a few months. Other men of Iditarod and Flat rushed to the newest goldfields, at Ruby on the Yukon River. Iditarod continued to produce gold, but the population dwindled rapidly. In 1914, Iditarod's population was 500, Flat's 300; at its peak in the summer of 1910, Iditarod had boasted of 2,500 residents. The *Iditarod Pioneer* ceased publication in 1915. By 1917, many of the town's buildings had been moved to Flat. Before many more years elapsed, both Iditarod and Flat had become ghost towns; the "inland empire" promised by editor Strong of the *Nugget* had been of short duration.

Ruby

Ruby was stampeded in 1911 and 1912. For a change, the goldfields were conveniently located. They were on Long Creek not far from the

Yukon River bank were the town sprang up in a hollow between two
bluffs. The booming town on the lower Yukon was easily served by the
river's steamboats, and soon after the discovery it had a population of
1,000 miners and camp followers. In the usual frenzied fashion, cabins,
hotels, stores, and saloons were constructed.

For a time two newspapers were published, but as the population dwindled from the first season's peak, a merger of the two took place. The
Ruby Record-Citizen insisted that the district would prove to be the biggest in Alaska; but, in fact, the placers were to be practically worked out
in a few years. Following the demise of a town through its newspaper is a
sad affair: the efforts of the editor to infuse his readers with his own
optimism and spirit wear thin as the decline continues. Of course, we are
spared the last days of any mining center because the newspaper quits
publishing before the end. In Ruby, as elsewhere, the year 1918 marked
the end of the golden era of Alaska. The *Record-Citizen* published its last
issue on August 3. Just previously its editorials had become petulant:

> *In these war times, the* Record-Citizen *has not raised its prices and yet
> its business is shrinking steadily . . . Do your part, and help support the
> paper. Advertise and subscribe and you will be a loyal citizen, and also
> get your money's worth . . . in this connection we have used up a number
> of pencils and a lot of paper trying to figure a way to keep this paper going
> but it seems a hopeless cause and we feel we must shortly announce our
> final issue; simply lack of support.*[8]

Upper Koyukuk

The 554-mile length of the Koyukuk River drains an area of 32,600
square miles. Gold discoveries on the upper river north of the Arctic Circle
led to a stampede of about 200 men to the region in 1898. Gordon
Bettles, a veteran sourdough, founded a store, and a town named after
him developed. Later Coldfoot, then Wiseman, became the principal
towns.

The upper Koyukuk was almost as remote as the neighboring Chandalar district. Because larger steamboats could not make it to the upper
river, the cost of living was very high there. The population of the region
never reached the level capable of supporting a newspaper. Wiseman's
permanent residents never exceeded 350. It was a tough country; yet,
because it held gold, men mined there for years. New stampedes in 1905
and 1908 attracted several hundred men but most did not stay long. Gold
deposits were sparsely located, but some were rich. Together, several
produced more than $1 million over several seasons. From 1900 to 1918
annual production averaged well over $200,000, hitting peaks of $420,-

ooo in 1909 and $368,000 in 1913. Estimated total production from 1900 to 1931 exceeded $5 million.[9] From 1918 on the district declined rapidly as employment opportunities elsewhere drew men out of the country. Gains totaling $5 million seem modest when compared with the gains for districts like Nome, Fairbanks, and even Iditarod, yet the upper Koyukuk holds first place by far among mining areas located north of the Arctic Circle.

Above the Arctic Circle

I am not making any claim on which to cause a stampede. I am simply going back to open a new district in a quiet way . . . There are many gold camps of similar importance to Caribou, Klondike, Nome, etc., yet to be struck in the North by men who dare face the conditions, and let me say right here, that Alaska has many of these men who dare face the conditions . . . men who are not posing for notoriety but are quietly blazing the trails for others to follow.[10]

Thus prospector Sam J. Marsh wrote to his backer, U.S. Congressman William Sulzer of New York. Marsh's trail was one of the longest and most severe ever blazed in the North. Marsh, Tom Carter, and Frank Yasuda developed the Chandalar River district north of the Arctic Circle, a region unmarked by roads, trails, or navigable rivers. To reach Fairbanks, Nome, Iditarod, Ruby, and the other Alaskan camps even in the early days was a cakewalk compared to the travails of journeying to the Chandalar country. Today, except by bush plane, the area is not much easier to get to than it was in 1902–1903, when it was first explored. The Chandalar was not very rich country, but the effort to develop it is certainly an essential part of the mining frontier story. It was tough country and needed tough men to exploit it—as was the case with much of Alaska.

In the fall of 1901, on their initial prospecting trips, Marsh and Carter loaded a schooner with supplies enough for two years and set sail from Port Clarence on the Seward Peninsula. From the mouth of the Colville River, the largest of the rivers draining the Brooks Range and flowing into the Arctic Ocean, they intended to cross the mountains to the headwaters of the Koyukuk River, a northern tributary of the Yukon. They had calculated on the rigors of the country—both were well-experienced mining men—but their woes began even before they reached the Colville.

Soon after the party voyaged past Point Barrow, the northernmost tip of North America, a fierce Arctic storm struck their path. For nine days their little vessel was battered by winds raging from 30 to 60 miles an hour. The storm drove ice floes through the wild waters, threatening to smash the schooner to the bottom. Sometimes, exhausted from the strain of dodging the huge icebergs, the crew anchored her to one and drifted with it for a time. The 35-ton schooner was a sturdy craft with nine feet of solid oak on its bow, especially built for ice navigation.

Even so, by the eighth day, the vessel's decks were so thick with ice from sea spray that she was almost waterlogged. The men anchored behind some large bergs, 300 feet high, which were aground and seemingly stable. All but a single watchman went below to sleep. In the middle of the night came a terrible cry: "For God's sake all hands on deck!" Hurrying up, the men saw with horror that the very berg they had anchored to was bearing down on the schooner. Because every part of the ship was encased in ice, it was impossible to get onto the berg to cast off the line. The captain hacked at the hawser with an axe, but it was too late. Before they could get up the sail, the ship collided with a berg that tore away the bowsprit and forward bulwarks—"Then with a roar as if hell were loose, came a blast that seemed to pick the vessel out of the water and carry her along through the air."[11]

For 10 minutes the uncontrolled ship banged into other icebergs. Finally she grounded on the beach, dumping the deck cargo into the water. As the stunned men were trying to collect their wits, nine of the eleven sled dogs housed on deck broke loose. Maddened by the storm and shipwreck, the snarling malemutes had to be destroyed. Before this was accomplished, the dogs bit the captain badly.

The ship's crew were picked up by another vessel but Marsh and Carter did not give up. They recovered what supplies they could and built winter quarters out of driftwood on the shore. After an uneventful winter, the prospectors were eager to continue their journey. Unfortunately, however, the two remaining sled dogs died, leaving them without means of hauling their freight into the interior. Thus the men decided to separate: Carter set out to the west hoping to acquire dogs from natives, while Marsh headed into the interior alone.

It is sometimes difficult to understand how prospectors could endure so much hardship in their quest for gold. Indeed, Marsh was of the breed "who dare face the conditions" of the North. He built a sled out of driftwood and hauled provisions about 100 miles into the interior, where he cached what he could not carry on his back. Then he proceeded as far as the summit of the Endicott Mountains, working his way along the northern slope, exploring the basins of the Canning, Sagavanirktot, Shaviovik, and Sadlerochit rivers. To cross these streams he often had to build a raft of willows to support his pack while he swam behind it in the icy waters. He sank innumerable prospect holes without finding any signs of gold. It was a frustrating, arduous, and lonely summer—a stretch of 128 days without seeing another person. With fall, he was glad to meet

Frank Yasuda and to build winter quarters with the Japanese trader's party.

Frank Yasuda was another legendary figure of the gold era above the Arctic Circle. He had worked with Charles Brower at the latter's whaling –trading station at Barrow and had traveled all over the Arctic trading for furs; so he knew the region intimately. Marsh jumped at the chance to join forces with Yasuda. The Japanese was married to an Eskimo woman and was traveling with a group of her relatives. Eskimos along the Arctic coast had been having a tough time since the decline of the whaling industry and Yasuda persuaded his wife's family to relocate in the interior. Eventually, other Eskimos followed suit and joined Yasuda's party at Beaver, the town Yasuda founded on the Yukon some 50 miles southwest of Fort Yukon.

After rendezvousing with Carter in the spring of 1903, Marsh was ready to continue prospecting in the Brooks Range. Yasuda traveled with Carter to the southeast, while Marsh traveled southwest. Marsh ran short of food in July, just after discovering some interesting prospects. Since he was closer to the Yukon settlements than to Barrow he headed for the great river by way of the Chandalar River. For the first 14 days of his trek, he subsisted on little more than a daily handful of flour and salt. Reaching a navigable stream, the tough prospector built a raft and floated down the Yukon River in comfort and style until he encountered rapids that upset his raft and nearly drowned him. Having no recourse save pushing on, he built another raft. After four more days he reached an Indian village where he obtained some dried moose meat. As hard as were the travails of the prospector in the North, they could have been far worse but for native samaritans—many an ill-fed Eskimo and Athabaskan family shared its food with men who otherwise would have perished.

When Marsh finally limped into Fort Yukon he decided to call it quits for a spell. He drew maps of the unknown country for the members of a United States Geological Survey party at the fort, then caught passage on a government steamboat for St. Michael and Nome. Marsh needed a rest but it was hard for a determined prospector to sit around Nome for long. He started off again, this time choosing another route to the Colville River, via Kotzebue Sound and the Kobuk River. The freeze-up caught his boat at the mouth of the Kobuk, where he wintered. With the spring of 1904 he boated his provisions to the headwaters of the Kobuk, packed across to the Noatak River, and finally reached the Colville by late summer, a journey of hundreds of miles across formidable mountain ranges. Once there, he found that his supplies were not ample enough for the winter and the following prospecting season, so he returned to Nome. From Nome he went Outside to raise a grubstake that would allow him to return to the region that had seemed promising on his earlier trip. Only a man convinced that he was on the verge of a great discovery could have persisted.

In Washington, D.C., Marsh met United States Congressman William Sulzer of New York. Born in 1863 Sulzer was a practicing attorney and politician in New York at the time of the Nome stampede. He rushed to the Seward Peninsula and invested in properties there, then returned to New York where he remained affected by the gold bug. Political office as governor and congressman did not dampen his enthusiasm for the North. Impressed by Marsh's explorations and confidence Sulzer guaranteed his support. The story of northern gold mining should not ignore the contribution of men like this backer. Investing in untried ground was high-risk speculation, and it took a special type of person to do it; it was, after all, safer to buy blue chip stocks. But capitalists also knew the pangs of gold fever. Over the years, Sulzer was to pour $200,000 into the Chandalar country and realize only very minute returns on his investment. At the time he met Marsh, Sulzer was most optimistic about the North; he could not know then how rugged a region was the Chandalar.

While Marsh was Outside, Carter and Yasuda continued to prospect the southern slope of the Brooks Range. Provisioning was always a problem. Carter traveled alone in 1904 to the Koyukuk River, where the new gold camp of Wiseman had developed. There he worked for wages to get a grubstake. The next year he and Yasuda traveled together to Barrow to reprovision and to meet Marsh. Marsh did not show up that summer, so the men crossed the Brooks Range to the headwaters of the Koyukuk. They established a winter camp on the Dietrich River, where the Eskimos of their party saw their first evergreen trees.

Caribou were plentiful there. In one day the Eskimos killed ninety, rolling the carcasses down the snow-covered hill to waiting dog sleds. The party put in the winter marketing caribou and mountain sheep to miners on Hammond River and Nolan Creek, the gold-bearing tributaries of the Koyukuk. The upper Koyukuk diggings, for which Wiseman was the trading center, were just 60 miles west of where the Chandalar discoveries would be made. The two camps accounted for most of the gold mined above the Arctic Circle.

In the early spring of 1906, Carter heard that Marsh had returned to the Chandalar by way of the Yukon. The Carter–Yasuda led party broke camp and set out for the Chandalar, hoping to encounter Marsh. In the summer that year, Carter found good signs of paydirt on Little Squaw Creek, a tributary of the Chandalar. Soon, 200 men stampeded there from the Koyukuk. Marsh arrived there in December, holding an appointment as United States commissioner and postmaster obtained through Sulzer's influence. More men were expected to stampede in from Rampart, Circle, and Dawson. The town of Caro rapidly developed. Carter mined a couple of hundred dollars in gold before winter shut down his operation. Over the winter the men concentrated on getting supplies in from Circle via Fort Yukon. That spring Marsh took out $27,000 from three claims he had located on other creeks. Things were looking up in the Arctic goldfields.

In 1907 Marsh reported his progress to Sulzer; he had been successful in staking claims but his work had been slowed because he had not received necessary supplies. A supply shipment to Herschel Island off the Arctic coast had been arranged for the summer of 1906. A tender serving the whaling fleet was supposed to deliver them to Herschel Island, where Eskimos were waiting to mush them into the interior, but it had not arrived. This was Marsh's last attempt to provision by way of the Arctic Ocean.

While waiting at Herschel Island, Marsh got wind of the murder of an Eskimo by a whaler seaman. As a United States commissioner he was the law enforcement officer rseponsible for the region. After a 400-mile journey to the Chandalar, "including a rafting of the Salmon—which can only be described by the word Hell in pronounced capitals," he heard of Carter's discovery and the subsequent stampede. Though he and his men were "worked down to shadows," Marsh continued on to Fairbanks to report the crime before looking for Carter.[12] His exertions were wasted. Law enforcement officials in Fairbanks telegraphed Nome, but nothing was done because the crime was thought to have been committed within the jurisdiction of Canada's North-West Mounted Police. The Mounties considered the affair a matter of American jurisdiction.

Most of the Marsh–Sulzer correspondence is taken up with the Marsh's pleas for more money. It may be that their company failed to prosper because the backing came in such small dribbles. "You cannot make any mistake in getting your forces in line," wrote Marsh to Sulzer in 1907. "The time is now ripe; I am not mistaken, neither is my judgment colored by the flash of gold; I have seen every important camp in Alaska bud and blossom and I am not dreaming when I say, that here is every earmark of a great camp."[13]

In 1908–1909, Marsh investigated quartz-mining possibilities. Carter had found some promising gold ore systems that, combined with the placer discoveries already being worked, made the region appear of great potential. Of course, the hard-rock mining of gold from quartz demanded more machinery than did placer mining, most notably a stamp mill to crush the quartz to release the gold. But without a trail it would be impossible to get any heavy equipment into the country. Marsh alerted the Alaska Road Commission to the development of the Chandalar, and in 1908 he helped Captain Phillsbury survey a trail from the Yukon to Caro.

The trail was to commence from the site of Beaver, on the Yukon, which is why Frank Yasuda and his Arctic Eskimo companions located there. By 1910, the trail was pushed through.

The same year, Sulzer bought a giant Allis–Chalmers four-stamp mill and shipped it to Beaver. Virtually anywhere else in the North the machinery would have soon been put into operation, but the forbidding Arctic region forestalled sporadic efforts over a 20-year period to get the mill to the mines. Although Marsh was not able to produce much over the years, Sulzer continued to back the operation. Irving McK. Reed was commissioned to report on the Little Squaw claims that Sulzer acquired from Carter, and he raised the New Yorker's hopes: "In all my experience, as a Mining Engineer," wrote Reed, "I do not know of any place, in Alaska, where such rich gold showings of free milling gold quartz ore can be seen, and so easily and economically developed."[14]

Tom Carter remained in the country. He sold his claims to Sulzer, then took them back when payments on the sales price were not maintained. In 1910, Carter offered his services as manager to Sulzer's Alaska–Chandalar Mining Company. His criticisms of his former partner, Marsh, were harsh. Carter figured that Marsh was spending too much money on his operation for the little he was gaining. "It takes a business man here that knows the country and its needs and *Horse Sense*." You have the best of miners, Carter went on; if the mines fail, "it will be the fault of management."[15]

Marsh managed to get a small stamp mill into operation but failed to get the huge Allis–Chalmers mill to the mines. It was 75 miles from Beaver to Caro and another 40 miles to the mines, and the massive stamp mill weighed 28 tons. Parts of the mill reached the destination, but other parts were strung out over the entire length of the trail.

The constant refrain echoed down the years was Sulzer's urging action on his managers. In 1922, C. W. Schultz was hired to freight the mill in. Heavy snow conditions defeated him though he got within a few miles of the mines. Two of his horses were frozen in the effort. In 1927, Schultz was still at it. "I supise [sic] you will be very much disappointed," he wrote Sulzer, "when you lirn [sic] that I haven't moved any of the machinery." Then Schultz recited the usual catalogue of woes that fills the files of the Alaska–Chandalar Mining Company. He was out 40 days. "It stormed forty days and has been stormined [sic] ever since. In all my days in Alaska I never saw such a winter. I do all I could do. Hope you will look at this in the right manner."[16] In 1930, Schultz had still not given up. Manager Carlson had to report to Sulzer another failure to deliver the mill. Other catastrophes occurred. Manager Patterson accidently shot himself. Two miners, Shaw and Dunlap, were injured by the explosion of dynamite. They were flown out on the first airplane flight from the Chandalar country.

Even in its early operating days the Alaska–Chandalar Company found it difficult to attract capital. "Everybody in the East is knocking mining properties, and gilt edged dividend paying stocks are going begging," wrote the company's secretary-treasurer to manager Marsh in 1910. "Whenever we try to sell any stock we get the same old song, 'It is too Far From the Bowery,' " he complained. Thus, the financial burden was chiefly thrown on the shoulders of Sulzer.[17]

With the Great Depression the money situation worsened. Sometimes the correspondence between the company's New York office and Beaver, Alaska, betrayed the tensions of the period. In 1932, the company secretary tried to explain things to manager Murphy. "The financial panic grows worse. Fear and starvation grip the people. Those who have no money can do nothing. Do you realize this? Do you understand the terrible financial conditions of the country?"[18]

The Allis–Chalmers stamp mill still lies spread out along the northern trail, an effective symbol of the travails of gold mining above the Arctic Circle. If the Chandalar region had held anything like the millions in gold of Nome or Fairbanks, it would undoubtedly have been developed fully. As it was, the paydirt existed in just enough quantity to keep a few men at it, men of courage and will. But it did not exist in bonanza proportions. The visionaries, Marsh, Carter, Yasuda, Sulzer, and a few others like them, did not realize their golden dreams in the Chandalar.

Part IV

THE DIFFERENT FRONTIER?

In the foregoing chapters, something of the story of the North's mineral and social development has been recounted, but the necessity of some evaluation remains. The biggest question is posed by the heading of this section—how different was the Alaskan frontier from those of other western regions? Individual assessments of law enforcement, the overall role of government, the impact on native peoples, journalism, labor struggles, politics, and the literature inspired by the gold stampedes provide some focus for clarification.

28

Law and Order

There's never a law of God or man runs north of Fifty Three.

So said Rudyard Kipling in a much quoted phrase, and to many witnesses of the disorder at Skagway and Nome from 1898 to 1900, it seemed a fair summary of Alaskan conditions during the gold rush. Whether, in fact, the North compared in lawlessness to other frontier communities of the American West—to Dodge City, Tombstone, Deadwood, Virginia City, or Abilene—is a difficult, perhaps moot, question. Comparative statistics of homicides, robberies, swindles, and other skulduggeries would not be very enlightening because of differences in time and conditions on the two frontiers. Nor would it help much to equate cattle-rustling with claim-jumping, horse thefts with dog thefts, or San Francisco vigilante actions with Alaska's miners' meetings. We can only examine the particular progress of Alaskan law enforcement in the context of its time and circumstances to reach a subjective judgment, a generalized appraisal that takes into account the several factors involved. Attention can be focused on four towns at different periods: Circle before the Klondike discovery; Skagway in 1898–99 during Soapy Smith's reign of disorder; Nome in 1899–1900 in the throes of its stampede excitement; and Fairbanks from 1903 to 1907.

Miners' Meeting

For 20 years, from the time of the first penetration of the interior by prospectors to the demise of Circle in 1896, law enforcement was in the hands of the miners' meeting. This institution had its limitations, and, as some of the incidents related to justice in Circle indicated, its performance was sometimes questionable. Still, the meeting was the only mechanism available to the early miners, and, crude as it was, historical precedent for its function as a court could be found on the earlier American frontiers. Its value in holding a mixed lot of men to some accountability for their conduct cannot be underestimated. It provided a forum for bringing complaints and a procedure for pushing miscreants. As it was organized, it worked best in dealing with comparatively simple matters like theft. In general, it was supported by the mining community because its members practiced restraint in meting out sanctions to offenders.

Imprisonment was out of the question, and corporal punishment did not appeal to everyone; thus the meeting usually dealt with transgressions by banishing the culprit. Nothing could be a more effective deterrent to a recurrence of the wrongdoing, nor a more satisfactory solution for the community. Once banished by decree, the offender had to stay banished. He had to leave the country entirely; there was no place to hide. There was no temptation on his part to attempt a circumvention of the decision —the threat of rough treatment and the certainty of social ostracism made the country unattractive to him. By leaving, he escaped an untenable situation.

Obviously, the miners' meeting was effective only in certain instances. When it grappled with problems evolving from personal relationships, it overextended its competence. Earlier cited instances of the meeting forcing miners to marry "wronged" women are amusing as long as one does not consider the inappropriateness of such rough-and-ready dealings to delicate matters. The same reservation must be made for all civil matters more complex than the most blatant kind of claim-jumping. Trader John J. Healy was certainly justified in resenting the interference of miners in the domestic arrangements of his household at Forty Mile.

Even more obviously, the miners' meeting either failed to remedy grievances or acted in a dubious manner virtually every time it was resorted to after the Klondike stampede. It failed to check Soapy Smith's gang in Skagway because the town's population was too large and transitory. On the crowded stampede trails, meetings were inconvenient, and conditions militated against the likelihood of fair judgment. In Nome a meeting did organize town government, but at another meeting, frustrated miners tried to dispossess legitimate holders of wealthy claims. Also in Nome the meeting could accomplish nothing against the McKenzie–Noyes conspiracy.

The miners' meeting was an expedient suitable to the pristine days of Forty Mile and Circle in the 1880s and '90s—and not even above criticism in those camps. Under the pressure of a great influx of population, the expedient faltered; it simply could not cope with circumstances altered by the increase in number of people.

Latecomers to the Yukon heard much of the miners' meeting from old-timers and formed their own impressions. Lieutenant J. C. Cantwell of the U.S. Revenue Service, who patrolled the Yukon from 1899 to 1901, knew something of the traditions of the meeting, but as a military officer, he was not favorably impressed. He commented that it "frequently happened that the miners' meetings were assemblages of disorderly persons whose decisions were manifestly unjust and the whole proceedings were so irregular as to cause them to be little better than examples of mob rule."[1] Cantwell had little faith in the order-keeping ability of the miners he encountered and had no first-hand experience in Alaska before 1899. Most stampeders of the Klondike and the later era would have had little reason to bemoan the decline of the miners' meeting. It would have been foreign to their experience and background, and hence a backward step in law enforcement.

For the pre-Klondike pioneers, however, the veneration of the primitive institution was unreserved. The miners' meeting made up a part of the legend of the "good old days," the period of manly directness in coping with disturbances to order, when, as old-timer Arthur Walden put it, "life, property, and honor were safe, justice was swift and sure, and punishments were made to fit the case."[2] The opinion of Walden and other pioneers on the efficacy of the meeting cannot be disregarded, particularly as it was corroborated by witnesses who were not directly involved. Alfred H. Brooks of the United States Geological Survey was perhaps best suited to give an objective judgment on Circle and other early camps. He had seen them all, as a government official rather than as a miner, and described the community life in terms of glowing praise.

[Circle] was thoroughly democratic and entirely American. The close contact between its members welded them together and Americanization went on unconsciously. Nowhere was the typical American, with his self-confidence, energy, perseverance, and democratic ideals, more definitely developed than in these little communities along the Yukon.[3]

Clearly, the conditions were perfect for the effective operation of the miners' meeting at Circle. Breaches of law must have been few; the miners showed a great deal of self-restraint. Morale was high and the moral quality of the men equally so. Whatever other reasons contributed to the near Utopian harmony of Circle—it was not to last. When the gold-seeking hordes poured into the North after the Klondike discovery, the days of innocence were over. For several years, the struggle for law and order was a long, uphill one. New, unwholesome attitudes prevailed. Laws did not matter. Customs were not respected.

Skagway and the Klondike

The lawlessness of Skagway has been described in an earlier chapter. (*See* Chapter 7, pages 37–43.) Its legend of disorder has been as well preserved as that of Circle's harmony, and is as richly deserved. Given the elements of the Lynn Canal scene—the tens of thousands of stampeders, the presence of a well-organized den of scoundrels, and the absence of effective law enforcement officials—Skagway's turbulence was inevitable. If for a time the crime and insecurity there made the town as wild and woolly as any that ever roared on the frontier of the Old West, it was not a milieu that dishonored the mass of its people. Klondikers, most of whom were Americans, proved that they were essentially law-abiding as soon as they crossed the border into Canada. A few miles of mountain pass did not alter their characters, but gave striking evidence of the difference between the rule of Canada's government and the neglect of that of the United States.

Canadian officials anticipated the effects of a stampede to the Yukon and provided for it; fear of the expansionist tendencies of the United States provided a strong motivation. Canada possessed a national police force admirably suited to the law enforcement task, one that was adaptable and efficient, experienced and well led. The United States government, on the other hand, was painfully slow in setting up machinery for the orderly development of Alaska. When it got around to assessing the problem, it did not have in existence a mobile constabulary force like the North-West Mounted Police, and available agencies were inadequate to Alaska's demands. The U.S. Army had never been effective as a police agency on the frontier. It was not constituted for such a purpose; nor was it acceptable to settlers in such a role. Skagway's disorders were permitted to run their course. The rule of law was eventually established after Skagway's frenzied days had passed and after the community had been cleansed of its rough crowd by an armed mob of outraged citizens. The one thing that is clearly established by a review of law and order during the Klondike rush is the ineptitude and inflexibility of the United States government. If Skagway constituted the only example of northern frontier lawlessness, the government's tardy response could be more easily dismissed as an isolated phenomenon. Regrettably for the record of the federal government, the story of Nome was a further, more grievous blemish.

Nome

In previous chapters the prevalence of crime and disorder in early Nome has been recounted in detail, and the bold conspiracy of the "Spoilers" has been described. The high incidence of violence, theft, and claim-jumping did not follow from the rogueries of a gang like Soapy Smith's, but the lawlessness on the Seward Peninsula surpassed that of Skagway in some respects and lasted over a longer time span.

Although the stampede to the Peninsula occurred suddenly, it did not come with the shock of the Klondike rush. By the time the major wave of argonauts hit Nome in 1900, events in the North had precipitated world-wide interest in Alaska, and the district had gained a substantial population. This time, the United States government had no excuse for being caught flat-footed by the new gold rush; yet, once again, miners had to bear the consequences of the federal government's unpreparedness. Many a veteran of Dawson wished himself once more under Canadian jurisdiction and protection of the North-West Mounted Police. Some were even manly enough to repent openly of criticisms they had uttered against the Mounties in Dawson.

The U.S. Army did dispatch a garrison to Nome early in the stampede. Fort Davis was established near the booming camp, and the soldiers helped keep the lid on the seething community, most notably when they broke up a miners' meeting that was deliberating a general takeover of valid claims on a flimsy pretense. The Army resisted a vociferous minority's pleas for complete military control of Nome on several occasions, and was probably wise in doing so. Martial law could arouse widespread resentment and political repercussions. It was considered the last resort, a measure not to be imposed upon Americans except in cases of dire necessity. But the military assisted in other ways. On occasion, squads of soldiers patrolled the streets to guard against open disorder, but only when requested to do so by Nome's businessmen. Soldiers also assisted in rounding up suspected bad men in 1899 and 1900, again at the request of civilians. On these occasions arrests were not made; indeed, no legal formalities were observed. The suspects were simply marched to the dock and loaded on the last ships to depart before the navigation season closed.

Thus, by its presence and collaboration in illegal punishment—what the enforced banishment amounted to—the Army lent support to civilian efforts at law enforcement. But much more policing was needed in Nome than was provided. Civil police authority existed only because the town fathers constituted it illegally. No provision of federal law prior to June 6, 1900, authorized the formation of a community police force in Alaska. In fact, the elected city council, which appointed Nome's police chief was itself unauthorized by federal law. Nome's citizens can hardly be blamed for asserting themselves in a legal vacuum. Unable to look to the federal treasury for police salaries, Nome relied instead upon private subscriptions for the purpose. Businessmen with valuable premises to protect contributed willingly, but the ordinary miner preferred to carry his own

weapon for protection against assailants. Such freelance police work made
Nome a lively and well-armed settlement, and added to the woes of law
enforcers.

During Nome's second season the federal officials were unable to check
the rate of crime and violence. In desperation they sought out Albert J.
Cody, formerly a Portland police officer, then a successful miner. Cody's
reputation attracted the beleagured government men. According to the
author of a biographical sketch, Cody possessed "great physical strength,
although a man of not extraordinary size, agile and alert, with a mind
quick of perception and an intuitive grasp of human motive, devoid of
fear, yet cautious, and having withal a keen analytical mind, Mr. Cody has
the traits of character that Conan Doyle has given to the hero of his great
detective stories."

United States Marshal C. L. Vawter needed a Sherlock Holmes to deal
with Nome's bad men. How could he lure Cody from mining to crime
detection? Cody was somewhat reluctant, but Vawter's appeal to his civic
conscience induced him to accept a deputy marshal's appointment—but
his terms must be met. "He agreed to undertake the work upon the conditions that warrants should be issued at his request and the arrested men
confined in jail without the privilege of anyone visiting them, and that
there should be not writs of habeas corpus,"[4] Present at this interview
were the federal officials charged with law enforcement: Judge Arthur
Noyes, District Attorney Joseph Wood, United States Commissioner
R. N. Stevens, and Marshal Vawter. All solemnly agreed to Cody's terms.
Without fanfare, the ancient right of *habeas corpus* was suspended in Nome.

With such means, Cody swiftly dispersed the criminals who had ter-
rorized the town. Suspects were rounded up, confessions were extorted,
charges were brought, and convictions summarily handed down. Winking
at conventional standards of justice enabled federal officials to establish
control of the situation. It is perhaps not surprising that all the officials
except Marshal Vawter and Cody were later charged with corruption in
other matters not related to Cody's cleanup.

Congress had to act to institute the means of civil government in Alaska
and did so belatedly in June, 1900. Civil government was extended by
legislation, which provided that town officials could be elected, local police appointed, and taxes levied. The act also provided for the addition of
two district court judges, making the total three in Alaska. No action was
taken to augment the federal police force with a more mobile branch.
Each of the three judicial districts was assigned to the charge of a United
States marshal who would be assisted by a handful of deputy marshals;
each district had its district attorney and staff appointed by the Department of Justice; and each district judge had authority to appoint United

States commissioners to act as judges for misdemeanor prosecutions and minor civil actions. Nothing very radical here, but at last Congress had acknowledged that Alaskan communities might have need of more governance than the military or a single federal judge could give.

Nome's gain of civil authority was more than offset by the assignment of Arthur Noyes as judge for the district. By the fall of 1900 the persistent crime waves had been checked, the streets were safe, and small-time thievery had been much reduced. But the large-scale frauds of the Mc-Kenzie–Noyes conspiracy kept the town seething for months more as Judge Noyes dallied over his court calendar and alarmed mine owners defended their claims by force of arms. In the summer of 1901, when Noyes was replaced by Judge James Wickersham, the serious work of cleaning up Nome began.

Fairbanks and Other Towns

Fairbanks did not have to endure lawlessness as Skagway and Nome had, for it had Judge Wickersham, virtually one of the town's founders because of his early move of the Third District court there. Fairbanks benefited by the presence of the court from 1904, and its citizens had legal authority to establish a town government. Other towns founded later also gained from the better organized judicial system and the privilege of civil government.

Fairbanks was not without crime, but its police officers kept order. The military was never called upon for aid despite the slight hysteria incident to the predations of the "Blue Parka" bandit and during the labor strife, although a formidable number of citizens were deputized as a precautionary measure on the latter occasion. Alaskans were no more criminally inclined than other frontier settlers and could live peaceably once the normal support of the federal laws and agencies was granted to their communities. Additionally, peace officers gained from the restrictions imposed by the climate and inaccessibility. A criminal fleeing Fairbanks and other interior camps had few options in any season. In the summer he could dash for the coast by way of Dawson and Whitehorse, take the Valdez Trail to reach Outside shipping, or catch a riverboat down the Tanana and Yukon to St. Michael. But long before he could hope to reach the coast, the telegraph would have alerted officers at all ports of exit. Over the winter months his escape opportunities were even more limited, and his progress to an ocean port would be slower yet. Furthermore, the district did not attract large numbers of tough characters after the gold bustle declined. A town like Fairbanks was not as open to criminally inclined opportunists as San Francisco or Seattle; Alaskan towns were small, and the actions of strangers were easily noted.

Alaskans had no reason to boast overmuch their law-abiding ways, however, though this did not inhibit their temptation to do so anyway. Judge Wickersham was typical of Alaskans in this respect. Even the Nome stampeders "constituted a special and picked class of people . . . young, strong, and healthy; the mentally and physically defective, the lazy, the incompetent, and the unthrifty did not come." Unfortunately, the 1899–1900 Nome record does not entirely bear out Wickersham's conclusions, but the judge's personal experience of Nome dated from 1901. One can, however, agree with Wickersham that "Nome's most serious law-breaking problems originated in the United States Senate."[5]

Pioneers of Alaska tended to forget the harder days. Dan Sutherland, a miner in Nome and Fairbanks before he replaced Wickersham as congressional delegate, also recalled Nome as a peaceful community—and he was there in 1899–1900. Alfred Brooks, a fervent supporter of Alaska, had a different view of Nome and did not forget that he deemed it necessary to carry a revolver for defensive purposes. Wickersham and Sutherland, it should be noted, were politicians, and vote-getters tend to look on the sunny side of things. Against the testimony of Wickersham, Sutherland, and a few others, there exists a much greater weight of evidence to substantiate the ill-fame of early Nome. It is not necessary to detract from the merits of the overwhelming proportion of peaceful men and women to present a balanced view of Nome.

Plainly enough, despite the rosy hue endowed retrospectively to the miners' meeting by some pioneers, the American system of governance—or rather, the lack of some components of the system—failed to meet the exigencies of the Skagway and Nome stampedes for much the same reasons that it sometimes failed on other frontiers. Settlers of virgin regions did not evolve orderly peace-keeping processes solely through their own exertions in the mining camps of California and Montana, nor in the cattle towns of Texas and Kansas. At times they were forced either to accept criminal oppression or take mob action against it. Neither of these options was particularly commendable, nor led to happy consequences for the general well-being. Given Alaska's circumstances, there was no reason its populace should have fared better than that of the Old West. And it did not.[6]

29

The U.S. Government's Role in Alaska

BECAUSE OF Alaska's territorial status, people looked to the federal government not only for law enforcement but also for all other basic services. Government contributions in exploration and trail construction, telegraphic communication, and relief for destitute miners were all carried out under the pressure of fast-moving events and the urgent demands of Alaskans. Because so little had been done during the first 30 years of United States' sovereignty, the activities were hurriedly undertaken. Harbors had to be surveyed, geographical explorations and geological investigations carried out, mail service instituted, and the best solutions found to communication, transportation, and law enforcement problems.

Washington, D.C., officials, faced with all these tasks, had limited resources. Alaska's requirements did not rank above those of other sections of the country, and certainly the territory's scant population did not command strong political power. Considering the competition for personnel and funds, officials concerned with the North felt that the government response represented achievements of substantial if not heroic proportions; Alaskans did not agree. Neither the mail service nor the transportation efforts were provided with the speed and substance Alaskans desired.

All Alaskans believed fervently that the federal government provided far too little in services and developmental aid in return for the gold Alaska poured into the economy. In his memoir, *Old Yukon*, James Wickersham used statistics to point out the misbalance, as follows[1]:

Balance of Accounts — United States with Alaska, 1867–1932	
Purchase price of Alaska	$ 7,200,000
Total "expenditures" by the United States in Alaska	200,117,286
Total cash account, United States against Alaska	207,317,286
Less total Treasury "receipts" from Alaska	50,357,660
United States cash balance against Alaska	$156,959,626

Alaska's trade credit with the United States:

Merchandise purchased by Alaska	$ 889,233,561
Alaska exports (gold, etc.) to United States	1,691,717,221
Total Alaska trade credits	2,580,950,782
Less balance United States "expenditures"	156,959,626
Balance trade credits due Alaska	$2,423,991,156

Although such statistics helped prove Wickersham's point and backed the refrain of imbalance and neglect he and other Alaskans sang, they did not convince Congress to raise Alaska's fiscal priority. If there was one issue on which it would be impossible to set two Alaskans arguing—this was it. Whether Alaska was misgoverned and neglected by the federal government might have been debated Outside, but there is no question that Alaskans felt intensely that this was the case.

Alaska's gold stampede and early development occurred simultaneously with the Spanish–American War and the Philippine insurrection. Although Alaskans cheered the defeat of the Spanish, they were unhappy about involvement with the Filipinos. An uneasy feeling that Uncle Sam was catering to them at the expense of Alaskans was often expressed. As editor Strong of the *Iditarod Nugget* saw it:

> There is not a native village from Cavite to Mindanao or Bontoc, but has [sic] mail service superior to Iditarod. Furthermore, every one of that treacherous bunch knows more about bolos than books. In the eyes of the federal government the Filipino is a man, and more than a mere brother. The Alaskan is a peon, and may be damned![2]

All American frontier newspapers had occasion to criticize the federal government, but nowhere did vituperation and outrage develop to as high and persistent a form of art as in Alaska. This feeling existed among Alaskans prior to the gold rushes but was greatly intensified by the mineral development. The same basic complaints were voiced continuously throughout the territorial period. Always, Washington, D.C., seemed so far away and so persistently deaf to the urgent needs of Alaskans, who urged that their requirements be met by men who knew their conditions through personal experience and insisted that all too often "carpetbaggers" from the Outside were given preference over Alaskans for official positions.

The first editorial in newspapers of most new camps would include strident calls for postal service. As likely as not, the next issue would demand a railroad. When, as editor of the *Nome News* Strong learned that postal service could not be expected for the 1899–1900 winter, he raged:

It is simply the continuation of the policy of misgovernment that has obtained in Alaska since it became a possession of the United States with a perversity that is culpable and an indifference to our needs that is heartless.[3]

Actually, the United States government made a heavy investment in carrying mail to the people of Alaska in the early days. Low postal rates were one bargain enjoyed by Alaskans. The first class letter rate was two cents but federal postal officials estimated that it cost 50 cents to get a letter to the Yukon valley. In the fall of 1899, mail service from Valdez to Eagle was inaugurated. A mail carrier started from the coast in October of that year with a pack train of eleven horses. Christmas was near when he finally staggered into Eagle, the mail sack slung over his shoulder. His horses had long since died of cold and exhaustion. All the town turned out in anticipation of mail. Alas! The sack contained only three letters.

On the whole, it appears that the post office did very well, considering the distances and expenses involved. In 1903 the postmaster at Point Barrow, the most northerly point of United States territory, sent a report to Washington, D.C. The route taken in delivering the report and the time elapsed—some five months—illustrate the difficulties involved. On the first leg, 650 miles between Barrow and Kotzebue, the mail was carried by reindeer. Both dogs and reindeer were utilized on the second stretch, between Kotzebue and Nome. From Nome to Unalakleet, dogs went forward for another 230 miles, then another 363 miles to Tanana, and 567 miles farther up the Yukon River to Eagle. Thus, the Alaskan mileage had already totaled 2,200 miles. The next stage was from Eagle to the port of Skagway via Dawson City, accounting for 594 miles, only 22 of which were in United States territory. The White Pass railroad carried the report for 112 miles of this stretch, while horses and dogs took care of the rest of the Canadian mileage. A steamer carried the mail the 1,000 miles to Seattle, and at last, the railroad carried the report across the continent to Washington, D.C., a grand total of 6,904 miles.

The estimated cost of such a trip, regardless of quantity of mail carried, was $2,329. The figures are based on the contractor's rates for his services:

Barrow to Kotzebue	$375
Kotzebue to Nome	259
Nome to Unalakleet	263
Unalakleet to Tanana	402
Tanana to Eagle	529

The Canadian government paid for the portion of the route passing through the Yukon territory, but the steamer rate to Seattle and the railroad rate from Seattle added $169 and $341, respectively.[4]

At best, during the winter, a miner anxious to have an answer to a letter could expect a reply 100 days later if travel conditions were good. The key figure in the winter mail service was the dog-team driver, whose stamina and skill were all important. What other frontier role demanded such a combination of strength and knowledge? The state of the Yukon River ice varied from year to year, but it was never a smooth surface. In the early stages of freeze-up, the current of the river tossed the floes about and carried wedges of ice that would crash against others and create jams. Thus, the surface was rugged and uneven, a hummocky mass that taxed the carriers to the limit of their endurance. Danger as well as discomfort threatened the postman. In the fall and spring he had to be extremely cautious lest the heavy sled break through ice too thin to carry its weight. Such a mishap could mean the end for driver, dogs, and the precious mail they carried. Often enough, camp newspapers carried the notice that the mail was "too wet for distribution."

Carriers were not employees of the United States postal service, but private contractors who bid for the season's mail contract. Early Yukon carriers could expect to get $1 per letter delivered and a good commission on any gold carried. Later, competition drove the bids down and carriers got smaller gain from their efforts. Dogs were not the only source of power. In 1899 and 1900 the post office contracted with the Superintendent of Reindeer in Alaska to carry the mail between St. Michael and Nome, and from Nome to Kotzebue. These 500-mile round trips through a roadless country were accomplished in 12 to 15 days. Reindeer covered the ground much faster than dogs did, but there were fewer skilled drivers for them.

Now for a Railroad

Railroads loomed large in the imagination of Alaskans, who never tired of demanding that the government undertake major projects. Soon after the founding of Nome and Fairbanks, track was laid to provide rail service between those town and their mines. These short-line railroads were financed by private interests without any government assistance. Such local railroads, however useful, failed to assuage the pioneers' craving for long-distance lines, lines that would tie Alaska to the continental United States, thus halting the tyrannies of high steamship rates and the limited navigation season.

It was so easy to draw the route lines on a map and envision puffing locomotives spanning the vast distances with ease—but the long-range railroads existed only as fantasies. Initial steps were not overlooked—government and private surveys were often made to establish the feasibility of routes from Valdez to Fairbanks, from the interior to Nome, from Cook Inlet to Nome, and other chimerical lines.

The longest private railroad was built by the Morgan–Guggenheim Syndicate, without government aid for a very limited purpose: to haul copper from the fabulously rich copper mines of the Chitina valley to the Prince William Sound port of Cordova. Over 200 miles of difficult, mountainous country was tamed by the builders at a total cost of $23 million. Completed in 1911, the line was abandoned in 1938 when the Kennecott mines were worked out after having yielded $200 million in copper and silver. Alaskans envied the Canadians of the Yukon territory, who were well served by a railroad that is still operating today. Skagway is the terminus for the White Pass and Yukon Railway, which was built in 1899 to serve the upper Yukon country. From the interior terminus of Whitehorse, steamers or stagecoaches traversed the short stretch to Dawson. Virtually the entire line lies within Canada.

Fairbanks eventually got its government-financed railroad, but it did not measure up to long-held dreams. Instead of a connection with transcontinental lines Outside along a route like the Alaska Highway that was constructed much later, the line was built from Seward on the coast to Fairbanks. At least this gave the interior access to an ice-free, year-round port. In 1923, as Alaskans gathered to watch President Harding drive the golden spike at Nenana, symbolizing the completion of the Alaska Railroad, they were grateful, but not wholly content with the government's record in transportation.

The Alaska Railroad got its start in 1912 with legislation appointing a commission to study routes. Early in 1913 the commission, whose members included Alfred H. Brooks of the United States Geological Survey, recommended that two railroads be built. One would start at Cordova, follow the Copper River to the Tanana River, and end at Fairbanks. The other would commence at Seward, run to the Susitna Valley, then swing over to the Kuskokwim River. In 1915 Congress authorized the construction of 1,000 miles of track at a cost of $35 million. Despite the recommendations of the commission, only one line was built into the interior. More than 400 miles of track were laid during the long construction period, with most of the work being done during the summer months. Although the railroad was not on the scale of the transcontinental lines, the rigors of the country made its construction a formidable task; the same conditions still make winter operation difficult. During World War II and subsequently, the railroad was much improved, and a line was built from Whittier to Portage to provide a terminus on Prince William Sound.

Congress had often held hearings on the potential for railroad building in Alaska, giving Alaskans and Outside promoters the opportunity to make their pleas and arguments. But the federal government could not be induced to subsidize private builders and stalled for years its own Seward –Fairbanks line. By the time of Alaska's gold era the railroad building momentum in the continental United States had ground to a stop. Muckrakers were questioning the policies that enabled the railroad moguls to amass fortunes from the disposition of huge portions of public land that had been given them. With this kind of adverse public reaction to the subsidizing of the transcontinental railroads, Alaskans were fortunate to get anything at all.

The costs involved in providing a rail network for Alaska were too staggering to attract private capital. The Morgan-Guggenheim Syndicate found it profitable to spend $23 million to transport $200 million worth of copper and silver, but nowhere else did the same arithmetic pertain. World War II alarms stimulated the military construction of, at incredible cost, the Alaska Highway from Dawson Creek to Fairbanks, but it was only accomplished strictly as a wartime measure.

The government did construct some trails and primitive wagon roads, most notably the Valdez Trail. Other government trails were built from Seward to Iditarod, from the Yukon to Nome, and even into the remote Chandalar country from the Yukon. These trails were welcome in an otherwise trackless wilderness, but did not satisfy the pleas of Alaskans for railroads. They obtained trails instead because the building costs were comparatively modest.

Weighing the Achievement

It is not easy to judge the total effectiveness of the government's work in providing services. During the gold era Alaskans believed passionately that they were not receiving the support they deserved, and their views have been supported by some historians. More recently, other historians, who identify themselves as "revisionists" of the traditional "neglect" opinion, have cautioned against a deprecation of the government's efforts.[5] These revisionists argue that the government's effort was insufficiently recognized by Alaskans and suggest that a comparison of Alaska's frontier history with that of other frontier regions would show the northern endeavors of the government in a more favorable light. Pioneers in every section of the West condemned the government's failure to respond swiftly to emerging demands, and perhaps Alaskans had less reason to complain than others.

Which view of the government's contribution is correct? Few comparative frontier studies have been made, nor is it clear that a comparison would actually answer the question. The question of the timeliness and substance of government aid to Alaska is not after all a relative one. A finding that Oklahoma and Nevada fared no better or worse in their frontier period does not resolve the issue. The question could be made one of relativity by asking whether a reasonable proportion of the federal budget was expended for Alaska; i.e., all things considered, did Alaska get a "fair" share of national revenue? But how could it be determined what constituted a fair share? Would a *per capita* assessment be rational?

If comparisons have any validity, it would seem once more that the Canadian example has more applicability than that of the American West. Police measures and the government surveys made in the Yukon have been discussed elsewhere, but other achievements of the Canadian government should be noted. Dawson had a telegraph line in 1899 that was relied upon by Alaskans for several years before Alaska enjoyed similar communication. In fact, the first construction undertaken by Capt. Charles Farnsworth and his U.S. Army telegraph crew was a link between Eagle and the border, so that the Canadian line could be utilized. Private enterprise provided the Skagway–Whitehorse railroad by 1899 so the Canadian government was relieved of that responsibility. Demands were made for other railroads, but the White Pass and Yukon route served the region's essential needs. Canadian explorers had done their work before the Klondike rush and were spared the embarrassment of their American counterparts in encountering stampeders along every trail they "opened." Canadian authorities knew the conditions of Yukon miners and attended to them promptly, thus avoiding the colorful comedy of the U.S. Army's reindeer relief drive. When the American mail service to Dawson broke down, the Mounties took on the chore and handled it efficiently. Thus, in all respects the timely efforts of the Canadian government contrasted with those of the American agencies.

It is interesting that revisionist historians have been chiefly those who have researched particular areas of government accomplishment, while traditionalists have been those looking at a broader portion of Alaska's history. My own review of the social history of the mining era, perhaps because of its scope, inclines me towards the traditional school of thought. I am influenced, in particular, by the inadequate law and order provisions made by the government, more than by its work in other fields. Yet the question can hardly be decided on quantitative grounds and must, it seems to me, be affected by subjective factors. One's attitudes and sympathies come into play in the resolution of historical issues. When much more research has been done on the role of the government in Alaska, it may be possible to assess it with greater confidence—but not before.

30

Natives and the Mining Frontier

DISRUPTION OF the way of life of Alaskan natives was a natural consequence of the northern stampedes. The process of cultural change, of
course, had been going on long before the gold era commenced on the
Yukon River and the Seward Peninsula. Russian fur traders made Pacific
coastal Alaska a province of the czars in the eighteenth century, and by
mid-nineteenth century, New England whaling fleets stood off the Bering
Sea and Arctic coasts each season. For the sparse and scattered population of interior natives, however, the contact with whites was minimal
before the gold rushes; a few traders and prospectors and fewer missionaries were the forerunners of a wave that was to affect drastically the
traditional native culture.

The 1880 census taker estimated that about 3,100 Eskimos inhabited
the Arctic, a very sparse population for such a great area. Nearly 7,000
natives were thought to dwell in the Yukon basin, while about 9,000, a
rather high estimate, were supposed to live on the Kuskokwim River.[1] In
1888, Alaska's Governor Alfred P. Swineford estimated the total population: "Whites, 6,500; Creoles (practically white) 1,900; Aleuts, 2,950;
Natives (partially educated and those who have adopted civilized ways of
living) 3,500; Natives wholly uncivilized, 35,000. Total 49,850."[2] A
smaller population was estimated in the 1890 census, 23,531 natives and
1,823 of mixed races. Of these, 14,012 were Eskimos scattered along the
lower Yukon and Kuskokwim rivers, Bristol Bay, and the Arctic, 3,439
were Athabaskans of the interior, while the remainder consisted of the
Tlingits, Haidas, and Tsimsheans of southeastern Alaska.[3] All these figures
were only educated guesses. It is impossible to say precisely how many
natives of ·Alaska were directly affected by the stampedes to the interior,
but their numbers were probably from 5,000 to 10,000.

Considerable relocation of natives was the immediate consequence of the gold stampedes. On the Tanana, for example, the natives of the upper river moved down to be closer to Fairbanks, where they could help provide food for the thousands of miners. Another inevitable result was the depletion of game in the regions where gold camps were founded. Even if every gold camp had passed out of existence after a few years, the game depletion would have forced further relocation.

Violent conflicts between whites and natives seldom occurred during frontier days. Alaskan natives were not aggressive warriors like the mounted hunters of the western plains. Stampeders were welcomed rather than resisted. Miners also were of a different stamp from the gun-packing cowboys of other regions. Somehow the rigors of the North compelled men of both races to more gentle deportment.

The northern mining frontier offered more natural hazards to the pioneer than anywhere else in America. It was fortunate that a kindly disposed aboriginal populace existed to ease the lot of the miners. Natives saved the lives of innumerable prospectors who lost their way along the trails. No record exists of the refusal of aid and hospitality by natives to whites, regardless of their own poverty. Explorers on occasion also owed their survival to such charity. In 1899, Lt. Joseph S. Herron led an expedition from Cook Inlet to explore the headwaters of the Kuskokwim River. This was one of several military explorations made in 1898 and 1899 in quest of an overland route to the Yukon that would bypass Canadian territory. Pack horses carried supplies for the twenty soldiers, a party far too large to do effective exploration. In attempting to traverse a trackless, swampy region, Herron lost his way; the horses mired in the muck and encumbered progress. In some panic, the horses were abandoned and the soldiers set out on foot for Fort Gibbon on the Yukon River. But for their discovery by the chief of the Tena Indians the lost explorers would have died of starvation and exposure before finding their way out of the swamps. For two months the Indians sheltered the soldiers in their village, before guiding them to the Tanana River, which they descended to Fort Gibbon.

During the same year, an Army expedition to the Tanana River ran out of provisions. The soldiers ate their mules and stumbled on with clothing in shreds, shoeless, suffering from exposure and hunger. Just in time, they reached Tanana village where they were mercifully received. As Lieutenant Castner reported:

— it is but justice to say a word for these friends of mine, who found us all but dead in the wilderness, with the Alaskan winter closing in around us. Entire strangers and of another race, they received us as no friend of mine, white or colored, ever did before or since. They asked no questions

*and required no credentials. They were men. It was enough that their
fellow-beings were starving. Unknown to them were the wrongs our race
have done theirs for centuries.*[4]

Before a network of roadhouses developed along established trails,
travelers could move lightly, without tent or stove, through any region
populated by natives. Miner N. N. Brown mushed from Nome to St.
Michael and back relying entirely on native hospitality. He was not disappointed. "They are the heartiest, kindest, most content people I have
ever met."[5]

White northerners were generally aware of their debt to the natives and
tried to treat them fairly. They learned to wear the native parka and
mukluks and adopted native travel techniques. Natives were informal
instructors in a school for survival, and whites who hoped to cope with the
harsh climate were quick to learn. This is not meant to suggest that racial
barriers did not exist in Alaska. The stampeders' attitudes on race were
fixed long before they journeyed north. In towns, if not on the trail, the
white man felt himself to be superior to the native and could be derisive, as
shown by the following newspaper doggerel:

> *Oh, look at the queer Esquimaux,*
> *His nose is too pudgy to blaux;*
> *His perfume is awful;*
> *To describe it unlawful,*
> *The thought of it fills me with waux.*[6]

Yet a closer relationship between races could be found in Alaska than
on the earlier western frontier. After all, there had been no bloody conflicts in the North to create intensely felt hostilities. Natives posed neither
a physical nor an economic threat to white settlement. Their contribution
to the newcomers' development of their native land was substantial. As
hunters they provided food; as trappers they gathered valuable furs for
trade. They were good customers as well, though this was detrimental to
them. The whites' canned goods and whiskey degraded their health and
culture—but were nonetheless eagerly demanded.

Natives of Alaska, unlike those in the continental United States, were
free to live where they liked, and their movements had economic consequences for the white man. Because of certain traders' "dirty work,"
warned the *Alaska Forum* editor, "Rampart's Indians will relocate near
Fairbanks. Better do something about this."[7] Natives were not scorned as
were the immigrant "Chinks" and "Japs" of the time. The despised orientals, unlike the natives, took jobs away from white men. Orientals were

considered dangerous and were forcibly expelled from Juneau by a vigilante mob in 1886.

Particular racial harmony existed outside of the towns. Men like George Pilcher, the woodcutter and trader of the lower Yukon, depended upon native society, entertaining his neighbors on long winter nights with gallons of tea and phonograph music. He and other similarly situated pioneers could hardly be intolerant. They traded with the men and bedded with the women—what more could one ask of neighborly good will and harmony?

Selling booze to natives was a violation of law, and attempts to halt this illicit traffic heavily engaged law enforcement officials. It was an impossible task. The fulminations of the press against the sellers indicate the frustration involved: "The fear of God and the law should be put into the gizzards (they have no hearts) of the reptiles who furnish natives with fiery hootch."[8] Six months' imprisonment was the standard penalty imposed upon convicted liquor sellers, and prosecution for violation was vigorous. But comparatively few incidents resulted in prosecution. To many, the easy money to be gained in liquor transactions was too great a temptation. Then too, "squaw men," whites with native families, could buy booze freely and often acted as suppliers. Although many recognized the ravages of liquor, all the white communities could do was to register a sense of responsibility.

Whites' adaptation to things native was always a positive gain. The reverse process usually proved unfortunate. Traditional Eskimo housing took the severity of the winter into consideration. Their half-buried dwellings heated by seal oil lamps proved adequate to the severity of the climate. Yet some Eskimos were impressed by the frame shacks the newcomers built, imitated the style, and suffered accordingly. In giving up traditional housing, they became economically dependent; fuel oil was needed to keep the shack warm and could only be acquired from the whites.

It was the same with food. Natives developed a taste for sugar and such luxury items as canned fruit and thereby committed themselves to a cash economy—a shift that was hardly suitable to the traditional pattern of subsistence. With a few exceptions like Creole John Minook, the discoverer of the Rampart goldfields, natives did not participate directly in prospecting and mining. They chopped wood, fished, and hunted for the miners in exchange for tobacco and other trading goods. At one time in the early mining period, most of the Yukon riverboats were piloted by natives. Captain Ellsworth West, whose *Corwin* was traditionally the first steamer to reach Nome each spring, always shipped an Eskimo crew because whites were too prone to jump ship and join the latest gold rush.

Hudson Stuck, the far-ranging Episcopal missionary, was a close observer of the natives through the latter part of the stampede era. His conclusion on the effect of the white miners on the aborigines was unequivocal: they "brought nothing but harm to the native people of Alaska." As one instance Stuck cited the situation at Fort Yukon during the 1897–98 winter, when 350 Klondike-bound miners were stranded by the freeze-up. The miners had nothing to do but amuse themselves with the natives and their large stores of whiskey: "There was gross debauchery and general demoralisation. It took Fort Yukon a long time to recover from the evil living of those winters and the evil name that followed."[9]

Missionaries were not loved by the lower classes of whites, who saw no wrong in debauching natives. Stuck and other missionaries were quick to report violations of the liquor law and this was resented. At Fort Yukon an indignant steamboat hand remonstrated with Stuck: "Why, it's got so . . . that a man can't give a squaw a drink of whiskey and take her out in the brush without getting into trouble!"[10]

The diseases brought to Alaska by whites were also devastating to the natives. Measles swept through the villages of the lower Yukon in the wake of the 1900 stampede to Nome. George Pilcher, the woodchopper, noted the decimation worked by that plague and applauded the Catholic missionaries' unselfish devotion to the sick at Holy Cross. Despite the existence of a hospital there, Holy Cross itself lost half its native population.

Missionaries were generally popular with miners, the low-life's opinion notwithstanding. Most miners shared the missionary view of the importance of spreading Christianity and the whites' ways among the natives and had no reason to be in conflict with the clergy. There were men, however, who argued that the natives should be free from the influences of missionaries and all other whites. Hudson Stuck addressed himself to this opinion on several occasions. He argued vigorously that the natives desperately needed the protection missionaries could give against the depredations of the white riffraff who followed explorers, traders, and prospectors into the country. He noted that a longing for an uncontaminated native people made no historical sense.

The natives most seriously affected by the influx of whites were those who abandoned their traditional pattern of life to live in mining towns. Some were women married to whites, whose children became an integral part of the white community, were educated in the local schools, and found employment within the mining economy. These town natives did not necessarily have a hard lot in making the transition to a new world. Even if the mixed-blood children were denied entry to the upper regions of society, they were, for the most part, treated decently by the tolerant white settlers. Other natives dwelled on the slum fringe of the community, sharing only marginally in its life, living between two worlds but fitting into neither. Their ghetto existence was unsanitary; they were ill-housed, likely to suffer from diseases, and often ravaged by alcoholism. Their fate was a visible reminder that the white intrusion brought disaster as well as prosperity.

But there were only a few scattered mining communities to attract natives and their number diminished as the gold placers were worked out. The great majority of Indians, Aleuts, and Eskimos maintained their village existence and avoided close, frequent encounters with whites. For thousands, the handful of missionaries and teachers provided the only contact with the white culture—not that their isolation assured them of a better fortune than town natives. Life for many was a hard struggle for sustenance—as it had always been. Famine and disease were very real specters.

How can the entire cultural impact of the rushes and subsequent development of the Alaskan interior be summed up? Did it actually bring "nothing but harm," as the Reverend Hudson Stuck affirmed? Most missionaries would probably have agreed with Stuck. Missionaries, with some justice, sometimes saw themselves as representing a thin line of shock troops trying to shield the aboriginal peoples against the more outrageous conduct of miners and other whites. Contemporary anthropologists have been inclined to decry the impact of *all* whites—missionaries, traders, and miners—on the native peoples. A historian has a harder time reaching such definite conclusions. Certain questions have no reliable answers. White pressure on the aborigines of the North dates back to the mid-eighteenth century. How much of the cultural disruption followed from the rushes and how much from the 150 years of contact that occurred before? And how can the effects be assessed? Surely Stuck's contention that the stampedes brought "nothing but harm" is open to question. Thousands of natives were affected only to a minor degree by the mining frontier, others made an apparently successful adaptation to the white culture.[11] Lacking the evidence that could only be the product of a case-by-case study of individual natives, it takes some temerity to reach conclusions as generalized as Stuck's.

It is not much easier for a historian to compare the native experience in the North with that of other aboriginal peoples on the western frontier. In the North there was no resistance to the white invasion, no Indian wars, no general reservation policy, none of the tensions of earlier frontiers.

Those who complained of the government's native policies in the North centered their grievances on neglect rather than aggression. But government failures or successes in education, welfare, and medical treatment were worked out in Washington, D.C., not by miners in Nome and Fairbanks. The role of the federal government in regard to natives is outside the scope of this study. In as much as Alaskan miners did influence these policies, they probably showed no more wisdom or ignorance than other frontiersmen, considering the particular age and situation. Newspaper editorials consistently complained that the government was flagrantly neglectful of the natives and called for a sound welfare policy. But the whole matter was far removed from the hands of Alaskans—and still remains so to a considerable degree today.

If a historian cannot answer some of the complex questions regarding the cultural impact, he can report on the attitudes of whites during the gold era. As might be expected, natives were praised or derided as their conduct and manners exemplified or varied from white standards. Few whites were scholarly or curious enough to attempt to gain an understanding of the native culture. Judge James Wickersham tried to gather and record native legends, and so did a few others, but most men were content with their superficial impressions. Native languages were rarely studied by any but missionaries who, of course, had very practical reasons for such labors. Yet such scholarship commanded respect among the whites, so long as the student was not a squaw man. Jack Hines, the "merry minstrel of Nome," was applauded for his facility in Eskimo by the author of an early history of Seward Peninsula mining activity. How much Eskimo Hines actually learned is another question, but certainly enough to impress some of his Nome cronies.

As has already been indicated, whites had good reason to appreciate native hospitality and their skills on the hunt and on the trail. Whites in the North understood that the original civilization of the natives, previous to contact with whites, had substantial merit, that it had to have or the natives could not have survived in a harsh land. Sourdough Lynn Smith expressed this consciousness of the aboriginal achievement: "When one realizes that four hundred years ago, there were more natives living in Alaska than now [1931]; that they were living off the country without any doctor except their own medicine men and women; and that they had to work out their own salvation—we can take off our hats to them—for their system of way of life worked."[12] Smith's sentiments were shared generally by whites and were the foundation for their basic respect for the natives, a respect that seems to have been greater than that extended by whites to aboriginal peoples on other frontiers. Human respect of northern people for other northern people derived from a shared experience that took the edge off racial antipathies and blurred distinctions in customs and manners that would otherwise raise unsurmountable barriers of disdain and suspicion.

Such mitigating factors did not, however, sweep away all vestiges of cultural arrogance even if they did have a leavening influence. Whites could not help elevating their institutions over those of the natives. A good Christian like Lynn Smith must "thank God for the missionaries and schools that have uplifted the poor, unfortunate natives until they are now partly civilized and live as we do." That the natives have the opportunity to "live as we do" was universally and inevitably the hope of well-meaning whites, a hope that extended to material and spiritual blessings alike. "Though they must have their seal oil even now," marveled Smith, "one cannot help but wonder how they managed years ago without the necessities of life."[13]

We can hardly expect men like Smith to have considered the dietary hazards of bacon, sugar, and tinned foods, any more than we can expect them to have doubted the advantages of stuffy, heated cabins or the truths of Christianity. The white's commitment to the values of his world and its benefits for aboriginal peoples was basic and unshakable. For all we might question today such convictions and their effects, it would be impossible to imagine what courses of the cultural disruption other attitudes might have directed. Attitudes towards natives have changed in recent times, a haunting consciousness of guilt has dictated new approaches, but the "native problem" has not disappeared. What has been done cannot be undone now and could not have been better done before. Perhaps it is as well to end on a fatalistic note as on one of thundering, meaningless recrimination. Or maybe it would be better yet to conclude with a sample from the ribald verses composed by Lynn Smith in less serious moments:

My Kobuk Queen, sweet sixteen, not too bold, not too clean
You're the simple child of nature, Kobuk Queen.
You've learned things from every nation and boast of white relations
For your kids are a combination, Kobuk Queen.[14]

31

Northern Journalism

The running of a newspaper is an easy job. All one has to do is to be able to write poems, discuss the tariff and money questions, umpire baseball, report a wedding, saw wood, describe a fire so that the readers will shed their wraps, make $1 do the work of $10, shine at a dance, measure calico, abuse the liquor habit, test whiskey, shoot craps, attend church, subscribe to charity, go without meals, attack free silver, defend bimetalism, snear at snobbery, wear diamonds, invent advertisements, overlook scandal, praise babies, delight pumpkin raisers, minister to the afflicted, heal the disgruntled, fight to a finish, set type, mould opinions, sweep the office, speak at prayer meeting, stand in with everything and everybody. Now if you think "it's easy" try it.[1]

One must agree with the editor of the *Sitka Cablegram* that the running of a northern frontier newspaper was not an easy job. Competition for ads and circulation was sharp and the remuneration could not have been great. The editor of another paper, the ubiquitous J. F. A. Strong, once pointed out that newsmen did not make good grubstakes and had no backers. They worked hard and could probably be good "farmers, blacksmiths, junk dealers and insane asylum trustees . . . so energetic are they—and strong backed, withal, albeit sometimes of a great weakness of mind."[2]

Numbers of newsmen joined the northern gold stampede, producing dailies and weeklies of surprisingly high caliber. Some stayed on after the initial boom, often moving from one town to another as the situation seemed propitious. Among the veteran Alaskan editors, besides J. F. A. Strong, were W. F. (Wrong Font) Thompson, John W. Troy, George B. Swinehart, Elmer J. "Stroller" White, Will and Harry Steel, O. W. Dunbar, George M. Arbuckle, George Bellows, and others.

J. F. A. Strong was an individual of surpassing interest. We have been able to follow Strong and document his editorial biases from Skagway in 1897, to Dawson in 1898, to Nome in 1899 through 1906, to Katalla in 1908, to Iditarod in 1910 and, finally, to Juneau in 1913. In Nome, Katalla, Iditarod, and Juneau, Strong established newspapers. All of these, save that in Juneau, were the first newspapers in new boom towns. Whether Strong represents the "typical" Alaskan editor of the pioneer era is impossible to say. Certainly he possessed the qualities common to the best of them: aggressiveness (even combativeness), public spirit, and a colorful, cogent prose style. Like other editors, he claimed to be independent and objective in his editorial policy. Naturally his rivals denied this and frequently charged Strong with selling out. Although Strong did not lack for enemies, his appointment as governor of Alaska in 1913 seemed to meet with general approval among Alaskans.

What were the predominant themes of mining frontier newspapers? They can be divided into two categories: those unique to the northern frontier and those common to all frontier communities. Uniqueness can be seen in Alaska's economic relationship with the Outside because of its remoteness. Also unique were the limited political options of the residents because of Alaska's territorial status. These factors did much to form the attitudes of Alaskans on a wide array of issues. In the category of things typical of the American frontier generally can be listed partisan politics, rivalries with other towns and other newspapers, community boosting, highly personalized editorship, and a commitment to law and order coupled with a tendency to disregard civil rights. But even in these, some distinctively Alaska facets can be noted that resulted from the isolation and the small size of the communities of the North.

Editor Strong and His Rivals

If we try to follow J. F. A. Strong's editorial adventures in Nome we can see how the personal element became interwoven with the issues of the day. No love was lost between newspaper editors competing for subscriptions and ads in the same town. Yet the virulence of editorial abuse that frequently burst forth could not be explained by mere economic rivalry. Personal antipathies were at the root of open eruptions between editors and seemed to affect editorial positions on civic and territorial issues. An examination of the feuds of Nome's editors is not productive for an impartial assessment of the justice of editorial causes, but allows one a delicious sampling of inflamed vituperation. Editorial language was colorful, and when disputes raged, no holds were barred. Strong's *Nome News* often beset the *Nome Gold Digger*, which Strong liked to label *Grave Digger*. Not only was the *Digger* a "half-moribund sheet," given to "lying" and "misrepresentation," but "its ways were Peeksniffian and its whining is that of Uriah Heep." Beyond that, "it has both our pity and contempt." In the same issue Strong found space to levy the ultimate insult in a mining community—the rival editor "is a lot jumper."[3]

When Strong moved from the *News* to found the *Nome Nugget*, he did not discontinue his sniping at the *Digger*. Naturally enough, the *Digger* editor responded in kind, and readers of both papers followed the exchange of slander for months. Occasionally, feuding editors would question whether their readers were really interested in a public airing of their personal spleens. They invariably concluded that the public was not interested and resolved to halt hostilities—but did not invariably hold to this resolution. Readers probably enjoyed such running feuds. The communities were small enough for the individuals to be known to all, and the issues were not beyond the ken of the average man.

The *Nome Nugget* also attacked the *Nome News*. The *News* ran a story on the Boer War based on a letter from Olaf Jackson of Dawson City. Strong smelled a rat and accused the "yellow *News*" of concocting a false report and offered to donate $100 to charity if Olaf Jackson actually existed.[4] A provincial newspaper, the *Council City News*, informed its readers that its telegraph bulletins appeared by arrangement with the *Nome News*. Not so, cried Strong, "The *Council City News* gets its telegraph news from our pages and should not indicate otherwise . . . if the paper relied solely upon the local contemporary for outside news, it would have a great deal of space left for other matters."[5]

Criminal Libel

A more serious adventure in the journalistic career of the editor Strong was a libel suit brought against him by John L. McGinn, the United States district attorney when Judge James Wickersham was cleaning up the mess left in Nome by the McKenzie–Noyes ring. McGinn successfully prosecuted United States Marshal Frank Richards for jury fixing, and Wickersham found Richards in contempt of court. Strong was an honest man, in no way implicated in Richards' misuse of office, yet he took strong exception to the marshal's prosecution and launched a vigorous editorial attack on Wickersham and McGinn. Presumably, Strong's friendship with Richards determined his editorial position.

Of course, the reasons for the *Nome Nugget's* attack seemed clear enough to the editor of the *News*. Will Steel, of the *News*, yearned to defend the court against Strong's assaults, but Wickersham restrained him. McGinn urged the judge to find Strong in contempt of court for questioning the Richards' decision, but Wickersham knew better than to inflame the issue. For months, Steel and Strong had been feuding, and Steel had charged Strong with fawning on Noyes and McKenzie while they were in power. In subsequent issues, the *News* pondered Strong's reasons for having attacked Judge Wickersham after supporting him initially—"it was a spectacle to strike men blind to see this great, lumbering buffoon toady to and beslobber a man who had shown himself to be an upright judge"—but then, according to the *News*, when Wickersham found Marshal Richards guilty of jury fixing, the *Nugget* thundered against "a gross miscarriage of justice and grave judicial error."[6]

The *News* wondered why its praise of McGinn's prosecution of Marshal Richards drew fire from Strong. Our praise of McGinn "rambles in the feeble brain of the antiquated editor of our semi-weekly competitor."[7] Strong's devotion of "great space" to attacking the *News* shed no light on his motivation. Wickersham became unavailable as a target when he returned to the interior, but McGinn was still on hand and Strong opened fire on him in prose and poetry. An example of the latter was "A Gambler's Soliloquy":

> *Of all speculations the market holds forth,*
> *The best that I know for a lover of self, is to buy*
> *Mc . . . n up at the price he is worth,*
> *And then sell him at which he sets on himself.*[8]

On another occasion the *Nugget* declaimed that "Mr. McGinn seems to be of that stripe of prosecuting attorney that would, without scruple, send an innocent man to the gallows merely for the sake of making a 'record'."[9] Nor did Strong's badgering of the attorney end with McGinn's resignation from the district attorney's office. "He disgraced the office which he unworthily filled, and at the twelfth hour he resigned well knowing that it was the most prudent course for him to pursue."[10]

McGinn finally reached the boiling point and filed a libel suit against Strong, asking $50,000 in damages on seven separate counts. A twenty-five page complaint mainly made up of quotations from *Nugget* articles published between August 9, 1902, and February 7, 1903, comprised McGinn's case. Strong remained unintimidated. The *Nugget* reported on the filing of the suit, but had "space for the publication of but one of McGinn's 'causes' for action, and it may be taken as a fair sample of all the others"; Strong reprinted "A Gambler's Soliloquy" and huffed, "for publishing the following he only wants $5,000."[11]

When the libel suit was brought to trial, the courtroom was jammed with spectators who anticipated a sparkling forensic display. They were not disappointed: McGinn was at the top of his form. The *Nome News* reported extensively on the trial, "one of the most notable ever heard in Nome." McGinn's summation before the jury received the highest praise: "Not within the history of the bar in Nome has there been a more eloquent

or forceful speech." Indeed, it was some effort. McGinn, commencing at
9:30 A.M., continued until the noon recess, then went on from 1:30 P.M.
until 3:15 P.M. "During the long argument not once did the jurors manifest any signs of weariness or impatience and the audience were on the
verge of breaking into loud applause a number of times," reported the
News.[12]

McGinn made much of the relationship between his prosecution of
Marshal Richards and of saloon keeper J. D. Jourdan for jury fixing and
Strong's vendetta against him: "Then it was that the cry went forth that
McGinn must be ruined—visit his haunts, search Nome, search Council
City, go over the whole district with a fine toothed comb . . . we must
annihilate him so that he won't annihilate us." The marshal's office watched
him very closely. Every drink he took in a saloon was recorded; each
occasion on which he laid a dollar on the roulette wheel was noted—"All
this was done simply because I had brought suit against them." Strong,
asserted McGinn, acted as hatchet man for the marshal: "The defendant
has circulated many slanders and malicious falsehoods concerning me and
has ever used the weapon of a fool since the foundation of the world."
Libel is difficult to establish at law, and McGinn needed to carry the jury
through an emotional appeal: "The heart of the libeler is more base and
low than the heart of the assassin or the heart of the man who commits
midnight arson." A lawyer's most precious asset was his reputation:
"Take away the reputation of a lawyer and what is there left?" One who
would circulate "these filthy libels and slanders is not worthy the attention
given to a mangy malemute dog . . . the editor of the character of the
defendant is ever ready to throw the stink pots of the scavenger at the
objects of his hatred."[13]

Strong testified on his own behalf with cool composure. Under cross-
examination he did not retract any of his charges against McGinn. It just
happened to be his opinion that McGinn was capable of judicial murder:
"I believe these things are true . . . you got drunk . . . you asked members
of the jury if they were A B's (Arctic Brotherhood members) . . . you
formed combinations to hold up the gamblers of the community . . .
therefore I draw the conclusion that you are the kind of man who would
send innocent men to the gallows."[14] The jury was sufficiently impressed
by McGinn's arguments to vote ten to two in favor of $5,000 damages on
the first ballot. In subsequent votes the damage figure went down to $100,
but there were still holdouts. The jury was hung and had to be dis-
charged. Strong had triumphed despite McGinn's brilliant attempt.

Other Rivalries

Equally fierce newspaper rivalries characterized Tanana valley journalism. The shrieking calumny exchanged between the *Fairbanks Times* and

the *Fairbanks News* matched the best abuse and slander delivered by the editors of Nome. Just as in early Nome, the personal biases of editors and publishers shone strongly. But an additional element intrudes after 1906 when federal legislation finally approved the election of a non-voting Alaskan delegate to Congress. Alaska was allotted one voice in Washington, D.C., one voice and one prime source of federal patronage. To say that the honor of holding the delegate's job was bitterly contested in each election is to understate the case. Every two years a Donnybrook erupted.

The intensity of Alaskan politics owed much to the bristling temperaments of leading figures like James Wickersham. But perhaps the chief fuel for the fire under the political cauldron was the small size of the poll, the small number of voters involved. In the first election of a delegate, in 1906, only 9,236 votes were cast. Out of the six candidates in the field in 1912, James Wickersham won with 3,335 votes of 8,220 cast. Decisions were brought about by a few votes, thus increasing the temptation to challenge election results.

Most Alaskan newspapers, despite all disclaimers of "independence" to the contrary, joined partisan politics with a vengeance. While averring that their partisanship sprang from civic duty and love of good government, editors freely sold editorial support for the campaign period. Northern journalism reached its nadir as each biennial election drew near.

Seattle and the Press

It was always considered good editorial form to attack Seattle. "Seattle spirit" was understood to express the higher reaches of rapacity and profiteering.

Alaskans sitting around a hot stove liked to exchange stories highlighting Seattle's greed. For example, there was the time a deceased Seattleite was rejected by both St. Peter and the devil. In order to resolve the issue, Peter and the devil decided to toss a coin; the loser would have to take in the unwanted soul. Up went the coin, the Seattle man grabbed it and departed. Editor Strong once reflected at large on the issue:

If the Seattle spirit is a good thing for Seattle the fact merely adds corroboration to the dictum that one man's meat is another man's poison. The suppurations of Seattle spirit have never benefited Alaska. . . . The joyous manner in which Seattle assumes that Alaska is a hackneyed feudatory of her vain and bragging self is the cause of the widespread dislike of Seattle which pervades all Alaska and is felt even by men who once lived in the Sound city. Seattle hands Alaska a green lemon on every possible occasion.

Seattle stands with the big mitt constantly extended toward Alaska. She grafts on the territory with both hands. She levies a wharfage tribute on Alaskan freight double that imposed upon other shipments, adds ficti-

*cious charges to the excessive freight rates extorted from Northern ports
and distends her elastic maw by every recourse of commercial piracy
which she can devise, or initiate.*

*Seattle has grown like Jack's beanstalk upon the outpouring of Alas-
ka's natural wealth and the industry of the territory's hardy and adventurous citizens, and now she wants to trade upon the Alaskan name.
She plans a mighty exposition for her own profit, but she does not call
it the Seattle Fair, the name would post it at once in the rogues' gallery.
She labels it the Alaska–Yukon–Pacific Exposition which is somewhat
like stealing the livery of heaven to serve the devil in.*[15]

Some of the buffeting of Seattle was outrageously unjust. Strong and
the other frontier editors gambled on the continued prosperity of the
communities in which they were located. As might be expected, editors
were always fervent boosters of their towns' prospects. When the Morgan–
Guggenheim Syndicate chose Katalla as the coastline terminus for the
railroad it had decided to build to its interior copper mines, Strong arrived
with his press just as the town was springing up in anticipation of a boom.
(*See* Chapter 26, pages 224–26.) Strong reacted harshly, later, when
the *Seattle Times* reported the syndicate's abandonment of the proposed
Katalla route. He complained that Seattle papers had been knocking Katalla for three months "palpably, glaringly and with so much unreason and
apparent mereticiousness, as to almost lead one to believe that those
newspapers were subsidized for that particular purpose." Seattle papers,
cried Strong, "welcome every derogatory statement whether made by land
or sea hobo." Seattle, "in its vaingloriousness and its swollen condition
forgets how Alaska saved it from bankruptcy a few years ago, and is now
doing it again."[16] It was hardly the fault of the *Seattle Times* that the
closure of Katalla's coal lands to development and the destruction of a harbor breakwater doomed the town, but boom town boosters were sensitive
men.

In an early issue of his next venture, the *Iditarod Nugget*, Strong caught
Seattle in another big lie. This time amusement overcame indignation. A
Seattle newspaper was impressed by the quantity and ferocity of the mosquitoes in the Iditarod mining district. Yet there were advantages, reported the paper, "mosquitoes stand guard over prisoners in Iditarod and
do so well that stone walls, iron bars or jailors are unnecessary."[17] On
their arrest, miscreants were placed in a mosquito-proof tent without their
clothes. Prisoners dared not venture outside. There were so many mosquitoes that the only way their numbers could be increased would be for
them to grow smaller. *Nugget* readers enjoyed this story, particularly since
the informant who had passed it off to the Seattle press was a Fairbanks
sourdough. Explorer Vilhjalmur Stefansson often said that the only dis-

comfort in the North that was not exaggerated was the mosquito plague. A minor exception may be allowed for the Iditarod jail story.

Even lower than a knocker from Seattle was an Alaskan who did not think the new camp—whether Skagway, Nome, Fairbanks, Iditarod, or Katalla—had infinite, long-range economic potential and was destined to be the wonder of the world. When Strong edited the *Nome Nugget*, he observed that pessimists and detractors never overlook a chance to knock —any excuse would do:

It may be that the grasses which grow on the tundra are not garnished with golden filigree work, or that the sands in the creeks are not all golden like those of "Africa's sunny fountains." Just because they mush out to new districts and find the creeks are not lined with working sluices, these modern Jeremiahs raise their voices in doleful lamentations. They cry aloud and spare not; on the streets and in public places they lift up their voices in denunciation like trumpets.[18]

Strong, like many other journalists, ventured successfully into politics. He served as governor of Alaska from 1913 through 1916. Although he had staunch enemies, his political appointment pleased many Alaskans; obviously his years of editorial fulminations had created more friends than enemies. Strong left Alaska in 1918 to retire in California but continued to enjoy associations with Alaskans. A visit to Seattle in those days was almost the equivalent of traveling to Alaska. Seattle was full of Alaskans who wintered or retired on Puget Sound or who were passing through on visits. The city no longer seemed an alien, exploitative place to Strong and other Alaskans who had numerous personal ties there. A good indication of this is reflected in a July, 1924, issue of the *Alaska Weekly* (published in Seattle), which reported on a visit Strong made shortly before his death. The former editor and governor's many friends made his progress through town something of a triumphant tour. Strong and his wife checked into the Frye Hotel, one of the favorite hostelries of Alaskans, then, after a night's rest, set out to walk up Third Avenue to Pike Street. Every minute along the way the Strongs were hailed by old sourdoughs from the North. Encounters were so frequent, noted the newspaper, that it took the Strongs a half day to walk those few blocks.

32

Labor Strife

ALASKA'S GOLD was discovered by the rugged, restless prospectors who roamed the tundra and hills, subsisting on beans and bacon, in unending quest for the telltale signs. These pioneers still existed after the development of the big camps of Nome and Fairbanks—indeed they went on to find Iditarod, Ruby, Wiseman, and Livengood, to name only a few towns. Throughout the territory, some producing mines were worked by individual men or pairs of partners, but the inevitable industrial transition proceeded in Alaska as elsewhere. Within a few years of the time when Nome was known as "a poor man's diggings" and Fairbanks' creeks were open to all, the major portion of production was dominated by large operators who employed hired labor.

Mining was tough work. Every miner was expected to pick free, load, and trundle 80 to 100 wheelbarrows full of earth in each 10-hour shift. It was heavy, grim work carried out in damp tunnels by flickering candlelight. Miners worked the 10-hour shifts for $6 to $8 a day plus bunk and board. Such wages seemed magnificent by Outside standards but not in view of Alaska's high cost of living and the short season—generally four to five months. Money did not go far. Neither a beer nor a newspaper could be had for less than 25 cents. Transportation to the Outside for those who were not year-round residents was a heavy burden. A steamer ticket to Seattle or San Francisco cost $250, added to the cost for the 376-mile stretch between Fairbanks and Valdez, which was $150 by coach with roadhouse costs of another $7 per day for 10 days.

In 1907 and 1908 the Western Federation of Miners organized the Tanana valley miners and struck for an eight-hour working day at a pay of $5 per day. Although this meant that the miners were willing to take a cut in average daily pay corresponding to the desired reduction in hours, mine operators responded in the same fashion as their counterparts in Idaho,

Washington, and Montana. Spies infiltrated meetings of miners; strike breakers were brought in; newspapers chorused litanies of abuse at "socialist agitators and anarchists"; law enforcement officials vigorously protected the operators' interests; and the workers resorted to violence. In 1908, the situation was especially chaotic.

A strike in an isolated town like Fairbanks created particular tensions. Essentially, the area depended on a single industry. Those not directly involved in mining served the industry. Businessmen—merchants, bankers, saloon keepers—needed to step warily, not daring to alienate either the operators or the miners. It was a relief to them when the strikers committed acts of violence; they could then embrace the operators' cause under the banner of the maintenance of law and order.

W. E. Priestly was a young miner, but he had "a gift of gab" plus a good bit of drive. He had organized the independent Tanana Miners Union before deciding to call upon the Western Federation of Miners (W.F.M.) for help and affiliation. The W.F.M., which had already organized the miners of southeastern Alaska, dispatched Thomas Steffenson to work with Priestly in Fairbanks. Priestly also took over the editing of the union-backed newspaper, the *Miners Union Bulletin* after its editor, W. F. Thompson, was fired for his anti-labor sentiments. In recalling his editorial work in later years, Priestly related how he had dipped his "pen into vitriol and started in to fight for the miners, clean up the community, and save suffering humanity and to make myself a general nuisance"; Priestly's "hot sheet" enjoyed a booming circulation.[1] But the established press was even hotter.

Among the Tanana valley newspapers, the *Fairbanks News* launched the most virulent attacks on the miners' union. For the *News* the issue was clear: "The miners say the ground would stand payment of $5 for eight hours and the operators—those who risk money and should know—say it will not." The Western Federation of Miners leadership, according to the paper, consisted of "rabid socialists and anarchists who led the more ignorant of the membership at will as a herder drives his sheep." Of course, "the *News* has no objection to a labor organization as such. But it does raise its voice in loud warning against invasion by anarchistic, socialistic organizations led by the foreign element now striving to get the Tanana in its grasp." There has never been peace and prosperity in a camp where the W.F.M. put a charter, the *News* alleged further. Then the *News* got to particulars concerning the W.F.M. leader, Thomas Steffenson. When interviewed after strikers stopped a stage carrying Russian strike breakers to the Ester diggings, Steffenson asserted that the Russians—invariably called Cossacks by union men—were a dangerous element in the camp, "being regarded as bandits." "Such gall," raged the *News*; the men detained were only trying to make a peaceful living. Steffenson "already shows himself possessed of the inherent instinct of the bandit in his conduct of the strike," and though a foreigner "not long ago," whose English is "not intelligible," he "assumes to revise our constitution," angrily asserted the *News*.[2]

The next week a front page cartoon, entitled "Behold the Alien Leaders!" revealed Steffenson and Priestly up to their nefarious tricks, trampling on the Constitution and setting off dynamite. An editorial asks whether "it will be necessary to have government aid (military) to drive the traitors out of the Tanana?"[3] Stridently, the United States marshal was urged to take action against the union men.

The determination of the operators to keep the 10-hour day can be seen in their attempt to use imported laborers. Russian miners were imported from the Outside and marched in from the coast. The "Cossacks" must have needed work badly to withstand a winter trek of 376 miles. In Katalla J. F. A. Strong, now publishing the *Katalla Herald*, thought the importation of foreign labor an outrage both to the strikers and the foreign strike breakers themselves, who were poorly dressed for the rigorous climate.[4]

Well before the Russian party reached Fairbanks they were intercepted by armed miners and ordered to turn back for the coast. The foot-weary Russians started back to Valdez, then were halted again by the United States marshal and a company of newly sworn deputies. Under heavy guard the strike breakers were conveyed to Fairbanks; to add insult to injury, they were lodged at the Miners' Hall! Growling numbers of miners gathered before the hall, but by this time the marshal had formed three companies of citizen deputies armed with rifles. A violent confrontation was avoided on this occasion, but the uneasy peace only endured as long as the Russians remained shut up in the closely guarded hall.

Former judge James Wickersham was practicing law in Fairbanks during the 1908 strike and was agonizing over whether he should become a candidate for congressional delegate. His sympathies did not lie with the Western Federation of Miners. Among Wickersham's arch political foes were the editors of the *Fairbanks Times*, who did not share the vitriolic line on labor leaders hewed to by the *Fairbanks News*—not that the two papers ever agreed on any issue. Wickersham expressed glee when businessmen apparently reacted against the *Times*' stand favorable to the miners' cause: "The *Times*, stripped of every advertisement, is whining like a whipped dog."[5]

Unlike the *News*, the *Times* editorialized on the labor situation in mild and reasonable terms. Its editors cried out against acts of violence and the interception of the Russian strike breakers, but otherwise remained neutral. To the *News* and its partisans like Wickersham, this neutrality was proof that the *Times* supported the W.F.M.

As Wickersham saw it, the labor struggle was intimately related to Alaskan politics and the forthcoming congressional election. He believed that John Clum, the pioneer postmaster and the Democratic candidate for delegate, the *Times,* and W.F.M. officials were forming a combination to swing Clum's election: "Fred Martin's saloon is the headquarters of the scheme—the worst 'bum' resort in the Tanana."[6] The former judge was a politician born and, despite disclaimers to friends, panted to enter the delegate race to succeed Thomas Cale. Both Wickersham and Cale were Republicans. All that held Wickersham back was the uncertainty regarding the incumbent; when Cale finally withdrew, Wickersham promptly announced his candidacy.

The "bum" resort referred to by Wickersham was the popular California Saloon. If patrons did not care to belly up to the bar on the street level, they could relax upstairs, where reading material, stationery, and pool tables were provided. It provided a pleasant retreat for miners, most of whom lodged in bunk houses. But to Wickersham and other law and order men, the California was a hot bed of radicalism, and the marshal ordered it closed. Wickersham believed the closing would "do more than a hundred deputy marshals to preserve order."[7]

Closing the California and another saloon, the Miners' Home, followed some gunplay at the railroad station. While strikers gathered to watch the escorted "Cossacks" board the train for the mines, one of them scattered a few shots. He didn't hit anyone, but the incident provided United States Marshal George Perry the excuse needed to bear down on the union. Warrants were issued for the arrest of the gunman and all the W.F.M. officials. Wickersham's diary records his satisfaction: "Steffenson, the organizer and inciter to riot, is in jail and liable to remain there."[8]

Ever since the first strike breakers had been brought in, the more apprehensive residents had been demanding army troops from Fort Gibbon. Fort Gibbon, on the Yukon River near the mouth of the Tanana, was the military installation closest to Fairbanks. Some mine operators wanted martial law imposed upon Fairbanks, as well as the posting of troopers along the Valdez Trail to prevent the interception of strike breakers. Marshal Perry, however, figured he could handle the situation without the army; his forces consisted of twenty paid deputies and 150 volunteers.

The resistance of the mine operators to the miners' demands seemed petty and selfish to some observers. Mining engineer T. A. Rickard, though a hater of the W.F.M., felt that the miners richly deserved $5 for an eight-hour day. On a visit to the mines in 1909 he noted that the deep bedrock made mining in the Tanana much more difficult than else-where.

In every western mining camp, the operators fought the union bitterly. Some of the most violent examples of class conflict in American history resulted. Peace-loving Alaskans had some cause for alarm when they reviewed the history of the W.F.M. strikes in Colorado and other west-ern states. The struggle for an eight-hour work day had been going on for years. Operators had infiltrated unions with Pinkerton spies, routed strik-ers with state militia, and blacklisted active union men. Strikers had been beaten by militia, herded into bull pens, and, on occasion, shipped out of state while compliant government officials looked on. Miners answered violence with violence. Strike breakers were assaulted with vengeance. Dynamite wrecked buildings and maimed operators.

Unquestionably, the W.F.M. leadership was radical. Big Bill Haywood was an officer of the union and of the International Workers of the World (Wobblies) as well. In one of the most frightful frame-ups in American labor history, operators stooped to murder in an effort to break Haywood and the union. Harry Orchard, a W.F.M. member, confessed to the murder of Idaho's governor, and implicated union leaders Haywood, Charles Moyer, and George Pettibone. Orchard, or his fiendish backers, had conceived the scheme of rigging a bomb at the governor's gate. In one of the most celebrated trials in America's judicial history, the great de-fense attorney Clarence Darrow unmasked the operators' plot and secured the acquittal of the labor leaders.

Haywood's acquittal did not convince the *Fairbanks News* editor of his innocence—men like Haywood and their Tanana valley cohorts, Steffen-son and Priestly, would stop at nothing to achieve their anarchistic goals. Perhaps, "like Haywood and Moyer," Steffenson and Priestly were "too smooth to be caught, but wherever there is a Moyer or a Haywood, there will be found an Orchard."[9] This kind of inflammatory rhetoric helped little to cool tempers in Fairbanks. T. A. Rickard blamed the Tanana's "reptile press" for inciting miners to reprisals.[10] Priestly believed that the press entirely misrepresented the union's efforts to restrain violence during the dispute.

Another gathering of miners was broken up by Marshal Perry and his deputies. Once more the union leaders were arrested for "rioting." Word came from Seattle that John Ronan, head of the Tanana Valley Operators Association, was benefiting from widespread unemployment there; he would hire 2,000 men and send them to the Fairbanks' mines. Harass-ment of union leaders went on. As editor of the *Miners Union Bulletin*, Priestly was convicted of libel and fined $400. He had exposed some scandalous doings at the Tanana Club, the operators' resort, that "had all the married men in Fairbanks explaining to their wives"[11]—his story suggested that sex orgies at the club were common events. Pressure began to tell on the miners. The strike was in its second year and prospects for success dimmed. In 1907 there were no cleanups and no wages because of the strike and because of the critical shortage of water. Missing the cleanup season meant impoverishment for the workers and their families. Nominally, the strike went on—but most miners went back to work.

An aftermath of the strike was a vigorous crackdown on vice in Fairbanks. Wickersham's successor as district court judge, Silas H. Reed, arrived in May and went hard at it. Judge Reed must have had instructions from the Justice Department to root out the town's more combustible elements. Wickersham's advice to Washington probably had something to do with this. Wickersham wrote the attorney general calling for an investigation of Fairbanks' district attorney concerning actions "with his woman" and jury fixing.[12] Perhaps the former judge put the finger on others as well. James Wickersham never missed a chance to punish his political opponents.

Grand jury indictments poured forth in scores against every pimp, prostitute, and bath house operator in town. Judge Reed closed all dance halls. Indictments were also issued against men cohabiting with women outside of marriage. To the surprise of most Fairbanks' residents, a prominent lawyer, Tom Marquam, was charged with adultery. It may not have been coincidental that Marquam headed the local anti-Wickersham forces and edited the Wick-baiting *Fairbanks Times*. Noting all this in his diary, Wickersham's joy abounds: "Go to it! This bunch wanted a change—they stood in with my enemies and especially with the Union and now they are getting it! I can now sit back and smile."[13]

By late June, things had quieted down in Fairbanks. The strike's back was broken, and the reform fever had peaked. As the time for the election neared, attention shifted to politics. Wickerhsam had entered the contest with a bang. At a meeting before an audience of 500, the former judge stated his views and, marvelously enough, "quoted every plank from the local labor platform"![14]

Writing in the *Alaska Weekly* in 1931, Priestly thought Alaska miners "can give me a good deal of credit for pioneer work as a youthful editor of the *Miners Union Bulletin*." He recalled his three arrests, the threats made against him and his unpopularity—even the women of the Row had vilified the union leader. When the Tanana Valley Railroad had refused to carry the *Miners Union Bulletin* to the creeks, 50 miners had organized a dog-team brigade to haul the papers. After being jailed as a consequence of the shooting affray, Priestly had still managed to get the miners' newspaper out, by writing in his cell and handing copy out the window for the

printer. The jury selected for his libel trial had been packed with businessmen: "If my penalty had been set by the jury I would still be in jail,"
wrote Priestly, who had acted as his own attorney for the trial, where he
had heard himself described by the prosecutor as a "foreign agitator trying
to tear down the pillars of freedom for which our forefathers bled and
died." In response, Priestly had "gently reminded" the judge that the
prosecutor had been born in Canada and that "his forefathers must have
been on the wrong side of the fence."[15]

Eventually the miners won all their demands. In 1909 they gained
protection by legislation providing workers with a mechanics' lien against
owners who refused to pay whenever the cleanup was sparse. In 1914,
mine safety inspection was instituted. And finally, in 1915, all Alaskan
workers were given the protection of a law limiting their work to an eight-
hour day.

33

James Wickersham and Gold Land Politics

THE INTERIOR OF ALASKA is remarkable for its clear, sparkling skies and fresh, invigorating air. Summer or winter, a sense of the open vastness of the land stimulates one. Some of the greatest rivers of the continent vie with the grandest mountains to delight and refresh the eye, though more intimate valleys and low-rolling hills charm the senses without overwhelming with their grandeur. It is a land to be wondered at; the Yukon River alone drains an area of 330,000 square miles. Its length is just short of 2,000 miles, while thirteen of its numberless tributaries exceed 1,000 miles in length.

In this fresh, clear, boundless land, a haven for men who did not care to be trammeled and confined by burgeoning cities or narrow, provincial towns, what should the political atmosphere be like? Lofty? Open? Detached? Irreproachably honest? The answer is none of these. Political battles in the North were waged with all the scurrility, corruption, vituperation, and mendacity of a Boston ward. Gutter politics prevailed in a land claiming very few gutters. After all, the transplantation of a man from Boston or Seattle to a fresher country did not make him an angel.

Federal Neglect and Home Rule

Given the vagaries of human personality and the labyrinthine ways of national politics, it would be daring to state that the Alaskan political scene during the gold rush era was simple. Policies concerning Alaska were determined in Washington, D.C.; all government officials, except the congressional delegate after 1906, were federal appointees. However involved the trade-off in the White House and Congress might have been on Alaskan issues, Alaskans themselves were not complex in their political stands, though there was always plenty of conflict.

Another source of conflict was even nearer at hand: the assertion of federal authority over matters Alaskans considered of municipal concern. Businessmen generally favored open gambling and it was tolerated for the first hectic years of the boom. But eventually the federal authorities clamped the lid on, and the high rollers had to take cover.

John B. Wallace, a Nome rusher, resented the efforts of Judge Alfred Moore to close the games and harass the whores of Nome. As he saw it, the judge was trying to pattern Nome after some small village in the East or Midwest. It seemed clear to Wallace that some of these "imported" federal officials failed to adjust to their new environment. Since "god is afar off and it is a long way to Washington," all that Alaskans could do was complain long and hard against particular judges, district attorneys, and marshals, but with no conviction that they would be heard. There was only one remedy to such a dilemma, which brings us to the leading article of political faith among Alaskans. Almost everyone agreed that viable solutions to the territory's problems required home rule. In the early days demand focused on congressional representation for Alaska. In 1906, this long felt need was granted by Congress; the election of a single non-voting delegate to the House of Representatives was provided for. Then the home rule campaign shifted to a call for a territorial legislature. In 1912, Congress acceded to this request, though sharply limiting the powers of the Juneau-based legislature. These successes did nothing to assuage the pangs of most Alaskans for a fuller measure of control over their own destinies. They wanted statehood, and finally achieved it in 1959. An appreciation of Alaskan attitudes towards the federal government helps to clarify the aspirations of her political leaders.

Re-enter James Wickersham

From his appointment as federal district judge in 1900 until his death in Juneau 38 years later, James Wickersham was the leading political figure of the territory. He served as judge for seven years, helped to found Fairbanks, and brought order to Nome after replacing the corrupt Judge Alfred Noyes. In 1908, he was elected congressional delegate, an office he enlivened for 18 years.

To his political foes—and he had an ample number of them—he was "Flickering Wick," a model of inconsistency, or "Terrible James," a man who never forgot or forgave anyone who opposed him. His friends and supporters lauded his honesty and courage whether on the bench or in baiting Congress. Nobody was neutral regarding Wick; one was all for him or all against him. Both factions agreed that he was a battler, either for "useless causes" like home rule or for the good of all Alaskans—depending on particular political views.

Wickersham's judicial stints on the Yukon, in Nome, and in early Fairbanks have been described elsewhere, but without detailed reference to the political repercussions evoked by the energetic official. Opposition to the judge grew strong in Washington, D.C., as an aftermath of his cleanup of Nome's mine claim mess and, particularly, his contempt conviction of United States Marshal Frank Richards. Reasons for the antagonism were always lucidly apparent to Wick: "The vindictiveness of human nature readily appears in a frontier mining camp peopled with men from all quarters of the globe intent only on getting a fortune as soon as possible." Their lust for gold, if frustrated by a court decision, drove them to malicious opposition to the judge, who commented, "Then no slander is too vile, no means of revenge is too base to satisfy the thirst for vengeance."[1]

In June, 1904, Wickersham's first term as district court judge ended. Though he had reason to expect commendation for his work at Nome and elsewhere and swift confirmation by the United States Senate of his reappointment, it was quite otherwise. Charges of misfeasance and malfeasance in office and of improper private conduct were brought before the Justice Department by McKenzie's associates and by some disappointed litigants, according to the judge.[2] William A. Day, first assistant to the United States attorney general, was ordered to conduct an investigation in Alaska—the first of three such harassments of the judge. Meanwhile, Wickersham was given a one-year recess appointment that did not require the Senate's approval.

The investigation was likened by Wick to a miners' meeting and he felt it helped clear the air, but the judge was annoyed because neither Day nor anyone else would fully specify the secret charges made against him. Day visited all the camps and heard whatever the men had to say about the court. At any rate, Day's report exonerated the judge, whose name President Theodore Roosevelt then sent to the Senate.

The Senate balked at confirming him as judge of the Third Judicial District. Senators McCumber and Hansbrough of North Dakota—friends of the Spoiler's leader Alexander McKenzie—were joined by Senator Nelson of Minnesota and others in a struggle against the appointee. A subcommittee of the Senate judiciary committee voted in favor of confirmation, but Wick's foes filibustered, holding up all other legislation, in an all-out effort against him. The appearance just then of Rex Beach's article on the Nome Spoilers, "The Looting of Alaska," helped the cause of Wick's opponents.[3] Beach had exposed the North Dakota senators for their relationship to McKenzie and the Nome mining claim swindle. The injured senators told colleagues that Beach's material came from Wick and appealed for closed ranks against senatorial muckraking. The filibuster kept the judge's appointment from coming before the Senate and once more the President gave the judge a recess appointment.

The struggle over Wickersham's appointment engaged his senatorial opponents from 1904 to 1907. They were successful each year in keeping the issue from a vote, but Roosevelt declared that Wickersham would be an Alaskan judge as long as he was president and made recess appointments each year. Those senators who were not interested in Alaska must have grown weary of hearing about the judge of the Third District.

Wickersham decided in the spring of 1907 to offer his resignation should another investigation be made of his office. Roosevelt assured him that none would be permitted. In the fall, the judge decided to resign anyway. His diary mentions concern for his wife's health and a desire to enter private law practice as reasons for resignation, but perhaps others were more compelling: Roosevelt's term would soon be up, and who then would protect his position?

Home Rule, the Syndicate, and the Delegate

Wickersham's exit from political life was of brief duration—in the summer of 1908 he offered his candidacy as Alaska's second congressional delegate. It cost money to buy political support of newspapers in Alaska—as much as $2,500 for the popular *Fairbanks News*—and he did not have it. But editorial support was not all important. His public speeches in Fairbanks, Nome, and in other towns made his views well enough known. He supported labor's platform, though his sympathies had previously never been warm to the workers' cause. Most important were his espousal of the home rule/anti-Syndicate views—however tardy in developing, his fine gift of public speaking, and his general popularity. He handily won a plurality of the votes cast, taking 3,802 of 9,636, to commence his long reign as Alaska's delegate. Wick won his last election in 1930. In 1932 he was buried in the Democratic landslide. He did not run again but remained a political force in Alaska until his death at the age of 82 in 1939. Even in his old age, Wick was a man of imposing appearance. He was a sturdy six-footer of erect carriage, hardened but not bent by his middle years when he had mushed the winter trails to hold court in the vastness of the North. When Wickersham announced his first campaign, editor Strong of the *Katalla Herald*, who knew him well but loved him not, admitted that Wick was a fighter. Nor did the judge care what weapons he fought with, according to Strong; "blades, war clubs/truth/lies" would do.[4] Old-timers among Alaskans today differ in assessing Wickersham. Some lionize him, while others are critical. But all remember his persuasiveness on the stump as he stood before a packed hall or on a town corner, defending his actions, damning his rivals in terms of striking eloquence and savage insult. The record indicates that he was equally persuasive in Congress, despite his fiery attacks on offending bureaucrats. His dominance of the northern political scene was challenged often, but dominate he did until the end.

34

The Literary Frontier

THE NORTH was a brutal frontier, raw and desolate, demanding of all the stamina and courage men could muster against it. Mesmerized by their lust for gold, they endured excruciating hardships on the trail, faced incredible obstacles of distance and a savage climate and struggled on to a triumphant achievement of their goal—or to failure and frustration. Their tenacious efforts in a harsh land were memorialized in contemporary journalism and autobiographical accounts, and in a popular literature that encapsulated all the drama and rugged romance of their collective experience. Countless millions shared vicariously in the travails of the gold seeker, welcoming avidly the birth of a new frontier hero in story and verse.

Towering over all those who enshrined the heroes and rogues of America's last frontier adventurers in popular fiction was Jack London. His rowdy youth as oyster pirate, hobo, and seal poacher was as colorful as that of any of his fictional characters, London stampeded to the Klondike in 1897. There he prospected, mined, suffered from scurvy—the miner's curse—and failed to strike a bonanza. All these were common enough vicissitudes but they provided the basis for a literary outpouring that was to springboard the young writer to worldwide fame. In eleven books London served up his highly seasoned conception of the northern scene, the violent world of the Malemute Kid, Sitka Charlie, Old Tarwater, and the indomitable Buck. He created characters of commanding strength—men, and women too, who strode over snowy mountains and frigid tundra in fulfillment of their unique destinies. They could not be intimidated; their courage, resourcefulness, and sagacity made their progress irresistible; they exemplified Thomas Huxley's theory that the fittest survive at the expense of inferiors. As one scholar put it, "the age of heroes was not dead, but they had emigrated to the frozen north."[1]

Among the strongest intellectual influences upon Jack London were

Thomas Huxley, Charles Darwin, and Rudyard Kipling. From the first two, the writer gleaned a particular interpretation of the theories of evolution and the survival of the fittest, concepts that easily supported London's reading of Kipling. Clearly, the Anglo–Saxons demonstrated a racial superiority condoned by the laws of the universe. It was obvious among the jungle fauna, on the Indian subcontinent, and equally so, with the inhabitants of the high latitudes who peopled London's stories. In novels like *Burning Daylight* and *Call of the Wild*, short stories like "Love of Life" and "Son of Wolf," London's characters loom huge to display their surmounting mettle.

London drew on his own Yukon and Alaskan travels and on the lore he gathered from others. Old Tarwater of "Like Argus of Ancient Times" was modeled on the aged rusher who joined London's party on their ascent of the Chilkoot; his would-be egg profiteer of "One Thousand Dozen" owed much to an actual incident related to the writer. These figures and others like them were transmuted by the novelist's alchemy into the dramatic personae of his literary world. Critics might dispute the verisimilitude of London's creatures, but his northern tales still exercise their fascination over readers. No other writer's depiction of events of the North has approached London's in popularity. Today, London's books are more widely read in some European countries than in America. In Russia he holds the place of best-known American writer. As one Russian put it, "This is the first cigar we smoke in our youth."[2]

In 1899 the *Overland Monthly* published nine of London's short stories, most of which later appeared in his first book. In 1900 eastern journals became aware of London's work and published ten more of his stories. For five years after his return from the Klondike, dead broke and scurvy-ridden, his output of novels and stories with northern settings was snapped up eagerly by editors anxious to assuage the appetite of magazine and book buyers. "I never realized a cent from any property I had interest in up there," London wrote a friend in 1900, "still, I have been managing to pan out a living since on the strength of the trip."[3] London discovered a literary mother lode and drew from it throughout his career.

Wilson Mizner, the wittiest of all the stampeders, once made fun of the "London school" of Klondike fiction, with "its supermen and superdogs, its abysmal brutes and exquisite ingenues."[4] Other critics have complained that London's craft consisted of turning men into brutes, and brutes into men. Yet a close examination of London's stories reveals their basic strength aside from any dependence on ideology. They are good stories that are well told.

What did pioneer northerners think of London's fiction? It is difficult to generalize about this beyond noting that they read London's work eagerly.

Obviously they did not accept every facet of the writer's interpretations. Will Ballou, the Rampart miner, read *Call of the Wild* in the spring of 1901 and remarked that it was one man's version of Alaskan life. The only feature he criticized in particular was London's endowment of squaw men, whites living with Indians, with heroic qualities. Miners did not view such men so favorably because they corrupted natives by getting liquor for them and because of racist attitudes.

Robert Service

Another writer who established a reputation through his northern residence was the poet Robert Service. The going was not easy for this Scot who threw up his bank clerk's position in the Old World to emigrate to North America. He hoboed his way to California, lived on oranges and an occasional mission handout, and read about the gold rush in the stories of Jack London and others, little dreaming that, "while other men were seeking Eldorado, they were also making one for me."[5] In 1904 the young Scot took a job with a Canadian bank and was sent to Whitehorse, the interior head of the railroad built in 1899 from Skagway to Whitehorse. As he steamed north on the passage, Service marveled at the rugged grandeur of the coastal mountain ranges and mused on his future. He hoped to be a writer, knowing himself as a "poor wretch with dreams, but somehow different from the crowd." From the steamer deck he reveled in the sublime, moonlit scenery "inspired . . . to sordid schemes of self-enrichment, because in the end they mean escape to freedom."[6] His years as bum and minstrel, thumping out his own songs on a guitar to unresponsive listeners, had not reconciled him to a resumption of a bank clerk's life. Yet, by an accident of fate, he was voyaging towards the land that would be his artistic catalyst and where all his dreams would find fulfillment.

The Skagway at which Service disembarked was a sleepy little town, very different from the wild port known to the Dawson argonauts. Now there were no crowds, no excitement, no threats from lawless gangs. Travelers to the interior could ride the White Pass and Yukon Railway safely and comfortably over the coastal range to the interior. Far below his coach Service could see the distinct markings of the stampeders' trail. It looked tough enough, and the poet did not long for its drama. "I was glad I had not been one of those grim stalwarts of the Great Stampede."[7] Strange comment from the writer whose verses were to romanticize the gold era for generations of enraptured readers of "The Cremation of Sam McGee" and "The Shooting of Dan McGrew," but quite in keeping with his no-nonsense character. Once established in Whitehorse, Service plugged away at his commercial duties, avoided the drinking crowd, and saved his money. This austere regime was to bring him closer to the old

Klondike mood than any amount of wassailing in saloons could have done.

In his spare time Service was in demand at social gatherings for his recitations of dramatic poems. "Casey at the Bat," "Gunga Din," and "The Face on the Bar-room Floor" were universal favorites of the day and his own verse efforts were in the same vein. Though he recited other mens' poems he had the satisfaction of seeing some of his own early work in print. Little fame or fortune attended the occasional appearance of a poem in the *Whitehorse Star*, the town's newspaper; still, it was an encouragement to his lonely aspirations.

Service's ambitions got a nudge in the proper direction from Stroller White of the *Star*, one of the best-known newsmen of the North. White urged the young banker, who had been asked to recite at a church concert, to do something original: "Give us something about our own little bit of earth . . . there's a rich paystreak waiting for someone to work. Why don't you go on in and stake it?"[8]

Musing on White's suggestion, Service took a long walk, searching for a poetic theme. Nothing came. Back in the bank, where he could work in quiet after closing, he gnawed a pencil and stared at his blank notepaper. Faintly he heard sounds of merriment from a neighboring saloon—it was Saturday night and revelry time. "A bunch of the boys were whooping it up in the Malemute Saloon," he wrote. Suddenly, there was the roar of a pistol in his ear. The bank's nightwatchman had mistaken Service for a burglar and fired at him. After calming the watchman, the poet scribbled feverishly through the night. His theme—a shooting at the Malemute Saloon, and the lurid narrative of unrequited love and vengeance unfolded itself. By 5 A.M. the ballad "was in the bag." "The Shooting of Dan McGrew" had taken form.

A delighted audience heard Service's "Dan McGrew" at a church concert. Afterwards, one of them, a Dawson mining man, buttonholed the poet to tell "a story Jack London never got." One wonders what Jack London might have done with the miner's story of the prospector who cremated his partner, but it gave Service a masterpiece. After the concert Service walked for hours, brooding on the incident and searching for a theme. Then it came—"There are strange things done in the midnight sun." Verse after verse fell into place as emerged "The Cremation of Sam McGee," which was to be the keystone of the poet's success. Before Service stumbled into bed he had completed the last verse celebrating the miner who finally got in from the cold.

And there sat Sam, looking cool and calm, in the heart of the furnace roar;
And he wore a smile you could see a mile, and he said: "Please close that door.

It's fine in here, but I greatly fear you'll let in the cold and storm —
Since I left Plumtree, down in Tennessee, it's the first time I've been
warm."[9]

The *Songs of a Sourdough*, Service's first book of poems, met with
instantaneous acclaim. Immensely readable and, even more important,
recitable, the ballads appeared in edition after edition—the twentieth by
1909, and never out of print since.

Rex Beach

Next to Jack London the most popular fictional portrayer of the northern gold scene was Rex Beach. Beach was a law student in Chicago when
he heard the call of the Klondike. The burly youth had joined the school's
football and water polo teams for the privilege of free dining and he was
eager to escape the playing field. The hardship and privation on the trail
did not worry him. "Freezing was far more pleasant than drowning . . .
and as for hunger, I was starved most of the time, anyhow."[10] With a
grubstake from his brothers, equipped with sleeping bag, rifle, doeskin
suit, and mandolin, Beach set out.

Beach spent two years at Rampart working at mining, logging, and
various odd jobs, including music-making. A writer's career did not cross
his mind at the time; he was just one of many drudging away to make a
living. The question of the literary possibilities of the northern frontier
was discussed on occasion, but mining men did not find their own work
glamorous. A journalist acquaintance at Rampart assured Beach that the
North would never produce a Mark Twain or Bret Harte—the writers
who immortalized the California gold era in fiction—"There's no drama
up here, no comedy, no warmth. Life is as pale and cold as the snow."
How could colorful stories be told of such a drab and dreary country?[11]

At the time Beach agreed with the journalist. Life did seem hard and
unromantic on the Yukon compared to sunny California. Later he reflected on this conversation in amazement at what he had almost missed.
"Color, comedy, drama indeed! There we were, some fifteen hundred
souls, and twelve saloon keepers, all dumped out on the bank of the
Yukon to shift for ourselves in a region unmapped and unexplored." The
men had arrived in Rampart late in the fall; grub was short; stoves were
scarce; and all were newcomers. "Not one in ten knew how to toss a
flapjack or tear a footrag." None knew what gold looked like in its "native
state." Neither roads nor well-marked trails existed. "Every valley was a no-
man's land, every rushing river was a highway to adventure and every
gulch [was] filled to the brim with a purple haze of mystery." Surely the
stuff of romance was there![12]

He was only 24 when he left the North and had not yet thought of becoming a writer. In Chicago he joined a building materials firm as a salesman and moved up rapidly in the business world. One day he met a Yukon acquaintance who had just earned $10 from the sale of an article on Alaska. "Here was news more incredible than the Klondike discovery, viz., paydirt on Michigan Avenue running ten dollars to the pan!" Beach exclaims, recounting this episode humorously in his memoirs. As he described it, he was fearful that the news of such easy money would leak out and start a literary stampede: "I implored my friend to keep it under his hat at least until I could get some stakes down." Exaggeration aside, the incident did, for some reason, stimulate Beach to try his hand at writing.[13]

His first story was based on an anecdote told to him by a Rampart miner. This piece was submitted to the popular *McClure's Magazine* and promptly accepted. With some pride the fledgling author displayed a $50 McClure's check to his boss who pretended amazement at such a windfall. His business colleagues' taunts did not divert Beach from further writing. By this time he had been promoted to a vice-presidency in his firm, but he devoted evenings, Sundays and holidays to authorship: "I wrote on railroad trains, in waiting rooms or wherever I could hold a suit case on my knees."[14] Before long his income from writing equaled his salary and Beach gave up business to become a full-time author.

S. S. McClure, the magazine editor, suggested that Beach try a novel. A good plot came readily to mind—the brazen conspiracy of Alexander McKenzie and Judge Noyes to oust the Nome discoverers from their rich claims. "About all I had to do was add a little imagination, flavor with love interest, season to taste and serve."[15] After completing *The Spoilers*, a fictional account of the "boldest buccaneering raid directed at the North," Beach wrote a muckraking article, "The Looting of Alaska," based on the same incident.[16] McClure liked the article but made the mistake of letting another publisher get the novel. *The Spoilers* became a best-selling book and a Hollywood film. In fact moviemen have liked *The Spoilers* well enough to base films on the story three times over the years.

Roy Glenister is the hero of *The Spoilers*. He is depicted as one of the mine owners whom the conspirators tried to defraud. To some extent former reindeer herdsman Jafet Lindeberg served as a model. The young miner proves himself too dominant a figure to stand aside in the face of judicial chicanery, and triumphs over the legal minions and thugs set against him. For all Glenister's gentlemanly qualities he was essentially an untamed force, bottling up under the veneer of civilized conduct a fierce, half-savage spirit. Glenister has to struggle against his demon and the consequences of his love for a girl, who happens to be a loyal niece of the perfidious judge.

Among Beach's thirty-two books are other novels set in Alaska. *The Barrier* draws on Beach's experiences on the Yukon at Rampart, but is not based upon actual events—and does not hang together as well as *The Spoilers*. Beach turned to another chapter of Alaskan history in *The Iron Trail*. Here the rivalry of railroad builders driving to complete a route to the rich Kennecott Company copper mines forms the substance of the plot. In Beach's works the secondary characters are pale foils to the leading hero and villain. Regardless of their efforts at humor and their varying vernacular, they cannot balance the overpowering weight of the main figures, men almost too good or evil to believe in.

Beach's stories still have readers, particularly *The Spoilers* and *The Iron Trail; The Iron Trail* has been recently reprinted in paperback. But Beach's popularity over the years has not kept pace with that of Jack London—and for obvious reasons. London was a craftsman of much superior ability, his plots and characters were much better than Beach's. Nor could Beach's descriptive powers approach those of London. London's North may have been somewhat unreal at times, but it never lacked vividness. Despite Beach's extensive experience at Rampart and Nome, he fails to communicate the atmosphere of those lively towns. His highly charged scenes set in saloons and elsewhere are dramatic enough, yet often are not marked by any particular quality of their northern background.

London and Beach have not had a long line of successors. For all the popularity of northern stories in the early years of the century, when noted writers like Jules Verne tried their hand, the interest has not been maintained. Popular fiction depends upon ready points of reference among readers, and the decline of interest in the North since the gold rush days has diminished the opportunities for such work. While the appeal of the colorful history of the Old West's frontier never wanes, and is encouraged endlessly by films and television, the fictional field of the North lies fallow. It is conceivable that popular writers might rediscover the North and exploit the material that brought prominence to London and Beach. Alaska's current oil boom might help to prepare the ground for tales of hearty dog mushers and the quest of fortune in frozen regions, but a resurgence cannot be predicted with any confidence. The weary cycle of Deadwood shoot-outs, Apache battles, and hard-riding cattle-rustling grinds on relentlessly while the rich adventures of northern mining camps are forgotten.

Perhaps the pessimistic prophecy of Ambrose Bierce has been partially fulfilled as far as the North's literary heritage is concerned. Bierce made his name writing about the California gold rush but could see nothing of permanent value resulting from the Klondike stampede. He doubted that even a "dog sled civilization and a reindeer religion" would survive,

---

Nothing will come of him [the stampeder]. He is a world in the wind, a brother to the fog. At the scene of his activity no memory of him will remain. The gravel that he thawed and sifted will freeze again .... The snows will cover over his trail and all be as before.[17]

But, of course, the North was changed radically and permanently by the gold developments. Some of the trails became roads. Yet the literary gravel did freeze up after it was worked brilliantly by London, Service, and Beach.

Too bad—but such neglect is understandable. America's Alaskan frontier experience has not fixed itself in the national consciousness. Fleetingly, in the skilled efforts of Jack London and Rex Beach, the North became part of the frontier legend, then was crowded from popular imagination by more familiar western exploits. Alaska was too strange, too distant and obscure to preserve its place. The handful of historians and creative writers of the North have not been able to reverse the trend. Soapy Smith, Wilson Mizner, Swiftwater Bill Gates, and other northern worthies toss restlessly in their graves, longing, one might suppose, for their just share of prime television time.

Epilogue

IN DISTANT EUROPE huge armies were fiercely engaged in the trench warfare of the Western Front as the little steamboat *Pelican* voyaged along the Yukon and its tributaries. The rivers themselves had not changed much over the 30-odd years since Lieutenant Schwatka's raft had floated down from the Yukon's headwaters to St. Michael. Waters yellow with silt poured into the Bering Sea as always, draining the great basin of the interior in an unending flow. Much that Lt. Frederick Schwatka had seen on his exploratory expedition in 1883 was observed also by Reverend Hudson Stuck from the deck of the *Pelican*. Of course there had been momentous changes as well. In the intervening years between these two voyages the North had boomed. Its ancient, gold encrusted stream beds had lured the adventurous, yielded up fortunes and created cities in the wilderness. The North known to Lieutenant Schwatka could never be again.

What evaluation can be made of this tumultuous chapter of the region's history? Stuck's reflections were gloomy indeed as the *Pelican* steamed downriver to Dawson and Forty Mile in the Yukon Territory, crossed the American border to Eagle, Circle, and Fort Yukon, then ascended the Tanana to Fairbanks. The Episcopal priest observed all the interior's principal gold camps, including Ruby on the lower Yukon, and Iditarod on the Innoku River, and reported on others: Wiseman, Coldfoot, Caro, and Nome. Few of the gold towns showed much bustle at the time of Stuck's visits, though many signs of former prosperity could be noted. A brief life was characteristic of a placer town: "However it may grow and flourish, however comfortable its homes and however attached to them people become, however . . . conditions of living become more and more pleasant, the whole thing is without substantial foundation, and inevitably temporary."[1] Unlike longer lasting quartz mines, placer deposits were soon worked out and when they failed after a few years, the communities dependent upon them also failed. Forty Mile, Eagle, Circle, and Rampart were dead, and elsewhere mining activity was

declining. Dawson was still alive, but the dredges operating there were
gathering the last remains of alluvial gold in the district and would soon
have all there was. Dawson was a "doomed city" and so were virtually all
the others that had not yet become ghost towns. Stuck thought that Fairbanks might survive with the aid of the government railroad to the coast,
"its market-gardens and its launderies," but he was not overly optimistic.[2]
With reason a Fairbanks newspaper had labeled the minister a Prophet of
Despair for uttering such sentiments on other occasions.

Surely the great boom had come and gone and with it had departed
Swiftwater Bill Gates, Wilson Mizner, Jack Hines, Tex Rickard, Rex
Beach, Jack Kearns, and thousands of lesser known stampeders. But the
collapse of the boom did not obviate community life in the interior. Alaska's population declined; yet a small mining industry sustained the pioneers of Nome, Fairbanks, and other towns. Tenacious men and women
defied the predictions of those who argued that a region without agricul-
tural potential could not survive. These northern settlers did not enjoy
great prosperity. The remoteness of the North and the high costs of trans-
porting most of the necessities from the Outside made their lives hard, yet
they had discovered other values that reconciled them to Alaskan conditions. Neither a romantic nor an adventurous spirit sustained them; it was
simply a preference for a life style that, for a variety of reasons, appealed
to them. Against all the formidable odds of isolation, distance, and a
harsh climate, they nurtured their frontier communities, ignoring the death
toll sounded by Reverend Stuck and other pessimists. Many could echo
the sentiments of George Pilcher whose adventures of 1898 ripened into a
lifetime commitment to life in the North:

---

*I came to this Alaska a young man full of energy, industry and a will to
win. I am now well into my 67th year and can feel the tug of time. I have
failed to win wealth but have maintained my self-respect and am convinced that I hold the respect of all—or most all—others. This is worth
more than gold.*[3]

But there was also a meaning in the northern experience for the tens of
thousands who did not settle permanently. Men like Fred Walker, an
Englishman, who was lured to the North in quest of adventure and
stopped only fleetingly in Alaska before moving on to other parts of the
world, looked back on his journeys there as one of "the high spots" of a
varied career.[4] Another favorable commentator, Johnny Walker, a veteran of the stampedes, had fond memories of his early experiences: "I'm
an old man now, but in those days of my youth I lived, ate, and slept

adventure. I made fortunes and spent them, lived like a prince, and like an Indian."[5]

Most of the argonauts seemed to have appreciated their individual gains as participants in the stirring events of the gold era. Very few of them expressed the disenchantment and bitterness of Arthur Dietz, whose sorry journey over the Malaspina Glacier was reported earlier in these pages. More typically, the rushers were like Charles Angel, who after suffering severe hardship on the trail and the climax of a near disaster at sea, watched from shipboard the land of so many golden dreams and shattered hopes recede.

True, I had found no gold. But I was no poorer than when I arrived; I enjoyed the best of health; and surely no more soul-satisfying adventures could have befallen me. No, I had no regrets.[6]

For Angel and others, the Alaskan adventure was well summed up in the verse of an anonymous poet:

A million dollar gold bond
Could never, never buy,
My memories of the Northland —
I'll keep them 'till I die.
I'll treasure them like a miser,
His hoard of gleaming gold —
My memories are my treasure,
And never may be sold.[7]

Notes[*]

Chapter 1
1. Wilson, *Campbell of the Yukon*, p. 97.
2. *Ibid.*
3. Schwatka, *Along Alaska's Great River*, p. 100.
4. *Ibid.*, p. 143.
5. *Ibid.*, p. 187.
6. *Ibid.*, p. 195.

Chapter 2
1. Kitchener, *Flag Over the North*, p. 154.
2. *Ibid.*, pp. 44–45.
3. *Ibid.*, p. 93.
4. *Ibid.*

Chapter 3
1. DeArmond, *Founding of Juneau*, p. vii.
2. Brooks, *Blazing Alaska's Trails*, p. 302.
3. Heller, *Sourdough Sagas*, p. 30.
4. *Ibid.*, pp. 43, 44.

Chapter 4
1. Brooks, *Blazing Alaska's Trails*, p. 372.
2. *Ibid.*

Chapter 5
1. Although Verdi and Wagner were not heard there. It was customary on the western frontier to term theaters as opera houses.
2. DeWindt, *Through the Gold-Fields of Alaska*, p. 157.
3. *Ibid.*, p. 161.

[*] Details about the works cited in these notes are given in the Bibliography (pp. 311–21).

4. *Ibid.*
5. Walden, *A Dog Puncher on the Yukon*, p. 42.
6. *Ibid.*, p. 43.
7. *Ibid.*, p. 44.
8. *Ibid.*, p. 45.
9. Heller, *Sourdough Sagas*, p. 90.
10. *Ibid.*
11. Spurr, *Through the Yukon Gold Diggings*, p. 167.
12. *Ibid.*, p. 193.
13. *Ibid.*, p. 203.
14. *Ibid.*, p. 204.
15. Wickersham, *Old Yukon*, p. 125.

Chapter 6
1. Winslow, *Big Pan-Out*, p. 30.
2. Alaska and the Klondike—Erastus Brainerd Scrapbook.
3. MacDonald, "Seattle, Vancouver, and the Klondike," p. 246.
4. Morgan, *Skid Road*, p. 5.
5. Ingersoll, *Gold Fields*, pp. 79, 80.
6. *Ibid.*
7. Ballou, letter to *Sommerville Citizen* [n.d.].
8. Lokke, *Klondike Saga*, pp. 31, 32.
9. Dietz, *Mad Rush for Gold*, pp. 20–21.
10. *Ibid.*, p. 19.
11. Lokke, *op. cit.*, p. 34.

Chapter 7
1. *Dyea Trail*, March 11, 1898.
2. *Skagway News*, October 15, 1897.
3. Munn, *Prairie Trails and Arctic By-Ways*, p. 86.
4. Steele, *Forty Years in Canada*, p. 297.
5. *Ibid.*, pp. 295, 296.
6. *Dyea Trail*, March 11, 1898.
7. *Ibid.*
8. *Ibid.*
9. *Ibid.*
10. Graves, *On the White Pass Payroll*, p. 23.
11. James Geoghegan Papers, p. 3.
12. Walden, *A Dog Puncher on the Yukon*, p. 132.
13. Heller, *Sourdough Sagas*, pp. 130, 131.

Chapter 8
1. Walker, *Jack London and the Klondike*, p. 58.
2. *Ibid.*

3. Brooks, *Blazing Alaska's Trails*, p. 360.
4. Lokke, *Klondike Saga*, p. 46.
5. Steele, *Forty Years in Canada*, p. 299.
6. Brooks, *op. cit.*, p. 357.
7. McLeod, pioneer broadcast tape.
8. Mizner, *Many Mizners*, pp. 111–112.
9. Steele, *op. cit.*, pp. 311, 312.

Chapter 9
1. *Compilation of Narratives of Explorations in Alaska*, p. 500.
2. *Ibid.*, p. 581.
3. *Ibid.*, p. 554.
4. Sherwood, *Exploration of Alaska*, p. 167.
5. Stewart, "From Rags to Riches," p. 10.
6. *Ibid.*, p. 11.

Chapter 10
1. Lynch, *Three Years in the Klondike*, p. 3.
2. *Ibid.*, p. 17.
3. *Ibid.*, p. 19.
4. Beach, *Personal Exposures*, p. 26.
5. Pilcher Diary, July 9, 1898.

Chapter 11
1. *Compilation of Narratives of Explorations in Alaska*, pp. 563–628.
2. *Sitka Alaskan*, February 20, 1898.
3. *Compilation of Narratives of Explorations in Alaska*, p. 586.
4. Abercrombie, *Copper River Exploring Expedition 1899*, p. 14.
5. *Ibid.*, p. 15.
6. *Ibid.*
7. *Ibid.*, p. 16.
8. *Ibid.*, p. 18.
9. *Ibid.*, pp. 19–20.
10. Dietz, *Mad Rush for Gold in Frozen North*, p. 15.
11. *Ibid.*, p. 13.
12. *Ibid.*, pp. 271–272.

Chapter 12
1. MacGregor, *Klondike Rush Through Edmonton*, pp. 1–3.
2. Underwood, *Alaska*, p. 35.
3. Steele, *Forty Years in Canada*, p. 292.
4. Brooks, *Blazing Alaska's Trails*, p. 358.
5. Tollemache, *Reminiscences of the Yukon*, p. 27.
6. Barbeau, *Pathfinders of the North Pacific*, p. 188.

7. Hamilton, *Yukon Story*, p. 10.
8. *Ibid.*, p. 11.
9. *Ibid.*, p. 15.
10. *Ibid.*, p. 16.
11. Garland, *Trail of the Gold-Seekers*, p. 8.
12. *Ibid.*, p. 100.
13. *Ibid.*, p. 217.
14. *Ibid.*, p. 237.
15. *Ibid.*, p. 241.

Chapter 13

1. Walden, *A Dog Puncher on the Yukon*, p. 106.
2. *Fairbanks Times*, November 22, 1906.
3. Walden, *op. cit.*, p. 148.
4. Steele, *Forty Years in Canada*, p. 327.
5. The most notable secondary account of the Klondike stampede is in Pierre Berton's *Klondike*.

Chapter 14

1. Cantwell, *Report of the Operations of the U.S. Revenue Steamer* Nunivak, p. 53.
2. Farnsworth to Rogers, January 30, 1900.
3. Cantwell, *op. cit.*, p. 59.
4. *Ibid.*, p. 60.
5. *Ibid.*
6. *Ibid.*, p. 63.
7. *Ibid.*, p. 69.
8. Ballou to brother Walt, June 2, 1899.
9. *Ibid.*, June 12, 1899.
10. *Ibid.*, September 20, 1899.
11. *Ibid.*, October 5, 1899.
12. *Ibid.*, June 22, 1900.

Chapter 15

1. Schrader and Brooks, *Preliminary Report on the Cape Nome Gold Region*, p. 31. Details and priorities of initial discoveries are always disputed. See also Lillo, *Alaska Gold Mining Company*, and Carlson, "Discovery of Gold at Nome, Alaska.
2. Carlson, *op. cit.*, p. 261.
3. Schrader and Brooks, *op. cit.*, p. 32.
4. Harrison, *Nome and the Seward Peninsula*, p. 57.
5. Beach, "The Looting of Alaska," January, 1906, p. 10.
6. *Nome News*, October 9, 1899.
7. Turner, "Chronology of Wyatt Earp," typescript sent to the author.

8. *Nome News*, October 14, 1899.
9. *Ibid.*, November 4, 1899.
10. *Ibid.*
11. *Ibid.*, November 11, 1899.
12. *Ibid.*, November 4, 1899.
13. *Ibid.*, October 21, 1899.
14. Robins, *Raymond and I*, p. 226.
15. *Ibid.*, p. 306.
16. *Ibid.*, p. 307.
17. *Nome News*, March 18, 1900.
18. *Ibid.*, April 7, 1900.
19. *Ibid.*
20. *Ibid.*
21. Reat, "From Dawson to Nome on a Bicycle," p. 69.
22. *Ibid.*, p. 72.

Chapter 16

1. French, *Seward's Land of Gold*, p. 2.
2. *Egg Island Yellow Journal*, June 21, 1900.
3. G. J. Lomen, manuscript, "In Reindeer Realms," unpaged. Lomen Family Papers.
4. Fell, *Threads of Alaskan Gold*, p. 28.
5. Kearns, *Million Dollar Gate*, p. 25.
6. *Ibid.*
7. Ballou to brother Walt, June 22, 1900.
8. *Nome News*, June 9, 1900.
9. *Ibid.*, June 23, 1900.
10. Beach, *Personal Exposures*, p. 28.
11. *Ibid.*
12. *Ibid.*
13. *Nome Chronicle*, August 11, 1900.
14. *Ibid.*
15. *Ibid.*, August 14, 1900.
16. *Ibid.*, August 21, 1900.
17. *Ibid.*, September 21, 1900.
18. *Ibid.*, November 14, 1900.
19. *Nome Gold Digger*, September 26, 1900.
20. *Nome Chronicle*, October 6, 1900.
21. *Ibid.*, November 17, 1900.
22. *Nome Gold Digger*, November 21, 1900.
23. *Nome Chronicle*, November 17, 1900.
24. *Ibid.*, November 21, 1900.

25. *Nome News*, December 5, 1900.
26. *Ibid.*, December 8, 1900.
27. *Ibid.*, December 12, 1900.
28. *Ibid.*, December 1, 1900.

Chapter 17
1. Starr, *My Adventures in the Klondike and Alaska*, p. 63.
2. Lillo, *Alaska Gold Mining Company and the Cape Nome Conspiracy*, pp. 29–31.
3. Wickersham, *Old Yukon*, p. 360.
4. Beach, "The Looting of Alaska," p. 41.
5. Lillo, *op. cit.*, p. 335.
6. *Ibid.*
7. Sutherland, *Memoirs*, p. 9.
8. Lillo, *op. cit.*, p. 288.
9. *Ibid.*, p. 293.
10. *Ibid.*, p. 294.
11. *Ibid.*, pp. 296–97.
12. Lillo, p. 298.
13. *Nome Nugget*, February 19, 1902.
14. Lillo, p. 331.

Chapter 18
1. Wickersham Diary, December 7, 1900.
2. *Ibid.*, December 11, 1900.
3. *Alaska Forum*, November 1, 1900.
4. *Ibid.* All quotations in this paragraph.
5. Wickersham, *Old Yukon*, pp. 60, 61.
6. *Nome Nugget*, August 2, 1901.
7. Wickersham, *op. cit.*, pp. 374–75.
8. *Ibid.*, p. 376; Wickersham Diary, March 17, 1902.
9. Wickersham Diary, May 17, 1902.
10. *Ibid.*, October 22, 1902.
11. *Ibid.*, October 30, 1902.

Chapter 19
1. *Fairbanks Daily News-Miner*, Pioneer Edition, June 30, 1958.
2. Wickersham, *Old Yukon*, p. 180.
3. *Ibid.*, p. 181.
4. Wickersham Diary, April 16, 1903.
5. *Ibid.*, May 5, 1903.
6. *Ibid.*, May, 9, 1903.
7. Young, *Hall Young of Alaska*, p. 411.
8. Wickersham, *op. cit.*, p. 126.

9. *Fairbanks Miner*, May, 1903.
10. Nogales, *Memoirs of a Soldier of Fortune*, p. 41.
11. *Ibid.*
12. *Ibid.*, p. 44.
13. *Ibid.*, pp. 44–45.
14. Mikkelsen, *Mirage in the Arctic*, pp. 189–90.
15. *Ibid.*, p. 162.
16. *Fairbanks Daily Times*, May 23, 1906.
17. *Ibid.*, May 25, 1906.
18. John Clum papers.
19. *Ibid.*
20. *Ibid.*
21. *Ibid.*

Chapter 20

1. *Fairbanks Times*, August 18, 1906.
2. *Ibid.*, August 12, 1905.
3. *Ibid.*
4. *Fairbanks Times*, August 18, 1906.
5. *Ibid.*, July 29, 1906.
6. *Iditarod Nugget*, August 30, 1911.
7. *Fairbanks Times*, November 21, 1906.
8. *Ibid.*
9. *Ibid.*, August 21, 1906.
10. *Ibid.*, July 21, 1906.
11. Heller, *Sourdough Sagas*, p. 270.
12. *Ibid.*, p. 271.
13. *Alaska Weekly*, May 4, 1923.
14. Brooks, *Blazing Alaska's Trails*, p. 358.
15. "Gold Rush Poetry." Author's files.
16. Wallace, "The People of Nome were Scandalized," p. 16.
17. *Fairbanks News*, July 18, 1905.
18. *Nome Nugget*, March 22, 1905.
19. Marshall, *Arctic Village*, pp. 37–38.
20. Unidentified newspaper clipping in Carl Lomen's Diary, March 11, 1907.
21. *Ibid.*
22. *Alaska Weekly*, May 18, 1923.
23. *Nome Gold Digger*, July 22, 1903.
24. *Alaska–Yukon Gold Book*, p. 72.
25. *Ibid.*

Chapter 21

1. Robe, *Penetration of an Alaskan Frontier*, p. 100.

2. *Alaska Forum*, March 28, 1903.
3. Badger radio recording.
4. *Ibid.*
5. *Alaska Forum*, December 26, 1903.
6. Wickersham Diary, May 5, 1904.
7. *Fairbanks Times*, July 23, 1906.
8. *Ibid.*, November 16, 1906.
9. *Ibid.*, November 29, 1906.
10. *Ibid.*, December 1, 1906.
11. Wickersham Diary, November 29, 1906.
12. *Ibid.*, January 12, 1907.
13. *Ibid.*, September 30, 1906.
14. *Fairbanks Times*, January 17, 1911.
15. *Ibid.*, February 2, 1911.
16. *Fairbanks Times*, March 10, 1911.
17. *Ibid.*, March 24, 1911.
18. *Ibid.*, March 28, 1911.
19. *Ibid.*, December 22, 1912.
20. Quoted by the *Iditarod Pioneer*, February 1, 1913.
21. *Cordova Daily Alaskan*, December 23, 1912.
22. *Alaska Dispatch*, January 6, 1920.
23. *Ibid.*, April 20, 1923.

Chapter 22
1. Beach, *Personal Exposures*, p. 124.
2. *Ibid.*, p. 125.
3. *Nome Nugget*, May 4, 1904.
4. *Ibid.*, October 26, 1904.
5. *Ibid.*, October 22, 1904.
6. *Ibid.*, July 19, 1905.
7. *Ibid.*, October 26, 1904.
8. *Ibid.*, December 11, 1901.
9. *Fairbanks Times*, December 10, 1906.
10. Bundy, *The Valdez–Fairbanks Trail*, pp. 26–27.
11. *Ibid.*
12. *Ibid.*, p. 29.
13. *Ibid.*, p. 60.
14. W. Ropstenz to L. Washburne, A.C.C.—Kodiak Station Correspondence, May 3, 1896.
15. L. B. Smith to Kodiak Station, N.C.C.—Kodiak Station Correspondence, June 28, 1901.

Chapter 23
1. Farnsworth Papers, Farnsworth to cousin Will, August 2, 1900.

2. *Ibid.*, Farnsworth to McCoy, December 23, 1900.
3. Henry David McCary recording.
4. Farnsworth to cousin Will, September 14, 1899.
5. *Ibid.*, February 1, 1900.

Chapter 24
1. Beach, *Personal Exposures*, p. 89.
2. Wickersham, 2 *Alaska Reports*, p. 274.
3. *Ibid.*, p. 275.
4. *Ibid.*, p. 270.
5. *Ibid.*, p. 272.
6. *Ibid.*, p. 269.
7. Johnston, *Legendary Mizners*, p. 103.
8. Hines, *Minstrel of the Yukon*, pp. 107–108.
9. Kearns, *Million Dollar Gate*, p. 27.
10. *Ibid.*
11. *Nome Nugget*, May 3, 1906.
12. Hines, *op. cit.*, p. 112
13. *Ibid.*, p. 229.
14. Beebe, *True Life Story of Swiftwater Bill Gates*, p. 20.
15. Berton, *Klondike*, pp. 81–82.
16. Beebe, *op. cit.*, p. 28.
17. *Ibid.*, p. 39.
18. *Ibid.*, p. 41.
19. *Ibid.*, p. 80.
20. *Ibid.*, p. 86.
21. *Fairbanks News*, June 29; July 1; July 11; July 13; July 18; July 25; August 9; August 16 (1906).
22. *Fairbanks Daily News-Miner*, Golden Days Edition, July, 1970. Reprint of an August 22, 1906 story.
23. Sutherland, *Memoirs*, p. 12.
24. Beebe, *op. cit.*, p. 110.
25. *Ibid.*, p. 134.
26. *Fairbanks Times*, August 16, 1906.

Chapter 25
1. Pilcher Diary, November 29, 1911.
2. Pilcher Diary, September 1, 1901.
3. *Nome Nugget*, April 13, 1908.
4. Pilcher Diary, January 16, 1906.
5. Pilcher letter to University of Alaska, May 2, 1935.
6. Ballou to brother Walt, March 3, 1901.
7. *Ibid.*, September 18, 1901.
8. *Ibid.*, September 25, 1901.

9. *Ibid.*, February 2, 1902.
10. *Ibid.*, July 11, 1902.
11. *Ibid.*
12. *Ibid.*, February 13, 1903.
13. *Ibid.*, May 15, 1903.
14. *Ibid.*, November 11, 1906.
15. *Ibid.*, October 1, 1909.
16. *Ibid.*, April 13, 1911.
17. *Ibid.*, November 29, 1911.
18. *Ibid.*, February 24, 1915.
19. Reed, "The Law and Gus Boltz," p. 12.
20. Carl Lomen Diary, November 9, 1900.

Chapter 26

1. *Nome Gold Digger*, November 29, 1907.
2. *Katalla Herald*, January 11, 1908.
3. *Ibid.*, January 18, 1908.
4. *Ibid.*
5. *Ibid.*, March 7, 1908.
6. Stearns, *The Morgan-Guggenheim Syndicate*, p. 222.
7. Wickersham to J. L. Osgood, June 2, 1910. Wickersham correspondence.

Chapter 27

1. *Iditarod Nugget*, September 3, 1910.
2. *Ibid.*, October 19, 1910.
3. *Ibid.*, September 21, 1910.
4. *Ibid.*, November 16, 1910.
5. Young, "Home Missions in Remotest Alaska," p. 313.
6. *Ibid.*, p. 315.
7. *Iditarod Nugget*, May 31, 1912.
8. Sherman, "Ruby's Gold Rush Newspapers," p. 24.
9. Marshall, *Arctic Village*, pp. 37–38.
10. Sulzer Collection, Marsh, "Adventures in the Arctic," unpublished manuscript, p. 5.
11. *Ibid.*, pp. 1–2.
12. *Ibid.*, Marsh to Sulzer, January 28, 1907.
13. *Ibid.*, Marsh to Sulzer, November 23, 1907.
14. *Ibid.*, Reed's report to Chandalar Gold Mines, Inc., undated.
15. *Ibid.*, Carter to Sulzer, October 17, 1910.
16. *Ibid.*, Schultz to Sulzer, April 2, 1927.
17. *Ibid.*, Levy to Marsh, January 3, 1910.
18. *Ibid.*, Leary to Murphy, June 21, 1932.

Chapter 28

1. Cantwell, *Report on the Operations of the U.S. Revenue Steamer* Nunivak, p. 182.
2. Walden, *A Dog Puncher on the Yukon*, p. 45.
3. Brooks, *Blazing Alaska's Trails*, p. 333.
4. Harrison, *Nome and Seward Peninsula*, pp. 259–60.
5. Wickersham, *Old Yukon*, pp. 407–408.
6. Watkins, "Golden Dreams and Silver Realities" rejects the rosy view of democracy advanced by Charles H. Shinn, *Mining Camps: A Study in American Government* (1884).

Chapter 29

1. Wickersham, *Old Yukon*, p. 486.
2. *Iditarod Nugget*, November 23, 1910.
3. *Nome News*, October 14, 1899.
4. Cavagnol, *Postmarked Alaska*, p. 45.
5. W. H. Wilson summarizes the dispute in "Alaska's Past, Alaska's Future."

Chapter 30

1. Ivan Petroff, *Tenth Census of the United States*, pp. 4–17.
2. *Annual Report of the Governor of Alaska, 1888*, p. 7.
3. Gruening, *Alaska*, p. 75.
4. *Compilation of Narratives of Explorations in Alaska*, p. 706.
5. *Nome News*, January 13, 1900.
6. *Ibid.*, October 9, 1899.
7. *Alaska Forum*, October 29, 1904.
8. *Nome Nugget*, January 3, 1903.
9. Stuck, *Yukon*, pp. 103, 104.
10. Stuck, *Winter Circuit*, p. 71.
11. Slobodin, "The Dawson Boys."
12. Heller, *Sourdough Sagas*, p. 169.
13. *Ibid.*, p. 180.
14. *Ibid.*, p. 186.

Chapter 31

1. *Sitka Cablegram*, February 8, 1906.
2. *Iditarod Nugget*, November 30, 1910.
3. *Nome News*, April 28, 1900.
4. *Ibid.*, January 25, 1902.
5. *Ibid.*, February 22, 1905.
6. *Ibid.*, September 5, 1902.
7. *Ibid.*, September 12, 1902.
8. *Nome Nugget*, February 7, 1903.
9. *Ibid.*, August 13, 1902.

10. *Ibid.*, February 7, 1903.
11. *Ibid.*, February 18, 1903.
12. *Nome News*, December 15, 1903.
13. *Ibid.*
14. *Ibid.*
15. *Fairbanks News*, December 5, 1906, reprinted in *Fairbanks Daily News-Miner*, Pioneer Edition, July, 1970.
16. *Katalla Herald*, February 15, 1908.
17. *Iditarod Nugget*, November 30, 1910.
18. *Nome Nugget*, July 30, 1901.

Chapter 32
1. *Alaska Weekly*, October 2, 1931.
2. *Fairbanks News*, February 7, 1908.
3. *Fairbanks News*, February 14, 1908.
4. *Katalla Herald*, February 15, 1908; February 29, 1908; April 4, 1908.
5. Wickersham Diary, February 15, 1908.
6. *Ibid.*, February 20, 1908.
7. *Ibid.*, March 18, 1908.
8. *Ibid.*
9. *Fairbanks News*, February 7, 1908.
10. Rickard, *Through the Yukon and Alaska*, p. 270.
11. *Alaska Weekly*, October 2, 1931.
12. Wickersham Diary, February 25, 1908.
13. *Ibid.*
14. Wickersham Diary, June 25, 1908.
15. *Alaska Weekly*, October 2, 1931.

Chapter 33
1. Wickersham, *Old Yukon*, p. 433.
2. *Ibid.*, p. 434.
3. Beach, "Looting of Alaska," *Appleton's Booklovers Magazine*, January, February, March, 1906.
4. *Katalla Herald*, July 4, 1908.

Chapter 34
1. Calder–Marshall, *Bodley Head Jack London*, Vol. IV, p. 10.
2. O'Connor, *Jack London*, p. 6.
3. Walker, *Jack London and the Klondike*, p. 213.
4. O'Connor, *op. cit.*, p. 84.
5. Service, *Ploughman of the Moon*, p. 257.
6. *Ibid.*, p. 262.
7. *Ibid.*
8. *Ibid.*, p. 274.

9. Service, *Collected Poems*, p. 36.
10. Beach, *Personal Exposures*, p. 20.
11. *Ibid.*, p. 28.
12. *Ibid.*, p. 32.
13. *Ibid.*, p. 27.
14. *Ibid.*, p. 24.
15. *Ibid.*, p. 22.
16. *Ibid.*, p. 28.
17. O'Conner, *op. cit.*, p. 81.

Epilogue
1. Stuck, *Yukon*, p. 51.
2. *Ibid.*
3. Pilcher Diary, December 31, 1930.
4. F. Walker, *Destination Unknown*, p. 106.
5. J. Walker, "Bonanza Days," p. 12.
6. C. Angel, "And Going Home We Lost the Rudder," p. 29.
7. Wickersham, *Old Yukon*, p. 24.

Bibliography

I. Archival Sources

Alaska Historical Library, Juneau, Alaska
Bryant, C. A. "Another Man's Life." Unpublished memoirs.
Nome Jail and Police Court Records, 1899–1900.
California Historical Society
Minutes of the Alaska Commercial Company's Meetings 1868–1918. (Microfilm copy in University of Alaska Archives.)
Dartmouth College, Baker Library, Stefansson Collection
Edwin Tappan Adney Papers. (Corrsepondence with and biography of John J. Healy.)
Library of Congress
Alaska and The Klondike. (Erastus Brainerd Correspondence.)
National Archives
Records of the United States Army Commands (Army Posts). Record Group 393, Fort Davis 1900–19; Fort Egbert 1899–1911; Fort Gibbon 1899–1923; Fort St. Michael 1897–1922.
Sheldon Jackson College, Sitka
C. L. Andrews Collection.
University of Alaska Archives, Fairbanks, Alaska
Alaska Commercial Company Records (Erskine Collection).
History of the Alaska Commercial Company—"310 Sansom Street."
Eskil Anderson Papers (Chandalar District).
William B. Ballou Papers.
Alfred H. Brooks Papers and Newspaper Clippings.
Garret Busch Papers.
Frank Buteau Papers.
Charles Lee Cadwallader Reminiscences.
W. J. Christian Diary.
Eagle, Alaska Collection.
Lulu M. Fairbanks Collection.
Charles S. Farnsworth Papers.

Fugitive Papers on Alaska.
James Geoghegan Papers.
R. H. Geoghegan Papers.
Margaret Harrais Collection.
Martin Harrais Collection.
L. A. Levensaler Letters.
Daniel B. Libby Manuscript.
Lomen Family Collection.
Carl Lomen Diaries.
Henry David McCary Recording.
Military Records, Fort Gibbon, 1906–11; Fort Egbert closing records.
George H. Pilcher Diaries and Journalism.
Pioneer Radio Broadcast Tapes (*See* VI. Other Sources.)
Governor J. F. A. Strong Papers.
William Sulzer Collection.
Dan Sutherland Correspondence.
Joseph Ulmer Collection.
James Wickersham Diaries and Correspondence, microfilm. Originals held
    by House of Wickersham, Juneau, Alaska.
James Wickersham Correspondence with A. J. Balliet, 1900–1901.
University of Arizona Library, Special Collections
    John P. Clum Papers.
University of California, Berkeley, Bancroft Library
    John W. Troy Papers.

II. Newspapers

Alaska Forum (Rampart), 1900–1902.
Alaska Dispatch, 1920–22.
Alaska Weekly, 1923–24.
Boston Alaskan, 1906–1907.
Council Evening Bulletin, 1915–19.
Dyea Trail, 1898 (scattered copies).
Fairbanks Daily News, 1903; 1905–11.
Fairbanks Times, 1904–14 (incomplete file).
Iditarod Nugget, 1910.
Iditarod Pioneer, 1912.
Juneau Mining Record, 1891.
Katalla Herald, 1908.
Miner's Union Bulletin (Fairbanks), 1908–1909.
Nome Chronicle, 1900–1901.
Nome Gold Digger, 1900–1901; 1907.
Nome News, 1899–1905; 1907.
Nome Nugget, 1901–1908.
Nome Pioneer Press, 1907–1908.
Rampart Miner, 1901–1902.
Sitka Alaskan, 1898–99.

Skagway News, 1898 (scattered copies).
Tanana Miner (Chena), 1908–1909 (incomplete file).
Valdez News, 1902–1905.
Yukon Press (various locations), 1894–99.
Yukon Valley News (various locations), 1904–1909 (incomplete file).

III. Government Publications*

Abercrombie, W. R. *Copper River Exploring Expedition 1899.* 1900.
Annual Report of the Governor of Alaska. 1885–1940.
Army's Role in the Building of Alaska. Pamphlet 360–5, April 1, 1969.
Brooks, Alfred H. *Geography and Geology of Alaska.* 1906.
Brooks, Alfred H. *A Reconnaissance in Cape Nome, 1900.* 1901.
Cantwell, J. C. *Report of the Operations of the U.S. Revenue Steamer* Nunivak *on the Yukon River Station, Alaska 1899–1901.* 1902.
Compililation of Narratives of Explorations in Alaska. 1900.
Dunham, Sam C. *Bulletin of the Department of Labor.* 1900.
Eakin, Henry M. *Iditarod–Ruby Region Alaska, United States Geological Survey.* 1914.
Orth, Donald J. *Dictionary of Alaska Place Names.* 1967.
Petroff, Ivan. *Population, Industries, and Resources of Alaska. Report for the Tenth Census of the United States.* 1880.
Prindle, L. M., and Katz, F. J. *A Detailed Description of the Fairbanks District.* 1913.
Report on Population and Resources of Alaska at the Eleventh Census; 1890. 1893.
Schrader, Frank C., and Brooks, Alfred H. *Preliminary Report on the Cape Nome Gold Region Alaska.* 1900.
Spurr, J. E. *Reconnaissance of S. W. Alaska in 1898.* 1900.
Wickersham, James. *Alaska Reports*, St. Paul: West, 1903–1906.
Canadian Yukon Territory, Ottawa: Minister of the Interior, 1916.

IV. Books

Adney, Edwin Tappan. *The Klondike Stampede of 1897–98.* New York: Harper, 1900.
Allan, A. A. "Scotty," *Gold, Men and Dogs.* New York: Putnam's Sons, 1931.
Alaska–Yukon Gold Book. Seattle: Sourdough Stampede, 1930.
Andrews, Clarence L. *Wrangell and the Gold of the Cassiar.* Seattle: Tinker, 1937.
Austin, Basil. *Diary of a Ninety-Eighter.* Mount Pleasant, Michigan: John Cumming, 1968.
Bankson, Russell A. *Klondike Nugget.* Caldwell, Idaho: Caxton, 1935.
Barbeau, Charles Marius. *Pathfinders in the North Pacific.* Caldwell: Caxton, 1958.

* These documents were all published by the United States Government Printing Office, Washington, D.C.

Barry, Mary J. *History of Mining on the Kenai Peninsula*. Anchorage: Alaska Northwest, 1973.

Beach, Rex. *The Barrier*. New York: Harper, 1908.

————. *Iron Trail*. New York: Harper, 1913.

————. *The Spoilers*. New York: Harper, 1906.

Beebe, Iola. *True Life Story of Swiftwater Bill Gates*. Seattle: Privately printed, 1908.

Berton, Pierre. *Klondike*. Toronto: McClelland and Steward, 1972.

Black, Mrs. George. *My 70 Years*. Toronto: Nelson, 1938.

Blount, Ellen S. *North of 53 — An Alaskan Journey*. London: Percy Lund Humphries [n.d.].

Bocca, Geoffrey. *Life and Death of Harry Oakes*. London: Weidenfeld and Nicolson [n.d.].

Brooks, Alfred H. *Blazing Alaska's Trails*. College: University of Alaska, 1953.

Bundy, Hallock C. *The Valdez–Fairbanks Trail*. Seattle: Alaska Publishing Company, 1910.

Caldwell, Elsie Noble. *Alaska Trail Dogs*. New York: Smith, 1945.

Cameron, Charlotte. *Cheechako in Alaska and the Yukon*. London: Stokes, 1920.

Carlson, L. H. *An Alaskan Gold Mine, The Story of No. 9 Above*. Evanston, Illinois: Northwestern University, 1951.

Carpenter, Herman. *Three Years in Alaska*. Philadelphia: Howard, 1901.

Carrol, James A. *The First Ten Years in Alaska: Memoirs of a Fort Yukon Trapper, 1911–1912*. New York: Exposition, 1957.

Cavagnol, Joseph J. *Postmarked Alaska*. Halton, Kansas: Gossip Printing, 1957.

Chapman, John. *A Camp on the Yukon*. Cornwall on Hudson, New York: Idlewild, 1948.

Chase, William H. *Pioneers of Alaska*, Kansas City: Burton, 1951.

Chicago Record's Book for Gold Seekers, Chicago: Chicago Record, 1897.

Clark, M. *Roadhouse Tales—Nome in 1900*. Girard, Kansas: Appeal, 1902.

Clifton, Violet. *The Book of Talbot*. London: Faber and Faber, 1933.

Cody, H. A. *An Apostle of the North—Memoirs of Bishop Bompas*. London: Seeley, 1908.

Coolidge, L. A. *Klondike and the Yukon Country*. Philadelphia: Henry Altemus, 1897.

Copper River Joe. *A Golden Cross* [?] Los Angeles: White–Thompson, 1939.

Curtin, W. R. *Yukon Voyage: Unofficial Log of the Steamer Yukoner*. Caldwell, Idaho: Caxton, 1938.

Dall, William H. *Alaska and Its Resources*. Boston: Lee and Shepard, 1870.

Davis, Mary Lee. *Sourdough Gold*. Boston: W. A. Wilde, 1933.

————. *Uncle Sam's Attic*. Boston: W. A. Wilde, 1930.

DeArmond, Robert. *Founding of Juneau*. Juneau: Gastineau Channel Centennial Association, 1967.

————. *"Stroller" White, Tales of a Klondike Newsman*. Vancouver: Mitchell, 1969.

Denison, Merrill. *Klondike Mike*. Cleveland: World, 1945.

Devine, E. J. *Across Widest America, Newfoundland to Alaska.* Montreal: Canadian Messenger, 1905.

DeWindt, Harry. *My Restless Life.* London: Grant Richards, 1909.

————. *Through the Gold-Fields of Alaska.* London: Harper, 1898.

Dietz, Arthur Arnold. *Mad Rush for Gold in Frozen North.* Los Angeles: *Times Mirror,* 1914.

Douthwaite, L. Charles. *Royal Canadian Mounted Police.* London: Blackie and Son, 1939.

Downie, Major William. *Hunting for Gold.* Palo Alto: American West, 1971.

Downs, Art. *Paddlewheels on the Frontier.* Sidney, British Columbia: Gray's, 1972.

Dubofsky, Melvyn. *We Shall Be All: A History of the IWW.* Chicago: Quadrangle, 1969.

Dufresne, Frank. *My Way Up North.* New York: Holt, Rinehart and Winston, 1966.

Dunham, Sam. *Goldsmith of Nome.* Washington, D.C.: Neal, 1901.

Edingtons, The. *Tundra: Romance and Adventure on Alaskan Trails,* as told by former Deputy U.S. Marshal Hansen. New York: Century, 1930.

Ellsworth, Lincoln. *Beyond Horizons.* London: Heinemann, 1938.

Fell, Sarah. *Threads of Alaskan Gold.* [n.p., n.d.]

Fitz, Frances. *Lady Sourdough.* New York: Macmillan, 1941.

Fraser, James D. *Gold Fever.* [Honolulu]: [n.p.], 1923.

French, L. H. *Seward's Land of Gold.* New York: Montross, Clarke and Emmons, 1905.

Garland, Hamlin. *Trial of the Gold-Seekers.* New York: Macmillan, 1899.

Goulet, Emil O. *Rugged Years on Alaska Frontier.* Philadelphia: Dorrance, 1949.

Graves, S. H. *On the White Pass Payroll.* New York: Paladin, 1970.

Green, Elmer. *Adventures of Carl Rydell.* London: Arnold, 1924.

Grinnell, Joseph. *Gold Hunting in Alaska.* Elgin, Illinois: David C. Cook, 1901.

Gruening, Ernest. *State of Alaska.* New York: Random House, 1954.

Hall, Olaf. *Youth North.* Caldwell, Idaho: Caxton, 1936.

Hamilton, Walter R. *Yukon Story.* Vancouver: Mitchell, 1967.

Hamlin, C. S. *Old Times on the Yukon.* Los Angeles: Wetzel, 1928.

Harris, A. C. *Alaska and the Klondike Gold Fields.* [n.p.], 1897.

Harrison, E. S. *Nome and the Seward Peninsula.* Seattle: E. S. Harrison, 1901.

Haskell, William B. *Two Years in the Klondike and Alaskan Gold-Fields.* Hartford: Hartford Publishing, 1898.

Hayne, M. H. E., and Taylor, H. W. *Pioneers of the Klondyke.* London: Sampson, Low, Marston, 1897.

Hegg, E. A. *Souvenir of Nome Alaska.* Seattle: [n.p.], 1900.

Heilprin, Angelo. *Alaska and the Klondike.* New York: Appleton, 1899.

Heller, Herbert L. *Sourdough Sagas.* Cleveland: World, 1967.

Hewitt, John Michael. *The Alaska Vagabond Doctor Skookum.* New York: Exposition, 1953.

Hicks, George. *The Account of a Pioneer Prospector's Search for Riches.* College, Alaska: University of Alaska, 1954.

Hildebrandt, James C. *History of Placer Mining in Alaska.* College, Alaska: University of Alaska, 1947.

Hinckley, Theodore C. *Americanization of Alaska.* Palo Alto: Pacific Books, 1972.

Hines, Jack. *Minstrel of the Yukon: An Alaska Adventure.* New York: Greenburg, 1948.

Hinton, A. Cherry, and Godsell, Philip H. *Yukon.* Philadelphia: Macrae Smith, 1955.

Hitchcock, Mary E. *Two Women in the Klondike.* New York: Putnam's, 1899.

Ingersoll, Ernest. *Gold Fields of the Klondike and the Wonders of Alaska.* Edgewood, 1897.

Jenkins, Thomas. *The Man of Alaska — Peter Trimble Rowe.* New York: Morehouse–Gorham, 1943.

Johnson, Alva. *Legendary Mizners.* New York: Farrar, Strauss and Young, 1953.

Jordan, Jed. *Fool's Gold: An Unrefined Account of Alaska in 1899.* New York: Day, 1960.

Jordan, Philip D. *Frontier Law and Order.* Lincoln: University of Nebraska, 1970.

Judge, Charles J. *An American Missionary.* New York: Catholic Foreign Missionary Society, 1907.

Karr, H. W. Seton. *Shores and Alps of Alaska.* London: Samson, Low, 1887.

Kearns, Jack, and Fraley, Oscar. *The Million Dollar Gate.* New York: Macmillan, 1966.

Keeler, N. *A Trip to Alaska and the Klondike in the Summer of 1905.* Cincinnati: Ebbert & Richardson, 1906.

Kirk, James W. *Pioneer Life in the Yukon Valley Alaska.* Buffalo: Presbyterian Church, 1935.

Kitchener, L. D. *Flag Over the North; The Story of the Northern Commercial Company.* Seattle: Superior, 1954.

Lillo, Waldermar E. *Alaska Gold Mining Company and the Cape Nome Conspiracy.* Fargo: North Dakota State University, 1933.

Lloyd–Owen, F. *Gold Nugget Charlie.* London: Harrup, 1939.

Lockley, Fred. *Alaska's First Free Mail Delivery in 1900.* Portland, Oregon: [n.p., n.d.].

Lokke, Carl T. *Klondike Saga: A Chronicle of a Minnesota Gold Mining Company.* Minneapolis: University of Minnesota, 1965.

Lomen, Carl J. *Fifty Years in Alaska.* New York: McKay, 1954.

London, Charmian. *Jack London.* London: Mills and Boon, 1921.

London, Jack. *Burning Daylight.* New York: Macmillan, 1910.

———. *A Daughter of the Snows.* New York: Archer House, 1963.

———. *Klondike Dream.* Edited by Arthur Calder Marshall. London: Bodley Head, 1966.

———. *Smoke Bellew.* New York: Century, 1912.

Lynch, Jeremiah. *Three Years in the Klondike.* London: Arnold, 1904.

McElwaine, E. *Truth About Alaska*. Chicago: [n.p.], 1901.

McGarvey, Lois. *Along Alaska Trails*. New York: Vantage, 1960.

MacGregor, J. G. *The Klondike Rush Through Edmonton*. Toronto: McClelland and Stewart, 1970.

McKee, L. *Land of Nome*. New York: Grafton, 1902.

McKeown, Martha F. *The Trail Led North*. Portland, Oregon: Binfords & Mort, 1948.

McLain, Carrie M. *Gold-Rush Nome*. Portland, Oregon: Graphic Arts Center, 1969.

McLain, John Scudder. *Alaska and the Klondike*. New York: McClure, Phillips, 1905.

McLean, Dora E. *Early Newspapers on the Upper Yukon Watershed, 1894–1907*. College: University of Alaska, 1963.

Macfie, Harry. *Wasa–Wasa*. New York: Norton, 1951.

Margeson, Charles A. *Experiences of Gold Hunters in Alaska*. [n.p.], 1899.

Marshall, Robert. *Arctic Village*. New York: Literary Guild, 1933.

Martinsen, Ella Lung. *Black Sand and Gold*. Portland, Oregon: Metropolitan, 1967.

Masik, August. *Arctic Nights Entertainment*. London: Blackie, 1938.

Mathews, Richard. *The Yukon*. New York: Holt, Rinehart and Winston, 1968.

Medill, Robert B. *Klondike Diary*. Portland, Oregon: Beattie, 1949.

Mikkelsen, Ejnar. *Mirage in the Arctic*. London: Rupert Hart–Davis, 1955.

Millard, Bailey. *The Lure of Gold*. New York: Clode, 1904.

Mizner, Addison. *Many Mizners*. New York: Sears, 1932.

Monahan, Robert L. *Development of Settlement in the Fairbanks Area, Alaska*. Montreal: McGill University, 1959.

Moore, J. Bernard. *Skagway in Days Primeval*. New York: Vantage, 1968.

Morgan, Edward, and Woods, Henry. *God's Loaded Dice*. Caldwell, Idaho: Caxton, 1948.

Morgan, Murray. *One Man's Gold Rush*. Seattle: University of Washington, 1967.

———. *Skid Road*. New York: Viking, 1962.

Morrell, W. P. *The Gold Rushes*. London: Black, 1968.

Munn, Captain Henry Toke, *Prairie Trails and Arctic By-Ways*. London: Hurst and Blackett, 1932.

Nelson, E. W. *The Eskimo About Bering Strait*. New York: Johnson Reprint, 1971.

Nelson, Klondy, with Corey Ford. *Daughter of the Gold Rush*. New York: Random House, 1958.

Nichols, Jeanette Paddock. *Alaska*. Cleveland: Clark, 1924.

Nogales, Rafael De. *Memories of a Soldier of Fortune*. London: Wright and Brown, [n.d.]

O'Connor, Richard. *High Jinks on the Klondike*. Indianapolis: Bobbs–Merrill, 1954.

———. *Jack London*. Boston: Little, Brown, 1964.

Ogilvie, William. *Early Days on the Yukon*. London: Lane, [n.d.].

———. *Klondike Official Guide*. Toronto: Hunter–Rose, 1898.

Palmer, Frederick. *In the Klondike.* New York: Scribner's Sons, 1899.

Parker, G. A. *Evolution of Placer Mining Methods in Alaska.* College: University of Alaska, 1929.

Polk's Alaska–Yukon Gazetteer and Business Directory. Seattle: R. L. Polk, 1900–35.

Purdy, Anne. *Dark Boundary.* New York: Vantage, 1954.

Quiett, Glenn Chesney. *Pay Dirt.* New York: Appleton–Century, 1936.

Raper, Fred. *Klondyke to Kenya.* London: Sheffington, 1938.

Reed, Irving McK. *Boyhood in the Nome Gold Camp.* College: University of Alaska, 1969.

Rickard, T. A. *Through the Yukon and Alaska.* San Francisco: Mining and Scientific Press, 1909.

Rickard, Mrs. Tex. *Everything Happened to Him.* London: Rich and Cowan, 1937.

Ricks, Melvin B. *Directory of Alaska Post Offices and Postmasters, 1867–1963.* Ketchikan, Alaska: Tongass, 1965.

Robe, Cecil F. *The Penetration of an Alaskan Frontier, the Tanana Valley and Fairbanks.* New Haven: Yale University, 1943.

Robertson, William Norrie. *Yukon Memories.* Toronto: Hunter–Rose, 1930.

Robins, Elizabeth. *Raymond and I.* New York: Macmillan, 1956.

Rydell, C. *On Pacific Frontiers.* Chicago: World, 1924.

Samson, Sam. *The Eskimo Princess—A Story of a Million Dollar Gold Discovery in the Cyrus Noble in Nome, Alaska.* As told to Mignon Maynard Chisam. Boston: Christopher, 1951.

Samuels, Charles. *The Magnificent Rube.* New York: McGraw–Hill. 1947.

Satterfield, Archie. *Chilkoot Pass Then and Now.* Anchorage: Alaska Northwest, 1973.

Schwatka, Frederick. *Along Alaska's Great River.* New York: Cassell, 1885.

Secretan, J. H. E. *To Klondyke and Back.* London: Hurst and Blackett, 1898.

Service, Robert W. *Collected Poems.* New York: Dodd, Mead, 1968.

———. *Ploughman of the Moon.* London: Benn, 1946.

Sheldon, Charles. *Wilderness of Denali.* New York: Scribner's Sons, 1960.

Sherwood, Morgan. *Alaska and Its History.* Seattle: University of Washington, 1967.

———. *Exploration of Alaska, 1865–1900.* New Haven: Yale University, 1965.

Sola, A. E. Ironmonger. *Klondyke: Truth and Facts of the New Eldorado.* London: Mining and Geographical Institute, 1897.

Spurr, J. E. *Through the Yukon Gold Diggings.* Boston: Eastern, 1900.

Stacey, John F. *To Alaska for Gold.* [n.p., n.d.].

Starr, Walter A. *My Adventures in the Klondike and Alaska 1898–1900.* [n.p.], 1960.

Stearns, Robert Alden. *The Morgan Guggenheim Syndicate and the Development of Alaska, 1906–15.* Santa Barbara: University of California, 1967.

Steele, Colonel S. B. *Forty Years in Canada.* London: Jenkins, 1915.

Stefansson, Vihlajalmur. *Northwest to Fortune.* New York: Duell, Sloan and Pearce, 1958.

Stuck, Hudson. *Voyages on the Yukon and Its Tributaries.* New York: Scribner's Sons, 1917.

————. *A Winter Circuit of Our Arctic Coast.* New York: Scribner, 1920.

Tanana Directory, Fairbanks: [n.p., n.d.].

Thornton, Harrison. *Among the Eskimos of Wales, Alaska, 1890–93.* Baltimore: Johns Hopkins Press, 1931.

Tollemache, Stratford. *Reminiscences of the Yukon.* Toronto: Briggs, 1912.

Trelawney–Ansell, Edward. *I Followed Gold.* New York: Lee Furman, 1939.

Underwood, John J. *Alaska an Empire in the Making.* New York: Dodd, Mead, 1913.

Vanderlip, W. P. *In Search of a Siberian Klondike.* New York: Century, 1903.

Verne, Jules. *The Claim on Forty Mile Creek.* Westport, Connecticut: Associated Booksellers, 1962.

Walden, Arthur T. *A Dog Puncher on the Yukon.* Boston: Houghton Mifflin, 1928.

Walker, Franklin. *Jack London and the Klondike.* San Marino: Huntington Library, 1966.

Walker, Fred. *Destination Unknown—The Autobiography of a Wandering Boy.* London: Harrap, 1934.

Weimer, M. D. K. *True Story of the Alaska Gold Fields.* [n.p.], 1903.

West, E. L., and Mayhew, E. R. *Captain's Papers.* Barre, Massachusetts: Barre, 1965.

Wharton, David B. *Alaska Gold Rush.* Bloomington: Indiana University, 1972.

Whiting, F. B. *Grit, Grief and Gold.* Seattle: Peacock, 1933.

Wickersham, James. *Old Yukon.* Washington: Washington Law Book, 1938.

Willoughby, Barrett. *Gentlemen Unafraid.* New York: Putnam's Sons, 1928.

Wilson, Clifford. *Campbell of the Yukon.* Toronto: Macmillan, 1970.

Winslow, Kathryn. *Big Pan-Out.* London: Phoenix House, 1952.

Wirt, Loyal. *Alaskan Adventurers.* New York: Revell, 1937.

Wolff, Ernest. *Handbook for the Alaskan Prospector.* College, Alaska: University of Alaska, 1969.

Young, Hall. *Hall Young of Alaska.* New York: Revell, 1927.

Zaslow, Morris. *Opening Canada's North 1870–1914.* Toronto: McClelland and Stewart, 1971.

V. Periodical Articles

Adams, C. W. "I Hauled 'Fairbanks' on a Sternwheeler," *Alaska Sportsman,* September, 1961, 14–15.

Angel, Charles Wilkes. "And Going Home We Lost the Rudder!" *Alaska Sportsman,* September, 1943, 16, 17, 25–30.

Beach, Rex E. "The Looting of Alaska," *Appleton's Booklovers Magazine,* 1906: January, 3–12; February, 131–40; March, 294–301; April, 540–47; May, 606–13.

Berton, Pierre. "Gold Rush Writings," *Canadian Literature,* No. 4, 1960, 59–67.

Carlson, L. H. "Discovery of Gold at Nome, Alaska," *Pacific Historical Review*, September, 1946, 259–78.

———. "First Mining Season at Nome, Alaska," *Pacific Historical Review*, May, 1947, 163–75.

———. "Nome: From Mining Camp to Civilized Community," *Pacific Northwest Quarterly*, July, 1947, 233–42.

Genini, Ronald. "Fraser–Cariboo Gold Rushes," *Journal of the West*, July, 1972, 470–87.

Gough, Barry M. " 'Turbulent Frontiers' and British Expansion: Governor James Douglas, The Royal Navy, and The British Columbia Gold Rushes," *Pacific Historical Review*, February, 1972, 15–32.

Hunt, William R. "Judge Ballou of Rampart," *Alaska Journal*, Winter, 1972, 41–47.

———. "A Soldier on the Yukon," *Journal of the West*, April, 1971, 319–36.

———. "I Chopped Wood: George M. Pilcher on the Yukon," *Pacific Northwest Quarterly*, April, 1972, 63–68.

Jarvis, Joseph Russell. "The Cape Nome Gold Rush," edited by Alan Probert, *Journal of the West*, April, 1970, 153–95.

King, Joe. "Alaska's Newest Mining Camp," *Alaska–Yukon Magazine*, June, 1910, 3–4.

McDonald, Donald. "I Remember Iditarod," *Alaska Sportsman*, September, 1969, 14–17.

MacDonald, Norbert. "Seattle, Vancouver, and the Klondike," *Canadian Historical Review*, September, 1968, 234–46.

McKennan, Robert A. "Athapaskan Groups of Central Alaska at the Time of White Contact," *Ethnohistory*, Fall, 1969, 335–43.

Nichols, Jeannette P. "Advertising and the Klondike," *Washington Historical Quarterly*, January, 1922, 20–26.

Reat, Ruth. "From Dawson to Nome on a Bicycle," *Pacific Northwest Quarterly*, July, 1956, 65–74.

Reed, Elmer. "The Law and Gus Boltz," *Alaska Sportsman*, April, 1945, 12–13, 27–29.

Reed, Irving McK. "Frank Yasuda, Pioneer in the Chandalar," *Alaska Sportsman*, June, 1963, 14–15, 42–45.

Ryan, Pat M. "John P. Clum in Alaska," *Alaska Sportsman*, October, 1965, 21–23.

Sherman, Steve. "Ruby's Gold Rush Newspapers," *Alaska Journal*, Autumn, 1971, 16–24.

Siddall, W. R. "The Yukon Waterway in the Development of Interior Alaska," *Pacific Historical Review*, November, 1959, 361–76.

Slobodin, Richard. " 'The Dawson Boys'—Peel River Indians and the Klondike Gold Rush," *Polar Notes*, June, 1963, 24–35.

Stewart, Thomas R., as told to Louis R. Huber. "From Rags to Riches," *Alaska Sportsman*, September, 1944, 10–11, 33–36.

Walker, Johnny, as told to Louis Whittaker. "Bonanza Days," *Alaska Sportsman*, November, 1943, 12–13, 26–28.

————. "We Killed the Dogs for Food," *Alaska Sportsman*, December, 1943, 18–19, 26–28.

Wallace, John B., "Nome Was Like That," *Alaska Sportsman*, October, 1939, 16–17, 31–33.

————. "The People of Nome Were Scandalized," *Alaska Sportsman*, December, 1939, 16–17, 20–21.

————. "Three Strikes Was Out!" *Alaska Sportsman*, November, 1939, 16–17, 23–25.

————. "We Settled Disputes with Our Fists," *Alaska Sportsman*, August, 1939, 14–15, 28.

Willey, George Franklyn, as told to Jules Archer. "Lady Luck and the Cold Deck," *Alaska Sportsman*, October, 1954, 14–17, 30–31.

Wilson, William H. "Alaska's Past, Alaska's Future," *Alaska Review*, Spring and Summer, 1970, 1–12.

Young, S. Hall. "Home Missions in Remotest Alaska," *Assembly Herald*, vol. 18, no. 16, June, 1912, 313–15.

VI. Other Sources

Douglass, William C. "A History of the Kennecott Mines." October, 1964. Typescript provided by the Kennecott Copper Corporation.

Pioneer radio broadcast tapes (*c.* 1955) (in University of Alaska Archives).
Harry Badger
Jessie Bloom
Robert Bloom
Gus Conrad
Frank Chapados
Bentley Falls
Ed Farrell
Rebecca Farrell
Mrs. George Gasser
Maurice Goding
George Goshaw
Charlie Jones
Al McLeod
A. G. McKenna
Mrs. Jessie Mather
George Preston
Frank Thiesen
Charlie Wilson
Eustice Paul Ziegler

Sutherland, Dan. Unpaged copy of unpublished memoirs. Elmer E. Rasmuson Library, University of Alaska.

Turner, Alfred E. "Chronology of Wyatt Earp." Typescript provided by Mr. Turner.

Wolff, Dr. Ernest. "Resumé of History of Chandalar." Typescript provided by Dr. Wolff.

Index